ENCOUNTERING RE\

EARLY AMERICA: HISTORY, CONTEXT, CULTURE
Joyce E. Chaplin and Philip D. Morgan, *Series Editors*

ENCOUNTERING
REVOLUTION

Haiti and the Making of the Early Republic

ASHLI WHITE

THE JOHNS HOPKINS UNIVERSITY PRESS
Baltimore

This book was brought to publication with the generous assistance of Columbia University.

© 2010 The Johns Hopkins University Press
All rights reserved. Published 2010
Printed in the United States of America on acid-free paper

Johns Hopkins Paperback edition, 2012
2 4 6 8 9 7 5 3 1

The Johns Hopkins University Press
2715 North Charles Street
Baltimore, Maryland 21218-4363
www.press.jhu.edu

*The Library of Congress has catalogued the
hardcover edition of this book as follows:*
White, Ashli.
Encountering revolution : Haiti and the making of the early republic /
Ashli White.
p. cm.
Includes bibliographical references and index.
ISBN-13: 978-0-8018-9415-2 (hardcover : alk. paper)
ISBN-10: 0-8018-9415-8 (hardcover : alk. paper)
1. Haitians—United States—History—18th century. 2. Haitians—
United States—History—19th century. 3. Refugees—United States—
History. 4. Haiti—History—Revolution, 1791–1804—
Refugees. 5. Haiti—History—Revolution, 1791–1804—Foreign public
opinion, American. 6. Public opinion—United States—
History. 7. National characteristics, American—History. 8. Political
culture—United States—History. 9. United States—Politics and
government—1789–1815. 10. United States—Ethnic relations—
Political aspects—History. I. Title.
E184.H27W458 2010
972.94'03—dc22
2009023835

A catalog record for this book is available from the British Library.

ISBN-13: 978-1-4214-0581-0
ISBN-10: 1-4214-0581-4

*Special discounts are available for bulk purchases of this book.
For more information, please contact Special Sales at 410-516-6936
or specialsales@press.jhu.edu.*

The Johns Hopkins University Press uses environmentally friendly
book materials, including recycled text paper that is composed
of at least 30 percent post-consumer waste, whenever possible.

CONTENTS

ACKNOWLEDGMENTS

The research and writing of this book would not have been possible without generous financial support from several institutions. While at Columbia University I received aid from the Graduate School of Arts and Sciences, the Institute for Research on Women and Gender, and the Whiting Foundation; the Bancroft Dissertation Award was also instrumental in bringing this book to publication. Fellowships at the John Carter Brown Library, the American Philosophical Society, and the Library Company of Philadelphia facilitated my research, and I want to thank their directors and staffs, who made working there so pleasant and productive. A predoctoral fellowship at the McNeil Center for Early American Studies provided an engaging and lively year during which to finish the dissertation. In the transition from dissertation to book, two Max Orovitz Summer Awards in the Arts and Humanities from the Provost's office at the University of Miami allowed me to dedicate time to writing, and a subvention from the College of Arts and Sciences Dean's Office went toward the indexing of the book. When I was making the final revisions to the manuscript, I had the good fortune to be a visiting professor at the UFR d'Etudes Anglophones Charles V, Université de Paris 7–Denis Diderot. Many thanks to Marie-Jeanne Rossignol for sponsoring my fruitful stay in Paris.

As a student of early American history, I found encouragement at every stage. Back when I was an undergraduate at the University of Virginia, Peter Onuf and Joseph Kett nurtured my interest in the age of revolutions and inspired me to pursue it further. During my time at the Winterthur Program in Early American Culture, Bernard Herman saw the potential of the topic of this book, and he and J. Ritchie Garrison urged me to think Atlanticly; Christine Heyrman and Cathy Matson at the University of Delaware helped me to consider narrative bridges between history and material culture. But above all, my dissertation committee at Columbia shaped my approach to this project. My advisor Eric Foner asked tough questions, pushed for clear answers, and has always given freely of his time. I have long relied on Elizabeth Blackmar for her wisdom and wit, while Herb Sloan has the last word on anything related to early America. Winston James guided me through the historiography of the Caribbean, and as an outside reader of the dissertation Ada Ferrer offered a fresh comparative perspective. It was a privilege to work with all of them, and I am grateful for their support over so many years.

I received valuable feedback on various aspects of this project from audiences and commentators at several venues and events: the Early American Seminar at Columbia University, the University of Miami Atlantic Studies Research Group, Florida International University history department, Université de Paris 7–Denis Diderot, University of Delaware history department, Université de Montréal history department, the John Carter Brown Library Conference on the Haitian Revolution, Washington State University and Portland State University, the Atlantic History Seminar at Harvard University, the McNeil Center for Early American Studies at the University of Pennsylvania, and the annual conferences of the Omohundro Institute for Early American History and Culture, the Society for Historians of the Early American Republic, the Organization of American Historians, the American Studies Association, and the Social Science History Association.

Scholars of the Francophone Atlantic and the early U.S. republic contributed to refining my arguments in important ways. Thanks to Rafe Blaufarb, Laurent Dubois, Yvie Fabella, Norman Fiering, François Furstenberg, John Garrigus, David Geggus, Malick Ghachem, Monica Henry, Chris Hodson, Darrell Meadows, Sue Peabody, Jeremy Popkin, and Marie-Jeanne Rossignol. Reflecting the best cooperative impulses of the profession, Rick Demirjian, Darrell Meadows, Jeremy Popkin, Donna Rilling, Seth Rockman, and Billy G. Smith kindly shared their research and in so doing, enriched my interpretations. Portions of chapters 2, 4, and 5 appeared in *Early American Studies, Historical Reflections/Réflexions historiques,* and *The World of the Haitian Revolution.* I thank the editors and outside readers for their comments and suggestions.

When it came time to get the book done, I could not have asked for better series editors than Joyce Chaplin and Philip Morgan, whose smart suggestions, probing questions, and overall good sense have improved this book beyond measure. Laurent Dubois spent more time and care on this manuscript than I had any right to expect, and I thank him for his attentive and enthusiastic reading. With his discerning eye my colleague Richard Godbeer encouraged me to think carefully about the arc of the book, while Jeremy Popkin's close look at chapter 3 tightened up the argument considerably. Over the years members of the Writers'

Kollektiv—Meri Clark, Eduardo Elena, Kristin Roth-Ey, and Todd Stevens—have read more versions of chapters than they (or I) would care to recall, and I am grateful for their sharp readings, even sharper senses of humor, and friendship. At the Johns Hopkins University Press, Robert J. Brugger and Anne Whitmore honed the text, and Josh Tong demystified the publication process. The John Carter Brown Library and the Library Company of Philadelphia graciously permitted the reproduction of several illustrations.

I have been privileged to work at institutions where teaching and research go hand-in-hand. At the State University of New York–Stony Brook I was fortunate to have excellent colleagues, and for several years now, the department of history at the University of Miami has proven a dynamic and supportive professional home. I thank my fellow historians at UM for making department life enjoyable. Also, the director and staff of UM's Richter Library fulfilled my every research request with speed and good cheer.

My extended family—the Whites, Hannigans, Serafins, and Fuscos—have sustained me in many ways. Special thanks go to my aunt and uncle, Barbara and Richard Serafin, who let me move in with them (twice) during lengthy stays in Philadelphia. I have never, in my adult life, eaten so well nor had such clean laundry. Over the years, friends up and down the East Coast have put me up on research trips and conferences, taken me out on the town, and cheered on the completion of this book. For that and much more, I thank Sanjay Arwade and Meri Clark, Ed and Rina Brown, Ellen and Bill Carpenter, Karina Corrigan, Jeff and Crisse Klee, Mike and Shannon Spaeder, Renée Stein, Dana Tepper, and Amanda Wunder. Ellen Carpenter deserves particular mention for flying all the way to Paris to help me out, while Mary Doyno and Ellen Wurtzel have been there at every turn. My brother P. M. White and his family have provided welcome diversions from research and writing, and my mother, Annemarie White, has backed all my endeavors. Her unconditional support is evident on every page of this book. And the latest member of the family, my daughter Paulina Elena, had the grace to arrive three days late so I could complete the manuscript.

To a certain extent, this book's publication is bittersweet because of the loss of two people who I wish were still around to read it. My grandfather, Joseph Fusco, loved history and loved to tell stories, and I hope that this one would have sparked his interest. My father, Paul White, had an infectious intellectual curiosity, and he instilled in me a love for books and the notion that what they said mattered. This work is a small tribute to his many gifts.

When all is said and done, however, this book belongs to Eduardo Elena, who makes everything possible.

ENCOUNTERING REVOLUTION

INTRODUCTION

The United States felt the impact of the slave insurrection in Saint-Domingue almost as soon as it began. The French possession, consisting of the western third of Hispaniola, was the most lucrative colony in the eighteenth-century West Indies, but its colonial regime came under threat in August 1791, when the enslaved majority rebelled, inaugurating what would become the Haitian Revolution. Over the next thirteen years, violence racked the island, as black and colored Saint-Dominguans faced intractable resistance to their bid for freedom and citizenship. Plantations went up in flames; Spanish, British, and French armies invaded; and thousands of residents, white and nonwhite, fled to other Caribbean islands, Europe, and North America. The rebels persevered, and finally, in 1804, the largest slave uprising in history ended with emancipation and national independence.

While this remarkable outcome was uncertain in the first stages of the revolution, Americans realized early on that the rebellion had important consequences for their own republic. In the summer of 1793, as he learned that boatloads of refugees were disembarking on American shores, Thomas Jefferson connected the fates of Saint-Domingue and the United States: "I become daily more and more convinced that all the West India islands will remain in the hands of the people of colour, and a total expulsion of the whites sooner or later take place. It is high time we should foresee the bloody scenes which our children certainly, and possibly ourselves (South of Patowmac) have to wade through, and try to avert them."[1] In the predicament of slaveowners in the French colony, Jefferson saw the destiny of his countrymen. Eventually, white Americans, too, because of their commitment to slavery, would experience civil war.

In light of events in the nineteenth century, Jefferson's prophecy was prescient. Yet in the same pen stroke, he also suggested that such "bloody scenes" could be staved off in the United States—that residents could "try to avert them" by drawing lessons from Saint-Domingue. Other Americans thought likewise, and the refugees inspired intense discussion over what the Haitian Revolution did and did not portend for the early U.S. republic. Throughout the revolutionary era, many locals had frequent contact with Saint-Dominguan exiles, for at least twenty thousand black, white, and colored refugees landed at ports from New York to New Orleans. Compared to other, more numerous migrant groups, the Saint-Dominguans attracted greater attention because of the controversial circumstances surrounding their flight. In the streets and markets, at coffeehouses and taverns, in boardinghouses and parlors, residents came face to face with the Haitian Revolution.

This study examines American responses to the Saint-Dominguan refugees in order to understand how the Haitian Revolution shaped the early United States, especially how the exiles forced Americans to confront the paradox of being a slaveholding republic. The refugees were not the only ones to stir debate on this score, but in the 1790s and early 1800s, no event more clearly laid bare the contradiction between republican principles and slavery than the Haitian Revolution. Slaves and free colored people in Saint-Domingue pushed republican ideals to the radical conclusion that all men, regardless of race, are free, equal, and entitled to the rights of citizens. The exiles were living examples of the repercussions of this assertion, and their very presence in American cities compelled residents—black and white, northern and southern, Federalist and Democratic Republican, pro- and antislavery—to ponder the implications of the Haitian Revolution for the viability of their nation. A lonely few looked to the revolution and its exiles to call publicly for the end of slavery, but not until much later could this argument be made forcefully. Although free and enslaved black Americans took heart from the bold campaign in the French Caribbean, they struggled to adapt the revolution's message to an increasingly hostile local context. Most white residents (even abolitionists) joined Jefferson in efforts to avoid replication of the Haitian Revolution in the United States, and in the process they bolstered and rationalized American slavery and racism.

Debates surrounding the crisis in Saint-Domingue and its refugees went beyond slavery. Time and again, white Americans evoked the case of the exiles in order to consider whether the U.S. version of republicanism might make them exceptional. They assessed not only political practice and policy but also the virtue and character of Americans—how they looked, spoke, and acted vis-à-vis Saint-Dominguans. These appraisals of republican-ness involved both races, as white Americans sought to differentiate U.S. society from that of the French colony, and African Americans, in spite of many constraints, turned to the example of the Haitian Revolution to support their vision of a nation inimical to slavery and racism. Thus, the Saint-Dominguan exiles raised as many questions about being a republic as they did about slaveholding, and in this regard the Haitian Revolution provoked some of the first articulations of U.S. nationalism.

Such an argument about the significance of Saint-Domingue for the early U.S. republic necessitates a new view of the Haitian Revolution. Jefferson's reduction of the revolution to "bloody scenes" was a derogatory sleight of hand that persisted for two centuries, at least outside Haiti. In general, white observers have intentionally overlooked the revolution because it challenged—and continues to challenge—the racial hierarchies fundamental to Western society. When it was discussed, the revolution was couched in dismissive terms—as an atrocious "race war" in which bloodthirsty, rebellious slaves exacted indiscriminate revenge on a helpless white population. These racist accounts cast Haitian revolutionaries as devoid of humanity, let alone political principle, and their authors cited the lamentable state of postwar Haiti as evidence of the dangers of liberty, equality, and independence for an "unprepared" people. Generations of historians excluded the Haitian Revolution from the prestigious ranks of its American and French peers.[2]

This interpretation disguised what contemporaries well knew (but some refused to admit) and what historians are now making clear: that the Haitian Revolution was as much about the meaning and application of republican principles as were the American and French examples. In the eighteenth century, the Caribbean was a crucible of republicanism, as slaves, free people of color, and white Saint-Dominguans experimented with republican ideology and practice.[3] After all, the Haitian Revolution sprang, in part, from opportunities presented by its continental counterpart. In the late 1780s, the socioeconomically divided white population of the island saw the new French National Assembly in Paris as an auspicious venue in which to press for their divergent ambitions. The *grands blancs*—the administrators, prominent planters, and wealthy merchants who controlled the colony's economic, political, and social life—sought to minimize oversight by the metropole and consolidate their own rule. These goals dismayed the *petits blancs*, recent migrants from France who, after the end of the Seven Years' War in 1763, had flooded into Saint-Domingue with dreams of making fortunes. Marginalized by their *grands* contemporaries, the *petits blancs* lobbied the National Assembly for a voice in colonial governance. In addition, the island sustained a large and vibrant community of *gens de couleur* (free people of color) who had long smarted under their inability to enjoy the full rights of citizens. Composed of people of varying proportions of African and European descent, the *gens de couleur* were numerically—and in some cases, economically—almost equal to white inhabitants. In an attempt to eradicate the discrimination and disenfranchisement that they endured, free men of color sent representatives to Paris in 1789 to ensure that the "Declaration of the Rights of Man and Citizen" included them as well.

The competing agendas of free residents sparked disputes and outright violence in Saint-Domingue, and the discord provided an opening for the enslaved majority to press for their liberty. The slaves' actions, combined with the Jacobin ascendancy in France, led to some of the most radical measures of the French Revolution, namely, those declaring the end of slavery and the extension of citizenship to black men. As a result of these developments, the actual slave rebellion lasted only a few years, after which former slaves, free people of color, and French republican forces spent most of the Haitian Revolution—from about 1793 to 1801—securing their achievements from foreign invaders (Britain and Spain) as well as from internal, counterrevolutionary foes. But when Napoleon Bonaparte decided that emancipation had been a mistake and in 1802 sent a military expedition to reinstate slavery, the former slaves became the sole guardians of liberty and equality. They launched a war for independence, seeing it as the only way to protect their rights; and in 1804 they emerged triumphant, establishing the second republic in the Americas.[4]

Given that the republican revolution in the United States had occurred just a decade or so before, people there could not help but take note of events in Saint-Domingue. Throughout the 1790s the press worked to satiate the curiosity about and demand for news from the island. Newspapers up and down the East Coast featured detailed, if not always accurate, coverage of the revolution—everything from accounts of battles and proclamations from leaders to forecasts of trade prospects and opinion pieces on potential resolutions.[5] Word about the revolution also circulated by less formal, but no less influential, means, as sailors, slaves, merchants, and exiles brought stories and rumors from the colony to residents of U.S. seaports and their reports rippled through networks of communication deep into the countryside.[6]

While these currents of news helped black and white Americans to imagine the war in Saint-Domingue, the arrival of the refugees quite literally put a face on the revolution: Americans could see with their own eyes the colonists, slaves, and free people of color they had read and heard so much about. Sightings and exchanges were most common in cities, but some exiles relocated to rural areas or traveled through them on their way from one port to another. These encounters spanned more than a decade, increasing the odds for interaction between Saint-Dominguans and Americans. Although the refugees began to appear in the United States as early as 1791, their most dramatic influx came in the summer of 1793, after the momentous battle of Cap Français, which led to the first declaration of emancipation in Saint-Domingue. The British withdrawal from the island in 1798 resulted in another surge of refugees, and in 1804 officials in U.S. cities noticed an appreciable rise in the numbers of Saint-Dominguan exiles. The last sizable migration occurred in 1809, when about ten thousand Saint-Dominguans fled from their first haven, Cuba, again seeking sanctuary, this time in the United States.

Each wave of refugees prompted heated discussion about the Haitian Revolution. Often the exiles threw themselves headlong into the debate, offering their perspectives on what had happened and why. Not surprisingly, Americans drew from these exchanges sundry conclusions about the future of slavery in the United States. But the exiles, and by extension the Haitian Revolution, ignited debate on a host of issues related to the republic—national character, migration policies, philanthropy, political practice, abolition of slavery, and even territorial expansion. Deeply invested in the success of republican projects at home and abroad, Americans discovered, via the exiles, that the Haitian Revolution shook their credentials to the core, and they attempted to adjust accordingly.[7] In response to the refugees in their midst, white Americans fabricated key tenets of their national myth, and black Americans turned to the larger Atlantic world to challenge those tenets.

The United States was enmeshed in a vast Atlantic world that stretched to Europe, Africa, and the rest of the Americas. Born out of European conquest and colonialism, the Atlantic world evolved throughout the early modern era, as peoples on all four continents cultivated networks of trade, migration, and information that knit them ever more tightly together. Brutal violence and destruction accompanied the forging of these links and resulted in subjugated and displaced populations, destroyed environments, and insidious ideologies (such as racism) which persist to this day. These Atlantic ties flouted the imperial and emerging national boundaries thought to divide the various New World colonies, and created an intricate web of interconnections in which Virginia looked to Barbados for cues, English Puritans and Spanish conquistadors shared sensibilities, coerced African migrants (and, in far smaller numbers, European settlers) molded societies, and so on.[8]

This vision of the Atlantic world has played a critical role in disrupting exceptionalist narratives that have read the colonial era, especially in the case of British North America, teleologically through the lenses of the American Revolution and U.S. nationhood. Within an Atlantic frame of reference, it is much harder to maintain that there was something distinctive about British North America that made its independence inevitably triumphant. Despite this important corrective, the revolutionary and early national periods still sit somewhat uneasily in the arc of Atlantic history—for the example of the United States as well as for other locations.[9] To be sure, the republican revolutions that marked the late eighteenth and early nineteenth centuries have long been viewed collectively as an Atlantic phenomenon, and it is in that historical moment (rather than earlier ones) that some of the first self-proclaimed Atlantic historians located the origins of an "Atlantic civilization."[10]

But the age of revolutions has been construed differently from—and to some extent problematically in comparison to—its colonial precursor. The dominant trope for the revolutionary decades is that of a chain, a sequence in which political principles and activity at one site inform revolution in another. The chain configuration follows the path of revolution in a linear fashion, moving from the United States to France to countries throughout Europe to Haiti (sometimes) to Latin America (maybe). While this approach has its virtues, it stands in stark contrast to the web model typically used to interpret the colonial period. The two constructions of the Atlantic world are almost opposites—one is organic, the other mechanistic. Consequently, the fluidity and contingency of the colonial era surrender, in most accounts, to the seemingly straightforward march of revolution and nation building.[11] The divergent emphases in histories of these two Atlantic eras exacerbate this conceptual disparity. Colonial scholarship tends to probe social, economic, and cultural connections, eschewing politics, yet the age of revolutions literature privileges ideology and collective conflict about the structure of the state and gives short shrift to social, economic, and cultural concerns.[12] There are noteworthy exceptions to this mutual exclusivity; however, by and large the incongruity of themes and the rival metaphors make it difficult to discern precisely what did and did not change in the Atlantic world with the rise of revolutions and nation-states.[13]

By focusing on the relationship between Saint-Domingue and the United

States, this book bridges the paradigms and themes that have separated studies of the colonial and revolutionary Atlantic worlds. Revolution generated ties that bound the French colony and the early U.S. republic, but not only in the ways that the chain metaphor suggests. With independence, the United States lost some of its previous trade routes; most significantly, the British West Indies became off limits (at least legally). Saint-Domingue helped to fill the breach, so much so that by the early 1790s the colony ranked second in volume and value of trade with the United States after Great Britain. The ever-growing traffic fostered social, intellectual, and cultural connections between the two regions' residents. In sum, Saint-Domingue was central to initial U.S. attempts to stake out a place as a sovereign nation in the thriving Atlantic system.

When the Haitian Revolution disrupted U.S. endeavors to assert its newfound autonomy, Americans had no choice but to react, reassessing and adjusting their position toward Saint-Domingue and the Atlantic world. This moment of upheaval offers an opportunity to reconsider the transformations brought about by Atlantic revolutions. Rather than follow the chain model and appraise how the ideology of one revolution influenced a subsequent one, this book highlights the weblike characteristics of the age. It contemplates the effects that a later revolution had on a previously revolutionary site—in this case, how events in Saint-Domingue shaped the United States. This approach helps us to understand a key juncture in the histories of these two places and of the Atlantic world as well, for the age of revolutions did not signal the end of the Atlantic system, as colonies gave way to nation-states. Nation making was as much of an Atlantic phenomenon as revolution, and national ventures responded to and were altered by revolutions throughout the basin.[14] Refugees are one manifestation of the tendency of governments and their residents to renegotiate—almost constantly—their situations within a broader context. At the turn of the nineteenth century, peoples throughout Africa, Europe, and the Americas had to adjust to the changes and tests wrought by revolutions; and in so doing, they remade the Atlantic world.

In examining this dynamic of revolutionary response, this book takes a somewhat unusual perspective on migrants and migration. The Saint-Dominguans were just one of several refugee groups—Huguenots, Acadians, American loyalists, and French continental exiles, to name but a few—who affected North America and the wider Atlantic world in the early modern period. Studying these diasporas produces vital insight into the ways that imperial or national power influenced the lives of individuals and collectives and vice versa.[15] This book pursues another interpretive tack: how Americans and Saint-Dominguans made sense of the latter's migration and its cause, the Haitian Revolution. Rather than providing quantitative breakdowns of population demographics or extensive biographies of exiles or an in-depth account of community building and identity formation, this work focuses on interactions between U.S. residents and Saint-Dominguan refugees.[16] As locals and exiles mingled, literally and figuratively, they came to grips with the multiple implications of this coerced migration—what it meant for individuals, cities, nation and colony, and the Atlantic world. While newspapers and government records informed many appraisals, commentaries also occurred on the American stage, in poems and popular fiction, and in person, as residents and refugees sized up one another in the public sphere. This book therefore treats diplomatic correspondence alongside analyses of clothing, the works of amateur authors next to those of leading thinkers, and the goings-on at the gaming table as well as those in the halls of Congress. The discussion was pervasive, and this work investigates as many of these sites as possible in order to illustrate the far-reaching impact of the refugees and the Haitian Revolution.

Although this exploration is attuned to the unique circumstances of specific locales, the story is national. This study considers how inhabitants of, for example, Charleston, Baltimore, and New York responded to the same challenges—be they social, cultural, or political. In this case, geography—whether the city was in the North or the South—conditioned conclusions far less than one might expect. Race was a powerful factor in shaping American reactions to the exiles and to the Haitian Revolution, yet even here, black and white cannot be starkly disaggregated. During the Haitian Revolution, race and politics did not always align neatly, and this book explores the intertwined histories of black, white, and colored Saint-Dominguans and Americans. Without a doubt, formidable racism barred black and colored exiles and locals from particular arenas of public discussion in the United States, and certain subjects engaged some sectors of the American population more than others. Because the voices of people of African descent resonate much less than those of their white counterparts in the surviving sources, many questions remain unanswered. Still, in spite of these gaps, a picture emerges that illustrates the complex impact of the Haitian Revolution on Americans—black and white.

Five questions drive this narrative about encounters between U.S. residents and Saint-Dominguan exiles in the 1790s and early 1800s. First, how did Americans and refugees respond to their social and cultural exchanges in U.S. cities, and then, how did locals react to the pressures the exiles placed on the republican ideal of asylum? How did the refugees influence political life in the early republic, and what did residents make of the possibility for the importation of slave rebellion from Saint-Domingue to the United States? And finally, how did the last wave of exiles, in 1809, figure into national debates over territorial expansion? The answers to these questions allow us to appreciate more fully the Haitian Revolution's impact on the United States and to think more deeply about what it meant to live in an era of revolutionary change. Contrary to engrained ideas about exceptionalism, it is only by looking outside the nation's borders and appraising its engagement with the wider world that we come to understand the making of the early American republic.

CHAPTER ONE

THE "NEW CAPE"

In the summer of 1793, Charles Laurent, a fifty-six-year-old white man born and raised in Cap Français, a city on the north coast of Saint-Domingue, found himself, as he put it, a "fugitive" from his own country. He owned sugar and coffee plantations in one of the fertile parishes just outside of Le Cap, but as a slave insurrection ripped through the northern plain, Laurent and his family took refuge in the fortified city. The streets of the Cape became war zones, too, though; and Laurent, his wife, brother, two children, and two slaves, Sambore and Azor, left the port "while it was actually in Flames" and boarded a vessel bound for Philadelphia. It took almost two years for the entire family to reach the "City of Brotherly Love," as they were separated and suffered "various accidents" along the way—perhaps falling prey to bad weather, privateers, and other vagaries that plagued Atlantic travel. By June 1795, the Laurent family was reunited in Philadelphia, but Madame Laurent and the brother died shortly thereafter, and so Laurent, his children, Sambore, and Azor took up residence in a hat factory on Sixth Street, opposite the State House garden.[1]

Laurent, his family, and his slaves, as well as the thousands of other Saint-Dominguan refugees who arrived on U.S. shores during the 1790s must have felt their dislocation keenly. Not only had they suffered a tumultuous, coerced migration, but they disembarked in a place that in many respects was quite different from their home. After all, they had been reared in a torrid climate, in a

colony about the size of Maryland which was dominated by plantation agriculture, an overwhelming slave majority, and French imperialism. They must have
found their new environments—in most cases temperate, urban, and English-
speaking—alien, if not downright hostile. Yet Saint-Domingue had much more
in common with North America than a first glance suggests. During the eighteenth century, Saint-Domingue and the United States followed analogous trajec-
tories: both were slave societies, both had contentious relationships to their respective metropoles, and both saw the rise of colonial elites who wanted to assert
their status. These parallel paths intersected in the 1780s as the French colony
and United States cultivated more complex ties.

In fact, in the view of merchants—those conduits of Atlantic connectivity—the
United States and Saint-Domingue had become inextricably linked by the early
1790s. As a merchant in New Orleans declared to an American associate, "they
call Philadelphia the New Cape."[2] Initially, this assertion seems counterintuitive,
almost absurd: Philadelphia, the so-called Quaker City, was the new Cap Français,
with all the tropical, luxurious, and French associations that went along with it?
New Orleans would have better filled this bill. Although under Spanish jurisdiction since the 1760s, the port was unmistakably Francophone in its population,
culture, and outlook, with a sultry climate, to boot. How was it that Philadelphia
and not New Orleans came to be referred to as the New Cape?

The answer, in part, can be found in trade. The United States and Saint-
Domingue had enjoyed close communication since the American war for independence, thanks to alliance and trade agreements brokered in the 1780s. In the
following decade, a quicker tempo characterized exchange between the two
places, as American merchants sought to capitalize even more aggressively on
Caribbean markets, especially after France lifted previous restrictions on its colonies in February 1793.[3] In light of this brisk traffic, it is not so surprising that
merchants might see one city as tantamount to the other. And, increasingly in the
1790s, the vessels that ferried between Saint-Domingue and the United States
carried not only goods but people. As the revolution gathered steam in the French
West Indies, colonists, slaves, and free people of color secured passage to U.S.
cities by the thousands. Not since the Huguenot immigration in the late seventeenth century had Anglophone America seen so many French-speaking migrants
arrive so suddenly.[4] Frenchmen had been a fixture along the western frontier, and
during the war for independence, French soldiers, including regiments from
Saint-Domingue, had made their presence felt along the East Coast. Throughout
the 1780s, French West Indians had traveled to North America for business and
"for their health," but in the 1790s almost every major city—New York, Philadel-

Eighteenth-Century Saint-Domingue. Map drawn by Bill Nelson.

phia, Baltimore, Norfolk, Charleston, Savannah—witnessed an influx of Saint-Dominguans.[5] In the words of one newspaper report, "our cities are crowded with them."[6] This migration introduced a new dimension to the relationship between Saint-Domingue and the United States—one that, indeed, had the potential to transform American cities.

To what extent were U.S. cities "New Capes" from the perspectives of locals and exiles as they encountered one another on the streets? The social and cultural interaction of Americans and Saint-Dominguans is important to answering this question. For years, each had drawn conclusions about the other from tracts, pamphlets, and various reports; but with more direct contact in the 1790s, they also eyed the smallest, most quotidian aspects of ordinary life—appearance, behavior, living circumstances. These observations resulted in judgments about an individual's character that were frequently extrapolated to an entire people.[7] Republican revolution changed the standards of assessment somewhat by disrupting centuries-old hierarchies of status (at least for white men), and appraisals took on even more urgency as onlookers struggled to understand what the revolutions meant for various peoples throughout the Atlantic world. This issue was critical for residents of the United States, who were formerly colonists but now citizens of a new nation, and for Saint-Dominguans, who were displaced by a revolution in progress.

The arrival of the refugees to the United States offered each group ample opportunity for the intimate scrutiny that went into sizing up another population, and what emerges is a dynamic not of stark difference taken for granted—of each side simply affirming the foreignness of the other. In fact, from an Atlantic perspective, Saint-Domingue and the United States shared key traits that made them comparable, particularly their urban areas—the contexts in which most exiles and locals came into contact. Although the refugees did indeed feel the pains of dislocation, their everyday lives in U.S. cities show that this displacement was due more to the tumult of revolution and exile than to their new surroundings. Many refugees had planned their migration to North America and were familiar with what they would find as they sought to live and work there. Nevertheless, as Saint-Dominguans and locals came into contact on city streets, in parlors, and elsewhere, they dwelled on the disparities, from the clothes they wore to interracial relations. The interactions between locals and refugees were marked by the process of drawing finer distinctions: they often elided their similarities and drew attention to perceived differences in an attempt to justify the virtues of their societies in a rapidly changing Atlantic world. Each side tried to use the other to claim an exceptional character.

THE TWO AMERICAS

Today "America" is a shorthand appellation for the United States (in North Atlantic circles), but in the eighteenth century this was not the case. Saint-Domingue and the United States were both at times referred to as "America." After all, both places were located in the New World, and in the 1790s they still bore the imprints of early modern European colonialism on their economies, infrastructure, and populations. People born in both of these areas were also called "Americans" and "Creoles," the theory being that the unique environments and societies of the New World made them distinct from Europeans. Common features mattered in how inhabitants experienced life in Saint-Domingue and in the United States and how they were perceived throughout the Atlantic world. Therefore, it is worth considering from an eighteenth-century view what qualities made Saint-Domingue and the United States alike.

Although small in comparison to the United States, the French colony of Saint-Domingue was remarkably diverse in its geography, economy, and population, and in this way, was much like its North American neighbor. As many commentators noted then and have since, eighteenth-century Saint-Domingue was essentially three colonies within one, in that a series of mountain ranges carved the territory into discrete regions: the North, South, and West. Settled at different times and at different paces, each district developed into a distinct, albeit constantly evolving, society. They shared plantation agriculture and all had populations made up of white, black, and free people of color; French laws, institutions, and customs shaped the three provinces, and African cultures left their mark as well. Yet the differences among the regions were apparent to islanders and to visitors. Attracting few European immigrants because of its rough terrain, the South was noted for its frontier ethos, its large and powerful free colored community, and its orientation toward the rest of the Caribbean rather than toward France, while the North was renowned for its grand estates, its influential and outspoken white elite, and close cultural associations with France and the North Atlantic world. The West was the site of the colony's capital, Port-au-Prince, but it had a rough-and-ready quality—more of a "tartar camp," in the words of one Frenchman, than a seat of government. Thanks to ambitious irrigation projects in the second half of the eighteenth century, the arid plains surrounding Port-au-Prince were transformed into lush plantations, attracting fortune seekers from across the Atlantic.[8]

All three provinces grew sugar, but with uneven success, and so diversification was critical to the economic vibrancy of the island. Cotton, indigo, and coffee were significant exports; in fact, by 1789 coffee plantations outnumbered sugar plantations in both the West and the North.[9] Restricted by mercantilist policies known collectively as the *exclusif*, much of Saint-Domingue's produce went to the mother country before it was re-exported throughout Europe, but in the 1780s the French government allowed selected ports in Saint-Domingue to trade with other nations. As a result, on any given day, 170 or more ships—say, 80 from France (often by way of Africa), 50 from the United States, another dozen or more from Louisiana, Cuba, Spanish America, and the Windward Islands, and 30 local vessels and ferries—dropped anchor at Cap Français alone. During the dangerous, yet also flush, times of war, witnesses spied as many as 600 ships in the harbor at one time; and like almost every other port in the Americas, illicit trade augmented, if not outstripped, official activity. By some accounts, two-thirds of the exports from the United States to Saint-Domingue were contraband.[10] No matter the terms of trade, the Atlantic world wanted what "the pearl of the Antilles" had to offer.

The emphasis on agricultural exports meant that most of the population, as in the United States, lived in the countryside. But in Saint-Domingue slaves outnumbered free men and women handily, while in the U.S. republic only a few parishes in the South Carolina Lowcountry approached a slave majority. Slaves dominated every region of the French colony—in some areas to a staggering degree, with ratios of fourteen slaves for every free white person.[11] In addition, every year thousands of Africans joined the ranks of the enslaved in Saint-Domingue, resulting in an enslaved population with closer and more recent ties to Africa in contrast to the increasingly "country-born" slave population in North America.

Conspicuous from a North American perspective was the colony's relatively large community of free people of color. Composed of people of various degrees of African descent who were manumitted by their masters or were born of already free parents, the free people of color, or *gens de couleur*, rivaled their white counterparts in terms of numbers and in some cases wealth. Over the course of the eighteenth century, many *gens de couleur* managed, through paternal inheritance, intermarriage, and hard work, to consolidate economic might and to accrue the material, social, and cultural trappings to go along with it. Some accumulated large plantations and were educated in France, and a few married white Frenchmen or -women.[12] The free African American population in the United States was growing in the 1780s and 1790s, reaching almost 50,000 in the northern states and making significant strides in the upper south as well. Nevertheless, this was by all accounts a new group; they lacked the economic and social collateral of free colored Saint-Dominguans. Perhaps the only place on the U.S. Atlantic coast that came close on this score was the lower south, the areas around Charleston and Savannah. There, free people of color carved out a niche: segregated from the white ruling class by racism, they distanced themselves from slaves, and in the process, helped to create tri-caste societies.[13]

The profiles of enslaved and free colored Saint-Dominguans suggest an "America" in the French West Indies that was very different from North America—a divergence so stark that it would seem to overshadow any similarities. Yet, eighteenth-century Atlantic observers continued to comment on the commonalities between Saint-Domingue and the United States, especially their urban areas. As the points of departure and entry for refugees, urban centers were critical contexts for the interactions of these two groups of Americans.[14] Contrasts certainly existed, yet more noteworthy are the common characteristics that made the evocation of Philadelphia (or any other U.S. city for that matter) as the "New Cape" feasible. At a basic level, U.S. and Saint-Dominguan urban areas shared a similar status as second-tier New World cities. At the end of the eighteenth century, the leading cities in the Western Hemisphere were in the Iberian domains; places like Mexico City, Salvador de Bahia, and Lima far surpassed their English and French rivals in terms of population as well as cultural, social, and economic complexity. In 1790, of the fifty largest cities in the Americas, five were in the United States and one was in Saint-Domingue, and none of these ranked in the top ten.[15] Urban growth in Saint-Domingue and North America had been held in check by several factors, most of them related to the restrictive nature of mercantilism. In Saint-Domingue the tremendous slave majority, the centrality of slaves for both rural and urban work, and the rate of absenteeism among planters restrained urban expansion.[16]

The close resemblance of U.S. and Saint-Dominguan cities from a broad Atlantic perspective translated to a personal scale—that which refugees and residents experienced firsthand as they came into sustained contact in the 1790s. Just as rivers connected rural North Americans to their many ports along the coast, Saint-Dominguans were oriented to their island's shores. The colony supported thirteen ports, and although regional isolation ensured that no single city completely dominated trade, Port-au-Prince in the West, Cap Français in the North, and Les Cayes in the South saw the greatest volume. The export trade attracted merchants and agents as well as a host of people who supported commerce: artisans, sailors, lawyers, doctors, soldiers, keepers of taverns and boardinghouses and shops, stevedores, domestic slaves, and prostitutes, among others. By 1789 the population of Cap Français hovered around 19,000 persons—about the size of Boston at that time. As in the countryside, slaves made up the majority of residents in Le Cap, but white inhabitants outnumbered free colored ones by over two to one.[17]

The Cape—and Saint-Dominguan cities generally—were "blacker" than their U.S. counterparts, yet in the 1780s and 1790s the number of African American inhabitants in early republican cities increased markedly. Fleeing the harsh conditions of rural life, freed black men and women made their way to Boston, New York, and Philadelphia by the thousands, much to the consternation of those cities' white residents.[18] In the upper south, older ports, such as Baltimore and Norfolk, expanded rapidly, and new towns, like Richmond and Petersburg, cropped up inland. The slave and free colored population grew apace with these southern cities, in some places exceeding the white population.[19] In almost every U.S. city in the 1790s, slaves and free people of color were pervasive and their presence more pronounced than it had been in previous decades.

The imprint of slavery distinguished towns such as Le Cap and Philadelphia from European ones. For centuries there had been slaves in European cities; however, during the eighteenth century both France and Great Britain asserted, albeit it with some profound contradictions, the "freedom principle"—essentially that African slavery did not and could not exist in Europe.[20] Slavery was gradually cast as an exclusively New World phenomenon: the fiction of European freedom was built on the foil of American slavery, and this was especially true during the era of Atlantic revolutions. Britons found solace and moral high ground in the Somerset case of 1772 that guaranteed freedom for black men in Britain (or so it was interpreted), while in France early revolutionaries tackled the questions of racism and slavery and sought to redefine their republic as one based on, among other principles, racial equality. Unlike their Saint-Dominguan peers, several northern U.S. cities were caught up in the transatlantic abolitionist impulse during this era and were making the transition toward the prohibition of slavery. This protracted process would not be complete until several decades later, and slavery remained a visible feature of these urban landscapes.[21]

Despite the taint of slavery, both Saint-Dominguan and North American cities were cosmopolitan in other ways. From 1730 to 1790 each of the prominent towns of Saint-Domingue swelled, as more and more immigrants and locals took up residence there, and starting in 1790 the major U.S. seaports began a population boom that would last for the next forty years.[22] Cities in both places attracted migrants from all over Europe, creating urbane enclaves. The variety was astounding. One chronicler described walking through the streets of the Cape as like "running through the whole of France in an instant, [as] the Gascon accent takes the place of the Norman, and the Provençal gives way to the Dunkirk dialect."[23] Added to these were the cadences of assorted African languages, the local patois, English, Spanish, Dutch, and other European tongues. In U.S. cities the vocal din resounded with more English lilts, but the swirl of peoples and languages was similar.

These bustling and burgeoning populations—both permanent and transient—instigated a rash of urban building in the eighteenth century. Much of this new construction followed the latest Atlantic trends. The sixteenth- and seventeenth-century European endeavor to rationalize the jumbled plans of cities was applied to colonial towns throughout the Americas, and perhaps nowhere is this better seen than in Cap Français. In its layout Le Cap, like Philadelphia, Balti-

Plan of Cap Français and Environs in Saint-Domingue (Paris, 1786). This view of Le Cap shows how it, like many U.S. cities, reflected the impulse of early modern reformers to rationalize urban spaces, using a grid plan, open squares, and carefully placed public buildings. (Note that the compass is pointing west, not north.) Courtesy John Carter Brown Library at Brown University.

more, Savannah, and elsewhere, reflected the vogue for a regular grid of evenly divided city blocks running on north-south and east-west axes.[24] Warehouses and docks lined the harbor, and noteworthy civil and sacred buildings stood several blocks back from the shore. Although few streets were paved, most included brick or stone sidewalks. After fire ravaged the town at least twice in the early 1700s, reforms required Le Cap residents to construct new buildings of masonry rather than wood (comparable legislation was passed in North American cities).[25] An enlightened impulse for improvement inspired all sorts of building in Cap Français in the 1780s, just as it did in its North American counterparts. Tax revenue supported the construction of aqueducts, bridges, fountains, and seventy-nine public buildings—an exchange, government headquarters, hospitals, churches.[26]

As part of this progressive ethos, local leaders in Saint-Domingue and the United States invested in institutions designed to promote and cater to a refined citizenry. White Saint-Dominguans established a reading room, assembly rooms, scientific societies, and newspapers, although the French crown censored the press, which the locals resented.[27] These spheres of sociability and learning were intended mostly for the literate white elite, but Cap Français hosted other amusements that brought men and women of all races and classes together. The most popular was the theater; one resident noted, "It would be impossible to pass up a play at the Cape, especially when one has contracted the habit." Seating fifteen hundred people at least three times week, the theater drew a cross-section of Saint-Dominguan society—colonial administrators and the white elite in the prominent balconies, the military guard on a bench near the band, "mulatto women" and "negresses" in boxes at the back, and standing on the floor sailors and poorer locals.[28] Markets, taverns, billiard halls, bathhouses, Masonic lodges, and churches were also places where Saint-Dominguans interacted.[29] Cultural developments in Saint-Dominguan cities echoed the hottest craze in France: shops sold the newest fashion within weeks of its being sighted on the streets of Paris, the theater at the Cape performed Molière's plays soon after their metropolitan premieres, and white men read and debated the most current philosophic treatises, political predicaments, and scientific findings.

White Saint-Dominguans, like creoles elsewhere in the Americas, were ambivalent about colonial life. On the one hand, elites lamented the coarseness of Saint-Dominguan society, regretting, for example, the absence of a university in the colony or griping about the questionable quality of theaterical performances.[30] Such deficiencies smacked of a provincialism that embarrassed white elites. But this was not the provincialism of small-town France: it was *creole* provincialism, with all of the intellectual and cultural baggage that went with it. White Saint-

Dominguans suffered under the disparaging characterization Europeans attributed to all people born in the Americas—in sum, that the New World environment compromised their bodies and intellects to such a degree that they degenerated drastically from their European origins.[31]

Slavery and racism were part and parcel of this creole characterization. As Europeans celebrated their "free air" and "free soil," they chided Americans throughout the Atlantic world for their lack of both. This critique proved potent in the age of revolutions, leading to Samuel Johnson's famous quip in 1775 about hearing the loudest cries for freedom from North American slaveholders. Perhaps even more unsettling for white creoles, however, were the populations of free people of color. They represented a dangerous transgression, a violation of the equation of white with freedom and black with slavery. Whereas in other eighteenth-century Atlantic societies (such as Jamaica and Brazil), free people of color could be "whitened" through wealth and legal procedures, in both the United States and Saint-Domingue white residents became obsessed with maintaining racial distinctions. Both Médéric-Louis-Elie Moreau de St. Méry, one of Saint-Domingue's leaders and its greatest ethnographer, and Benjamin Franklin dabbled in convoluted racial taxonomies (Franklin, unlike Moreau, recanted his musings on the subject). In both jurisdictions legislatures put in place one restrictive law after another in an attempt to check the liberties of their non-white free populations. In Ira Berlin's poignant phrase for the U.S. case, white residents sought to ensure that freedmen were, in essence, "slaves without masters."[32]

On the other hand, white Saint-Dominguans, like North Americans, praised their home and its people. Although the society of the Caribbean colony was admittedly somewhat unsophisticated by European standards, its very roughness held great promise for some white Frenchmen looking for a better life. One memoirist recorded about Saint-Domingue: "The European who sees the American country for the first time can hardly cope with what he experiences. He is stirred by a confused medley of the most varied ideas. Not only is there the joy of arrival, there are also the regrets as to things he left behind. His imagination exaggerates both the advantages which he promises himself and the difficulties which he fears. . . . You jump into a ship's boat, sail, go ashore, and with still unsteady foot, you tread on American soil."[33] Such descriptions have been trotted out so often in romantic descriptions of immigrants' arrivals at Philadelphia or New York as to have become almost pedestrian, but Cap Français stirred similar emotions and hopes in this era. In the second half of the eighteenth century, white Saint-Dominguans worked to counter more forcefully the derisive remarks of Europeans. Like Thomas Jefferson in his *Notes on the State of Virginia* (1780), Moreau wrote his magisterial three-volume *Description topographique, physique, civile, politque et historique* (1797) of colonial Saint-Domingue as a retort to derogatory European claims regarding creoles.[34]

Some defenses of Saint-Domingue made explicit links to North America, as an appeal to and recognition of their shared status as Americans. In 1784, the first scientific society formed in Cap Français decided to call itself the Cercle des Philadelphes in homage to its brother institution in Philadelphia, the American Philosophical Society, and the two groups corresponded throughout the 1780s, with each electing members of the other to its ranks.[35] Saint-Dominguans lauded their role in the American Revolution in varied ways, for instance, by naming a reservoir after the former Governor-General of the colony, Count d'Estaing, who was an admiral in the American Revolution; going to see a wax rendition of George Washington in his full military regalia drew crowds as well.[36] The array of vindications points to a sense among white Saint-Dominguans and North Americans of their common experience as "Americans" in the Atlantic world. They smarted from the same criticism, had the same potential, and on some occasions, contemplated collective efforts that might prove mutually beneficial in attaining the social and cultural legitimacy they craved.

U.S. and Saint-Dominguan seaports were also critical conduits linking African Americans throughout the Atlantic world. To borrow from historian Julius Scott, port cities were "capitals of Afro-America," where local African Americans met up with those who lived in the hinterland as well as with black and colored travelers passing through. In Cap Français and Philadelphia (as well as in Havana, Kingston, New York, Charleston, and elsewhere), free and enslaved black and colored people created fragile but persistent sanctuaries in a hostile world and fostered connections by swapping news, knowledge, and goods. These networks were facilitated by sailors, runaways, hucksters, and other men and women of the "masterless" classes who enjoyed some mobility to and within urban areas and beyond. During their travels they picked up the latest reports and rumors and passed them on. Most dangerously for the white ruling class, these ties abetted rebellious activity, especially in the age of revolutions when emancipatory rhetoric went hand-in-hand with the growth of free African American urban communities.[37] Given the amount of traffic between Saint-Domingue and the United States, African Americans in both places had ample opportunity for contact and exchange, a fact that was not lost on white and black inhabitants in the United States.

While they had begun in the seventeenth century, Saint-Dominguan and North American cities were eighteenth-century upstarts. They fed and fed off of the commercial and agricultural dynamism of the era; they were centers of civic life; and they embraced new ideas about urban planning, learning, and sociability. They were similar in development—more so than in comparison to other Atlantic cities—and their populations shared important features and sensibilities. For all their ethnic and racial diversity, these cities were riven by stratification and discrimination: the white residents toasted and bemoaned their American-ness; the enslaved were denied political, civil, and human rights and worked to make cultures and Atlantic connections of their own; and free people of color became more predominant, more disgruntled, and more feared. In light of these resemblances, perhaps it was not so inconceivable that Philadelphia—even with its cold winters, gruff manners, and by all accounts, bad food—could become, as the New Orleans merchant attested in 1792, the "New Cape."

EXPERIENCING ANOTHER AMERICA

Although by the 1790s U.S. and Saint-Dominguan cities had much in common and had enjoyed frequent contact for at least a decade, it remained to be seen whether structural parity would translate into a comparable experience on the ground for refugees as they lived, gathered, and worked in American cities. The tumult of revolution and flight compromised their ability to reconstruct their lives. Nevertheless, their everyday routines in the United States were familiar, in that many aspects of city life—conditions, institutions, and work—rang true to their earlier experience. Yet, it was by playing up their foreign, French background that many white exiles were able to make ends meet.

Saint-Dominguans knew what to expect in the United States—or at least they thought they did. Many refugees had chosen the new nation as their destination. After over a decade of trade and travel between the two areas, some Saint-Dominguans had contacts—near or distant—in the United States on whom they relied for credit and support. Others sought to take advantage of the professed (although not always heeded) U.S. neutrality, seeing it as a safer bet than sites in the Caribbean, which, as the seventeenth and eighteenth centuries had made clear time and again, were vulnerable during international war. (This calculation was confirmed when Saint-Dominguan refugees who settled in Cuba and Jamaica were, within a matter of years, expelled.[38]) While neutrality was a boon, the location of the United States was also critical: it was close enough to allow quick return to Saint-Domingue, and it afforded relatively easy access to Europe. For the exiles—white, black, and colored, this criterion was crucial; many hoped to return to the island or to France, and some, at different points during the revolution, did so.

The motivations of free people of color and slaves to migrate to the United States present a much more complex picture. Upon first reflection, it seems strange that free people of color and slaves would leave a colony that was in the process of achieving liberty, equality, and citizenship for all men. No doubt some were coerced into leaving, but given the powerful counterrevolutionary forces that continued to thwart the implementation of freedom and citizenship in Saint-Domingue, many slaves and free people of color saw asylum elsewhere as more secure than life on the island. In addition, complicated personal relationships bound some masters and slaves together, and in other cases, slaves struck bargains with their owners for compensation and even freedom if they traveled with them.

For lucky migrants, the trip was smooth: they obtained berths, met with few troubles along the way, and arrived swiftly at their intended port. For Charles Laurent and many others, the voyage to the United States was arduous, despite the best-laid plans. White, would-be exiles in the Saint-Dominguan countryside faced possible attack as they made their way to the nearest port. Once there, they frequently found that vessels were full, fares were high, and officials barred their departure; families were sometimes split up in the scramble to find passage. Not even setting sail guaranteed success. The trip from Saint-Domingue to the United States usually took two to three weeks, but the revolution exacerbated the hazards and length of sea travel.[39] Boats were overcrowded and ill-equipped to handle so many passengers, some of whom were sick or injured from their ordeals in the colony; and the vessels were susceptible to inclement weather and privateer raids, during which many slaves and free people of color were seized as contraband. Under duress, personalities clashed, and disputes broke out among passengers as well as with crew members.[40]

When refugees arrived in the United States, the first order of business was to locate housing; and whether the exiles found themselves in Charleston, New York, or somewhere in between, the architectural stock was different from that of Saint-Domingue. In Le Cap most houses were built to cope with the challenges of the tropical environment: they stood only one story, although rooms had high ceilings to draw off the heat and jalousied windows to catch the breeze, and the exteriors were painted white to reflect the sunlight (an effect that was picturesque, but brutal on the eyes, in the opinion of one resident).[41] Houses in early U.S. cities, however, had to make no such allowances for tropical living. They were multiple stories, ranging from at least two stories to on rare occasions, four, and residents worried more about the months of cold, and so fireplaces were prevalent.[42]

The exiles' housing situations in American cities ran the gamut of possible arrangements. On one end of the spectrum were those who owned grand homes. Doctor Jean Louis Polony purchased and lived in a house in Charleston, but also had a fully outfitted working plantation in St. Andrew's Parish on the Stono River.[43] Most refugees, however, ended up renting rooms in boardinghouses, taverns, or private residences. Exiles often noted in their last wills and testaments that the documents were executed "in the room [or rooms] which I occupy."[44]

Renting suited many refugees. It offered the flexibility to come and go as they pleased, and many exiles roamed from city to city in search of better prospects or trying to find relatives and friends. The story of Pierre Andre François Thebaudieres suggests the wide range and frequency of this movement. After leaving Saint-Domingue, he and his family landed in Baltimore and then moved to Elizabeth, New Jersey. They stayed there for less than a year before he returned to Jérémie in Saint-Domingue. Within a matter of months, Thebaudieres came back to the United States, this time choosing to settle down in Philadelphia with his wife, while their eleven-year-old daughter resided in New York, and his son, only seven years old, remained in Baltimore. Unfortunately the records reveal only where his children lived, not with whom or under what circumstances.[45] In the early 1790s, exiles anticipated that their sojourn in the United States would be brief; they thought that the slave revolution would be crushed quickly and that they would soon return to the island. Renting fit this presumed eventuality. Finally, renting appealed because lodgings were furnished, a necessary amenity since the majority of exiles had not brought with them—and in many cases, could not afford to purchase on arrival—the implements needed for a household.[46] For all these reasons, many refugees decided not to purchase houses.

Normally the exiles found accommodation in boardinghouses, but at peak moments of migration, there were no vacancies. The inns were so crowded in Norfolk that exiles "sought out the canopies of the marketplaces, which gave some shelter from the inclemencies of the night."[47] Even before the refugees arrived in the 1790s, the demand for housing exceeded the supply in several prominent cities; New York, Philadelphia, and Baltimore all suffered from overcrowding, despite their relatively small populations.[48] As a result, Saint-Dominguans found that they had to pay dearly for what space they could procure. Although in Norfolk refugees spent what was considered a reasonable $4.50 a week for their lodgings, James Pongaudin paid almost twice as much in Charleston—$32 per month for room and board in Mr. Paince's house.[49] Given that, according to one estimate at the time, the costs of living in the countryside for several months were $22 per person, including provisions, the figures for room and board show the high price of city living, and these costs could add up to substantial debt. When Pierre Bonnell died in 1796, he owed his landlord $100.[50] Some refugees moved into less expensive neighborhoods and the suburbs, yet many preferred to stay in the heart of the city (as did the locals), to keep tabs on the latest news from the island, to be near fellow colonists, and to find work more easily.[51]

In general, these living arrangements reflected a decline in circumstances for the refugees. On moving to Philadelphia, François Hyacinth Brocas resided in one "room upstairs on the Second floor fronting the Street" in John Boulanger's boardinghouse on Sassafras Street, and many other refugees lived in similarly tight conditions that altered their daily routines.[52] Close quarters were not necessarily foreign to the exiles nor were they unusual in this period. City dwellings throughout the Atlantic world were crowded, multipurpose spaces on constricted lots. In both North America and Saint-Domingue, urban houses were complexes that supported, on average, seven or eight people of varying ranks (from slave to master) and numerous animals (horses, cows, pigs, chickens). Some had interior courtyards with working spaces that served as offices, kitchens, sheds, waste pits, gardens, wells, and so on.[53] Seaports being central to the economic, cultural, and political life of Saint-Domingue, many refugees were familiar with living—even if briefly—in dense but articulated urban settings. François Brocas, for example, was born in Bordeaux, migrated to Saint-Domingue, and established a mercantile house in Cap Français. Although being reduced to one room was certainly a change for him, he would have recognized the form and function of John Boulanger's boardinghouse.

The same held true for black and colored exiles, especially those who continued to live with their masters and mistresses in the United States. Domestic slaves in Saint-Domingue's port towns lived in ramshackle backyard sheds or slept inside their masters' houses on the floor. When slaveowner François Testas migrated to Philadelphia from the Quartier Grand Anse in the parish of Jérémie, he rented one room for himself and two black servants, Lesperance and Pelagie, whom he described as residing "here with me."[54] Testas's papers provide little information as to exactly where in the house Lesperance and Pelagie lodged. They may have lived together in the attic, the cellar, an outbuilding, or a separate room, depending on the size, plan, and other occupants of the building. Regardless of their specific location in the house, their cramped living and working conditions increased the potential for closer scrutiny by Testas. Such circumstances were typical of urban slavery and servitude throughout the North Atlantic world. Exiled bondsmen may have been all too well acquainted with such conditions and, like their peers elsewhere, have become adept at carving out privacy, whenever and wherever possible.[55]

No matter where and how the refugees lived, rents had to be paid, and the exiles employed several strategies to achieve this end. Specie was always in short supply, and so was credit, because white refugee credit rested on the value of their estates—an unpredictable quantity in the midst of a revolution. With specie precious and credit compromised, many exiles found a more reliable source of wealth in goods, and they brought with them property of substantial value. In one sense, the migration of the Saint-Dominguan refugees was as much about the movement of property as of people.

The most common possessions brought by white refugees were textiles, silver, and slaves. In comparison to other valuable objects, textiles and silver were easier to transport; they were durable and small and had high resale values. Secondhand clothing in good condition (along with other types of linens) found an eager market in the United States.[56] When executors assessed Jean Aubin's estate in Philadelphia, they found among his possessions a trunk belonging to Hortense, his free black servant, who had been kidnapped en route to the United States by privateers. The trunk contained sixteen petticoats, eleven shifts, six handkerchiefs, "three small pieces of dimity," as well as a quantity of child's clothing—the latter presumably for her three children who had accompanied her, but were also captured in transit. The trunk's contents reveal that Hortense had invested what capital she had in textiles, a sure commodity. Of course, not all black and colored Saint-Dominguans had Hortense's means, but her trunk suggests that when they did, their strategies complemented those of white colonists.[57] Silver plate was as good as currency and possibly more prized, for its workmanship and style. An account of the auction of exile Jean Mares's estate in 1798 provides some insight into how much money these goods fetched. A silver coffee pot sold for $32, and five silver soupspoons and three forks brought $27—together, enough to cover basic expenses for a few months.[58] Refugees with larger caches of goods sometimes sold them and invested the profits in various business schemes in order to earn a steady income.[59]

In slave states (which included New York until 1799 and New Jersey until 1804), enslaved exiles added substantially to their masters' assets. Bills of sale for Saint-Dominguan slaves are scarce; however, estimates in inventories denote their possible value. Appraisals of slaves depended on their age, sex, health, skills, and the market; when George Dupirct of Charleston died in 1817, his slave Rose, a twenty-two-year-old "born in the Island of St. Domingo," was listed as worth

$500, the most valuable "item" in his estate.[60] The sale of slaves was also common in "free" states, such as Pennsylvania and Massachusetts, where a master could sell the remaining time of a former slave who had been manumitted but was indentured for a number of years, often to his ex-owner. In Philadelphia a Saint-Dominguan exile named Marinette sold the last eighteen years of her servant's indenture for £50, while another refugee, called Somayrac, received $112 for the contract of his servant, Clere.[61]

The sale of a slave could bring a large, one-time cash infusion for a refugee, but renting out one's bondsmen could produce a steady income. François-Alexandre-Frédéric La Rochefoucauld-Liancourt, the famous reformer and exile from the French Revolution, claimed that in Charleston Saint-Dominguan refugees lived "on the product of the renting-out of some of their negroes whom they brought with them."[62] According to one observer, a master in the lower south could bring in between $6 and $10 per month by renting out a slave.[63] White and colored refugee slaveowners put their bondsmen to work in other profitable ways, for instance as labor in home industries. Lewis John Baptist Grand, an exile in Charleston, owned two men who were cigar makers; during an inventory of Grand's estate, appraisers found 380,740 cigars along with almost 200 pounds of tobacco, testaments to the productivity of the two slaves.[64] In Baltimore, assessors counted as part of Danse Fabre's estate three enslaved male bakers whose skills provided their master's income.[65] These household enterprises suited the urban environment, catering to the tastes and needs of residents, but it is clear that these slaves most likely migrated with such skills. Enslaved men in the towns of Saint-Domingue worked on the docks as well as in craft and retail trades.[66] For them, employment as bakers and cigar makers was probably a holdover from their time in the colony.

White exiles from Saint-Domingue brought other property that could be hawked, but these items appear with less frequency than silver, textiles, and slaves. Some refugees salvaged barrels of sugar and coffee from their plantations and sold them to U.S. merchants; they were able to get high prices, thanks to the disruption of trade caused by the revolution. In September 1795, "some Frenchmen arrived from the West-Indies" advertised the sale of a large collection of books.[67] Others carried jewelry, watches, and gold trinkets that, like silver, could be pawned or sold for significant sums.[68] Saint-Dominguan professionals and artisans migrated with the tools of their trades, yet these instruments were among the last items with which they would part, for they enabled the refugees to practice their occupations and generate income.[69]

While useful for its monetary value, this property, when retained, served another purpose: it connected the refugees' lives in Saint-Domingue to their exile lives in the United States. These objects helped create the "New Cape" in everyday settings; a soupspoon, a chemise, or a book evoked Saint-Domingue, transforming a tiny room in a boardinghouse into something that resembled home. This function of personal property explains the more unusual items that turned up in exiles' luggage. Stowed in General de Rouvray's trunk, for example, were two "African Pipes," and a C. Guillaud carried with him "a large dog, of the bull breed, cropt ears, grey hair, but striped like a tyger."[70] Having sentimental value or reflecting the curiosities of their owners, these goods signal personal rather than commercial priorities.[71] Some refugees displayed their sensibilities by acquiring new items once they settled in the United States. Set among the nondescript furnishings at Peter Benjamin Maingault's residence in Philadelphia was an expensive billiard table with all of the appropriate accessories, suggesting that he valued male sociability and envisioned entertaining guests.[72]

Maingault's billiard table points to another important aspect of refugee life in the United States: they acted collectively, fostering community development and, in some cases, altering the physical and social landscapes of American cities. Social networks eased the displacement of exiles, and the compactness of early American cities made it likely that refugees would come across one another in the streets. They took rooms in the same boardinghouses or lodgings, and they found public spaces to gather.[73] Among the most frequent meeting places for Saint-Dominguans were Roman Catholic churches. Like many North Americans, the exiles rejected the challenges to religion made during the radical phases of the French Revolution: Pierre Jaronay, an exile in New York, professed on his deathbed in 1796, "[I was never] as much convinced of [Catholicism's] sublimity than I am this day and pray therefore the person charged with the care of my children to educate them according to those principles and to banish from their minds the wish and the knowledge of these new doctrines rather invented to corrupt men than to render them better."[74] Many other Saint-Dominguans shared Jaronay's sentiment and became active members in local Catholic churches, attending masses and other spiritual rites.

Black and colored exiles also attended American Catholic churches. While several historians have documented the importance of vodou to slave life in Saint-Domingue and in particular to sparking the Haitian Revolution, there is little direct evidence of its transfer to the U.S. eastern seaboard in the 1790s. This absence of documentation is not surprising, given that the master class in Saint-Domingue worked to suppress vodou during the eighteenth century, and so its practitioners had long been in the habit of disguising their worship. Vodou was, and still is, a syncretic religion; it combines African religious beliefs and local experiences with Catholic frameworks and rituals, and among practitioners, vodou and Catholicism are not mutually exclusive but reinforcing.[75] In addition, certain gestures, objects, and phrases associated with vodou permeated the everyday lives of Saint-Dominguan adherents and could easily have continued in the United States. Therefore, black and colored refugees may have practiced vodou within the structures of Catholicism and daily life.

Catholic churches in Philadelphia, Baltimore, and Savannah saw a high level of participation by black and colored Saint-Dominguans. Consider the records for Holy Trinity and St. Joseph's Catholic churches in Philadelphia, where scores of black and colored exiles were married and baptized.[76] In 1794 Father Cibot baptized Felicitas, the daughter of Justina, "a free negress, of the Island of San Domingo," at St. Joseph's, while in 1801, John Louis Lindor and Louisa Rosette, "negroes, of San Domingo" were married there.[77] Black and colored exiles in Savannah were godparents for one another's children and witnesses at weddings, suggesting a sense of community among these populations.[78] At times, white refugees served in these roles as well. On the one hand, this phenomenon could be read as testimony to the continued power of white over black and colored Saint-Dominguans. On the other hand, it was a tactic whereby black and colored refugees made these white people responsible to them. As godparents or witnesses, white Saint-Dominguans pledged before God to look after the spiritual welfare of the subjects, and while this relationship was paternalistic to be sure, it also enabled these black and colored refugees to call on their white guardians for support—a potentially helpful safeguard in a virulently racist world.

With their numbers alone, black, white, and colored refugees transformed American Catholic churches. Saint-Dominguans doubled the size of Baltimore's Catholic population in the 1790s, but just as importantly, the exiles changed the make-up of congregations.[79] For decades, American Catholic churches had been dominated by Irish, English, and German adherents, and the arrival of a French-speaking, multiracial membership presented new opportunities and challenges. Sulpician priests in Baltimore accommodated their Francophone constituents by offering catechism classes in French at St. Mary's Lower Chapel, a church with a strong black and colored refugee membership. As late as 1810, priests were appointed to minister specifically to the needs of "French negroes."[80] With several priests and nuns among them, the white exiles bolstered the resident Catholic leadership throughout Maryland, in Wilmington, Delaware, and even in New London, Connecticut.[81] Although black and colored refugees were denied access to positions of rank, Pierre Toussaint, an enslaved exile later freed by his owner, aided the black Catholic community in antebellum New York City by founding the *Frères Réunis*, a social outreach organization.[82]

Exiles literally helped to build U.S. Catholic churches. Edmond Suire left a bequest of $200 for "finishing and compleating the Roman Chapel now building at Fells Point," and the widow Leroi donated her "Cinamon Coloured and Embroidered" gown to the same chapel, most likely for the church to sell for revenue.[83] The mark of refugees was apparent in a Catholic chapel in Philadelphia, where on the wall hung "a small oil painting about one and a half feet wide by two feet high, representing a brig with a shattered foremast; the Virgin is in the sky, with her Son near her, and seems to be protecting the vessel. On one of the sides of the picture on the canvas itself one reads *Ex Voto* and at the bottom of the canvas 'Made the 1st of November 1791 by the passengers of the brig *Minerva*, coming from Cap François to Philadelphia.'"[84] The painting gave thanks for the refugees' safe delivery to American shores, and its presence in the chapel as a devotional centerpiece called on parishioners to ponder God's power again and again within the frame of the exiles' flight from the Haitian Revolution.

This Francophone Caribbean infusion into American Catholic churches provoked discord when the practices of the Saint-Dominguans clashed with those of other members. Saint-Dominguans and Irish congregants in Charleston quarreled for decades, and they exchanged insults in other cities as well.[85] As one refugee traveled from city to city, he recorded his consistently negative impressions of local priests. Of a Philadelphia congregation, he remarked, "The priests of this chapel are Irish and consequently fanatics." In Norfolk, he disagreed with the theological tenets of "a zealous, red-faced Hibernian" who "came among the unhappy French San Domingan refugees to preach humility and submission to the will of God and the necessity of accepting gladly a miserable lot with which the Church and the priest are in harmony."[86] For this observer, the refugees' fate was not the will of God. If it was, then the slave rebellion would have been justified, and that was an ideological leap that few white refugees—or white Americans for that matter—wanted to make.

In almost every U.S. city, Saint-Dominguans marked out establishments where they gathered. Certain taverns, boardinghouse parlors, shops, and bathhouses became known as the stomping grounds of island refugees. In some cases these businesses were run by Frenchmen or the owners catered to the tastes and longings of exiles by stocking goods and providing services that reminded them of home: from French bread to French baths. While principally the haunts of white exiles, these sites facilitated interaction among black and colored refugees as well. Free people of color were not barred from certain spaces, and as enslaved and indentured exiles accompanied their masters and mistresses or were sent out on errands, they met up, swapped stories, exchanged gossip, and enjoyed the company of fellow French- and Creole-speakers—in much the same way as did their white counterparts.

Perhaps nowhere was the sociability of the Saint-Dominguan white diaspora more evident than in Moreau de St. Méry's printing shop and bookstore in Philadelphia. It was a magnet for exiles, and Moreau was their shrewdest observer. Born into the white elite of Martinique in 1750, Médéric-Louis-Elie Moreau de St. Méry went to Paris for his education in the law, and set up shop in Cap Français in the 1770s. There, his career flourished, and so, too, did his role in the colonial Enlightenment as he became a freemason and member of the Cercle des Philadelphes and penned numerous political, cultural, and ethnographic texts. In the 1780s Moreau spent much of his time in Paris, advising the government on all things related to the colonies, including advocating against free men of color and slaves and promoting greater political and economic autonomy for white colonists. Despite his brilliant success, Moreau soon found himself on the wrong side of the French and Haitian revolutions and made his escape to the United States in the early 1790s.[87]

Moreau traveled extensively between Norfolk and New York before settling—for a few years at least—in Philadelphia. At the corner of First and Walnut, he established his print shop and bookstore. There, employing two refugees to work the press, Moreau reprinted the latest tracts from France and Saint-Domingue and printed original publications, such as a newspaper edited by a refugee named Gatereau that featured news from France, the colonies, and the local exile community. Ever the entrepreneur, Moreau offered other goods that he thought would appeal to his colonial comrades, among which were "a stock of certain small contrivances—ingenious things said to have been suggested by the stork," in other words, condoms. Of these "contrivances" he noted that, "while they were primarily intended for the use of French colonials, they were in great demand among Americans, in spite of the false shame so prevalent among the latter." Never weighed down by humility, Moreau proudly concluded, "Thus the use of this medium on the vast American continent dates from this time."[88]

Moreau was not the only refugee to realize the power of the press. Several exile-run newspapers sprang up in the 1790s. In addition to the *Courier of France and the Colonies* printed out of Moreau's shop, there was *The American Star* (Philadelphia), *Gazette française et americaine* (New York), and *The Level of Europe* (New York), among others. Printed in French or sometimes in double columns of French and English, these newspapers courted subscribers outside their local vicinity, relying on contacts up and down the East Coast to advertise and reach refugees in their areas.[89] Many of these enterprises lasted only a year or two before folding, yet they constituted attempts to maintain a sense of community in the diaspora. Other transfers of goods and services are also illustrative: for example, Moreau acquired his supply of condoms from a refugee in Baltimore.

In housing and churches, shops and taverns, and in products and print culture, the refugees found and constructed an infrastructure in American cities that was recognizable and conducive enough to allow them to continue aspects of their daily lives back in the colony. Saint-Dominguans also parlayed their island background into profit as they sought to find work in U.S. cities. Some managed to sustain themselves without working, but most Saint-Dominguans discovered that their exile outlasted their resources. The white refugees tried to turn their displacement and foreignness to their advantage, highlighting both their refugee status and their French background to curry the favor of potential bosses and customers.

Saint-Dominguans entered almost every line of employment. They were bakers, hairdressers, pastry cooks, and ice cream makers; boardinghouse keepers, planters, merchants, and musicians; teachers, fencing instructors, tin workers, and watchmakers; lacemakers, storekeepers, coppersmiths, barbers, and coopers; dockworkers, domestics, laundresses, and painters, to name but a few.[90] For some skilled artisans and professionals, these jobs represented continuations of their occupations in Saint-Domingue. Several free men of color in Savannah translated their thriving tailoring businesses on the island to their new surroundings, but many white and free colored men found it impossible to resume their customary occupations.[91] Language proved a formidable obstacle: everyone from bookkeepers to actors stumbled over this barrier.[92] Others had professions that failed to transplant readily to the American context. Lawyers, like Maurice Parfait Daligny, needed time to acquire "sufficient Knowledge of the Laws of the US" before they could practice their profession.[93] A few circumvented linguistic problems by obtaining jobs with the French consulate or with Frenchmen already established in the United States, but these positions were few and far between, leaving most refugees to compete in local job markets.[94]

Some turned their refinement into profit. Paster Laval in Charleston, "finding himself here divested of any other means of acquiring a decent livelihood, than those which his education have procured him," opened a fencing academy.[95] A group of young Saint-Dominguan men roamed New Jersey giving concerts and balls in order to earn money, while two exiles in Baltimore gave classes in drawing, painting, and music.[96] Others faced more desperate circumstances: Charles

Laurent "endeavored to support his Family by every kind of Work he was able to perform such as making wood Boxes or mending Umbrellas or any Thing he could work or execute with the Help of two Negroes." Five years later, Laurent was working in the hat factory and his family and slaves were living there.[97] His path points to the dire straits into which some refugees were driven.

Exile compelled many white and free colored women to join the work force, too, though for some, this was nothing new. Middling white and colored women in Cap Français ran small shops and other establishments, and several white women ranked among the elite plantation owners.[98] This experience and know-how served them well in the United States. Jacqueline Françoise Pebarte Courtin, a white exile, went into business with Andrew Anthony Charles Lechais to establish a boardinghouse in Charleston in 1804, while Manette Tardieu, a free colored seamstress, purchased property in Savannah and established a flourishing enterprise.[99] Nevertheless, for many white women in particular, working was a challenge. Some fell back on their educations, becoming teachers of French, fine sewing, and music.[100] Although this work signaled a decline in fortune for them, it was well within the realm of respectability. At times, however, white refugee women found themselves in humbler circumstances. On a visit to New Jersey to see the former colonel of a Saint-Dominguan regiment, a young gentleman noted with surprise that the colonel's wife, "her hair bound in a red kerchief, was vigorously polishing the furniture in the parlor; and Miss Polly [the colonel's daughter], with bare legs and feet, was busy milking the cows." The women were doing the kind of work that they had previously ordered slaves to perform and, most strikingly, in a similar manner—barefoot with kerchiefs around their heads. Despite these transgressions of class, the author was careful to make clear, Miss Polly was still "as white as the milk which gushes through her fingers."[101] The work and the accompanying dress did not undercut their status as white women. Looking to diffuse the potentially subversive situation, the author painted the scene in pastoral terms—an aesthetic that was popular in late eighteenth-century France thanks to Marie Antoinette's getups as she played shepherdess and milkmaid at her faux village on the Versailles estate.[102]

Compared to the occupations of the majority of their masters and mistresses, the labor of enslaved Saint-Dominguans remained essentially the same in exile as it had in the colony. Most of the migrating slaves were probably domestic servants who cooked, cleaned, laundered, looked after children, and attended to the toilettes of their owners, or they were skilled in a craft, such as baking or cigar making, that they continued on arrival.[103] While the actual labor performed by most black refugees did not change, the conditions of their work did. Usually, black migrants toiled in their masters' households, but many slaves, especially those who were rented out, found themselves working for locals.[104] In addition, as the example of Charles Laurent demonstrates, black refugees sometimes labored with their masters. Finally, because of the gradual manumission laws in a few northern states, some enslaved Saint-Dominguans became free. As a result, many entered the wage labor market—albeit at times in the homes of their former masters and mistresses. Jean Jacques, for example, nursed the ailing Alexandre Heguy, who promised him $20, "over and above the Wages that may be due him," if Jean Jacques stayed with him until his death.[105] Some freed refugees used the exigencies of exile to bargain with their former owners for better pay and better terms.

Whether they found new situations or continued in their previous occupations, the refugees had to make their services appealing to the American consumer. After all, why should a Philadelphian decide to patronize a Saint-Dominguan doctor or cooper over a local one? Aware of the competition, exiles played up their backgrounds to bring in business, and they did so in two ways. First, the refugees used their experiences as practitioners in Saint-Domingue as selling points. One physician, Dr. Courbe, publicized his expertise in treating yellow fever, adding that the epidemic in Philadelphia in the fall of 1793 could have been averted had the Saint-Dominguan method of treatment been applied.[106] Men like Courbe made clear that they knew the particularities of the New World environment (in some cases, better than North Americans), and as such, their services were superior to competitors'.

Second, in their solicitations for work, white Saint-Dominguans highlighted their recent traumas, occasionally in mini-narratives. Michael Fronty, a doctor from Le Cap, began his notice with an account of his recent tribulations, how he lost his fortune in the slave uprising and was robbed of what little property he had left by the notorious pirate, Captain Tucker.[107] Such pathetic tales were designed to arouse pity among readers, who, so moved, the exiles hoped, would patronize the authors. Most often, the white refugees denoted their plight with the simple phrase "an unfortunate from St. Domingo," or as one of "the unfortunate French from St. Domingo." The wording here is important and deliberate. "Unfortunate" encapsulated how the refugees saw their situation: they were blameless victims of a slave rebellion that was beyond their control. Given the extensive coverage of the Haitian Revolution in the United States, every reader would have known the circumstances on "St. Domingo" to which the exiles alluded.

The variant "unfortunate French" worked in a slightly different manner. While it, too, argued for the innocence of white refugees, the phrase also brought out their Frenchness. This was significant for two reasons. It helped to differentiate them from continental French exiles in the United States whose politics were frequently denounced as "aristocratic." The white Saint-Dominguans labored under this allegation as well and worked doggedly against it; distinguishing themselves from their continental peers was central to this aim. Also, the Saint-Dominguans wanted to accentuate their Frenchness in order to market themselves more lucratively. At first glance, this decision seems somewhat odd: British North Americans had cultivated a rather vigorous Francophobia, thanks to war and rivalry between Britain and France. Britons and their colonial counterparts derided Frenchmen for their Catholicism, their political system, and for just about anything else (food, social mores, character), and Anglophone colonists' experiences battling Frenchmen and their Indian allies fueled this acrimony.

American reservations about the French lingered during and after the U.S. revolution, but, that said, French goods and services were the height of fashion in the 1790s. In part, this fascination with things French was associated with U.S. supporters of the French Revolution; however, even among the revolution's American detractors, French fashion carried a certain cachet. This cultural clout persisted regardless of the political incarnation of the revolution—from its radical, Jacobin phase through Bonaparte's self-declaration as emperor. French became part of the curricula of U.S. colleges, and interest in learning the language stretched beyond the academy, as evidenced by the numerous advertisements for French instruction in newspapers. Americans, especially the elite, followed French manners, style, and taste avidly, reading the fashion magazines and demanding imports from the Continent.[108] By underscoring their French affiliations, the refugees tapped into this market for refined French goods and services, claiming to know the most up-to-date styles. Two pastry chefs advertised to New York residents that their delicacies were "dressed to the French new fashion," while Madame Deseze's dancing school featured all the "new French steps."[109] This marketing strategy made their products and services tempting and hence, saleable to those local consumers concerned with keeping up appearances.

In their advertisements the white Saint-Dominguans insisted that they possessed the best of both worlds: they had the savvy of creoles and the sophistication of Frenchmen. Much as North Americans maintained on the eve of their revolution that the best qualities of Britons were preserved and flourished in the New World (more so than in Britain), so, too, did the white exiles from Saint-Domingue aver to represent the best of France. Yet some observers begged to differ. A Parisian school master in New York named Hyacinth Agnel published a scathing condemnation of the exiles that dismissed them on the basis of their creoleness:

> The subscriber . . . finds himself under the necessity of warning [the public] against a set of people, who pretend to teach the French language, and who . . . are so far from being qualified for their art, that they do not so much as suspect that it is one. Teaching French is become now-a-days the profession of foreigners of all sorts, who know not how to shift for a living, and often have no qualification at all; the most part of them are refugees, from the islands.[110]

Agnel's withering contempt stemmed from longstanding notions about the inferiority of islanders. In his eyes the exiles were backward bumpkins, ill-prepared to teach anyone anything French, yet his outburst also suggests that the Saint-Dominguans' pleas to U.S. audiences were convincing. Regrettably, no refugee account books have been discovered, but that Agnel felt compelled to post such a notice and that so many exiles relied on "Frenchness" in their advertisements indicate the success of such themes.

There was one area in which the Saint-Dominguans did not advertise their heritage. However strapped they may have been, white exiles shied away from invoking "creoleness" or "Frenchness" when advertising the labor of refugee slaves. This silence is particularly revealing, given that some white colonists saw "creoleness" as a cultural phenomenon shared by black, white, and colored born in Saint-Domingue. In the late eighteenth century, commentators on the island, most famously Moreau de St. Méry, claimed that certain characteristics of native-born Saint-Dominguans united the population across racial lines. Not surprisingly, this vision of "creoleness" was used by some white Saint-Dominguans to support slavery and the continued subjugation of free people of color.[111] But this aspect of Saint-Dominguan "creoleness" was not present in the U.S. context. Among white Americans, black and colored exiles were not considered as among the "unfortunates" from Saint-Domingue, and the combination of "French" with "negro" carried very different connotations indeed.

The ploys of the white Saint-Dominguans are strong testimony of their degree of familiarity with the United States. Not only were the urban landscapes of U.S. cities recognizable in many respects, but the refugees had some sense of their new neighbors' wishes as well. This familiarity, however, did not spill over into a celebration of similarities between these two groups of "Americans." The more Saint-Dominguans and locals interacted socially in the 1790s, the more each saw the other as distinct, and these differences played important roles in an age of revolution.

THE OTHER AMERICANS

A Maryland charity group summed up what it saw as the awkward predicament of Saint-Dominguan refugees in U.S. cities: "Their embarrassments here, and need of assistance, must be encreased by a wide difference in manners and customs, and a difference in language."[112] In the view of white Americans, the refugees were, in short, a different people: the way they spoke, looked, and acted, all deviated from local norms, and in the eighteenth century such distinctions mattered. In more hierarchical eras and cultures, clothing, deportment, and speech were critical signs of status as well as national origin, and while the age of republican revolution challenged some of these notions, appearance and behavior were still crucial indicators of virtue—the bedrock of republics. The attributes of individuals were cited to encapsulate the temperament of entire populations and to judge whether they were worthy of membership in enlightened republics. In the case of North Americans and Saint-Dominguans, the evaluative process included not only white men, but also white women, the enslaved, and free people of color. The condition of these subordinates reflected on the character of white men and the society they had built.

U.S. residents' assessments of the Saint-Dominguans reveal as much about what they liked to think of themselves as about what they thought of the refugees. Their appraisals indicate both an attraction to the exiles, as with the goods and services that they offered, and locals' desire to distance themselves from their Caribbean peers. The white exiles, in turn, had their own take on the members of the first New World republic. More often than not, the refugees were frustrated by Americans' views and contended that the locals could stand to learn a thing or two from Saint-Dominguans. Their interactions in the social and cultural spheres of U.S. cities reveal how each group compared itself favorably with the other and argued for its own merits in the new revolutionary republican milieu.

One of the starkest dissimilarities between locals and exiles could be heard rather than seen: language. Prior to the arrival of the Saint-Dominguans, it was unusual to hear French on the streets of U.S. cities. Enthusiasm for the French Revolution inspired some white Americans to study the language, yet few achieved true proficiency, let alone mastery. And, according to scholars' best estimates, African Americans in the northeastern states during the colonial and revolutionary periods were more likely to know Dutch than French.[113] However, Americans noted an increased presence of French in the local soundscape with the arrival of the refugees. As late as 1805, Philadelphia merchant Stephen Girard declared that one "would find, daily, opportunities to speak French," and the white refugees certainly contributed to this linguistic diversity.[114] The role of black exiles in this change in the linguistic environment was less noticeable, since some enslaved Saint-Dominguans spoke French "indifferent[ly]" at best, probably because of their relatively recent arrival from Africa.[115] Advertisements for runaway enslaved refugees in the United States occasionally noted the slave's African place of origin, such as "Congo," "Nago," "Ebo," "Arada," and "Mozabie."[116] The eighteenth-century linguistic collision of African languages and French led to the development of a new vernacular, called, appropriately enough, Creole, which was (or at least could be) spoken by native-born Saint-Dominguans of all races and was particularly prominent among the enslaved.[117]

The exiles' Caribbean background per se was critical to American appraisals of the manners and customs of the exiles in their midst. According to popular notions of the day, "the burning heat of the sun in the torrid zone, must produce such effects on the organs of the inhabitants, as to make them considerably differ from those of the people of more moderate climes."[118] Being born in the tropics meant that Saint-Dominguans were physically different from European Frenchmen and from North Americans, and these distinctions were supposedly apparent to any acute observer. White refugee women and both genders of black and colored people were the subjects of great scrutiny in this regard. White creole men elicited commentary, but their physiques were judged more in discussions about their military performances in Saint-Domingue than in the American social scene. Similarly, refugees took only passing notice of white American men, whom they found "tall and thin" but "listless," and spilled much more ink describing the women, free people of color, and slaves they saw in the United States.[119] This apportionment of observers' attention may follow the gaze of white men, resident and immigrant, who were the most represented recorders, yet there is no reason to suppose that men were not interested in appraising other men. In this era they did so constantly.[120] Rather, it seems that observers found the most telling features of a society at what they deemed its nadir rather than its apex.

Commentators declared that white Saint-Dominguan women had a beauty as unique as the colony itself. They were celebrated for their "elegant shape," possessing "an activity and suppleness" of their limbs produced by the "temperature of the climate," and they were lauded for "their delicacy of features," "majestic walk," and "their large eyes [which] exhibit a happy medium between languor and vivacity."[121] Significantly, white creole women were depicted as knowing how to handle their beauty, as they struck an uncanny balance between ease of movement and erect posture—a guise that was important to the genteel class of the eighteenth-century Atlantic world.[122] According to the refugees, white American women were not without their charms. Moreau de St. Méry noted that they were, in general, "pretty," but he noted that this beauty was ephemeral: after eighteen, their faces became pale, their hair "scanty," their teeth "bad," and "their breasts, never large, already have vanished."[123]

The best evidence of visible distinctiveness between North Americans and Saint-Dominguans concerns enslaved populations. In part, this reflects the nature of available documentation: we lack a body of evidence for the appearance of white refugees that is comparable to the scores of descriptions of runaway black exiles. The advertisements indicate that certain aspects of appearance were associated with black Saint-Dominguans—or as Americans called them, "French negroes." At times, this nationalized terminology operated as a kind of shorthand. In a notice for the runaway slave Breland, his owner warned other masters not to be fooled—that although Breland was a "French Negro Man," he "looks very much like an American negro."[124] Master Thomas Keen in Charleston noted that his slave Tom was "African born, but has much the appearance of a French negro."[125] These notices suggest that some slaves may have used masters' categories—"French," "American," and "African"—to their advantage, disguising themselves with the attributes of another "type" and turning a tool of oppression into a means of individual rebellion. But the classifications also reveal a shared visual culture between masters and slaves in the Atlantic world—a common, but certainly not the sole vocabulary for appraising people and their origins.

Enslaved Saint-Dominguans were remarkable in the U.S. context because of the visible marks of West Indian slavery on their bodies. As a way to keep track of their slaves, Saint-Dominguan masters and mistresses branded or "stamped" them on the chest with the owners' last name or initials. Moreau contended defensively that branding was used exclusively on African not creole slaves, but given that the overwhelming majority of slaves in the colony were African-born, the practice was obviously commonplace.[126] Notices for runaway "French negroes" in the United States mention these marks repeatedly; usually, American slaves did not bear such scars. Branding had been employed in the British colonies earlier in the eighteenth century; however, in the revolutionary era masters generally frowned on the practice. In a letter from merchant Jean Girard written in Cap Français to his brother Stephen in Philadelphia in December 1786, Jean wrote concerning a young slave, Sam, who belonged to Stephen but was on loan to Jean. According to Jean, Sam ran away constantly and cost Jean much money to recover him each time. Jean complained that he was at his wit's end and so had decided to take drastic measures: "I will stop this by branding him in fear of losing him." Anticipating his brother's censure for such a step, Jean added, "I must do something."[127]

But the advertisements for runaway "French negroes" in the United States imply that recognition of an enslaved Saint-Dominguan was almost instantaneous: it did not require a conversation to hear what language was spoken or an inspection for branding scars. Instead, clothing was key, and this held true not just for differentiating a "French negro" from an "American" one, but for assessing all members of local and refugee populations. Clothing was as crucial to discerning individual identity as were physical features, and dress operated in more general terms to signal status, nationality, and gender.[128] One exile noted that in the United States "more than anywhere else, it is the clothes that make the man" and in this case, the woman, freedman, and slave as well.[129] Some white refugees, unable to bring their whole wardrobe with them or forced to sell their best clothes, worried that migration had compromised their appearance, leading locals to misread them. Foreseeing this possibility, one exile, whose clothes were in tatters when he boarded a ship for North America, wrote, "[I] carefully guarded my hat and shoes, so that they would honor me at my debarkation."[130] Notwithstanding the financial straits of many white refugees, the inventories of their estates attest to substantial investments in everything from smart clothes to pounds of hair powder.[131] Clearly, they were concerned that their look match the level of respectability that they claimed.

In the United States Saint-Dominguan slaves, free people of color, and white women were all identifiable by their clothes. Commentators pointed to the white refugee ladies' "thinness of . . . dress," which suited the tropical climate and emphasized their "exotic" origins.[132] Loose, flowing, diaphanous fabrics were fashionable in France, especially in the second half of the decade when neoclassicism was all the rage, and elite women donned white, transparent dresses that, in the words of one wry observer, "did not leave the beholder to divine, but to perceive, every secret charm."[133] Fashion-conscious American women followed the Parisian scene, and some, not without scandal, adopted the "semi-nude" chemise gowns, albeit not to the same effect. In the refugees' estimation they could not "imitate that elegance of style possessed by Frenchwomen." American ladies came off as unsophisticated, cluttering their dresses with all sorts of ribbons and notions; they were "greatly addicted to finery" rather than in command of it.[134] In the exiles' opinion, these women had much to learn about taste from the white women of Saint-Domingue.

Slave clothing in both the United States and Saint-Domingue was by and large flimsy, not by choice but by imposition; yet the dress of slaves and masters sometimes intersected among the refugees. Enslaved exiles were noted as dressing in the "West-India creole manner," and in comparing the notices for runaway black Saint-Dominguans with those for U.S. slaves, a few distinguishing, although not hard-and-fast, features come to light.[135] While American slaves, especially women, often wore handkerchiefs tied around their heads, "French negroes," it seems, stood out because of the style or material of their handkerchiefs; and according to the advertisements, black Saint-Dominguans pierced either one or both ears, sporting a gold hoop, with greater frequency than did American slaves. Also, several are described as tying their shoes with ribbons.[136] Interestingly, these accoutrements—handkerchiefs, earrings, and laced (rather than buckled) shoes— were popular fashions among white and free colored Saint-Dominguans as well. Elaborately tied kerchiefs and shoes with ribbons were trendy in France and its colonies during the 1790s, and some white men were known to wear gold hoop earrings.[137] This borrowing is not a simple case of enslaved Saint-Dominguans imitating their masters; it points to complicated exchanges back and forth across racial lines, in which the direction of mimicry did not follow strict hierarchies. In the colony this phenomenon was witnessed most often among white women, who imitated the styles of colored women, as both vied for the attentions of white men. This can be most clearly seen with the wearing of madras handkerchiefs, which began as a punitive sumptuary law against free women of color, but because their mode of folding the handkerchiefs was so alluring, white women in the colony, including Bonaparte's sister, Madame Leclerc, took up the accessory.[138] The blurring of lines between white and colored women persisted in exile, and Americans were taken aback by the "obnoxious luxury" enjoyed by some Saint-Dominguan women of color.[139]

In the eyes of black and white Americans, Saint-Dominguan refugees looked different; their features and clothing made them stand out on city streets. Some Americans appropriated aspects of the refugees' appearance—some in the name of fashion, others when attempting to escape bondage—and in so doing reflected a degree of admiration. But the branding of slaves, the skimpy dress of white Saint-Dominguan women, and the sumptuous circumstances of free women of color gave other Americans pause; they suggested a society too violent and salacious, too ruled by passion to be truly virtuous. For their part, the white refugees

Dress of Free People of Color and Slaves in the Colonies. Nicolas Ponce, *Recueil de vues des lieux principaux de la colonie françoise de Saint-Domingue* (Paris, 1791). Courtesy John Carter Brown Library at Brown University.

thought that the look of Americans, even slaves in the United States, signaled a crassness that compromised any pretensions to virtue. Not only were the white women unrefined, but the master class seemed determined to maintain the wretched condition of slaves, and of freedmen as well. Moreau de St. Méry professed his shock when buying fabric in Philadelphia for a slave and being "shown only the coarsest and ugliest material." He asked for "something better," and the shopkeeper retorted that the cheap cloth was "good enough for Negroes."[140] What white Americans celebrated as the noble simplicity of their society the white refugees saw as baseness.

Late-eighteenth-century men and women were also keen observers of comportment, and U.S. residents and Saint-Dominguans had ample opportunity to take stock of each other. Refugees and locals passed one another on the street, rubbed elbows in taverns, coffeehouses, shops, clubs, theaters, and churches, and attended the same balls, parties, and amusements. Americans occasionally advocated such interaction. In the early 1790s, notices for plays and concerts were frequently printed in both French and English so as to include exiles in the festivities. One advertisement for a ball in Baltimore offered to instruct "strangers" in the English style of dancing.[141] Centers of learning welcomed educated exiles, and city residents invited Saint-Dominguans—at least those with status—into their parlors to partake of tea, dinner, and conversation.[142]

In these meetings, refugees and locals found much delight in each other's company, and some interactions between individual exiles and residents went so well that they married.[143] The perceived affronts during these encounters are perhaps more telling, however, and reactions ranged from the amused to the indignant. A young white Saint-Dominguan recounted his gaffe at a ball where he had gained the attentions of three or four ladies thanks to his witty repartee but had lost their interest when he executed a "fatal pirouette" on the dance floor.[144] In several cities refugee men earned a reputation for their "luxury" and "lack of reason" at the gaming table.[145] One recalled a conversation with an Ameri-

Slaves Playing Baton. Nicolas Ponce, *Recueil de vues des lieux principaux de la colonie fran-çoise de Saint-Domingue* (Paris, 1791). While no doubt stylized, these images of slaves and free people of color in Saint-Domingue offer insight into aspects of their appearance that made them distinctive in the American context. Before his exile in the United States, Moreau de St. Méry had a hand in the publication of this work. Courtesy John Carter Brown Library at Brown University.

can woman in which she peppered him with questions about eating frogs.[146] The gentleman wrote off the woman's comments as ignorance rather than malice, but a Francophilic writer in a Charleston newspaper protested that the prejudice against Frenchmen was so great that one was lucky "not to be knocked down with a brick bat, and hear the polite expressions of '*God dam Frenchman.*'"[147]

Such disparaging remarks were informed by longstanding notions about colonial *and* continental Frenchmen (hence, the questions about frogs). Yet, what set white Saint-Dominguans apart from their continental counterparts was the overwhelming presence in the West Indian colonies of enslaved and free people of color. This feature persisted to a certain extent in the refugee population, and Americans included appraisals of the behavior of black and colored refugees in drawing their conclusions about Saint-Dominguan society. Even prosaic activities raised eyebrows. In 1817 several local men petitioned the mayor of Baltimore to intervene with a group of enslaved Saint-Dominguan women. The petitioners complained that when the women gathered in their neighborhood to do laundry, they stripped "almost naked" with "a number of Black Men" present. This practice was not in any way clandestine; the writers expressed "no doubt" that the mayor himself had borne witness to "many instances."[148] Throughout the eighteenth century, commentators in France pointed to the behavior of free women of color as a sign of the lascivious nature of the colony and its residents, and white Americans did the same when refugees arrived on their shores. Free women of color were a sensitive subject for white Saint-Dominguan men. In the 1790s white residents of the United States claimed to be stunned to see white refugee men walking arm-in-arm with colored women in broad daylight.[149] Moreau de St. Méry viewed these reactions as hypocritical, pointing out that there were plenty of surreptitious "favors" between local white men and free and enslaved women of color.[150] In his estimation white Americans' astonishment at the Saint-Dominguans was a front to disguise their own infelicities.

Whether they had actually witnessed these notorious behaviors or merely heard them rumored, white Americans found the resulting characterizations of Saint-Dominguans convenient, in that they helped to distinguish Americans from their French Caribbean peers. The implication that ran throughout these assessments of refugee behavior was that white Americans were more virtuous than white Saint-Dominguans: they avoided foppish dance moves, the vagaries of the gambling table, and the temptations of black and colored women. These images were reinforced in popular culture, which perpetuated stereotypes about free Saint-Dominguan women—both white and colored.[151] Consider these two examples. The first is a 1795 fireworks display in Philadelphia. The elaborate

Washerwomen. Nicolas Ponce, *Recueil de vues des lieux principaux de la colonie françoise de Saint-Domingue* (Paris, 1791). This portrayal of black Saint-Dominguan laundresses plays on and perpetuates their eroticized reputation. Courtesy John Carter Brown Library at Brown University.

exhibition featured explosions that resembled wheels, vessels, and the sun as well as more abstract representations of folly, love, and friendship. Most interesting for our purposes was the tenth display in the line-up, "a great mechanical piece" that illustrated "the caprices of the French Creole ladies."[152] No eyewitness accounts of this spectacle survive, but the brief description in the newspaper suggests that the piece included a built set (sometimes called a *machina*) of the "ladies," probably posed in a vignette, with fireworks set off around or from it. The exact nature of their "caprices" is unclear: they could be sexual, racial, or, in a less vicious vein, fashionable. Most fireworks displays in this period came with a program that explained what the audience was supposed to see—a handy aid, given the unpredictability of the fiery medium.[153] Even if the scene required identification as "the caprices of French Creole ladies," the exhibitors assumed that once told, the spectators would get the joke. While the name of the firm that designed the show, Ambroise and Company, hints at a French origin, the event was clearly tailored to an American audience; for example, one piece featured fifteen stars, an allusion, so an advertisement explained, to the United States. The choice to include the "French Creole ladies" in the program indicates an understanding that jokes at their expense were just as "American" as the flag.

A more narrative typecasting of female refugees turned up on the American stage. Some exile women performed in traveling troupes in the 1790s, looking to make ends meet; and American playwrights incorporated refugee characters into their plays, as did the author of *The Triumphs of Love; or Happy Reconciliation*.[154] This comedy was written by John Murdock, a native of Philadelphia and a hairdresser by profession, who claimed that he was moved to compose his own theatrical works after being "at times, much disgusted, to see and hear pieces performed, so foreign to the circumstances of a republican people." He wanted to offer "drama, which would be more consonant to the ears of Americans." *The Triumphs of Love* was his first effort in this regard.[155]

The plot of the play is simple: it is a story of young men looking and finding love. Keeping in mind that Murdock intended his tale to ring true for local audiences, the importance is in the details—what made it, in Murdock's view at least, American. Some of the main characters are Quakers (a decision not surprising in Philadelphia), but a more interesting decision is that Saint-Dominguan refugees are central to the plot: a pair of exiles—a white brother and sister—are befriended by the aptly, if somewhat obviously, named Quaker family, the Friendlys. George Friendly, Jr., falls in love with the Saint-Dominguan maiden, named Clementina. Clementina's story of her arrival is typical of those told by white refugees. Alone in her room, she laments, "Oh, who is like unto me—in so short a time to experience such a reverse of fortune? Some few months ago, I was in the full enjoyment of all the luxuries of life—and in one day, obliged to fly my country and possessions, with some few hundred dollars: thought myself fortunate in getting a passage for this famed country of liberty and tranquility. But was arrested by the way, by cruel pirates, and stripped of the remnant of my fortune, save a few dollars the relentfull savages left me: and here I am, a wretched refugee; reduced almost to the last extremity."[156] The quintessential damsel in distress, with her story and her beauty Clementina charms the prosperous George Friendly, Jr., who, within minutes of their first meeting, proposes marriage, relishing the role of protector. George—like the nation he represents—provides asylum for the distressed, beautiful, and suppliant.

As this love story unfolds, another episode involves a refugee with quite different overtones and resolution. George's friend, the unsubtly named Trifle, announces he has fallen in love and challenges George to guess with whom. Knowing that Trifle is, as George puts it, "fond of variety," he speculates that Trifle is smitten with a black woman. Trifle denies such an allegation, attesting that he has "not quite so strong a stomach." Instead he is enamored "with one of those called people of colour," who, he thinks, possesses a complexion "superior to all our boasted fair whites and reds: 'tis a fine standing colour: oh, such soft, such sweet, languishing, melting, dissolving looks."[157] Goading Trifle on, George asks to see "this yellow piece of perfection," and here, Trifle tells of his encounter with the woman of color on the street: "As I was addressing her in her own language, you know I speak French very well," a dog that was chasing a pig ran between his legs and sent him crashing to the ground.[158] In the confusion Trifle lost sight of his "love," to the comedic benefit, it is presumed, of the audience. However, the episode underscores assumptions that white Americans held about themselves and their society: that "people of colour" were not indigenous (only "whites" and "reds" were) but "French" and that no respectable member of society would be attracted to them (and that not even a trifler could "stomach" black women). Trifle's tale reasserts an emerging U.S. fiction regarding interracial relations, denying that miscegenation existed. This fiction asserted that such relations were incompatible with American virtue and attributed them instead to the French Caribbean.

In such popular performances, white Saint-Dominguan women were derided, but there was hope for some, at least those who fit the model of Clementina and found an American guardian. For black and colored women from the colony, their inclusion into U.S. society was impossible. They were exotic and foreign, and white Americans looked for assurance that they would stay that way. But for their part, many exiles were not so sure that they wanted to be incorporated into U.S. society. They protested disdainful treatment at the hands of Americans and thought their new neighbors repugnant on several fronts. In the few surviving accounts left by refugees, the authors lambasted Americans' poor hygiene, awful food, crass manners, and tiresome society. The exiles were particularly affronted by the American refusal to acknowledge these shortcomings. As one refugee groused, "I only wish that when each day they ridicule national pride (in others), they would not gracelessly terminate their tirade with a pompous eulogy of themselves. To hear them, their nation is already the most enlightened and the most powerful in the universe. The deuce! What airs!"[159]

Moreau de St. Méry pointed to U.S. slavery as another point of conceit. While not an abolitionist (far from it), he fumed that since the onset of the Haitian Revolution, Frenchmen had praised the practice of slavery in the United States as a counterpoint to that in the French West Indies. Yet Moreau countered that in the American South slaves were "held in a state of debasement which astounds even the inhabitants of the colonies." Some states may have begun the gradual process of emancipation, but, he noted, "Free Men of Color are no better treated than the slaves, except for the fact that no one is allowed to beat them. They too are in an abject condition."[160] Judging from the treatment of enslaved and freedmen, the United States—even "free" Philadelphia—fell far short of its self-congratulatory rhetoric.

The exiles' critiques reveal an attempt to expose flaws in the visions of the United States that persisted in France. Since the American Revolution, many Frenchmen had expressed their enthusiasm for the republican experiment. The United States was seen as a place where even modest men could flourish and emerge as prosperous, tolerant, enlightened, and virtuous; Philadelphian Benjamin Franklin represented the apogee of this ideal—the runaway apprentice who became not only a successful printer but also a man of charm, letters, science, and republican revolution. Although in the 1780s some blemishes began to appear on this portrayal, Frenchmen still regarded North America with admiration well into the 1790s.[161] Moreau's descriptions cast Americans in a less favorable light—one that emphasized their vulgarity and fierce racism rather than honorable simplicity. In part, his and other refugees' impulse to do so reflected their frustration at being held up to and criticized by continental Frenchmen for their supposed failure to match the standards of North Americans.

As an antidote for U.S. ills, the refugees typically prescribed a strong dose of immigration—in particular, people like the Saint-Dominguans. The exiles commended themselves on serving as purveyors of refinement to the young republic. With tongue firmly in cheek, one refugee observed, "Already . . . the custom of blowing one's nose in the fingers has ceded to that of using a pocket handkerchief . . . and they now actually believe that it is not polite to belch in public in such a way that causes the house to shake."[162] An exile in Norfolk claimed that the orchestra of West and Bignall's theater company had benefited from the addition of Saint-Dominguan musicians.[163] Cities and towns throughout the United States could improve, they pointed out, by becoming, thanks to the presence of the exiles, New Capes. Americans would then have better amusements and services, better dressed women and slaves, and better manners. In short, they would become better Americans because of the influence of the refugees, and perhaps then they would deserve the high esteem in which they already held themselves.

Some exiles, however, concluded that the prospects for uplift of the resident population were hopeless. Traveling throughout the country at the end of the eighteenth century, the famous gastronome Anthelme Brillat-Savarin recalled meeting a refugee "who had lived two years in New York, and still did not know enough English to be able to ask for bread. I expressed my astonishment at this; 'Bah,' he replied, shrugging his shoulders, 'do you suppose I would ever trouble to learn the language of so dull a race?'"[164] In his opinion, because of the backwardness of its people, neither New York nor any other U.S. city could possibly become the New Cape. The United States and its citizens paled in comparison to Saint-Domingue: it was an America that, while young and new, was already socially and culturally moribund. This feeling was, to some extent, mutual. Many white Americans would prefer to be "dull" than take on the attributes which they—and Europeans—associated with the refugees. Even as they socialized with Saint-Dominguans, hired their services, bought their products, or admired their fashions, white Americans resuscitated stereotypes about the exiles in an attempt to hold them at arm's length and to claim the distinctiveness of North Americans and their singular suitability for republican life.

Despite the structural similarities between Saint-Dominguan and U.S. cities and the ability of exiles to translate much of their earlier everyday lives into practice in their new locations, and despite polite, productive, or friendly relationships that did develop between locals and refugees, the two groups generally played up their differences—in appearance, in language, and in behavior—making each, by the standards of the day, a discrete people. White Saint-Dominguan refugees cultivated and relied on these distinctions in order to market their services and products more effectively. At the same time, they resented the negative connotations given to these attributes, which dogged them, and they parried these characterizations with their own indictments of locals and their society. Americans resisted self-scrutiny and found derogatory depictions of the Saint-Dominguans convenient as they sought to articulate their own unique American-ness. Although the voices of enslaved and free colored refugees were largely excluded from these discussions, their presence shaped how white Americans and exiles appraised each other and they provided points of convergence with and divergence from the resident African American communities. On the whole, the differences between Americans and Saint-Dominguans were a product rather than a condition of the 1790s, and one that white locals and exiles worked hard to maintain. From the vantage points of both groups, albeit it for different reasons, U.S. cities were a far cry from being New Capes.

Whatever their perceived—and created—differences as people, the Saint-Dominguans were fellow men (or at least the whites among them were), and this appeal to common humanity exacted demands from citizens of a purportedly enlightened republic. As they disembarked on U.S. shores, the white refugees called on Americans and their government to sympathize with their predicament and to aid them in their distress. This plea brought up for debate another key component of self-proclaimed American-ness—the commitment of the young nation and its citizens to provide an "asylum for mankind."

CHAPTER TWO

THE DANGERS OF PHILANTHROPY

When Saint-Dominguans sought refuge from the Haitian Revolution, their arrival in American cities initiated debate over what exactly constituted asylum. The notion of asylum as famously articulated by Thomas Paine carried connotations that went beyond mere acceptance of newcomers. As the story went in *Common Sense*, many immigrants, having been persecuted in their mother countries, would be in need of assistance when they reached U.S. shores. For the nation to function as a real haven, then, Americans must aid migrants in their transition from the Old World to the New. This kind of action fell under the term "philanthropy."

The term "philanthropy" came into vogue in the United States and Europe during the revolutionary era. Meaning literally "love of mankind," the word drew on the emotional—or in eighteenth-century speak, the affective—side of the Enlightenment ethos. In that age, affection as much as reason defined the "universal citizen." Sympathy for one's fellow man—the power to identify with another—was celebrated as a virtue of enlightened people and enlightened societies and was seen as fundamental to building a republic, as it facilitated connections and good will among citizens.[1] The capacity for sympathy allowed men and women to recognize when the rights and happiness of others were in jeopardy and moved them to take steps to alleviate affliction. "Philanthropy" joins this aptitude for sympathy and a mandate to act. While an older vocabulary of "charity" and "benevolence" was sometimes used along side or interchangeably with "philanthropy," they all had broad political implications in the revolutionary context.[2]

Throughout the eighteenth century, reformers in Europe had extolled British North America as a place where philanthropic feeling flourished; they created an idyllic vision that, not surprisingly, Americans embraced.[3] During their revolution and in its aftermath, Americans turned to the language of philanthropy to articulate the optimistic belief that they, as citizens of a republic, had the faculty to cure society's ills. The 1790s and early 1800s witnessed an explosion in the building of altruistic institutions, all designed to make good on the promise to attend to the needy and the oppressed.[4] But Americans struggled as they put this ideal into effect. Part of the allure of philanthropy was its universalist bent, yet this impulse had profoundly disconcerting implications. In its most radical interpretation, philanthropy could require sympathy for every person, regardless of politics, class, character, race, and gender, among other attributes central to the maintenance of social distinctions. Philanthropy, through its handmaiden, sympathy, could be a great leveler, inspiring democratic feeling toward and action on behalf of the enfranchised and disenfranchised alike.[5] More practically, but no less importantly, philanthropy assumed unlimited resources; and although Americans celebrated the bounty and potential of their nation, they worried about their ability to keep pace with philanthropy's demands.

The Saint-Dominguan refugees brought the problems of philanthropy into sharp relief. First, Americans doubted that all Saint-Dominguans were deserving of support, and one of their criteria of worthiness was race. When most white Americans deliberated over their philanthropic duty toward the refugees, they were thinking of the white exiles, not those who were black or colored. The direction of this racial bias was not a given, however. In this period, abolitionists saw slaves, not slaveowners, as worthy candidates for philanthropy, and manumission societies did work on behalf of enslaved refugees throughout the 1790s. In addition, during the early years of the Haitian Revolution, white Americans were critical of their peers on the island, although dramatic events there in the summer of 1793 would cause most of them to set aside misgivings about white Saint-Dominguans in the name of racial solidarity.

Despite strong associations forged between white Americans and white Saint-Dominguans, U.S. residents and officials faced difficulties as they tried to aid the exiles. City and state campaigns, while impressive, were plagued with logistical troubles; and by 1794, relief for the refugees became an issue at the federal level, as Congress debated the question of its philanthropic powers. Whereas the Constitution laid the foundation for an enlightened republic, it was unclear what the federal government's obligation was in dollars and cents for cultivating a benevolent nation. Congress's decision—more accurately its lack of decision—regarding the exiles had repercussions for years to come, not only for needy migrants, but for domestic petitioners as well. It helped to define the federal state's philanthropic obligations toward various populations.

Finally, the exiles themselves weighed in on the notion of philanthropy and highlighted what they saw as its ideological pitfalls. In their attempts to explain the Haitian Revolution, some white Saint-Dominguans laid part of the blame for the slave rebellion at the feet of philanthropists who had promoted the abolition of slavery. In doing so, they racialized philanthropy, tying it to equal rights and abolition, as a way to show how the French Enlightenment project had gone astray. Their interpretation was exculpation for their own role in their displacement and it was a warning to American audiences that misguided philanthropy led to a world turned upside down, where white men lost their rights, property, and lives, and black men were accorded all kinds of privileges that they did not deserve. These white exiles presented themselves as living proof that, in the hands of the wrong kind of men, philanthropy—and its emotional engine, sympathy—operated as a cloak for tyranny. In its application in the Americas, philanthropy could threaten the social order on which white dominion rested; and, drawing lessons from the white refugees' experiences, some white Americans worked to rein in the radical potential of philanthropy.

SYMPATHIZING WITH WHITE SAINT-DOMINGUANS

When word of the uprising in Saint-Domingue reached the United States in late summer of 1791, white Americans recoiled in horror, as they had to news about other slave rebellions in the eighteenth-century Atlantic world. The U.S. government responded to colonists' requests for aid in suppressing the insurrection by extending them credit (via the French consul, stationed in Philadelphia) to purchase provisions and military supplies.[6] But in 1792 and early 1793, as the uprising spread instead of abating, commentators in the U.S. press became suspicious of white colonists on the island and those showing up on American shores. In particular, U.S. residents' doubts reflected gender stereotypes. White women and children were seen as hapless victims of circumstances beyond their control because they were, according to social norms of the day, dependent, weak, and irrational. White men, however, were held to a different standard. As patriarchs they were accountable for preserving order, and consequently, when it disinte-

grated in Saint-Domingue, the actions of the colony's white men came into question in the American press.

A 1792 article in the *Virginia Herald* accused white male inhabitants of aban-
doning "their public duty" by emigrating to the United States. The anonymous
author directed his criticism at the largest proprietors—the very ones who were,
in light of their elevated social and economic status, supposed to head the campaign to defeat the insurrection. The writer hinted that by leaving the island, these
men had shirked their responsibilities.[7] Other observers criticized the military
competency of white Saint-Dominguan men. In an April 1793 letter to a London
correspondent, Philadelphia merchant Stephen Girard wondered why the colonists, who he thought had every advantage, had not yet vanquished the rebel
slaves.[8] A newspaper report attributed the ongoing rebellion to laziness in the
white population, claiming that military service was "not performed with very
great ardour on the part of the citizens."[9] In the view of these critics, the slave
rebellion endured because of the failure of white male residents to act with conviction. If anything, the Saint-Dominguans' military maneuvers proved their
ineptitude; as one account scoffed, "Now and then a small detachment of whites
makes a sudden excursion into the plantations, expends considerable quantities
of ammunition without doing much execution, and gives the insulting rebels
convincing proof of weakness."[10] They were paying the price for their indolence
and incompetence.

These assessments tapped into long-held stereotypes about men living in the
West Indies. The sultry Caribbean climate was thought to debilitate Europeans,
and commentators from elsewhere in the Atlantic world maintained that the
opulent creole lifestyle compounded the detrimental effects of the environment.
In the eyes of contemporaries, the West Indian appetite for amusement knew no
bounds; Saint-Dominguans were renowned for the luxury with which they surrounded themselves. Throughout the eighteenth century, continental French
authors contended that the notoriously wanton ways of white creole men had
compromised their manliness altogether. By 1781 the situation was so dire that
the marquis de Condorcet quipped, "If you were to search for a man in the American islands, you would not find him about the whites."[11]

To some extent, the U.S. perspective on Saint-Dominguans was informed
by French literature that for decades had been translated and published in the
American press. A prime example is a 1789 article in a Philadelphia magazine
that reiterated the conclusions of European writers for the benefit of American
readers. The author explained that white Saint-Dominguan men lost "sight of
every thing that is not qualified to satisfy desire; they disdain every thing that

does not wear the aspect of pleasure, and yield to the attacks and the tumults of passion."[12] Instead of following the dictates of reason, these men caved to the caprices of pleasure like silly women. They were like the heroines of popular novels of the time, who, because of their excessive passion, were complicit in their own ruin.[13]

In an age of revolution these accusations had grave political consequences. Eighteenth-century French *philosophes* and reformers railed against what they saw as the feminization of politics and people. They argued that the nation and its citizenry had deteriorated, besmirched by a penchant for sensual delights and frivolity and by the prominent role of women in the public sphere. While continental corruption had not descended to the level of that in the colonies, nevertheless, they claimed, both men and nation were in need of rehabilitation before it was too late, and this urgent "masculine republicanism" infused the rhetoric of French revolutionaries in the 1780s and 1790s.[14]

The language was mirrored on the other side of the Atlantic. Ever since their own revolution, American writers had noted that decadence led to the demise of entire countries. This refrain continued to resonate in the early 1790s, as the new nation struggled to gain a foothold and as the French Revolution corroborated such claims. Hence, both constituencies brought this view to bear on the Haitian Revolution. In a 1792 editorial in the *New-York Journal*, "Oranoak" described the enfeeblement of West Indian men and went on to warn about its consequences: "it is well known, luxury and intemperance enervates both mind and body; as was exemplified in the fall of the Roman empire. At this period her citizens were strangely depreciated; instead of being fired with an active spirit, and a manly fortitude, they sunk under the burthen, and fell like an emaciated effeminate race."[15] The follies of ancient Rome—always a compelling example for the United States—were being repeated in Saint-Domingue.

Most of these derogatory claims about West Indian men (by white Americans at least) were made before Saint-Dominguan refugees started to arrive in significant numbers. After the burning of Cap Français in the summer of 1793, Saint-Dominguans landed by the thousands, and Americans set aside some of their skepticism about white colonial men in the face of new reports. Letters from the Cape described forces of destruction that not even the most spartan men could overcome. The account by one U.S. merchant working on the island is typical: "We have done everything in our power to save our own, as well as the property entrusted to our care—we have exposed our lives twice, and guarded it until we were obliged to quit. . . . The Brigands from the country have come into town, and general massacre and destruction has taken place. To-morrow we shall be obliged to run—the whole town is now on fire, and the sailors all mad—if we yet escape with life, we shall be fortunate."[16] Not only did the merchant recount mayhem in Cap Français, but he also contended that city residents—men included—had no choice but to flee; they were, to use his terms, "obliged" to do so.[17] An article in *Dunlap's American Daily Advertiser* echoed the language of duty and cast the flight of Saint-Dominguan men in terms of their responsibilities as good patriarchs. The men were "obliged to fly from the city of Cape Francois, to save themselves and their wives and children from imminent danger."[18] Unable to withstand the enemy, the duty of Saint-Dominguan men now was to guide their dependents to safety.

Nevertheless, the question persisted: Why did colonists fail to subdue the rebelling slaves? This question took on greater urgency in the wake of the battle of Cap Français, which was essentially a clash between rival political factions. On one side were supporters of Léger-Felicité Sonthonax, one of the commissioners sent by the republican government to quell the slave insurrection and resistance to the republic; and on the other were the adherents of Thomas Galbaud, the governor-general of the colony, who was also appointed by the French revolutionary regime. In the thick of battle and fearing a loss, Sonthonax appealed to rebel slaves in and around Le Cap, offering freedom to any who would fight for his forces. He later expanded this measure, in effect declaring emancipation throughout the colony. In one stroke, rebelling slaves became republican soldiers, and when the National Assembly condoned Sonthonax's decree and made emancipation the order of the empire, revolutionaries in France turned to military action as the conduit to transform French Caribbean slaves to citizens. Commentators proclaimed that service to the republic would "awaken honor in the souls of these new men" and allow them to slough off the depravity that lingered from their days of enslavement. From this perspective, the formerly enslaved soldier emerged as the embodiment of republican virtue, sacrifice, and revolutionary commitment. As black men in Saint-Domingue (like others throughout the French Caribbean) pledged to fight and die for the French Republic, Sonthonax declared that the former slaves, not white colonists, were the only ones worthy of defending the nation.[19]

White refugees angrily denied this assertion for the remainder of the war, consistently portraying events in Saint-Domingue as a slave rebellion, *not* a republican revolution. They insisted that former slaves were not true soldiers and that the conduct of the war proved their point. Europeans who engaged in "honorable" warfare obeyed protocol, as lines of men met each other in open fields, but in Saint-Domingue these standards went by the wayside as former slaves and free people of color often relied on guerilla tactics that exhausted white forces. While colonists admitted that this mode of fighting was effective, they interpreted it as indicative of the flawed character of the enemy. A refugee who had served in a creole militia during the revolution put his opinions into verse: "Each tree, each hole, each piece of rock / Hid from our unseeing eyes a cowardly assassin, / Who, if undiscovered, came to pierce our breasts; / But who fled or begged for mercy / When we found him face to face."[20] Guerilla strategies transgressed the so-called "civilized" rules of conventional warfare, and in the eyes of white colonists, this was evidence of the spinelessness of their foes, who consequently were considered not honorable soldiers but "assassins."[21]

According to white refugees, the actions of black and colored soldiers also confirmed their barbarism. Tale after tale from the island referred to black and colored men as "cannibals," "unchained tigers," "savages," and "monsters, thirsting after blood, and unsated with carnage."[22] Infamous stories circulated about brutality. Very early on in the insurrection, the *Augusta Chronicle* related how "some unfortunate planters who were seized by the Negroes were most inhumanely murdered, after which canes were planted as if growing out of their bowels."[23] In the United States these tales grew in number, as the refugees recounted the circumstances of their flight. They became emblematic of the revolution: white babies held aloft on pikes by rebelling slaves; women raped by black men literally over the lifeless bodies of their husbands, sons, and brothers; and white colonists meeting their deaths by calculated dismemberment. Isolated incidents were represented as commonplace, and accounts avoided any mention of provocation or atrocities committed by white colonists—of which there were many.[24] These narratives sought to eradicate the possibility that black and colored men were worthy opponents. In trying to encapsulate the nature of the war, white observers in the colonies often called it a "volcano," equating black and colored soldiers to a powerful, unpredictable, and destructive force of nature (rather than civilization) that was impossible for any man—no matter how honorable—to contain.

Such depictions of the revolution played into white Americans' racist attitudes toward black and colored people and were reminiscent of white Americans' accounts of their centuries of conflict with Indians. Subsequently, these stories made the white refugees pitiable. Accounts that dehumanized the black republican soldiers and portrayed the white exiles as victims of a malevolent force of nature allowed white Americans to suspend doubts—for the moment—about the refugees' complicity in their own condition. In the summer of 1793, articles published everywhere from Charleston to Boston employed a language of happen-

The Burning of Cap Français. *L'incendie du Cap, ou Le Règne de Toussaint-Louverture* (Paris, 1802). Published to promote the expedition to Saint-Domingue of General Charles Leclerc, this scene includes many of the tropes about the war that the white exiles helped disseminate. As the city goes up in flames, marauding black men brandish swords and torches over the bodies of white men, while white women, children, and aged men huddle together in the foreground looking for protection. In the background are lines of French soldiers whose arrival promises to bring order to stance to describe the incoming exiles, using words like "unfortunate," "miserable," and "distressed." This vocabulary intimated accident instead of guilt: the exiles' situation was the result of an inexplicable twist of fate.[25]

The severity of the refugees' decline inspired pathos. Americans saw the exiles' "reverse of fortune" as particularly "cruel" because it was precipitous. A Charleston official found the case of the Saint-Dominguan refugees "the most striking example ever exhibited, of the changeableness of human affairs," and he reminded his fellow Charlestonians, "it is your duty not to measure your bounty by the frigid rules of economy, or to deal it out as if you were helping that unhappy part of our fellow creatures on whom habitual poverty has stamped contempt."[26] Dramatic sudden poverty registered more powerfully with American audiences than did the plight of the chronically indigent. For example, in 1795 *The Philadelphia Minerva* published "A French Story" about "a respectable character, . . . having long figured away in the gay world at Paris" who fell "victim of severe and unforeseen misfortunes" that left him dependent on the parish charity. When the curate upbraided him for requesting food for his dog, "the poor man, weeping," replied, "'and if I should lose my dog, who is there then to love me?' The good pastor, melting into tears, took his purse, and giving it to him, 'Take this, sir,' said he, 'this is mine—this I *can* give.'"[27] Importantly for white male refugees, this episode featured the displacement of a man and provided another case (albeit continental French) in which men (and animals) warranted sympathy and aid.[28]

If stories moved white American readers, then encounters with living examples of such "misfortune" were sure to elicit charity. The fascination with the refugees' fall explains how characteristics that had previously been invoked to doubt the exiles' actions now justified compassion on their behalf. John Huger of the Charleston Benevolent Society pointed out, "The inhabitants of St. Domingo have not been accustomed to the distress of poverty. . . . they all of them lived in ease, and most of them in affluence; and from affluence they are reduced to absolute beggary." White Caribbean creoles, who had been reared "in the lap of ease, affluence & plenty," were unexpectedly "stripped of almost every thing."[29] On the island or back in France, some of the exiled families had been benefactors rather than beneficiaries of charity. In Cap Français notable men helped to oversee three almshouses and infirmaries for the poor and supported their operations by soliciting private donations from the community.[30] The irony of the change in circumstances was not lost on Americans, and it compelled them to act.

The refugees' gruesome circumstances sparked the imaginations of white Americans in much the way that the popular sentimental novels of the era did. This dynamic can best be seen in appeals that asked readers to picture themselves in similar straits: "Oh! my dear country-women, let us for a moment fancy our-selves one of them; a husband perhaps, or other dear relation murdered, helpless children, looking up to our empty hand for food; driven from affluence, from our comfortable houses, and our native land, to depend on the cold charity of strang-ers, for the common means of subsistence. Let us reflect, that as our feelings in this situation would be, such are actually now their's; as *we* should then be anx-iously expecting the effects of *their* humanity, so are they now looking up for ours."[31] The writers, in this case a group of women in Charleston, dwell—and it seems, almost relish—the gripping details of the refugees' circumstances, em-ploying the exiles' own language (such as "murder") to conjure a vicarious experi-ence to stir their audience.

These anecdotes played on readers' sense of common humanity, but at the same time they reinforced the differences between Americans and Saint-Domin-guans. Imagining themselves in the role of the Saint-Dominguans highlighted white Americans' "comfortable" situations—how far away they were from such straits. The Charleston group's described plan of action underscores this point: they vowed to "sacrifice at the shrine of charity, every unnecessary luxury, every superfluous ornament" in order to "make it fashionable to be economists, and take delight in applying the precious savings, to wipe the tear from the mournful widow's eye, and give bread to the helpless orphan."[32] What constituted this "sac-rifice" was up for interpretation, as the phrases "unnecessary luxury" and "super-fluous ornament" reveal. For these women, the act of giving confirmed their secure status: the occasion proffered "delight" and "fashion" while for the benefi-ciaries it constituted a means of survival. This example reveals the ambivalent nature of sympathy—its power to cross and reinforce lines that divide people. As scholar Amit Rai puts it, "sympathy produces the very inequalities it decries and seeks to bridge."[33] Even as Charleston's women reached out to Saint-Dominguans, their philanthropic action accentuated their difference.

In response to the narratives being told during the summer of 1793, Ameri-cans regarded the white refugees sympathetically—with all that the term implied. One article from Philadelphia encapsulated the depth of feeling for the exiles, who "would excite sentiments of sympathy in the most ferocious of mankind."[34] It became a point of national pride that the refugees turned to the United States for succor: "those . . . who escaped the fury of their assailants have fled to the hospitable shores of America for asylum. . . . The man who would withhold his assistance, under these circumstances, we hope, does not reside in America."[35] The exiles offered white Americans an opportunity to show that they practiced the Enlightenment principles that they preached—to demonstrate that the United

States was truly the asylum that it purported to be, all the while skirting philanthropy's challenge to racism. Between 1791 and the summer of 1793, white Saint-Dominguans had gone from being objects of suspicion to being objects of sympathy. Now, U.S. citizens had to put their words into action, and this transition proved more difficult than they anticipated.

PHILANTHROPY IN ACTION

Although criticism of white Saint-Dominguans' emigration generally abated during the summer of 1793, Americans were unable to set aside all of their preconceptions as they translated sympathy into practice. City and state governments mounted impressive relief campaigns under the banner of republican philanthropy, but their efforts labored under many colonial trappings. As it became clear that locals would be unable to fulfill their aspirations, they set additional parameters on aid for the refugees and argued over who was responsible for footing the bill.

In the 1790s there was no centralized, state- or nationwide organization for coping with destitute persons. Employing practices that dated to the seventeenth century, each city, town, county, or parish was responsible for its own poor. Communities elected men to serve as Overseers of the Poor, a board in charge of distributing aid to needy locals. Public charity usually took two forms. Officials provided out-relief, which consisted of either small sums of money (regularly or sporadically handed out) or aid in kind (specific necessities such as fuel, clothing, and food). Another means of assistance was the city almshouse, where paupers were confined and often forced to work for their keep. To receive either type of aid, a supplicant required a recommendation from an upright citizen or a member of the poor-relief committee. Overseers wanted to ensure that candidates merited the assistance they sought—that they were "orderly & respectable Poor" rather than "immoral, loose & abandoned people."[36]

Only community residents could apply for assistance. Throughout the seventeenth and eighteenth centuries, poor-relief officials warned indigent strangers out of town, to avoid the expense of supporting them.[37] Notwithstanding this cost-saving measure, cities found it difficult to keep up with the local indigent population as their numbers swelled in the late eighteenth century. In federal-period Philadelphia, the nation's most prosperous city, the circumstances of the "lower sort" worsened. The most modest ranks met with fewer opportunities to improve their economic situation and relied on charitable support more frequently.[38] Increasing demands for charity strained the resources of existing insti-

tutions. As early as the 1760s, Philadelphians complained about the rising numbers of needy residents and the escalating costs of poor relief.[39] In response, the
Overseers of the Poor in Philadelphia and elsewhere tested innovations—stricter
regulations for almshouse and workhouse inmates, longer terms of service for
officials, new approaches to managing budgets.

While well-intentioned and sometimes effective, these experiments failed to
keep pace with the poor population. Some citizens took matters into their own
hands and established private charitable organizations. Various occupational,
ethnic, and religious groups founded mutual aid societies to help fellow members
in need. There were associations for German, English, and Irish immigrants, for
shipmasters, carpenters, and bricklayers, and for Moravians and African American Christians. Other citizens gathered together to aid vulnerable members of
the community, working on behalf of prisoners, widows, and mentally and physically compromised individuals. Inhabitants organized in response to catastro-
phes. When fire or disease afflicted cities or inclement weather closed ports, residents raised funds for those affected by the calamity.[40]

Given the already strapped situations of city institutions in the 1790s, the
arrival of Saint-Dominguan exiles threatened to overwhelm local systems. Citizens hoped that the French consuls stationed in several U.S. seaports would
contribute resources to the cause, and throughout the 1790s French consuls dis-
pensed significant amounts of aid to the exiles in the form of cash payments,
transportation to Saint-Domingue and France, and other means. This support
was critical to sustaining the exiles, yet it was not without controversy, especially
as the refugees found themselves increasingly at odds with revolutionary policies.
But even with substantial French aid to the refugees, Americans felt pressured to
prove their commitment to the United States as an asylum and hence made an
effort to extend support to the exiles.[41]

Americans turned to an old form of charity, namely, impromptu out-relief, to
cope with the influx of refugees. Although eighteenth-century officials had been
seeking to replace out-relief with institutionalization for resident poor, in the
case of the exiles, out-relief offered the flexibility essential to managing a large
population with diverse wants. Nevertheless, the size of the problem required
tremendous organization, and citizens in all cities designated leaders to spear-
head the efforts. The conventional process of selection of these leaders was a
mixture of appointment and election by ballot.[42] In Philadelphia, for example,
nine men, in addition to a chairman, oversaw the collection and disbursement of
funds for the refugees. These men, in turn, chose agents to canvass each of the

city's fourteen wards.[43] Efforts in New York, Baltimore, and Charleston were similarly structured.[44]

Many members of the relief committees had experience with charitable organizations. Their names appear on the rolls of city and medical dispensaries, free
schools for the poor, prisoner relief, and even the "Humane Society," a group
dedicated to "the recovery of persons apparently dead from drowning, and other
causes of suspended animation."[45] Their participation in altruistic associations
made these men obvious candidates for leading the refugee relief effort. Some
possessed the wherewithal to assist the campaign not only logistically but financially. Although financial records of individual subscriptions to refugee relief
funds have not survived, those for other benevolent groups suggest levels of giving to the exiles. In 1802, for instance, a dozen men from Philadelphia who had
been refugee charity organizers a few years before donated to the city dispensary.
Contributions ranged from $5 to $100, with $50 being the median pledge.[46] Con-
sidering that at the end of the century, a journeyman earned about $6.50 per
week, their donations indicate a degree of wealth well above the average.[47]

Relief committee members came from a variety of occupational backgrounds.
Professional men, such as lawyers and physicians, as well as successful artisans,
like goldsmiths and brewers, lent their energies. In Charleston several planters
offered their services. In both northern and southern cities, the majority of the
relief committee members made their money as merchants—a fact not surprising for seaport cities. In the eighteenth century the label "merchant" applied to a
diverse lot of both large and small entrepreneurs. In 1791, 440 self-described
merchants appeared in Philadelphia directories. Whatever the scale of their operations or the levels of their success, American merchants usually acted as whole-
salers in the foreign market.[48] This interest prompted concern for the refugees
among merchants, and the influence of trade was important to cities and states
as well. The Maryland House of Delegates justified aid in economic terms: "Before
the present war, the French Santo-Domingo opened to us a very great, constant
and certain market for our flour, and furnished to us the means of a very extensive
and lucrative commerce."[49] In light of this tie, the delegates argued, the exiles
deserved American support. Also, since most observers in the early 1790s saw
the rebellion in Saint-Domingue as a temporary rupture, relief committees hoped
that their benevolent actions would strengthen trade relations once the exiles
returned to the island and revived the plantation economy.

While refugee relief efforts reflected, to some extent, cities' economic interests, the campaign was not driven by partisan politics. Several organizers were

prominent politicians, holding city, state, or national offices or appointments, or later entered politics. Robert Wharton, a member of Philadelphia's common council in 1792, subsequently served as alderman and then mayor of the city. Of the Charleston committee, Edward Rutledge had been elected to the First Continental Congress and both the state House and Senate, and Henry William DeSaussure, also in the state legislature, headed the U.S. Mint in 1795 under George Washington and would serve as state chancellor for twenty years. As the decade wore on, these men identified with either the Federalists or the Democratic Republicans, but no one party dominated the relief efforts. Political rivals served together: Matthew Clarkson, a Federalist, and Samuel Osgood, a Democratic Republican, were two leaders of the New York subscription campaign.

Charity for the white refugees attracted both proponents and opponents of abolition. The Charleston relief committee included owners of some of the largest plantations in South Carolina, while antislavery activists participated in the New York group: Matthew Clarkson introduced a bill proposing the gradual abolition of slavery in 1789–90, and John Murray Jr. served as treasurer of the Society for Promoting the Manumission of Slaves. In the minds of these men, working on behalf of American slaves and of slaveowning white Saint-Dominguans did not represent a conflict of interests. Their disapproval of the way in which abolition was being attempted in Saint-Domingue made them sympathetic to the island's slaveholders.

Relief committee members had to address the needs of the exile population quickly in order to minimize the potential for disorder in their places of refuge. Although primarily concerned with exiles in their own communities, city organizations did see themselves as part of a multistate effort. Norfolk and Baltimore witnessed the first waves of Saint-Dominguan exiles, and as responsible parties in other localities learned of the exigencies, they rushed to help. The Baltimore committee thanked Philadelphia, admitting, "our fund cannot long sustain the heavy drafts that are continually made upon it . . . without the aid of the benevolent in other places."[50] When other cities along the eastern seaboard received hundreds of refugees who warranted attention, relief representatives corresponded with one another, sharing experiences and tips. The Philadelphia committee turned to Baltimore for advice and "data . . . on which to found [its] calculation of required supply." In response, Robert Gilmer and Samuel Sterett explained how demands had overwhelmed efforts in Baltimore: "the doors of our houses were thrown open and crowds admitted without any form or ceremony by which to number them." Since the initial influx, the committee had adopted a system to keep track of the exiles; however, they still struggled to ascertain exactly how many

Saint-Dominguans had arrived and needed help. The Baltimore society warned Philadelphians to ready themselves to provide not only shelter, but also clothes. It had not anticipated this want or expense and scrambled as many refugees disembarked "totally destitute of clothing."[51]

As city committees handled the everyday affairs of collecting and dispensing charity, they had to answer to their larger communities. Contributors demanded a say in how their money was spent, and throughout the relief campaign benevolent societies held public meetings to field questions, complaints, and suggestions. In July 1793 John Huger, chairman of the Charleston committee, requested the presence of contributors so that they could "agree on a plan for the distribution of the money collected, and for adopting proper regulations for the relief of the objects of the subscription."[52] Similar meetings for subscribers took place in Boston and Baltimore.[53]

In most cities, relief committee representatives solicited donations door to door.[54] Residents pledged amounts and paid in installments when requests were issued. In Baltimore, Samuel Sterett posted a notice in the local papers in July, asking subscribers to send in the first third of their pledged sums.[55] In August Charlestonians promised £1,700, but of this total, only £1,272 "were paid down" on the spot.[56] Reports about subscriptions for each city vary, making it difficult to calculate reliable totals. A Charleston paper claimed that Baltimoreans had pledged $15,000, while the *Boston Gazette* reported a sum of $12,000. Still another article asserted that the Baltimore fund reached $11,000.[57] Whatever the exact figures, these were substantial sums.

Although less directly affected by the Saint-Dominguans, smaller towns and rural areas participated in relief efforts as well. Norfolk received funds from towns and counties throughout Virginia, including nearby Williamsburg and Portsmouth and more distant Richmond and Petersburg.[58] The Patriotic Society of Newark, New Jersey, opened a subscription and voted to spend the money on shoes for the exiles.[59] These examples reflect rural and small-town residents' willingness to help their urban counterparts and the Saint-Dominguans. In addition, some of these areas expected that exiles would soon arrive in their communities. Boston, for instance, saw few refugees, yet its benevolent committee declared (with a good deal of self-promotion and pomp), "we are happy to acquaint the world, that this town, ever foremost in those acts which dignify and adorn human nature, has anticipated the wants of these children of distress, and a very liberal subscription is now making for their immediate relief, should they seek an asylum in this metropolis."[60] Some places preferred, if not prided themselves on, preparation.

As part of their fundraising, major cities hosted benefit events. In July 1793 a Baltimore theater staged a performance to raise money for the refugees. A *Baltimore Evening Post* advertisement for the event noted, "as compassion for the unfortunate objects of this Benefit happily pervades every rank, 'tis thought expedient . . . to do away with all distinction in the price of Tickets." Any seat in the house was available for a dollar.[61] A few days later, the Baltimore Exchange hosted a concert on behalf of "our distressed brethren, the *French*" in the hopes that "the Ladies and Gentlemen of the Town" would "display their usual *liberality* and *charity*."[62] Similar events took place in Philadelphia, New York, and Charleston. Philadelphians donated the proceeds from recent circus shows.[63] In Charleston, churches of various denominations passed the collection basket for the Saint-Dominguans, Sunday after Sunday.[64]

Relief committees solicited other forms of support. Norfolk committee members called on "every friend to humanity" to bring clean rags for ill refugees.[65] In the fall of 1793 members of the benevolent committee in Charleston advertised for donations of firewood to help the exiles survive the approaching winter.[66] One of the most pressing problems was finding shelter for the refugees, and locals opened their doors. In Baltimore and Charleston, inhabitants "generously relinquished a part of [their] houses for the accommodation of the strangers, and politely furnished them with the participation of their tables," that is, invited the refugees to dine with them. According to a letter in a Baltimore newspaper, an anonymous gentleman from Annapolis offered up two houses, stocked with provisions, for the refugees.[67]

Although the identities of contributors and the size of their individual donations remain, for the most part, unknown, the variety of donors demonstrates that concern for the Saint-Dominguan exiles did indeed, in the words of the Baltimore theater managers, "pervade every rank." Gentlemen weighed in with substantial sums, and less privileged citizens offered their mite by turning out for performances, sharing their houses, and donating rags and fuel. It is clear that the white Saint-Dominguans struck a philanthropic chord with wide swaths of the white American population.

This sympathy had a competitive edge. Newspapers broadcasted updates about relief efforts throughout the nation, and accounts of flourishing fundraising in other parts of the country spurred locals to contribute. The women of Charleston refused to be outdone by their contemporaries. In a call for action, they pointed out how "the ladies of Baltimore, upon a like occasion, have been celebrated for exerting their beneficence." The article asked, "Shall *we* submit to be excelled by them—surely no."[68] Another Charleston resident proposed that local newspapers publish the names of contributors in order to spur activity in other cities. The scheme had the added advantage of "afford[ing] great pleasure to those who shall be benefited by the subscriptions made here."[69] Up and down the seaboard, residents were trying to out-republican one another, goading ever more virtuous deeds from their fellow citizens.

In the midst of this good-natured competition, residents congratulated each other on their successes. The need for recognition was an integral part of the relief efforts. A letter to the *Connecticut Courant* opined that "the human attentions of our brethren of the middle states" deserved "the applause of all good men."[70] Bostonians remarked that such good works in American cities could not escape divine notice: "the eye of *omniscience* must view with peculiar benignity, the offerings made on the altar of disinterested Benevolence and Charity."[71] The campaign for the refugees became a point of national celebration—proof that the United States was living up to its revolutionary rhetoric. Whereas previously the world's "unhappy wretches" had looked to Great Britain for protection and hence brought that nation "glory," now the United States—as it had claimed during its revolution—was the true asylum for liberty and mankind.[72] Americans argued that the willingness of citizens at all levels to give generously for the refugees attested to the depth and breadth of republican conviction.

Despite the acclamation and the impressive outpouring that characterized the summer and fall of 1793, demand outstripped resources. Pocketbooks could not keep pace with principle, and American philanthropy for the exiles fell short of its universalist goals. Tensions mounted within exile communities, as refugees accused one another of collecting subsidies that they did not require.[73] Moreau de St. Méry normally admired the stoicism and pluck of his fellow exiles (although with characteristic egotism, he later remarked, "None of them seemed to me to be enduring our common ruin with as much courage as I"). But one meeting with Saint-Dominguan exiles in Norfolk provoked his ridicule: "I couldn't help smiling scornfully when I heard one of them bewailing the fate that had reduced him to only two Negro servants."[74] Clearly, not all refugees agreed on the line between luxury and necessity.

In an attempt to resolve disagreements and to stretch their limited budgets, relief committee members established criteria to determine who among the white Saint-Dominguans was the most worthy of support. These parameters followed gender stereotypes, as had sympathy for the Saint-Dominguans in the first phase of the war. Throughout the colonial period, benevolence had become increasingly influenced by ideas about the different natures of men and women. Widows, orphans, the elderly, and incapacitated were classified as dependent and seen as the most worthy candidates for relief. Able-bodied men were associated with independence, and in theory, did not—or at least should not—require charity. Colonial and American relief organizations operated within these assumptions, doling out monies or admitting people into institutions based on whether petitioners were truly "dependent" or not.[75]

Exile-relief campaigns reflected the gender standards of the time in their distribution of funds. Before receiving aid, a refugee applied to his or her local committee, which ascertained whether the petitioner qualified for assistance. For example, in the spring of 1794, the Boston relief society asked Saint-Dominguans "in want of support" to send in their names and addresses, along with "proper vouchers of their being persons of that description" (i.e., a Saint-Dominguan refugee and in need of assistance) to the committee's representatives within three weeks.[76] The emphasis on appropriate documentation points to the committee's concern that well-heeled exiles (or people posing as exiles) would defraud the system. Even after establishing their credentials and identities, many male refugees were refused aid. When Charles Menut, a refugee in Charleston, complained in a local newspaper that he had been unjustly denied support, committee members retorted that Menut was "*undeserving.*" They explained that "the most immediate objects of their care . . . [were] women and children," and Menut, as a healthy man, was not among the worthy poor.[77]

Local groups did extend support to men, but on certain terms. Consider the case of Philadelphia. During a general meeting of subscription contributors in August 1793, the Philadelphia committee agreed on a scheme for classifying applicants. In the first category were refugees with some property, probably men and women who, in the eyes of the benevolent society, had arrived with enough goods or slaves to meet their everyday needs. "Although subjects of commiseration," these Saint-Dominguans were denied aid. The second and third groups comprised people who were appealing for assistance to return to France or to Saint-Domingue. Mechanics and tradesmen belonged in the fourth category, skilled workers, and in the fifth group were refugees who wanted to settle in the American countryside but lacked funds to relocate. Widows made up the sixth class; the committee considered them "in an helpless condition, and from whose exertion for their own support, nothing ought to be expected."[78]

For each category the association set a monetary allocation. Members in Philadelphia calculated that passage to either France or Saint-Domingue cost $20 per person, and the price of establishing a refugee in the country "with 5 months provisions" ran about $22. The committee anticipated that after a four-week period of adjustment bankrolled by the committee, skilled refugees would find jobs, and so awarded them only $8 each. The committee then estimated how many exiles in each category would apply. They budgeted for sending 350 people to France or Saint-Domingue and for locally supporting 100 mechanics and tradesmen, 200 rural settlers, and 50 widows—a total cost of $12,200, not including the widows. Their computations exceeded their treasury, but the committee relied on future public donations to make up a discrepancy of $3,600.[79]

Similar schemes were implemented in other cities, and in all cases three assumptions underlay the plans. First the committees and their contributors thought that able-bodied men should work to support themselves and their families—be it in the seaports, the countryside, France, or Saint-Domingue. Any relief given to such a person was a temporary measure, part of a transition for which the refugees needed only momentary assistance. Second, members took for granted that employment was available, yet finding work proved difficult for many refugees. René Lambert, exiled in Wilmington, Delaware, described his exasperation in an appeal for a job: "I have lived in this city for 8 months doing nothing but spending money and I accordingly ask you, my dear sire, if possible to procure me some occupation. . . . I have no other way to keep from being a charge to somebody in a strange country."[80] Women, too, must have experienced this aggravation, given that some had been economically active on the island.

Third, relief committees based their budgets on the supposition that the influx of refugees would be short, yet exiles continued to arrive in significant numbers. As early as August 1793, the Norfolk organization complained, "the funds received are nearly exhausted, [and] unless the hand of Charity is kept open for [the refugees'] relief, their sufferings must be dreadful even to think of."[81] Committees struggled not only because of the volume of "deserving" refugees, but also because of rising costs. While the benevolent societies encouraged inhabitants to donate goods and accommodations, in many cases, members had to pay citizens for their services. To some extent, committees expected and calculated for these expenditures; occasionally they invited local entrepreneurs to bid for contracts to supply the refugees with needed items.[82] But, given their limited resources, committees sometimes only grudgingly offered compensation to "such as require payment."[83] In addition, accusations surfaced that some residents contributed to the refugees' troubles and the benefactors' expenses by price gouging. In August 1793 the New York Chamber of Commerce issued a warning to shopkeepers and grocers about the sudden inflation in the prices of provisions. Playing on the competitive spirit among the cities, the committee members commented, "Tis hoped that none of our citizens will demean themselves, as we hear has been done in several other states, by imposing on the distressed strangers (who are ignorant of our language and our prices) larger demands than usual for these necessary articles; or, thro' avarice grasp from them the little they have left, or what the hand of philanthropy has bestowed upon them."[84] One correspondent pointed out that inflated prices hurt locals: "The exorbitant Prices of Provisions are severely felt as well by the Honest, but poor Labourers of our own Country, as by the plundered People who have fled the Cape."[85] If appeals about the dire straits of strangers failed to resonate, officials hoped that civic pride and concern would curb the temptation to profit from distress.

Although cities attempted to stretch their funds by working within the criteria established by their relief boards, communities found that they lacked sufficient resources for even the "worthiest" of exiles. Practical concerns as well as assumptions about race and gender compromised the universalist impulse of the philanthropic ideal. As cities realized that they were coming up short, they looked for other avenues to pursue. In the late fall of 1793 and early 1794, benevolent societies turned to state governments and to the federal government to finance efforts and thereby alleviate mounting expenses and shortfalls. This appeal sparked a series of debates about federal power and the limits of asylum in the early republic.

GOVERNMENT AND PHILANTHROPY

In the summer of 1791, the federal government as well as the state of South Carolina aided white Saint-Dominguans, extending thousands of dollars in credit to finance their response to the slave rebellion. These loans were brokered with the approval of the French consul, but just two years later the question of assistance for the Saint-Dominguans was a different matter. After the momentous battle at Le Cap, the previously rebel slaves became—potentially—defenders of the French Revolution, should the French Assembly condone Sonthonax's decree. However, in the latter part of 1793 and in early 1794—when cities were turning to state and federal governments for help with the exiles—the French Assembly had yet to address the question of the abolition of slavery in Saint-Domingue. The U.S. government, then, was in a quagmire: if it aided the white refugees (who, obviously, resented Sonthonax's 1793 decree) and the decree was endorsed, then the Americans could be seen as abetting an antirepublican movement. But if Sonthonax was denounced and slavery upheld, then the U.S. government wanted to help the exiles in order to stay on the right side of revolution. How the French Assembly would respond, given its volatility during this period, was anybody's guess, and the tenuousness of the situation shaped Congress's reaction to the dilemma of the refugees.

There was another wrinkle in the 1794 congressional debates. When representatives voted to give aid in 1791, it was for a population most of whom lived outside the United States; three years later, the people they were considering supporting were a resident group. When Representative Samuel Smith of Maryland addressed the U.S. House of Representatives early in 1794 about federal relief for the refugees, he declared, "such a scene of distress had never before been seen in America." He emphasized both the size of the population and the acuteness of their misery.[86] Yet, the issue for congressmen was not the hardship suffered by the refugees but whether the federal government had the authority to intervene. The Saint-Dominguan exiles forced legislators to consider the boundaries of constitutional power and inaugurated a debate about the relationship between the federal government and philanthropy.

The Saint-Dominguans started appearing in the United States just after the ratification of the Constitution. The document outlined a new organization and vision for republican government; nevertheless, the boundaries of authority within that government were contested, in particular the appropriation of funds. This ambiguity affected the question of aid for the refugees. In the summer of 1793, Thomas Jefferson, even as he called for "pity and charity" for the exiles, argued that Congress could not allocate resources for the Saint-Dominguans' relief: "I deny the power of the general government to apply money to such a purpose but I deny it with a bleeding heart. It belongs to the state governments. Pray urge ours [Virginia's] to be liberal."[87] Quite simply, in Jefferson's interpretation, the situation lay outside the powers of the federal government.

State governments had stepped in to assist city campaigns in the fall of 1793. In South Carolina, for example, Charleston's dwindling resources compelled Governor William Moultrie to entreat the state legislature to help shoulder the burden of caring for the exiles.[88] Moved by the "helpless and distressed situation of the unfortunate French," the legislature earmarked £3,000 for the refugees— the "most affectionate and effectual provision which the public situation will allow."[89] Later in the year, the South Carolina House of Representatives agreed to appropriate the taxes from properties sold in Charleston to the relief of the exiles.[90] States passed such measures, however, with the expectation that they were stopgap solutions until the federal government could relieve them. In November 1793 the Maryland House of Delegates agreed to spend $500 a week for the exiles in Baltimore, but only until February 1794—the next scheduled meeting of the U.S.

Congress, when state representatives anticipated handing over the onus of aid to federal lawmakers.[91]

Although state governments were often as "liberal" as Jefferson could have hoped, they soon exhausted their means, or willingness, to pay, and several pressured Congress in January 1794. The issue of constitutionality permeated the discussion. James Madison echoed Jefferson's sentiments when "he acknowledged, for his own part, that he could not undertake to lay his finger on that article in the Federal Constitution which granted a right to Congress of expending, on objects of benevolence, the money of their constituents."[92] John Nicholas, also from Virginia, proposed that the members of Congress donate their individual salaries instead of meting out public monies.[93] Southern delegates were not the only ones worried about constitutional legitimacy. Samuel Dexter of Massachusetts asked to delay deliberating on the bill so that he might have time to formulate a cohesive case for its passage.[94]

Yet, several congressmen found no constitutional impediment to allocating monies for the refugees. Elias Boudinot of New Jersey contended that withholding assistance would violate the Constitution in both "theory and practice." He interpreted the first clause in section eight, which permitted Congress "to provide for exigencies regarding *the general welfare*," as justification for rendering aid. According to its supporters, the relief bill served the "general welfare" because it bestowed relief on the Saint-Dominguans and on American citizens as well. Thomas Scott of Pennsylvania stated that the inhabitants of Baltimore were virtually under siege by refugees. "If they were invaded by an army, we certainly would assist them; and where is the difference . . . whether they be an army of fighters, or an army of eaters?"[95] Both exiles and locals suffered from the strain, and Congress, in Scott's view, was obliged by the Constitution to act.

To bolster arguments in favor of the bill, Boudinot cited other expenditures not explicitly stipulated in the Constitution, such as congressional provisions for prisoners of war and the president's payment of the expenses of visiting Indian emissaries. Since the refugees were "citizens of our allies [France]," Boudinot maintained that the United States had a greater duty to Saint-Dominguans than to either Indians or prisoners of war.[96] Samuel Smith carried this reasoning further. He pointed to the assistance distressed Americans had received from other governments. Recently, both Portugal and Britain had aided U.S. sailors, and Smith queried, "Are we to stand up here, and tell the world that we dare not perform an act of benevolence?"[97] Legislation for the refugees offered Congress an opportunity to prove its philanthropic principles on the world stage. For a young republic struggling to assert its credibility, this was a test of its republican ardor.

Some exiles participated in the effort to lobby the federal government for relief. During the debates in Congress, Peter Gauvain and Louis Debourg, two exiles from Cap Français residing in Baltimore, presented a petition that implored representatives to approve funding for their assistance. A few months earlier, the refugees had successfully pressed for remission from tonnage duties. The exiles argued that because of their dire circumstances, they could not spare the money for taxes on the property they had brought with them from the island, and President Washington's cabinet concurred.[98]

In February 1794 the Saint-Dominguans and their advocates scored another legislative victory. Congress agreed to appropriate up to $15,000 for the exiles. The act left the distribution of funds to President Washington's discretion. In March the president remitted $2,000 for the relief effort in Baltimore and $600 for that in Philadelphia.[99] A month later, the Norfolk newspaper, the *Virginia Chronicle*, advertised that a committee had been authorized to distribute federal funds and invited applications from exiles "in want of relief."[100] Refugees in Charleston were notified to appear at City Hall in order to enter claims for federal assistance.[101] By the end of April, only $1,800 of the total congressional appropriation remained, and the president, at the suggestion of his cabinet members, applied the rest to outfitting several vessels to carry refugees back to Saint-Domingue.[102]

The allocation of funds for the exiles, however, did not signal a consensus on the federal government's role in creating an "asylum for mankind." Instead, the bill represented a bargain that skirted the constitutional issues at hand: the United States deducted the funds for the refugees from the balance owed on its enormous debt to France from the American Revolution.[103] If the French Republic failed to acknowledge this form of payment, relief would terminate in six months.[104] This arrangement borrowed from the provisions dictated in the 1791 aid bill, but in early 1794 this decision had different implications. In 1791 the slave uprising was still just that—a rebellion against the French government. With Sonthonax's decree, the slave uprising had been (possibly) transformed into a republican revolution. So, with this second bill, Americans were hedging their bets about how the French Assembly would vote regarding Sonthonax's move in Saint-Domingue. Less than certain about the tide of the French Revolution, the U.S. government sought to steer a middle course—to offer aid on terms that left the ultimate decision to the French government.

For the refugees, the federal decision fell short of the ringing endorsement (and long-term committed support) that they had hoped for, yet they tried to turn the situation to their advantage. Because the federal aid was couched as a settling

of debts, a Saint-Dominguan exile named Cesar Duny argued that previous qualifications for assistance should be lifted. In an editorial in the exile mouthpiece
American Star (a Philadelphia newspaper simultaneously published in French
and English), Duny criticized, in guarded terms, the city charity campaigns. He
praised members for their zeal, but worried that they had confined their aid "to
certain individuals, to the exclusion of others, not less unhappy." Duny suggested
instead that since "the inhabitants and proprietors of St. Domingo will all contribute to the reimbursement of this sum—of consequence, they should all
equally partake of the benefit of the advance." He admitted that of course, old
men, women, and children should be first to receive support, but he urged the
president to look carefully at the case of the men. Appealing to the "virtuous"
Washington, Duny assured his fellow colonists that the president "knows, no
doubt, that those who speak most and make the greatest noise, are not always the
most meritorious. He knows, that amongst the unfortunate, those who tell the
most distressing tale are not always the most needy; and that there are here
respectable men who live in silence, and the humility of their sad estate."[105]
According to Duny, Americans had been deceived in their assessment of male
refugees, and the new federal campaign offered an opportunity to rectify their
mistakes.

Duny's proposed reforms had little chance to materialize. The funds from the
1794 bill dried up in two months rather than the anticipated six, and the Saint-
Dominguans received no more support from the U.S. government. The reason
behind the cessation of funds was threefold. First, the federal government, like
its local and state counterparts, thought of the refugees as a temporary problem,
assuming that the exiles would soon return to Saint-Domingue. Even advocates
of relief postulated that the United States could recoup its expenditures because
the exiles were "expected to return to their settlements before the first of May
[1794], and they would then be very able and very willing to repay the money
themselves."[106] Second, rapid turnovers in the French government made Alexander Hamilton, the secretary of the treasury, apprehensive that France would fail
to recognize these payments, and so he warned against additional allocations.[107]
And last, word reached the United States that the French Assembly had expanded
on General Sonthonax's measure by abolishing slavery throughout its colonies
and granting all free men (no matter their color) the rights of citizens. To tender
another round of aid to white Saint-Dominguan exiles would suggest that the
United States was interfering with the course of republican revolution abroad—a
move that the federal government, although growing wary of events in France
and Saint-Domingue, was unwilling to admit openly.

Despite its short life, the 1794 bill proved significant for congressional debates about federal aid on the domestic front. Later in the decade petitioners used the Saint-Dominguan example as part of their arguments for federal funds for other charitable purposes. In December 1796 Representative William Smith asked the House to help rebuild Savannah in the wake of a ruinous fire. His descriptions of the situation mirrored those invoked by the refugees a few years before, emphasizing the destruction and the innocence of the victims; and he contended that "surely, if it were justifiable to grant relief to foreigners in distress, it was at least equally so when the objects were our own citizens." Thomas Hartley, a representative from Pennsylvania, seconded Smith's sentiments: "Shall we . . . treat the citizens of Savannah with more disrespect than the people of St. Domingo?"[108] According to these men, American philanthropy should start at home.

Opponents to the bill pointed out that Saint-Dominguan refugee relief was not a precedent for federally funded charity: Congress had simply paid an installment on the nation's debt to France, albeit through the exiles.[109] It was not a policy of philanthropic action. The provision rescued those congressmen who worried that approving relief for Savannah would open the floodgates for other petitions and overwhelm the precarious federal treasury with claims.[110] That same year, fires had also swept through New York, Baltimore, and Charleston. Small towns were affected as well; Lexington, Virginia, for example, had lost every house but two in a fire. William Giles warned that "if the present resolution passed it would make [Congress] answerable for all future losses by fire."[111] In the eyes of the challengers to the amendment, insurance offices and individual contributions were the appropriate sites for Savannah's inhabitants—and others down the road seeking aid.[112]

William Smith's resolution for Savannah was voted down, 55 to 24. Its defeat made clear that the responsibility for coping with needy populations—whether foreign or domestic—fell to the states, cities, private organizations, and individuals. For the refugees, this decision had important repercussions: they lost federal funding, and state, city, and local organizations took their cues from the federal decision. When federal aid was exhausted in March 1794, the Baltimore relief society declared that they considered "our task at an end."[113] The refugees stressed the consequences of this withdrawal to American audiences. In April 1794 the *American Star* ran a story, reporting that a "French gentleman" in New York had committed suicide by overdosing on laudanum. The New York paper from which the article was cribbed had been unable to learn the cause of the suicide, but the editor of the *American Star*, the refugee Tanguy de la Boissière, provided it: a notice from the treasurer of the local relief committee had been issued announcing the termination of support to Saint-Dominguans.[114] To Tanguy, the cessation of aid was as good as a death warrant for the exiles; the United States—the purported asylum—was killing the needy who sought refuge on its shores.

Federal precedent aside, state and city efforts on behalf of the refugees dwindled because other charitable causes had garnered attention. A deadly yellow fever epidemic struck Philadelphia in the fall of 1793, overwhelmed the population, and sapped manpower and funds. When the scourge ended in November, the relief committee had spent over $36,000.[115] As Mathew Carey, a printer, noted in his 1794 *Short Account of the Malignant Fever*, "Little, alas! did many of the contributors [to the refugee relief fund], then in easy circumstances, imagine, that a few weeks would leave their wives and children dependent on public charity, as has since unfortunately happened."[116] Yellow fever beset Philadelphia again in 1797, and Baltimore and Norfolk periodically reeled from the outbreaks of the disease, placing frequent demands on resources and residents.

Philanthropy was affected by international events as well. News that Barbary pirates had seized and enslaved one hundred Americans in early 1794 provoked incensed outcries from U.S. citizens, who looked for ways to ransom captives and collected donations in their communities. To encourage support for that cause, advocates alluded to recent American benevolence for the Saint-Dominguan refugees. "Humanus" in Charleston hoped that "that generous sympathy which poured balm into the wounds of unfortunate allies, will not be withheld from the misery of countrymen. Those hands which were so readily stretched out to relieve the wretched fugitives from St. Domingo, will not be withdrawn from the assistance of imprisoned and enchain'd brethren."[117] "A Citizen" in New York postulated that, "many of our citizens . . . who had not an opportunity to give to the late unfortunates of St. Domingo . . . would give their mite" toward a fund for the Barbary captives.[118]

These local and foreign crises captured American notice and dollars, but campaigners for more mundane causes stepped up their efforts to regain public interest. Some charitable groups argued that the refugees had had their moment and it was someone else's turn. In December 1793, for example, the Society for the Institution and Support of the First-Day or Sunday Schools reopened its appeal for subscriptions from Philadelphia residents. The committee stated that although the society had found its funds insufficient in the summer and fall, members "conceived it necessary to decline their applications to their fellow-citizens for their assistance in favor of these schools, in order that there might be no interruption from them to the solicitations then made in behalf of their unfortunate brethren from Cape Francois."[119] Other organizations had seen their ventures undercut by the arrival of the Saint-Dominguan refugees. Just before the arrival of the exiles in the summer of 1793, the black community in Philadelphia had initiated a campaign to raise funds for a church. Soon, some black locals observed that contributions that could have gone for the church were being stuffed into the pockets of Caribbean slaveholders.[120]

Despite competing causes, subsequent years saw renewed campaigns for the exiles, although the giving was at rates significantly lower than in the 1793 campaign. Urban leaders made sporadic requests to state legislatures for funds. In 1796 John Jay addressed the New York State Assembly for support for refugees, and after federal monies were spent, the Pennsylvania legislature continued to earmark funds for the exiles up to 1797, but in smaller amounts and with more restrictions.[121] In 1796 the South Carolina House of Representatives borrowed a strategy from federal lawmakers by deducting its contributions to Saint-Dominguans from the state's debt owed to France.[122]

Local committees went into action more vigorously when a wave of refugees arrived in 1804, following the declaration of Haitian independence. By then, the international political situation had changed dramatically: white Americans were, in general, wary of Napoleon Bonaparte in France and of the establishment of the first black republic, in the former Saint-Domingue. This sentiment translated into financial support for the white exiles. In Charleston, the city council initiated a subscription, and managers of local theaters staged performances, the proceeds of which went to refugee relief.[123] Residents even entertained the idea of opening a public kitchen for the exiles, but the plan was squashed when a citizen pointed out that such an establishment was suitable for a "certain class," namely for "privates," "non-commissioned officers," and "for all those who are cursed with the inveterate itch for gambling" (which, he editorialized, "is so much the misfortune of the French in general"). But "at the same time, honour and humanity recoil from the idea of letting those who have known high days of happiness and independence resort to such a thing."[124] The public kitchen, in other words, would add insult to the exiles' injury.

Campaigns throughout the 1790s certainly mitigated the hardships of many exiles, but the inconsistency of donations required many refugees to fend for themselves, look to private organizations or the French state, or enter charitable institutions such as almshouses, workhouses, and orphanages. Even within the larger system of charitable support, though, Saint-Dominguans were often distinguished from other poor people. Petitioned by "indigent refugee families," the New York City Common Council allocated money in the almshouse budget specifically for the exiles. Amounts ranged from $40 to $300. These sums were doled out sporadically, but they persisted from 1796 to at least January 1805.[125] Within such local institutions, the refugees were still a distinct population and the objects of an extra measure of consideration, even if they did not garner the levels of public support they had in years past.

The very presence of the Saint-Dominguan exiles pressed Americans to define the parameters of philanthropy more explicitly. As local and state governments turned to Congress to take the lead in funding charitable endeavors, representatives looked for a way to maintain the philanthropic ideal without falling into the crossfire of contentious French revolutionary politics and without being overwhelmed by petitions from their own citizens. Debates over the issue reveal that lawmakers felt the tension between the principles they embraced and the document that was supposed to guarantee them, and in the end, federal officials handed the burden of realizing the philanthropic ideal back to the state and city governments and to individuals. But the Saint-Dominguan exiles were not simply the spark for debate and uneasy resolution, they participated in the discussions as well, making their own case for what philanthropy meant in an age of revolution.

THE "CLOAK" OF PHILANTHROPY

The disputes over philanthropy in the United States were important to the Saint-Dominguan exiles for two reasons. Most obviously, the outcome determined if they could rely on financial aid in their new asylum and for how long. Also, the debates figured in refugees' arguments about the reasons for the Haitian Revolution. In their view they were the victims of French revolutionary philanthropy gone awry, and over the next two decades, the exiles railed against what they called the "cloak" of French philanthropy. Their warnings about the dangers of misguided philanthropy resonated with an American public grappling with the problem of slavery in an enlightened republic.

On the practical side, the unpredictability of support and its restrictions triggered bitterness among some exiles, yet most expressed their gratitude to American audiences throughout the 1790s. In private correspondence to individual benefactors and in published proclamations, the exiles thanked residents for their efforts. In an open letter to the *New-York Journal and Patriotic Register*, a group of exiles living on Vesey Street lavished praise on city residents: "Words are wanting to express our feelings, and the lively sense of gratitude. May you, O good people! be happy as long as our posterity will remember deeds of charity so rare, as almost to obliterate the painful recollection of the calumnies and atrocities to which we are victims."[126] Some refugees were moved to immortalize their appreciation in verse. In January 1794 M. Decolland in Charleston offered up a poem that celebrated "a country for asylum, a generous people / who alone can soften our great misfortunes."[127] Benefactors, to some extent, expected testimonies of gratitude as repayment for their kindness and as acknowledgement that assistance had indeed reached its intended objects. These demonstrations served to massage the givers' egos and to demonstrate the success of the charity campaigns.[128]

When the exiles lauded the generosity of their hosts, they held up American aid as a counterexample to the French revolutionary government's philanthropy. As one exile put it, "it is a great pleasure during such a revolution as this of ours in France and St. Domingo to know that people who are as generous as they are virtuous are relieving their fellow-men in one hemisphere while in the other they are all conspiring to destroy their kind."[129] In particular, the white refugees associated French philanthropy with abolitionist sentiments. The connection between the two was lifted from the language of slavery opponents, who identified their cause as a philanthropic endeavor: Henri Grégoire's famous 1790 treatise about *gens de couleur* was called *Lettre aux Philanthropes*. But the white exiles set out to prove that the philanthropy of Grégoire and his circle was, in their words, "false." Their attacks on false philanthropy responded to the increasingly radical course of French abolition during the early 1790s, as the movement developed from calls for slave trade abolition to equal rights for free people of color to demands for universal emancipation.

As slaves rebelled in the summer of 1791, some white observers both in and outside of Saint-Domingue attributed the uprising to the influence of slave trade abolitionists. In their petition to the governor of Jamaica in 1791, white residents cautioned that the British colony could suffer a similar end since "the spirit of philosophy" afflicting Saint-Domingue was "equally inimical to your system."[130] Slaveowners singled out William Wilberforce, a leader in the British anti–slave trade movement, as the main spokesman of this inflammatory ideology. Using the same language with which the Saint-Dominguans later described their own circumstances, Wilberforce saw enslaved Africans as an "unfortunate people"— the victims of a traffic that "outraged every principle of humanity," whose alleviation should appeal to all those "who were susceptible of a sentiment of humanity."[131] In his mind, the slaves, not the masters, were worthy of sympathy. Wilberforce's critics, however, reasoned that he and his colleagues, in light of this imprudent sympathy, had goaded slaves throughout the New World to revolt, and Saint-Domingue was the first manifestation of this provocation (and, the exiles warned, probably not its last). According to a 1792 account in the *New-York Journal and Patriotic Register*, "Mr. Wilberforce's wild visions respecting the emancipation of the Negroes . . . are so many exhortations to the blacks to destroy the whites."[132] Because of Wilberforce's unbridled rhetoric and misdirected sympathy, his critics contended, slave rebellion could happen to any slaveholding country or colony.

In the first few years of the revolt, when planters on the island looked to Jamaica and the United States for aid, the colonists cast Wilberforce as an international threat to the social and racial order common to the Americas. He also figured in exiles' arguments in a French revolutionary context, but in a very different way. Wilberforce's movement in Britain supposedly helped to inspire the establishment of the French antislavery society, the Amis des Noirs (Friends of the Blacks) in 1788. In the ranks of the Amis were men from a variety of backgrounds—journalists, *philosophes*, and noblemen, many of whom participated prominently in the early phases of the French Revolution. One of the group's founders, Jacques-Pierre Brissot de Warville, emerged in 1791 as the major leader of the revolution during its Girondist phase. The Saint-Dominguan refugees hoped that playing up the British connections of the Amis would tarnish its members' republican credentials. After all, Wilberforce was politically conservative (a close ally of William Pitt) and committed to maintaining the standing order in Britain. When the French legislative assembly awarded Wilberforce honorary citizenship, white Saint-Dominguans could claim that this act endorsed the very aristocracy and privilege that the French Revolution sought to overturn. In sum, the Amis' philanthropy was corrupt from the start.[133]

Early on, then, white Saint-Dominguans invoked Wilberforce for two almost contradictory purposes. On the one hand, they reviled him for disrupting the status quo throughout the Americas, and on the other they argued that he was a bulwark of the old regime. This criticism, to some extent, reflected Wilberforce's own complicated politics, but perhaps more importantly, it was an attempt to negotiate the uncertain path of the French Revolution. (Brissot was a case in point of the fickleness of French revolutionary politics: his dizzying ascent matched his equally swift decline.)

While Wilberforce represented one avenue of argument against "philanthropy," the refugees unleashed their rancor toward the Amis in much more straightforward terms. Initially the Amis had limited aims: its members sought to curb the slave trade with a view to the gradual abolition of slavery altogether. Saint-Dominguan planters bristled at the prospect of slave trade abolition, for the French slave trade was at its height in the years right before the Haitian Revolution. Any threat to this traffic was denounced as "the fruit of the false philanthropy of Brissot, for assuredly hastening the ruin of the commerce of France."[134]

The opportunities afforded by the French Revolution broadened the Amis' platform, and the group, under pressure from free people of color, became involved
in promoting their equal rights. In the minds of white refugees, the Amis' efforts
set in motion a transformation that ran amuck in Saint-Domingue.

One of the most vehement articulations of this view came from the pen of
Bernard-Barnabe O'Shiell. Exiled in Philadelphia in the mid-1790s, O'Shiell had
lived in southern Saint-Domingue, an area with a powerful *gens de couleur* population, and his family had earned its fortune from the slave trade. In a treatise sold
in several cities along the U.S. East Coast, O'Shiell blamed the revolt on the
"machinations of philanthropists," by which he meant the Amis des Noirs. According to O'Shiell, the pro-colored group encouraged the *gens de couleur* in Saint-
Domingue to agitate for political and civil rights. In France, representatives of the
Amis lobbied the government aggressively, bidding it to apply the Rights of Man
and Citizen to free people of color, while on the island *gens de couleur* took up arms
in the name of realizing equality and often enlisted slaves in the process. As a
result, O'Shiell concluded that the *gens de couleur* were "the direct and immediate
force of the slave revolt." He contended that "if [they] did not exist, there would
have been no uprising."[135] Of course, O'Shiell conveniently neglected to point out
that the very existence of the free colored population was the doing of white
French men.

By the white refugees' account, the *gens de couleur* provided not only opportunity and example for Saint-Dominguan slaves, but their sponsoring group, the
Amis, began to appeal openly to the enslaved population as well. In December
1791, soon after the first slave uprising in the northern plain, the marquis de
Rouvray, who the following year would become an exile in the United States,
explained to his daughter: "The Amis des Noirs have been, without doubt, the
first cause of our misfortunes, my dear child. It is clear to me that they have sent
us many of their emissaries and two were hanged who were convinced to preach
their dogma among our slaves."[136] In Rouvray's estimation, the consequence of
the Amis' designs would be nothing less than the downfall of the nation and
perhaps of civilization itself. A few years later he reflected, "Do you recall, my
daughter, all my predictions announced in my three pamphlets against the Amis
des Noirs and the Jacobins? It was the month of June 1789 that I wrote that the
sect of the Amis des Noirs contemplated the destruction of all thrones, all forms
of government, all religions, of the globe."[137] The philanthropic doctrine of the
Amis des Noirs, he felt, had led to anarchy.

The refugees' cries against "false philanthropy" grew more strident in the
wake of the abolition decrees of 1793 and 1794. In the words of a Monsieur Chô-

tard, a leader among refugees in Philadelphia who had been a mayor on the island, the laws proved that French officials operated "under the cloak of philanthropy." With this phrase Chôtard picked up on the Jacobin mania for transparency—their desire to unmask conspiracies that lurked, it seemed, almost everywhere, compromising the French Republic. Chôtard claimed that the case of Saint-Domingue confirmed that the Jacobins were the conspirators, hiding underneath a philanthropic mantle. He argued that "true philanthropy is a friend of its homeland; its homeland is the universe"; its actions could not result in the "carnage" and "devastation" witnessed in Saint-Domingue.[138] Therefore, the turmoil in the colony was proof of the corruption of philanthropic principles. As another exile elaborated in an American newspaper, "To give liberty to so considerable a body of slaves, at the expense of their masters, and that of the French merchants, it has been necessary to excite them to insurrection—to arm them with torches and daggers, to burn the country, and kill their masters; and to banish therefrom the industrious proprietors of the Colony."[139] How, the exiles queried, could emancipation be "philanthropy" when the rights and lives of others—both in Saint-Domingue and in France—were violated in the process? The problems that wracked the colony in the aftermath of abolition, wrote an anonymous refugee, demonstrated that the "friends of the African races" were nothing but "egoistic pedants who, from the depths of their libraries, judge everything by hearsay, and make a pretence of feeling compassion for some unfortunates whom they have never seen or known, so they may claim the right to lodge complaint against those people whom they do see daily. . . . theirs is an irremediable crime, and they do not overwhelm me with all the sonorous and high-sounding words of four or five syllables which they can find in the dictionary."[140] In the opinion of the white exiles, the lofty language of philanthropy was a verbal façade to legitimate nefarious designs.

At times, the "false" philanthropy of French officials led the refugees to defend their own controversial actions. In March 1796 the *Gazette française*, a French-language newspaper in New York City, ran an article about how the British army planned to use mastiffs to hunt down black foes in Saint-Domingue. The author celebrated the decision as economical and effective in the face of objections from those who found the measure barbaric. In a caustic and sarcastic response, he accused these "gentle" philanthropists of hypocrisy, charging that they had, while claiming to perform "an important service to humanity, let loose on the white race 500,000 black and yellow tigers" who wanted "to drink the blood" of their former masters. Had the enemy been "loyal" and "generous," the author contended, the army would not have been driven to this kind of defense. The so-called philan-thropists had brought it on themselves.[141]

This line of argument—that philanthropy had been botched in the French colonies—was eventually embraced by Bonaparte's regime. In 1802, the French government asserted that racial equality had brought only desolation and that the results cried out for correction: the "accents of a philanthropy that was falsely applied produced in our colonies the effort of the siren's song: with them came miseries of all kinds, despair, and death."[142] When the expedition of General Charles Leclerc failed to achieve this "correction" in Saint-Domingue and Haiti declared its independence in 1804, white Saint-Dominguan exiles continued to rail against the vagaries of philanthropy. In fact, the consequences of the revolu-tion persuaded some exiles that the word and its associated ideals had been so corrupted by events in Saint-Domingue that it should be abandoned altogether.

In January 1809 white refugees in Baltimore, along with their sympathizers, staged a festive tribute to Duncan McIntosh, an American merchant who traded with the French army in Saint-Domingue. McIntosh had, it was estimated, helped 2,400 colonists escape the island in 1804. According to depositions by exiles, ship captains, and merchants, McIntosh spent his own money to spare the lives of residents by bribing black officials.[143] At the fête, exiles and other attendees (French and American alike) honored McIntosh's deeds with testimonials. His actions were even commemorated in an allegorical drawing by Maximilian Gode-froy, a French artist who had migrated to the United States in 1805 and taught at St. Mary's College in Baltimore, a Catholic seminary patronized by many Saint-Dominguan exiles.[144] The sketch featured McIntosh as a "protecting Genius," standing between "an affrighted woman pressing her infant children to her bosom" and "a Monster, half negro and half tiger, who has already seized her garments in his teeth."[145] Well after the revolution, refugees harped on the same racist and gendered tropes that had elicited sympathy from Americans in 1793—and they still worked. As Eliza Boudinot, a young woman who attended the trib-ute, described to a friend, the scene and accounts were so moving that "there was scarcely a dry eye in the room."[146]

Throughout the gala, the refugees hailed McIntosh as the embodiment of virtue. An address by C. Loigerot, one of the "managers" of the evening, noted that the honoree was a "stranger by birth to the unfortunates who surrounded him—having no language in common with them but a sympathy of soul" and referred to him as "this Champion of Humanity (I will not say *philanthropy*)." "Philanthropy," Loigerot made clear, was "an expression unnaturally perverted by

"The mode of training Blood Hounds in St. Domingo, and of exercising them by Chasseurs." Marcus Rainsford, *An Historical Account of the Black Empire of Hayti* (London, 1805). In his account, Rainsford, an Englishman who traveled to Saint-Domingue during the final years of the Haitian Revolution, criticizes the French campaign to reconquer the island and reenslave its inhabitants. In particular, Rainsford condemns the controversial practice of using mastiffs to hunt down black adversaries, and this plate makes his reproach clear: a leering French soldier displays the sympathetically depicted black woman, with her breast bared, to the snarling hounds; and in the background, black Saint-Dominguans are being torn apart by dogs. Courtesy of the John Carter Brown Library at Brown University.

the pretended friends of humanity, who in France, aimed the destruction of the whites, under the veil of an affected pity for the negroes of the Colonies."[147] McIntosh, not the abolitionists, he said, exhibited the qualities of compassion, disinterestedness, and courage—the "*reflecting* sensibility" that characterized a man of enlightenment. To add further credibility to their claims, the event's hosts bedecked McIntosh with ancient Roman emblems of tribute. He was adorned with a medal and a civic crown, distinctions meant to recall those "appreciated by the Romans, because they knew the worth of a citizen."[148] His hosts also compared McIntosh to Titus, who had led the Roman siege of Jerusalem, and who, in light of subsequent good actions enjoyed "the sweetness of undisturbed sleep."[149] Among Americans, ancient Rome represented the pinnacle of republican government, endowed with a virtuous, active citizenry. In the refugees' view, men like McIntosh—men who worked to preserve Saint-Domingue for the colonists—were the true inheritors of Roman virtues.

From start to finish, the celebration of Duncan McIntosh was a performed argument in which the white exiles sought to show how things had gone awry in Saint-Domingue and, by extension, in France. McIntosh served as the perfect counterpoint for "false" philanthropy and misdirected sympathy. The French revolutionary application of "philanthropy"—namely, abolition of slavery and granting of equal rights for all freemen—bred mayhem, as unchecked sympathy led to the very tyranny that it was supposed to overturn. This view of philanthropy as articulated in public displays and proclamations throughout the 1790s and early 1800s attracted exiles of various political stripes as they courted American sympathy. The discussions of this perception provided a neutral ground of sorts, permitting critiques of the French and Haitian revolutions without requiring the disclosure of party loyalties or direct attacks on the revolutionary government. Republicans and aristocrats rallied around the philanthropy argument. A refugee known only as Mr. Gros contended in *Historick Recital* (a dramatic autobiography of his time in Saint-Domingue) that philanthropy was the philosophical guise that European aristocrats wore to cover their "infernal Machinations."[150] Others who denounced French philanthropy, such as McIntosh's supporters, were known for their royalist leanings. A poem commemorating the baptism of several Saint-Dominguan infants in New Orleans in 1808 lauded McIntosh's virtues (who stood as the children's godfather) and called the white Saint-Dominguans "the last brave friends of great St. Louis' line."[151]

Philanthropy, in this regard, proved a powerful language for the white refugees, especially in the context of the United States. With their racialized definition of philanthropy, white Saint-Dominguans cemented sympathetic ties with white

Americans in the summer of 1793, and the exiles continued to play on this common bond throughout the 1790s and early 1800s. The refugees' contentions about the pitfalls of philanthropy as applied in Saint-Domingue helped convince white Americans that they had to be careful how they practiced philanthropy in their own slaveholding republic: aid and empathy had to avoid challenging racial hierarchies. In general, distressed masters were seen as more worthy candidates of sympathy than bondsmen, yet white Americans at the local, city, state, and federal level also checked support for their peers—whether Saint-Dominguan exiles or other distressed populations. Asylum would extend only so far.

While the language of philanthropy failed to secure lasting financial commitment (as federal authorities skirted the issue and state and city governments could not keep pace with demand), it did provide the exiles with one ideological compass with which to navigate the treacherous and ever-changing political waters of the revolutionary era. But philanthropy was only one keyword of the age of revolutions, and it was clear that this appeal would not be enough to see the refugees through. Try though they might, white refugees could not avoid the vicious political battles under way on both sides of the Atlantic. Relief campaigns attempted to sidestep the issue of the exiles' political alliances when soliciting aid. The New York committee stated that philanthropy should be blind to politics: "Whatever causes may have led to the event [in Cap Français], it is not the business of charity to enquire; it is sufficient that they are men, and miserable!"[152] Yet American audiences could not resist asking, and the white exiles in order to bolster their claims to being worthy of sympathy and support, went on the political attack.

CHAPTER THREE

REPUBLICAN REFUGEES?

A fter hearing about the destruction of Cap Français in the summer of 1793, Philadelphia merchant Stephen Girard wrote to associates in Le Cap, offering them passage on his vessels and extolling the benefits of refuge in the United States: "come here and enjoy the peace which our republican government, founded as it is on the rights of man, assures to all its inhabitants."[1] Thousands took Girard's advice, but his breezy assertion elided the heated contest over republican government and the rights of man that was taking place, not only in the United States, but also in France and its premier colony, Saint-Domingue. With the exiles' arrival in North America, the discussion intensified, as the political landscape in all three sites changed in dramatic and interconnected ways during the 1790s.

Given the timing of the slave rebellion in Saint-Domingue in an Atlantic context—that it followed closely on the heels of the American Revolution and that it began during the first flush of republican fervor in France—it was almost inevitable that observers would wonder about the relationship between politics and events in the colony. In the case of Saint-Domingue, the appraisal of the revolution in these terms was, however, usually limited to the politics of the white population. While black and colored witnesses may have well understood the ideological impulses behind the actions of the rebels, most white commentators—from the most radical Jacobin to the staunchest defender of slavery—were unwilling to recognize the political motivations of enslaved Saint-Dominguans. To have done so would have challenged the racism fundamental to Western societies, even "enlightened" ones. Instead, the majority of white onlookers insisted that the slaves were the pawns of white and colored colonists who marshaled, for their own political and military ends, the raw and unthinking manpower of the enslaved.[2]

The ideological inspiration behind the campaign for rights by free men of color was acknowledged (if denigrated), for *gens de couleur* operated mainly through orderly channels of republican reform: sending delegates to Paris, petitioning the legislature, appropriating revolutionary language, and so on. Also, in comparison to the enslaved rebels, the goals of the *gens de couleur* were much less radical; in the early days of the Haitian Revolution, they wanted political and civil rights for themselves alone and looked to preserve slavery. Although their trajectory is, as many scholars have demonstrated, important and fascinating, white Americans were most interested in the political agenda of the white population. Perhaps because the United States lacked a free colored population with as much clout as that of the *gens de couleur* in Saint-Domingue, white Americans worried less about what this group's actions portended for their society. Instead, bystanders in the United States deliberated over the ideological affiliations of the white population. Ascertaining the white population's loyalties was no easy task, what with the diversity of views, conflicting reports, and the fast pace of revolution in France and its colony, yet doing so was crucial for commentators in the United States. While Americans were outspoken supporters of republican revolution, the nation did not seek to apply its ideals to enslaved people. The U.S. Constitution, for all intents and purposes, defended the institution. Saint-Domingue would test whether republican rhetoric and abolition of slavery necessarily went hand-in-hand.

American appraisals of white Saint-Dominguans' politics ran the gamut. In the early years of the slave rebellion, writers were quick to blame the white population's errant politics for the troubles in the colony. Even those Americans who were petitioning the public on behalf of the refugees made the link between suspect alliances and the slave revolt. In an appeal for aid for the exiles, members of the Philadelphia French Patriotic Society asserted that the refugees' "prejudices and their aristocracy, not less absurd and prejudicial to mankind than that of the heretofore French nobles, have been the principal cause of all the evils which now assail them."[3] Their predicament, the statement implied, was the product of their politics—just as the aristocrats in France were getting what they deserved, the white exiles from Saint-Domingue were reaping what they had sown.

With the Jacobin turn in France in 1793–94 and the sudden transformation of slaves into citizens in the Caribbean, this position became harder to maintain, and the refugees were not passive recipients of admonition. White Saint-Dominguans worked to dispel the aristocratic image and actively promoted themselves as "true" republicans. They took advantage of the burgeoning print culture on both sides of the Atlantic to enter political debates. With one eye on France and the other on their fellow U.S. residents, the refugees explained, in political terms, the reasons for their displacement. They depicted themselves as hapless victims, not only of an atrocious slave rebellion, but also of a republican government gone awry. In the minds of white colonists, these two circumstances—slave rebellion and corrupt republicanism—were intertwined; and during their exile in the United States, they tried to convince their American and French counterparts of the same. This argument mattered for the futures of white Saint-Dominguans: by persuading the French government to their point of view, they hoped to reclaim control of the colony and reverse what they saw as foolhardy Jacobin policies. From their U.S. hosts the refugees sought continued sympathy and financial support, and if the Americans took the side of the exiled Saint-Dominguans, then perhaps it would give France pause. Such a move could be read as the first republic chastising the second.

The discussion surrounding the white refugees reverberated in the turbulent political climate of the 1790s. The issues involved in the debate about the Saint-Dominguans—the French Revolution, relations with Great Britain, and U.S. immigration policies, to name a few—were hotly disputed in the early republic. Although the refugees hoped for exculpation, most white Americans drew another conclusion about the upshot of conditions in Saint-Domingue, namely the dangers of faction, especially in a slave society. The vicious political wrangling of white islanders, they concluded, diverted attention from a shared foe and gave the slaves an opportunity to rebel. The first political parties of the United States, the Federalists and Democratic Republicans, used this example to urge unity among Americans, but each party had a different idea about what that consensus should be built upon and who should participate in politics. This discrepancy widened as the decade wore on, feeding the development of party politics in the United States, and the refugees found themselves caught in the middle.

ARISTOCRATIC ACCUSATIONS

In the early years of the slave rebellion in Saint-Domingue—from 1791 to about 1794—continental Frenchmen and white American observers claimed that the "aristocratic" politics of the white colonists accounted for the insurrection. Hoping to subvert the republican cause, the explanation went, white Saint-Dominguans had provoked their bondsmen to revolt, with the intent of blaming the French Revolution for inciting the rebellion. The colonists would then use these rebel forces to fight republican reforms and reinstate the status quo. Some slave rebels did allude to the King of France in their bid for freedom, as rumors swirled that he had proclaimed emancipation but that the colonial assemblies refused to heed the decree. Royalist language made sense to the many African-born insurgents because monarchy was the predominant political organization in their homelands (although, of course, the content and practice of African kingships differed from European ones). In general, as scholars have shown, the royalist appeals did reflect the ideologies and political aims of the enslaved rebels; but during the revolution, white observers, determined not to recognize the political wherewithal of the enslaved, associated royalist language with the master class.[4] This reading of the rebellion resonated in the French and U.S. republics for two reasons. First, while the French may have pursued aristocrats in a more aggressive (even bloodthirsty) way, Americans and French alike attributed much of the disruption in their countries to those with royalist inclinations. It was, in other words, a shared vocabulary, and the trouble in Saint-Domingue seemed to fit the template. Second, the accusation of aristocracy was convenient in that it allowed white Frenchmen and Americans to avoid addressing the uneasy paradox of slavery in a republic. If servile insurrection was a symptom of counterrevolution, then perhaps enlightened republics had nothing to fear from the oppressed population in their midst.

The white refugees were not about to take lying down the charge of being aristocrats, but their ability to counter such allegations was hampered by the fact that some of them had royalist sympathies. In addition, the white colonial population was riven by political divisions that sometimes pitted factions against one another. From their exile in the United States, white Saint-Dominguans began to promulgate their own version of events—one in which the mother country had wronged its premier colony yet again.

Jacques Pierre Brissot de Warville, one of the most prominent leaders during the early phase of the French Revolution, leveled the most forceful accusation of creole "aristocracy" against the white colonists. Despite his egalitarian tendencies, Brissot doubted that slaves had the capacity for a large-scale, coordinated rebellion. In a famous address to the National Assembly in December 1791, he blamed "aristocratic" white planters who "abhorred" the revolution for inciting the insurrection. By encouraging the slaves to revolt, Brissot contended, the colonists, especially the *grands blancs*, hoped to force the government to meet their demands for more control over the economic and political life of Saint-Domingue. He saw the insurrection as a move to undercut the assembly's legislation and its principles: by instigating the rebellion and attributing it to recent French laws, the white ruling class sought to strong-arm the republican government into leaving its colonies to the colonists.[5]

Soon Brissot's speech, translated into English, turned up in U.S. newspapers. By the spring of 1792, subscribers read how "the infernal vanity of the whites . . . produced the effusion of blood" in Saint-Domingue. American observers in the colony seconded Brissot's interpretation.[6] Nathaniel Cutting, the U.S. consul in Le Cap, rehearsed for Secretary of State Thomas Jefferson a litany of atrocities that would "make a Nero blush," and then queried, "Is it possible that the French Aristocrates can be the stimulators and abettors of all the horrid proceedings which have deluged this Colony in blood and brought it to the brink of ruin, in the illusory hope of thereby effecting a Counter Revolution in France? Many circumstances go far to prove the affirmative."[7] It seemed as well that Americans had proof on their own soil of the refugees' aristocratic proclivities. The French minister to the United States, Jean-Baptiste de Ternant, clashed with a group of refugees when they supposedly drank a public toast to the Duke of Brunswick. (The duke, commander of the allied forces against republican France, had declared in his notorious July 1792 Manifesto that Prussian forces would fight to restore the king's authority in France—a development that was covered extensively in the U.S. press.)[8]

These allegations from Brissot, Ternant, Cutting, and others, were potent in the heady political climate of the United States. John Adams aside, most American onlookers were, at this moment, thrilled by events in France. In the early 1790s the French Revolution electrified Americans' imaginations: merchants and planters, laborers and artisans, religious and political leaders all celebrated the spread of liberty and congratulated themselves on initiating it.[9] The fact that white colonists challenged the French republican government seemed evidence enough of their designs against liberty. U.S. government officials, among them Jefferson, echoed the language of their French peers, denouncing the white refugees as "monocrats" who could stand to learn a lesson or two about liberty.[10]

The charges of aristocratic politics did not recede when Brissot's party, the Girondins, fell from power in June 1793; the allegations were elaborated on by the new leaders of the French government, the Jacobins. They exposed fresh plots of royalist treachery among white Saint-Dominguans, reports of which surfaced in the United States. According to a letter from the island published in a Virginia

newspaper, French commissioners had discovered that, "the counter revolutionists had made the negroes to believe that Capet [Louis XVI] had left a will by which
the negroes were to have their liberty, if by their exertions his son should come
to mount the throne."[11] Desperate yet determined, the white colonists, the rumor
intimated, hoped to convince slaves to fight for the restoration of monarchy in
the name of freedom.

But perhaps most damning in the eyes of Americans was the British invasion
of Saint-Domingue in 1793. France declared war on Britain in early 1793, and the
Caribbean, as it had during previous conflicts between these two empires, became
an active theater of battle and bloodshed.[12] Shortly after British forces landed in
Saint-Domingue, the news of their swift successes spread, adding credence to the
claim that the white colonists had aristocratic aspirations. A ship's captain recently
returned from the island informed Boston papers that the inhabitants of the Môle
Saint-Nicolas, a key port in the northwest, had declared themselves subjects of
the king of Britain.[13] The *Columbian Herald* in Charleston republished a message
from residents in Jérémie to the British people in which they declared, "Were it
possible, we would express to you the sensations that filled the breasts of our citizens at the sight of the English fleet, the satisfaction they showed at their landing,
and the sincere and cordial welcome we gave to our true and real friends."[14] A few
reports implied that the colonists suffered under and fought against British occupation, but for the most part, the U.S. press conveyed the impression that Saint-
Dominguans, especially those in the west, received the British with open arms
and were "perfectly satisfied under British protection."[15]

American officials also received dispatches from France cautioning that the
presence of Anglophilic colonists was not confined to Saint-Domingue. In early
1793, well before the British invasion, French authorities had notified ministers
abroad that "emissaries and partisans of George III"—French émigrés and Saint-
Dominguan exiles—had infiltrated cities in the United States, and those messages were passed along to the U.S. government.[16] These suspicions were seem-
ingly substantiated the following year in New York's *American Minerva* and in
other newspapers. An article averred that wealthy exiles in Baltimore had raised
"immense sums" to support the British at the Môle and Jérémie and that the
subscribers swore an oath "to shed even the last drop of [their] blood in support
of the British flag at St. Domingo, to fight until death against all Frenchmen . . . and
to perish rather than to acknowledge the French Republic."[17] Loyalty to the late
French king was bad enough, but in the eyes of Americans, allegiance to their old
enemy George III was even worse.

The charges of aristocracy by consuls in the United States, French officials at the metropole and on the island, and American commentators were not spurious: some counterrevolutionary Saint-Dominguan exiles had migrated to the United States, and they felt no remorse about their political affiliations. Consider the testimony in the "alien reports" taken from refugees in the late 1790s. These declarations included information about the place of origin, citizenship, occupations, and living circumstances of recent immigrants. White male heads of household usually filed the reports, but testimonies from the occasional white woman and even a few free men of color appear in the records as well. There was no official form, and so the language of each refugee's statement is revealing. In the briefest of terms, they narrated their past and accounted for their present; and for many, politics was central to their biographies. Several exiles underscored their disgust with the revolution by stating that they were "subjects" of the king of France, rejecting wholesale the brand of citizenship offered by the French Republic in favor of proclaiming tenacious loyalty to monarchy. Others had even more concrete ties to the *ancien régime*: Marie-Dominique-Jacques D'Orlic, for example, reported to American authorities that before his exile, he was "late employed in King's household commissioned by his majesty captain of Dragoons."[18] Pierre Andre François Thebaudieres had so resented French policies that, after emigrating to New Jersey in 1793, he returned to Saint-Domingue two years later to serve as the attorney general "for his Britannic majesty."[19] While not aristocrats in the most formal sense, the royalist sympathies of some refugees were hard to deny—nor did it seem that they wanted to.

Yet, for every white male exile in the United States who professed his fidelity to the French king, there was one, if not two, who proclaimed that they were "citizens" of the French Republic. To be sure, the refugees complained about the policies of the new French nation, especially their application to the colonies, and the definition of French citizenship was anything but stable in this period. However, many white male exiles were adamant that they were citizens. This assertion was critical: their arguments about the future of the colony, its relationship with France, and the reasons for the slave rebellion would only be given credence if the refugees affirmed that they were members, not outcasts, of the Republic. Aristocrats, they knew, could be simply disregarded—or worse, guillotined; but as citizens, white Saint-Dominguans could stay alive—literally and politically, as they tried to persuade all parties about what French citizenship should entail in a colonial context.[20] Occasionally, the refugees' proclamations on this subject reverberate with cognitive dissonance. John de la Fond, who had been "King's Attorney" at Petit-Goâve, a port town west of Port-au-Prince, described himself as a "citizen of the French Republic" but also as a "Gentleman."[21] Although his service to the king could, perhaps, be written off as part of his prerevolutionary past, his insistence on remaining a "gentleman" sits somewhat uneasily with his republican claims.

The divisions among white Saint-Dominguan exiles also reflected the political geography of the island. As one historian of the colony has remarked, "The natural isolation of each of the three provinces encouraged the development of local political and social differences and fostered interprovincial rivalries that could be intense."[22] Each region vied for power during the eighteenth century and pressed the French government for changes that suited its unique interests. The revolution inaugurated opportunity and discord, as each region jockeyed to have its voice heard in Paris. In October 1789, residents of the Petit-Goâve quarter complained about the "self-styled representatives" from the northern parishes who claimed to speak for the whole colony.[23]

Animosity among the white ruling classes in the different provinces escalated to violence. In March 1790, for instance, the National Assembly granted the white colonists the power to govern over "internal" issues (including legislation regarding slaves and free people of color), and the local assemblies acted independent of and in outright disagreement with one another. The most flagrant example of this disregard was the assembly in St. Marc, located on the western coast of the island, due north of Port-au-Prince. Members of the St. Marc assembly ran roughshod over the governor and drafted their own "Constitutional Principles," some of which blatantly contradicted laws passed in France. Perhaps the most egregious violation was the St. Marc assembly's declaration that all ports in Saint-Domingue were open to foreign trade—a policy the French National Assembly had expressly forbidden. The legal liberties being taken in St. Marc infuriated members of the assemblies in Le Cap and Port-au-Prince, who feared that their hard-won compromises in Paris would be revoked in light of St. Marc's recklessness, and they sent armies to bring the renegade representatives to heel.[24]

Differences among the white colonists did not give way in the face of the slave revolt of 1791. Rather than coming together to tackle a shared foe, the white ruling classes divided further still. Before his exile to the United States, Mayor Chôtard reminded white Saint-Dominguans (in vain) of their common grievances, in the hope of promoting agreement among the quarreling factions.[25] Yet the white colonists split over how to handle the insurrection—whom to turn to for help, what allowances (if any) to make to slaves and free people of color, and who, ultimately, was responsible. Verbal sparring frequently escalated to physical blows, and even in exile, the colonists' rifts flared into violence. In November 1793 a fight broke out on a vessel from Cap Français as it docked in Philadelphia harbor. A mob of refugees plotted to kill one of their number for crimes he allegedly committed on the island. After drawing him out on deck, they attacked him with swords, sticks, and fists, knocked him overboard, and then proceeded to pelt him with stones. The exile would have died were it not for the intervention of locals, who were appalled by the premeditated melee. Not dissuaded, a gang of white refugees had "the superlative audacity to assemble at the city-hall, where the wounded person had been brought to safety, and there insolently uttered threats of their future murderous intentions."[26] Officials chastised the exiles for insulting the laws of a nation that was extending them asylum. The incident, needless to say, did not reflect favorably on the refugees.

Aware that this acrimony would not serve the refugees' interests either in France or in the United States, several exiles looked to set aside their differences and unite in order to oppose the charge of counterrevolutionary sympathies that had been made against them. Thomas Millet, who had been the president of the first Colonial Assembly of Saint-Domingue as well as a member of the St. Marc assembly, published an appeal in French in the *Baltimore Evening Post* that exhorted "the citizens of Saint-Domingue" to "reject all the opinions, all the political systems which have divided you," and white refugees up and down the East Coast echoed his plea.[27] Perhaps the most interesting call came from the pen of Claude-Corentin Tanguy de la Boissière. Prior to his exile, Tanguy had been a planter in Les Platons near Les Cayes in southern Saint-Domingue and had been active in local politics, dashing off tract after tract that called for bolstering planter supremacy.[28] In 1793, residing in the United States but no less devoted to the cause of white hegemony on the island, Tanguy declared his intention to start a newspaper called *Journal des Révolutions de Saint-Domingue* that would, appropriately enough, focus on recent events in the colony. In his proposal for the journal, Tanguy tried to foster unity among his anticipated readership by narrating a history shared by all white colonists—one that, significantly, was steeped in republican allusions.

Tanguy's history began with the French colonization of Saint-Domingue in the seventeenth century. According to his account, his ancestors, along with those of all the exiles, had migrated to the French Caribbean because of tyrannical persecution at home: "Those Frenchmen, at the eve of being sacrificed in France, upon the sacred altar of religion, by their fathers and brethren, by their priests and kings, intoxicated with fanaticism, sought an asylum in the island of St. Domingo."[29] In other words, they descended from Huguenots, French Protestants who had left the country after the revocation of the Edict of Nantes in 1685 made Protestantism illegal (again) in France. Huguenots had been a presence in the French possession: the story went that the colony had its origins on the Isle de la Tortue, the small island off the north coast of Saint-Domingue, which had been a haven for adventuresome and liberty-seeking Huguenot privateers.[30] Although the ethos from this foundational era may have survived, it is doubtful that by the 1790s the majority of white Saint-Dominguans, let alone those exiled in the United States, were actually Huguenot progeny. As refugee wills attest, most white colonists were recent migrants or first-generation offspring, and almost all white Saint-Dominguans were avowed Catholics, who continued in their faith during their exile in the United States.

If somewhat misleading, Tanguy's emphasis on the Huguenot narrative functioned as a central trope of his history of Saint-Domingue: the colonists had long been the torchbearers of freedoms threatened in the mother country. The deflection of the refugees' Catholicism was important in an American context. Because of its strict hierarchical structure with the pope at its apex, Catholicism was seen as inimical to republicanism: throughout the American Revolution, propagandists spoke of British tyranny in Catholic terms; and well into the nineteenth century, Protestant Americans were wary of Catholics in their midst.[31] The reinvention of Saint-Dominguans into wronged Protestants shows Tanguy's sensitivity to this stream of American thought and his desire to encourage locals to picture their past and that of the exiles as occupying a similar Protestant and republican trajectory.

After asserting the colony's Huguenot ancestry and spirit, Tanguy went on to describe how the colonists had improved the land ("which had remained uncultivated under the hand of the inactive Spaniards, who seem to have invaded America only to deprive others of it") and established a flourishing society.[32] Effecting this transformation was testimony to their hard work and virtue: they had tamed a wilderness and made it productive—a theme Americans would have recognized from their own foundational stories. Tanguy asserted, however, that the colonists undertook this venture as good Frenchmen, so much so that they freely offered the fruits of their labors (noticeably not their slaves' labors) to the mother country.[33] The Saint-Dominguans gave and obeyed with good will, abiding by the metropole's exclusive mercantilist policies, even though, he hinted, they could have enjoyed greater profits by trading with other nations and colonies. This reference to trade would not have been lost on American merchants, who constantly assessed what Saint-Domingue meant for their ledgers.[34]

But more pressingly in his account, Tanguy tried to head off charges that the white colonists were, as he put it, "independentists"—an accusation that made them traitors to the French revolutionary cause.[35] Quite frankly, the allegation that the colonists sought independence from France was a bit of hyperbole generated by their political opponents. Even the Saint-Dominguans most disgusted with the French Revolution did not see independence as a viable option for maintaining the racial, political, and economic status quo. Nevertheless, the charge had to be countered, and Tanguy sought to do so. Unlike the American Revolution, in which republican politics and independence went hand-in-hand, such a suggestion among white Saint-Dominguans would have smacked of political corruption: after all, why would a colony want to break with a purportedly enlightened republic? The refugees insisted that their lobbying activities before the slave rebellion—their demands for free trade and for self-governance in local affairs—were not preparations for independence. The St. Marc assembly, with their wild claims, were outliers. So attached were Saint-Dominguans to the mother country, Tanguy wrote, that not even their deteriorated relationship would compel them to sever the tie: "Like those sons, the more respectful, the more attached to a deceived mother, as she seems to load them with despotism and motherly injustice; in like manner nature and the French blood, which flows in our veins, will cry aloud to us that we are Frenchmen—French republicans, and friends to true equality."[36] Although Tanguy's metaphor of dedication was odd, he affirmed emphatically the citizenship and Frenchness of Saint-Dominguans. If anything, he declared, their ardor for France and its cause had increased in the face of their tribulations.

Yet Tanguy by no means thought that Saint-Dominguan colonists should suffer quietly the "injustices" of their enemies' insults. His proposal included a clarion call to refugees to right the wrongs that had been heaped upon them. An early edition of *Journal des Révolutions* implored interested colonists to meet at Oehlers Hotel in Philadelphia, where in September of 1793 they formed the *Colons de Saint-Domingue réfugiés aux États-Unis*; similar associations had sprung up in Baltimore, New York, and other cities. Before commencing, the groups asked city mayors and magistrates for permission to organize; in testaments justifying their formation, the refugees employed the language of rights, referring to their property, individual safety, and legal representation.[37] With this rhetoric the exiles publicized that proper principles grounded their associations, and they reaffirmed this fact every time they met. Each group elected officers, usually a president and a few secretaries, to coordinate and oversee operations. More often than not, these men had held some sway back on the island: for example, Chô-tard, the secretary of the *colons réfugiés* in Philadelphia, had been mayor of Cayes-de-Jacmel.[38] The associations maintained close contact with Saint-Dominguans in France who were lobbying on their behalf.

As Tanguy's *Journal* makes clear, the refugees looked to newspapers to disseminate their political message far and wide. The same local and French-language newspapers that carried refugees' advertisements for goods for sale, services, and slaves on the lam, also included editorials and updates about the latest happenings in the French Atlantic. In addition, the exiles participated in and sometimes hosted events designed to celebrate the achievements of the French Republic. From New York to Charleston, they staged elaborate occasions to commemorate the execution of the king, Bastille Day, and any other accomplishment of the French Revolution that seemed noteworthy. Often including processions with music, toasts, and oaths of allegiance, these gatherings differed little in appearance from the parallel fêtes of their U.S. contemporaries and thus reinforced ties to American republicans.[39]

No matter the venue—whether a newspaper article, oath, or fête—the refugees in these organizations asserted over and over again that they were republicans. In fact, they argued that their very presence in the United States proved their republican character: "patriots" sought sanctuary in the United States from the slave rebellion, whereas liberty's foes hatched royalist plots on the island or in Britain.[40] But one event forced exile leaders to revise their assertion that *all* white Saint-Dominguans in the United States stood on the right side of revolution. In 1794 rumors circulated that exiles in Philadelphia had sponsored a funeral service for Louis XVI. The allegation was potentially damaging, since participation in such a commemoration would be evidence of aristocratic sympathies. In response, over ninety refugees renounced any involvement and signed an oath that pledged their fidelity to the revolutionary cause. They affirmed that they had always battled against "the first efforts of the aristocracy against liberty" but confessed that there were "some senseless royalists, some inhabitants of the French Antilles" in the United States who did support and engage in antirepublican activities.[41]

The same year, Pierre François Page and Augustin Jean Brulley, refugees leading the colonists' campaign in Paris, put a finer point on the distinctions among the exiles. In a tract aimed at government officials, they argued, "The colonists who are refugees in North America, are divided into two classes: the democrats or the friends of the republic; the counter-revolutionaries or the partisans of royalty."[42] Page and Brulley declared that the republicans could be differentiated from the monocrats in two ways. First, the democrats had been, in general, financially ruined in the upheaval in Saint-Domingue, while the royalists had capitalized on their enemies' misfortune and brought their loot with them; second, the republican refugees had formed assemblies in American cities, separating themselves from their counterrevolutionary peers. They cautioned officials not to condemn all for the actions of a few.

Regardless of how often the Saint-Dominguan exiles in the United States said they were republican, swore oaths to the cause, or toasted Louis XVI's demise, they found the epithet "aristocrat" hard to shake (at least those who sought to escape it) in both France and the United States. In the rhetoric of the French Revolution, their republican testimonies could all be dismissed as "cloaks" or "masks" intended to obfuscate the refugees' true counterrevolutionary tendencies. This accusation came from revolutionary leaders of all stripes: Brissot may have met his match in 1793, but the rising Jacobins continued to insist that the politics of white Saint-Dominguans were repugnant. In order to make their case more convincing—to both Americans and Frenchmen—the refugees realized that they had to do some unmasking of their own, and they went on the offensive, calling into question the actions of key French republican officials in Saint-Domingue and the United States. Tanguy summed up the sentiment: "By what strange destiny does it happen, that in the very times in which they doubt we are Frenchmen, whether we are men, whether we are useful to our mother country, whether she owes us protection and support, they conceived against us a sentiment of jealousy and envy so excessive, that they have taken upon themselves to be knowingly unjust to us, while they are possessed with the utmost concern for the unknown brutes and savages of the torrid zones."[43] In his view—and in that of many other white exiles—France's unfounded suspicions had caused the insurrection in the colony, and the actions of certain French officials, they argued, proved it.

THE LESSONS OF FACTION

As part of their bid for vindication, the white Saint-Dominguans attempted to turn the tables of revolution to show that members of the French republican government—not the colonists—were corrupt and deceitful. In particular, they set their sights on Léger-Félicité Sonthonax and Etienne Polverel, two of the civil commissioners assigned to Saint-Domingue from 1792 to 1794, and Edmond Charles Genet, the Minister Plenipotentiary of the French Republic in the United States in 1793. If the exiles could be persuasive in their denunciations of these men, the metropole might reverse its policies and give white Saint-Dominguans a greater voice in shaping the colonial application of the French Revolution. Regarding American favor, the advantages were more speculative, but no less important: the exiles wagered that an endorsement from the American republic might carry some weight with its European counterpart. In short, winning over both sides could be instrumental in helping the white refugees regain control of the colony.

The exiles' allegations about these officials were difficult for the French government to ignore; after all, they concerned the nation's premier colony. But perhaps more interestingly, the charges were impossible to disregard in the United States, for key players in the debate were in North America, and the refugees took their case to the American press for a public hearing. The significance of this strategy lay not just in the location of the discussion but in its content, too. In the contest over events in Saint-Domingue in 1793–94, white Americans witnessed the dangerous repercussions of faction, a menace that threatened their own fragile republic at that moment. Commentators turned to the situation in the French colony to draw lessons about how to avoid a fate similar to that of Saint-Domingue.

Well before they arrived to the United States, many white Saint-Dominguans resented Léger-Félicité Sonthonax and Etienne Polverel. The revolutionary government had sent the commissioners to the colony to rein in local assemblies, to restore order among the warring white, colored, and black Saint-Dominguans, and to enforce the law of April 4—the contentious legislation passed in 1792 that guaranteed full legal rights to all free men of color. The previous year's much more limited enfranchisement law for the *gens de couleur* had provoked uproar. The 1791 measure applied only to nonwhites born of two free parents and therefore affected a very small percentage of the free colored population, since most were the progeny of slave mothers and free fathers. Nevertheless, many white colonists refused to adhere to the law, and a few firebrands called for secession from France. As news of their reactions had reached France, the Constituent Assembly had reconsidered the prudence of colonial self-government and, seeking to reexert metropolitan influence, had sent troops and Sonthonax and Polverel.[44]

The white colonists not only begrudged the presence of the commissioners and their control over the colony but were also concerned about Sonthonax and Polverel's position on slavery. Rumors preceding their arrival claimed that Sonthonax intended to abolish slavery and that he brought with him twenty thousand rifles, with which to arm slaves for that purpose.[45] Although privately Sonthonax did see the issue of slavery as intertwined with the revolution, he publicly vowed that he would maintain the institution because it was permitted by French law; the same reasoning, however, applied to his determination to carry out the law of April 4.[46] White Saint-Dominguans balked at the implementation of the statute, but they feigned acceptance in a half-hearted attempt to pacify the war-torn colony and to preserve slavery.

Over the coming year, as the commissioners rewarded free men of color loyal to the republican cause by appointing them to coveted military posts and as they arrested and deported hundreds of colonists suspected of harboring antirevolutionary sentiment, the ire of the white population grew and found a sympathetic ear in Thomas-François Galbaud. A native of Port-au-Prince, Galbaud took over the post of Governor-General of Saint-Domingue in May 1793, and he was responsible for enforcing all laws in the colony.[47] Even though Galbaud was subordinate to Sonthonax and Polverel, the commissioners' success depended on the governor's willingness to demand adherence to their decrees, and disaffected white colonials tried to use this division of power to their advantage. They flocked around Galbaud and looked to him to overthrow the commissioners. Their intrigues set in motion a chain of events that culminated in June 1793 with the battle of Cap Français and the flight of thousands of Saint-Dominguans, including Galbaud, to the United States.[48]

The fighting at Le Cap was front-page news in U.S. cities for the next several months: refugees, French consuls, and American officials, merchants, and local residents all debated what had happened, why, and what it meant for the immediate future of the colony. The timing of the discussion was important in the U.S. context for several reasons. By the summer and fall of 1793 Americans were splitting in their responses to the French Revolution. On the one hand, some had recoiled in horror at the execution of Louis XVI earlier that year. The French king's support during the American Revolution had been critical to its success, and while many agreed that monarchy as a system left much to be desired, guillotining the king seemed excessive. Even Thomas Paine, the man who had done more than anyone else in North America to discredit the legitimacy of monarchy, had argued against regicide in France.[49] On the other hand, the arrival of Edmond Charles Genet, the minister of the French Republic to the United States, in the spring of 1793 had sparked a frenzy of support. During a tour he made along the East Coast, animated crowds from Charleston to Philadelphia greeted him with banquets, congratulatory addresses, bells, and cannon. Americans hailed Genet and his fellow Frenchmen for "struggling in the glorious cause of freedom," and scores of articles called on Americans to join France in the effort.[50]

American attitudes toward France combined with those toward Britain strongly influenced political life in the early American republic. War was declared between France and Britain in February 1793, and this had significant repercussions for the United States, as the Caribbean became a theater of battle between the two nations. U.S. shipping faced depredations by British privateers roving West Indian waters and looking for any excuse to board, raid, and seize vessels, and in many cases, the fact that American ships were bound to or returning from Saint-Domingue was reason enough. Captains cruising the Caribbean in July 1793 complained that "the seas swarm with privateers" and that "almost every American vessel is boarded, and on the least suspicion of their having French effects on board are carried into ports for investigation."[51] By the spring of 1794, more than 250 ships had been assailed, and Americans divided over how to handle the situation.[52] Some lobbied for a diplomatic solution, eager to remain on decent, if not good, footing with Britain, which was still the United States' top trading partner, while others interpreted the maritime molestation as yet further evidence of the heinousness of their old foe and saw Britain as an adversary who needed to be cut down to size again.

The emerging rifts among Americans over the French Revolution and the policies of Great Britain contributed to the development of the first political parties in the early republic—what would become the Federalists and the Democratic Republicans but at this stage they were, as one scholar has put it, "proto-parties." Neither side believed that consensus was impossible, and although later in the decade each would become convinced that the other had to be vanquished entirely, the lines had not been indelibly drawn in 1793–94.[53] Yet the discussions over the latest developments in Saint-Domingue resonated powerfully, as each proto-party drew its own conclusions about the effect which developments in the colony would have for the United States.

Initial reports in the American press set the responsibility for the conflagration squarely on Galbaud's shoulders. Just as the slave rebellion in 1791 had been described as a ploy by royalist colonists, the battle at Le Cap was interpreted as another desperate attempt to roll back the tide of liberty, equality, and fraternity. "Aristocratic motives" compelled the governor to devastate the port city in a reckless effort to subvert republican aims, these reports claimed. Articles reprinted from French newspapers warned that Galbaud might speak the language of freedom but that he wore only a "mask of Republicanism" and fellow republicans in North America should be careful: "Spirits of 76 arouse and be on your guard, beware of traitors, beware of the men of Lyons and Toulon, Dumouriez pleaded and pleads patriotism, so does Galbaud and his party."[54] The comparison made sense to U.S. readers who had been following the course of the French Revolution avidly: both Lyons and Toulon were antirevolutionary strongholds, and Charles François Dumouriez, a general who achieved stunning military victories for the

French Republic, defected to the enemy Austrians in April 1793. Turncoats and pockets of royalist resistance lurked throughout France and the Caribbean.

As summer gave way to autumn, the list of Galbaud's supposed crimes against the republican cause grew. He was now linked to the British invasion of the island under the reasoning that Galbaud would weaken the north at Le Cap as British forces attacked from the west. The *Baltimore Daily Intelligencer* averred that the reception of the British "with open arms" at the Môle and Jérémie, "added to Galbaud's flight into [British] Canada, shew who were the real conductors of . . . these two acts of treason [the easy capitulation of the Môle and Jérémie], and fully justify those who unmasked that man and his accomplices."[55] One of these "accomplices" surfaced in the United States. A bulletin from the French Republic published in Philadelphia in 1793 claimed that Tanguy de la Boissière, the outspoken defender of the refugees, was Galbaud's co-conspirator and that together in exile, they were hatching a new "abominable" scheme.[56]

This subversive activity, observers maintained, could have grave consequences for the United States. While Galbaud was the ringleader, his minions, like Tanguy, were fanning out along the East Coast. In letters to Secretary of State Thomas Jefferson, Genet warned about the machinations of the "so-called assemblies of colonists" in Charleston, Philadelphia, and Baltimore and their "gazettes contrerévolutionnaires." It was rumored that exiles in Philadelphia and Baltimore were outfitting privateers to sail to Jérémie and the Môle.[57] The implication was ominous: Le Cap represented the beginning rather than the end of the refugees' counterrevolutionary designs, and Americans should be wary, at the very least. Any group so intent on subterfuge against the French Republic could certainly turn its attentions toward the Unted States.

The fate of the entire white refugee community was, to some extent, tied to Galbaud. As soon as colonists joined him on the flotilla of ships waiting to leave Le Cap harbor, they were associated with the governor-general; the debate over Galbaud tested the republican mettle of all white exiles. In an open letter to the Philadelphia newspaper *Dunlap's American Daily Advertiser* in August 1793, the governor-general professed his innocence: "The love of the country alone dictated my actions, as I only wished to deliver St. Domingo from the power of two men, whose crimes are beyond comparison."[58] In Galbaud's view—and that of many of his fellow white refugees—the debacle was the commissioners' doing, and their misguided policies had wreaked havoc not just on Le Cap, but throughout the entire colony. Ever since Sonthonax and Polverel's arrival, Galbaud and his supporters maintained, tyranny, not freedom, had ruled in Saint-Domingue; and to make their point, the white refugees drew up a long list of the commissioners' misdeeds.

The exiles contended that the commissioners' despotism had been evident well before the showdown at Cap Français, as Sonthonax and Polverel sought to destroy anyone who stood in their way. In an editorial in the *New-York Daily Gazette*, a refugee with the Roman pseudonym "Juba" claimed that the commissioners were "men who *talk* so much of equality; but when they come to *act*, we find that, rather than endure the least supposed diminution of their power [the instating of Galbaud], they will hazard the total demolition of a great and flourishing city, and the shedding of the blood of all its inhabitants."[59] Since their arrival on the island, the commissioners had ordered the deportation or execution of hundreds of white Saint-Dominguans, even though those colonists were, by their testimony, good republicans. Tanguy was just one of many colonists banished by the French republican authorities.[60] Often, arrests and expulsions occurred without hearings or trials: some refugees protested that they did not know the exact charges leveled against them.[61] In the face of Sonthonax and Polverel's voracious hunger to consolidate power, the white exiles contended, the rule of law and justice had gone by the wayside.

According to the refugees, the commissioners' actions smacked of a new kind of prejudice. Under Sonthonax and Polverel, Saint-Domingue had become a world turned upside down, where black and colored men were favored over white because of their color. The exiles insisted that if the commissioners were truly interested in safeguarding liberty, they would have drawn distinctions along the political lines, instead of uniformly disparaging white colonists and rewarding men of color.[62] In their view this determination to deny the rights of white men came to a head at Le Cap in Sonthonax's battlefield emancipation. To white colonists and exiles, this measure was treachery—or in the words of a planter from Jérémie, "a fraudulent usurpation of my property that only despotism can justify."[63] As the white Saint-Dominguans had asserted time and again, the right to property was as sacred to "man" and "citizen" as any other, and by declaring the end of slavery on the island, Sonthonax and Polverel had violated this right. In addition, the colonists and refugees maintained that the emancipation decree indicated the commissioners' duplicitousness: only a year before, they had promised to uphold slavery because it was French law, yet suddenly they saw fit to run roughshod over the law and dismantle the institution. To add insult to injury, before the commissioners' overtures, many slaves had fought for the Spanish king "under the standards of and as servants to the aristocracy."[64] For the white colonists, this was more proof of Sonthonax and Polverel's perfidy under the guise of republican tenets.

Events in Saint-Domingue after the battle of Le Cap added more ammunition to the refugees' arguments, at least in their view. Fresh rumors cast further aspersions on the commissioners. In December 1793, the *Columbian Herald* in Charleston reported that Sonthonax "had formed the diabolical project of setting fire to [St. Marc], plundering the houses, and destroying the inhabitants." The "horrid plot," however, was discovered the day before it was to commence. The paper reported, "The inhabitants of St. Marc and ten other parishes have coalesced against the tyranny of Sonthonax and Polverel, and have succeeded in a great degree in restoring some kind of order."[65] News from Port-au-Prince relayed similar tales of Sonthonax's "cruelties," such as the construction of a guillotine in the town square to dispatch at least 500 "respectable inhabitants," while the *American Minerva* informed its readers that Sonthonax traveled with "12 waggon-loads of gold and silver bars," unscrupulously obtained.[66] White Saint-Dominguans claimed that because of these "Machiavellians," these "republican traitors," "despotism, driven from France, seems to have sheltered itself at St. Domingo, as its last asylum, or rather in a fortress, out of which it cannot be expunged."[67] What had once been, in Tanguy's reading, an asylum for liberty had now become a stronghold for metropolitan tyranny.

While this line of argument reflected some political posturing, the white colonists were not disingenuous. Many believed that their expulsions were unwarranted, and they held Sonthonax and Polverel personally responsible. Etienne Bellumeau Delavincendiere, a refugee who arrived in Charleston in February 1793, wrote in his will eight years later, "In order to avoid being murdered by the assassins armed by the Civil Commissioners Polverel and Sonthonax against all the planters of the said Island of St. Domingo, I shipped myself by furlow from the Municipality of St. Marc's . . . for North America."[68] "Citoyan" Larchevesque-Thibaud published a 176–page memoir with an additional 104 pages of "justifying documents" in which he described his mistreatment at the hands of Sonthonax, whom he called a "dictator."[69] Of course, these testimonies should be taken with a grain of salt. The old adage of "he who protests too much" seems to be at work here, yet many white Saint-Dominguans, like Delavincendiere and Larchevesque-Thibaud, felt betrayed as the increasingly radicalized National Assembly revoked its early promises to the colonists—jurisdiction over internal affairs, the establishment of colonial assemblies, and the upholding of slavery and the slave trade. Rather than lashing out at the Assembly directly, the white refugees took a safer route and attacked its handmaidens. The Republic's representatives, not the government itself, they charged with corruption. To have argued otherwise would have imperiled the refugees' aims.

Exiled white Saint-Dominguans were convinced that they were the victims of deceitful officials, and when they arrived in the United States, they turned not only to the American public for support but also to the resident French minister, Edmond Charles Genet, to rectify the situation. From the start, however, Genet had very little sympathy for the refugees. Like his fellow Girondin, Brissot, Genet saw the white Saint-Dominguans as thwarting the cause of liberty, and his suspicions were confirmed, if not deepened, when he read the briefs from his predecessor, Jean-Baptiste de Ternant, and the dispatches from Sonthonax and Polverel.[70] As a result, Genet was less than receptive to the refugees' version of events at Le Cap, and he had no reservations about sharing his opinions with others. Within weeks of the exiles' arrival in the United States, Genet expressed to Jefferson his contempt for the refugees who "abused asylum" in American cities in order "to plan new plots against their country." He blamed their "passions" and "prejudices" for the "evils" that had stricken the colony and urged the secretary of state, in the interest of France and America, to take measures to uncover "the web of the new conspiracy."[71]

As the summer of 1793 wore on, though, U.S. authorities were less inclined to listen to Genet. Despite his warm welcome in the United States, Genet's star was fading in official circles, as he clashed with almost every member of the administration within a matter of months. The minister's ridiculously tall order from his home government practically doomed him to disappointment, but Genet's fiery personality exacerbated the situation. In June he wrangled with Washington over the Neutrality Proclamation of 1793, in which the United States vowed to stay out of the war recently declared between Great Britain and France. Genet berated Alexander Hamilton for failing to back operations to spread the French Revolution to Canada, Louisiana, and Florida; and even Jefferson, usually quick to accommodate the French, refused Genet permission to outfit French privateers in American ports.[72] Furious with what he saw as the administration's caginess, Genet lambasted the president and his cabinet in the press. In Genet's view Washington's Neutrality Proclamation reflected the perspective of overly cautious government authorities rather than the American people. It is easy to see how Genet came to this conclusion, given his initial glowing reception, but his calculations misfired. His outburst was an embarrassment to the francophilic Democratic Republicans and a boon to Federalists, and afterward the U.S. government secretly demanded his recall.

The minister's rocky position offered the refugees an advantageous climate in which to approach him for backing. If he supported them, then they could benefit from his access to French funds—until his replacement took over. But if Genet spurned them, the exiles need not fear his continued influence, for having Genet's poor opinion was not necessarily a liability on either side of the Atlantic. After his diplomatic debacles in the United States, Genet's censure might bolster the refugees' appeal among Americans, and with the change in France from Genet's Girondins to the radical Jacobins in June 1793, the minister's fate became precarious. The following month, the French Ministry of Foreign Affairs reprimanded him for his "indiscrete enthusiasm," and a few months later, members of the Committee of Public Safety accused him of treason.[73]

The contentious relations between Genet and the exiles were not surprising, and the negative assessments of one for other were made public. In October of 1793 an intercity network of refugees asked Genet for financial support to send unauthorized delegates to the National Convention in France, and they also requested that the minister sponsor their planned military campaign to Saint-Domingue. Although Genet promised to "do a good turn to those colonists attached to the republic," he clearly thought that there were few republicans among them.[74] Genet refused to fund either venture, and by the end of October, the white exiles were irate. In letters to the National Assembly, they denounced Genet as a co-conspirator (with Polverel and Sonthonax) against liberty; they accused him of holding their rights as French citizens in contempt and implored the Assembly to rectify their grievances.[75] Genet retaliated by broadcasting in U.S. newspapers the views he had earlier shared with Jefferson privately. In a circular letter issued in mid-November, the minister lashed out at the refugees, "the counter-revolutionists, sheltered under the cloak of misfortune, [who] insinuate themselves into the people's favor, and after having disquieted their minds with apprehensions of evils similar to their own, they openly endeavor to alienate us from the confidence and affection of the nation." According to the minister, by blaming the slave rebellion on the commissioners, the white exiles preyed on white Americans' nightmares about slave insurrection in order to turn them against the French Republic. But Genet cautioned Americans that the refugees, not republican officials, were responsible for the uprising in Saint-Domingue, and that the fleeing colonists—the "boiling lava which overflows this continent"—"may possibly reproduce here the volcano which vomited it forth."[76] In Genet's judgment it was not unreasonable that the white exiles would also instigate a slave rebellion in the United States, in order to subvert the republican cause wherever they found it.

The refugees responded to Genet in kind. In an open letter to "generous Caro-linians," a "French West-Indian" expressed his outrage and indignation: "Who has appointed Mr. Genet to stand judge betwixt the commissaires, who are his friends, and us, whom he looked upon as enemies before he landed in America? How dare he thus continually and wantonly throw among our benefactors calum-nious hints against us, without the least provocation?" The anonymous author then implicated Genet in the demise of Saint-Domingue because of his associa-tion with the recently ousted Brissot and his "factious friends," who, the writer contended, had instigated "all the horrors committed in St. Domingo."[77] In a fol-low-up article another correspondent derided the witnesses whom Genet called to testify in his defense: they were "miscreants," party to "republican despo-tism."[78] In the refugees' view Genet was in league with Sonthonax and Polverel and shared their crimes.

Merely trading insults in the press did not satisfy either Genet or his Saint-Dominguan detractors: both wanted local residents and U.S. officials to take sides. Galbaud tried to force the issue when he insisted on standing trial in the United States for his alleged crimes. In a letter to Attorney General Edmund Randolph, published in the *Virginia Chronicle* in February 1794, Galbaud declared, "Since Mr. Genet offers to prove this accusation [against me], . . . I demand then to be made a prisoner, that a process be instituted, . . . and that I may be judged by a tribunal of the United States."[79] Perhaps Galbaud felt confident requesting such a measure in the same month that the new French minister arrived with orders to arrest Genet. Clearly Galbaud hoped that Genet's treatment of the refu-gees would be seen as one of the reasons that the U.S. government asked for the minister's removal.

But Americans were reluctant to take the bait—either in this specific instance or in any of the other spats that erupted among the French in 1793–94. In the rapid-fire exchange between the refugees and French republican officials, white Americans were at a loss to ascertain who was responsible for the current state of affairs in Saint-Domingue or the condition of the exiles. As one confused observer noted in the midst of the debate, "The partizans on each side bring railing accusa-tions against their opponents; who very punctually return the charges."[80] Unable to back one or the other completely, American observers drew a different conclu-sion from the situation—one that neither the refugees nor French officials antici-pated: one should beware the vagaries of faction.

Long before the refugees' migration, the term "faction" touched a sensitive nerve of the American body politic. During the constitutional debates just a few years earlier, James Madison had tried to allay fears about faction in his paper

Federalist No. 10, and in a series of essays in 1792 he refined his take on political parties. Nevertheless, the emergence of political divisions in the early 1790s deeply troubled many citizens.[81] Some predicted that political discord, if it grew, would imperil the young republic. In the words of "Cato," a contributor to the *American Museum* in 1792, "the present is a very momentous crisis in the affair of the united states—factious men are unusually active and noisy—they prove, by the violence of their efforts, the violence of their disease."[82] It was only a matter of time, some mused, until bitter verbal sparring would result in bloodshed and the dissolution of effective government; and for evidence of such deterioration, they said, one need only turn to Saint-Domingue.

Reports from the colony suggested that dissension among the colonists had provided the opportunity for slave rebellion. An account from Cap Français, a year before the battle there, described how "the colonial assembly were in a state of the most ruinous anarchy, the members having carried their difference on political opinions so far, that they actually drew their swords on each other."[83] Vicious clashes on the assembly floor spilled out onto the streets, and the white population was so occupied with its internal squabbles that it ignored larger threats. A "gentleman" from the island informed the *Baltimore Evening Post*, "Party spirit is wound up to a pitch that has seldom been equaled, even in the most violent and disastrous revolutions—The common and inveterate enemy to the white people (the rebel negroes) is nearly forgotten—and the colonists are totally absorbed in animosity against each other."[84] Official dispatches from U.S. consul Nathaniel Cutting reinforced this view, as he portrayed a government in shambles because of the "unparalleled degree of insubordination which pervades every department"—a situation "more evil . . . than . . . anything that Slaves or the intermediate class [the free people of color] can operate."[85] Thanks to the white population's factiousness, the entire colony faced ruin, he said.

The continuation, if not intensification, of vehement bickering during exile provided more proof to substantiate this reading of events. Americans witnessed in their own backyard the debilitating consequences of faction. This was a weighty example, given that in the eyes of some commentators, the United States was teetering on the same dangerous precipice. Even the language of contest between American rivals echoed that of the embattled colonists and the French republican officials. Democratic Republicans accused Federalists of "monarchical mystery" and "court intrigue," seeing Hamilton's party as "the fatal imitation here of the corrupt policy of trans-Atlantic monarchy and aristocracy." Federalists, "under the masque of Federalism," were turning the young republic into a vehicle for despotism. For their part Federalists charged that Jefferson's Democratic Republicans wanted "to subvert all governance, and introduce anarchy and confusion." They had jettisoned reason, and it was the Democratic Republicans' "intemperate zeal" and "ignorance and prejudice" that guided their heedless actions.[86] The accusations of aristocracy and corrupt republicanism had different meanings for Saint-Dominguans and Americans. In the French colony one stood the very real chance of having one's property seized, of being deported, and of meeting the guillotine; while several American politicians may have wished for such a fate for their rivals, the best they could hope for was that their opponents would be voted out of office. But the keywords of the debate—"aristocrat," "mask," "passion," "prejudice," and so on—suggested similarity between the United States and Saint-Domingue and left Americans wondering about the precariousness of their union.

Some Americans blamed the refugees for exacerbating local political discord. An unnamed commentator in the *Southern Centinel and Universal Gazette* of Augusta, Georgia, chastised the Saint-Dominguans for interfering: "Whilst our citizens exhibit daily proofs of their benevolence and humanity to the unfortunate people of Cape Francois, these very people, in their truly distressed situation, are continually endeavouring to sow the seeds of dissension among their generous donors. . . . The least they should do would be, to keep their political opinions to themselves." The very organizations that the refugees touted as proof of their republican credentials he saw as vehicles of disruption and wanted the organizers to "quit the practice of instituting societies in every part where they take refuge." With this particular line of censure the author sounded very much like Genet, deriding the refugees for inveigling residents with bogus assemblies. In the American version of the criticism, the Saint-Dominguans had learned their insidious ways from the French representative. The writer in the Augusta paper continued, "We need not, however, be astonished at this part of their conduct, when their minister was the very man who set the example; for, it is well known, that he was scarcely three days at Philadelphia before he placed himself at the head of a political club, from whence springs all the abuse we see leveled at our government."[87] The colonists and Genet were one and the same—disruptive meddlers who were taking advantage of American goodwill for malevolent ends, regardless of its disastrous effects on the young republic. This commentator implied that Americans would get along much better without the intrigues of Francophone foreigners.

In general, the refugees and Genet denied these allegations, but occasionally the exiles and the French minister found themselves frustrated by what they perceived as the superficial republicanism of Americans. In January 1794 the self-proclaimed "Citizen" Charles Menut, a colonist from Môle Saint-Nicolas in western Saint-Domingue exiled in Charleston, protested in a local newspaper that his application for aid was rejected because of committee members' pro-British politics. Menut remarked that he "could not help being very much incensed, at seeing new republicans, who owed their liberty to the French, deny him assistance because he would not remain with the British."[88] In almost Genet-like fashion Menut called into question—in a public forum, no less—the republican sensibilities of Americans and reminded them of the extent to which they owed their independence to French generosity. Moreau de St. Méry complained about the self-serving manner in which Americans appraised events in France: "As for Americans of all classes and all conditions, they expressed sincere sorrow for Robespierre and were filled with consternation at his loss. This was their reason why: *Robespierre made France uninhabitable for all the French. Every man, every gold piece, escaped at the earliest moment, and both took refuge with us, who are in need of men, of money, of industry. Consider, therefore, how the death of such a one will harm us!* I heard this view uttered a hundred times with a frankness which never made it any easier to tolerate."[89] Americans, in Moreau's view, were willing to support the architect of the Terror, who violated many of the republican principles that they supposedly held dear, as long as they consequently experienced an economic windfall. Moreau, Menut, and no doubt other Saint-Dominguan refugees, as they felt the bite of scrutiny themselves, doubted the republican sincerity of their North American peers.

For their part, white Americans, in reviewing the political landscape of Saint-Domingue and in their encounters with refugees on the streets, became even more chary of the ill consequences of faction. Faction had destroyed the colony, and in the minds of some, the political dissension among the exiles threatened to tear apart the fragile fabric of American union. Commentators, however, drew two different conclusions from this observation. An anonymous American author reflected in a Virginia newspaper that "the tragical scene lately exhibited at Cape Francois, shews the necessity of government and subordination. There we saw two authorities exist, and we saw . . . how soon disorder entered by the gap, and both devoured. The citizens of America may well rejoice, that their lines are cast in so goodly an inheritance."[90] Here, the emphasis was on "subordination" to a single authority—not to a monarch, to be sure, but to the federal government. The description held an implicit warning for Americans not to be swayed by foreign appeals and the factions they promoted; doing so, as the situation in Saint-Domingue proved, yielded only turmoil. Citizens should trust the working of the government and respect, in particular, its decision to remain neutral in the conflict between Britain and France. This was a very Federalist lesson to draw from the Le Cap episode, one that supported the Constitution and key decisions of the Washington administration in the face of ever more frequent and vociferous critiques.

But there was another reading of Saint-Dominguan factionalism that had powerful repercussions for the United States. Its interpreters, Democratic Republicans, emphasized the importance of racial consensus. Following the battle of Le Cap, the leaders of this party—men like Jefferson and Madison—saw the need to ensure unity among white Americans. This conclusion was not pronounced openly or even privately, rather it can be deduced from their actions. Prominent Democratic Republicans had steered clear of association with pockets of political ferment in urban areas, especially the Democratic societies which had their heyday in 1793–94 before disappearing from the public scene. Although characterized as "rabble," these groups were made up of ambitious men—merchants, craftsmen, newspaper and magazine editors, lawyers—who had not managed to penetrate the ranks of the social or political elite. Members were united in their enthusiasm for the French Revolution and contempt for Britain, and the societies worked to sway the public and politicians to embrace Francophilic policies.[91]

In the summer of 1793 and over the remainder of the decade, however, Democratic Republican leaders became more interested in courting support from these ranks, articulating a platform that included greater rights and status for white citizens, an agenda that appealed to those who felt that their political voice had gone unheeded and who, as was the case in several northern cities, faced a growing population of free African Americans. The shift in attitude by the Democratic Republicans was motivated, in part, by concerns that the Washington administration was far too accommodating to Great Britain; but, as scholar Robin Blackburn points out, it also was a consequence of how some southern Democratic Republicans understood events in Saint-Domingue. Le Cap made clear to Jefferson in particular that the future of the U.S. republic depended on white solidarity.[92] The counterpoint of Guadeloupe was perhaps influential in this regard. The French National Assembly's 1794 emancipation decree applied as well to this colony, the second largest French possession in the Caribbean and another critical center for sugar production; yet the outcome of abolition in Guadeloupe, according to observers, differed greatly from that in Saint-Domingue. Articles in the U.S. press described a relatively smooth transition from slavery to freedom, as consensus among freemen effectively checked slaves' endeavors to "raise commotions." The governor of Guadeloupe gloated that "had the inhabitants of St. Domingo been united, they would have had the same success."[93] He did not mention the conflict that did occur in the colony, for the move from slavery to freedom (and eventually back to slavery again) was anything but easy for the white ruling class or, for that matter, for people of color.[94] However, from the vantage point of white Americans in the United States and in comparison to Saint-Domingue, Guadeloupe did seem more stable, and many observers came to the conclusion that white consensus was the key to preserving the American republic.

While Federalists and Democratic Republicans invoked the example of Saint-Domingue in order to prevent divisions at home, faction nevertheless deepened. The parties' different views on faction in the French colony promoted the very antagonism that they sought to avoid. As the decade progressed, each party became convinced that its solution was the only option and that of its adversary would imperil the republic. The refugees tried to navigate this increasingly polarized political climate, which developed not only in the United States but in France as well; and in late 1790s the exiles faced judgments from both governments that called into question—again—their political credentials.

LEGISLATIVE DEBATES AND DÉBATS

Despite rigorous lobbying by many Saint-Dominguan refugees, the public—in the United States and France—remained unconvinced of their republican sympathies, however loosely defined. Too many contradictory reports, too much uncertainty clouded the discussion, yet as the political fortunes of each nation took another turn in the second half of the decade, the white exiles became the subject of public debate again—this time, on the floors of the American and French legislatures. In France the refugees were the subject of deliberation on at least two separate occasions, while in the United States the case of the Saint-Dominguans was part of larger discussions about the worthiness of various migrant groups for residence and citizenship. But on both sides of the Atlantic citizens pondered the same question: could the exiles, given their backgrounds, be fit members of a republic?

In late December 1794 and into January of the following year, the U.S. Congress reconsidered the country's laws regarding the naturalization of immigrants. Federalist and Democratic Republican representatives agreed that the qualifications for citizenship were too lenient, and they wanted the influence of incoming outsiders held in check. They divided over *which* aliens were disruptive to the young republic, but during debates over the bill, members from both parties introduced amendments that would create potential restrictions on refugees.[95] William Branch Giles of Virginia, a Democratic Republican, presented an amendment stating that an emigrant holding a noble title in any kingdom must renounce it before becoming a citizen of the United States. After making his proposal, Giles averred that such a "precaution" was necessary because "the prejudices of the aristocrats . . . were, upon the whole, more hostile to the spirit of the American Constitution than those of their antagonists."[96] Proponents of the addendum argued that an aristocrat's education and his experience with lording over other men made him unfit—without sufficient renunciation and reformation—to become a citizen of an enlightened republic of equals.

This proposal met with stiff resistance from Federalists—not so much because they wanted to welcome aristocrats to the United States, but because they saw nobles as posing little threat to the nation. Using the Democratic Republicans' own logic against them, Richard Bland Lee from Virginia pointed out that the same reasoning regarding aristocrats might be applied to slavemasters. After all, he queried, was not the relationship between master and slave even more degrading than that between lord and vassal?[97] Although Lee quickly added that he had no doubt that slaveholders were worthy of citizenship (he was one himself), the comparison, in his mind, undercut the grounds for excluding aristocrats. Federalist Samuel Dexter from Massachusetts pounced on Lee's point and offered up a devil's bargain: Dexter promised to vote for the rider concerning aristocrats as long as the new naturalization law included a further amendment that each immigrant seeking naturalization should "renounce all right and claim" to slaves and "declare that he holds all men free and equal."[98]

The impetuses behind these two amendments to the naturalization act lay in party politics. Federalists charged that Democratic Republicans introduced the anti-nobility rider because they hoped to paint the Federalists, who they knew would vote against such a measure, as plotting to establish an aristocracy in the United States. In retaliation, the Federalists, some of whom opposed slavery, sought to highlight the ideological hypocrisy of Democratic Republican slaveholders, especially their leader, Thomas Jefferson. But the amendments could also have real consequences for the white Saint-Dominguan refugees, whose republican sympathies were doubted and who had brought slaves into the United States.

Throughout the discussion of these two amendments, congressmen alluded directly and indirectly to many of the arguments made against, for, and by the Saint-Dominguan refugees. The debate about the "aristocracy" rider was, for the most part, uneventful. Some members worried that French aristocrats would "contaminate the purity and simplicity of the American character," while others retorted that several French noblemen, like the marquis de Lafayette, had fought gallantly for the cause of American independence.[99] But on the whole the discussion over aristocrats was less divisive than that over renouncing slavery. Joseph McDowell, a representative from North Carolina, vented the most spleen, lambasting Dexter's amendment as the most "monarchical" and "despotic" piece of legislation that he had ever seen. In words that echoed the white refugees' outrage with the republican government in France, McDowell wondered how the House could deny immigrants their right to property, and his tone became even more strident and indignant as he raised the specter of Saint-Domingue and its refugees: he "wished the gentleman [Dexter] to consider what might be the consequence of his motion, at this time, when the West Indies are transformed into an immense scene of slaughter. When thousands of people had been massacred, and thousands had fled for refuge to this country, when the proprietors of slaves in this country could only keep them in peace with the utmost difficulty, was this a time for such inflammatory motions?"[100] In light of the migration from Saint-Domingue and its circumstances, McDowell saw Dexter's proposal as irresponsible—and many white exiles agreed.

In the end Dexter's resolution failed and Giles's passed—a predictable outcome given the prevailing attitudes toward slavery. More importantly as it affected the Saint-Dominguan exiles, the debate over the two amendments to the naturalization act of 1795 reveals the strained political affiliations of the white refugees in the American context. In some respects, they reveled in the Federalists' increasing criticism of the French Revolution, yet at the same time, they found comfort in the Democratic Republicans' determination to uphold slavery and white property rights. They straddled American party lines, with the result that both Federalists and Democratic Republicans suspected the republican credentials of the exiles.

The French legislature had its qualms about the white Saint-Dominguans, but here the stakes were higher. In two separate episodes in the mid-1790s, the exiles faced legal judgment about their status as French citizens: the hearings of Sonthonax and Polverel before the Colonial Commission in 1795, and the Council of Five Hundred's discussion in 1797–98 over whether the Saint-Dominguans were "refugees" or "émigrés." The National Convention's decisions on both occasions determined the futures of white Saint-Dominguans as French citizens—what place and influence they would have in the Republic (until its next incarnation). These verdicts also reverberated on American shores, as the fates of Saint-Dominguan exiles in the United States were tied up in these rulings abroad.

As early as 1793, white Saint-Dominguans in the United States, France, and the colony had managed to hound enough members of the National Convention that it voted to summon Sonthonax and Polverel to Paris to account for their alleged crimes in the colony. But the execution of the order was delayed and almost abandoned altogether after the Convention abolished slavery throughout the Caribbean in February 1794. The Saint-Dominguans continued to lobby, however—a risky endeavor in the midst of the Terror, a wave of purges that swept through France and during which thousands of suspected antirevolutionaries, including Marie Antoinette, were killed. On unsure political footing, the refugees had plenty to fear from the Terror, but they took advantage of the prevailing paranoia to persist in their denunciations of Sonthonax and Polverel. In June 1794 the recall decree was finally carried out. By the time Sonthonax and Polverel returned to France later that year, however, the tide of revolutionary politics had turned once more, and Maximilien Robespierre, one of the main architects of the Terror, had fallen. The Thermidorian Convention that followed (1794–95) was exhausted from the Terror's excesses, and this weariness proved a boon for the refugees as the new government strove to return to measured legal processes. In addition, most members of the National Convention knew that the colonists would not go quietly; they had been ranting against colonial policies for years, and they wanted their day (or, as it turned out, months) in court. Perhaps Convention members hoped that providing the colonists a session before the Colonial Commission would settle the matter once and for all.[101]

While the procedure was not an official trial, Sonthonax and Polverel were required to listen to and refute the charges against them (and so the exchanges were referred to as "*débats*"). The hearing began in January 1795, with eight colonists participating as the accusers: Pierre François Page, Augustin Jean Brulley, César Duny, Thomas Millet, Louis Jean Clausson, René Ambroise Deaubonneau, a M. Sénac, and a M. Fondeviolle. Deaubonneau and Fondeviolle attended rarely, and later, Louis François Verneuil and Citoyen Larchevesque-Thibaud, who had published his complaints against Sonthonax, joined the group. Several of these men had connections with or had been refugees in the United States and claimed to act on their behalf.[102] Exiles in American cities wanted to follow the debates, since the judgment could have tremendous consequences for them: if the exiles' representatives managed to convince the panel that the commissioners' actions were crimes, then the colonists had some hope of restoring Saint-Domingue to their vision of it. However, following the debates from afar proved somewhat difficult. In a July 1795 advertisement addressed to the "Inhabitants of St. Domingo," the *Gazette française et américaine* noted that the debates "would set forth a picture in which the inhabitants of the other islands, and much more so our American subscribers would feel no concern." Possibly wary that the picture might be less than flattering, publishers promised to issue extracts from the proceedings separately, if a sufficient number of subscribers covered the expense.[103] The refugees anticipated an ugly fight, and they wanted to keep its contents out of the American public view.

The colonists had a long list of abuses—so long that the deliberations dragged on for eight months. Four months into the proceedings, in April, Polverel died. His death switched the focus to Sonthonax's affairs, and therefore, the hearing largely ignored events in the South and West, the regions that Polverel had administered.[104] The colonists' accusations against the commissioners brimmed with venom: at one point César Duny became so infuriated that he threatened Sonthonax's life and was barred from the proceedings for several days, while Larchevesque-Thibaud was thrown out permanently for similar behavior.[105] All told, the colonists leveled eleven actual charges, including usurpation of legislative, executive, and administrative powers; the ravaging of towns; provoking civil warfare in the colony, depleting the colonial treasury; and confiscating private fortunes. Some indictments were unique to exiles in the United States. The accusers blamed Sonthonax for turning Genet and Jefferson against them and for the unjust deportation of Galbaud and his supporters.[106] These experiences mattered in that the exiles had to account for their flight from the island (to prove it was not a counterrevolutionary move) and because the refugees were well aware that the American angle had the power to resonate in Paris.

Testimony on the first of the eleven charges took over three months, but at last the commissioners established that they had acted within their prescribed powers and in the best interests of the French revolutionary government. After Polverel's death, the pace of the trial quickened and so did Sonthonax's victories. While his rebuttals concentrated mostly on affairs in Saint-Domingue, he also drew attention to what he saw as the machinations of the refugees in the United States. During the proceedings, Sonthonax denounced the Saint-Dominguans as conspirators against the French Republic; and as evidence he cited the royalist leanings of Tanguy's newspaper, the exile-led funeral service for Louis XVI in Philadelphia, the refugees' failure to wear the national cockade, and their support for British invading forces—all allegations that the exiles in the United States had been laboring against for months.[107] The refugees, especially those who represented them in public, were schemers, he charged: they pled poverty in France, but they lived in luxury in America; and although they claimed allegiance to the Republic, they were firmly in the pocket of exiled French aristocrats, Alexander

Hamilton, and the rest of the "English committee" at the U.S. capital.[108] For Sonthonax, the exiles' American escapades reinforced his assertions about their colonial corruption.

In the end Sonthonax was exonerated. The Colonial Commission's closing statement admonished the colonists, including those in the United States, expressing disgust at their behavior and arguments. Their spokesmen were singled out for censure: César Duny and Thomas Millet, for example, were condemned for fomenting antirevolutionary activity among the refugees and for their mistreatment of Genet.[109] In general, the final report found the colonists' conduct "immoral" and "inhuman."[110] It seemed clear that the Thermidor was not a sympathetic venue for white Saint-Dominguans, and the ruling had a profound impact on the fate of the refugees in the United States. Following Sonthonax's acquittal, the French government, which became the Directory as of November 1795, reinstated him as one of the commissioners in the colony, and soon after his arrival at Le Cap in the summer of 1796, he wrote to Pierre Adet, the minister plenipotentiary in the United States, regarding the exiles. Significantly, this letter was translated and given to U.S. newspapers for publication. In it, Sonthonax stated that the *débats* had exposed the colonists as "eternal enemies of the principles of France and of its sacred laws," and he credited the close communication between the commissioners and French consuls in the United States in the preceding years with "frustrating the infamous plots of our emigrants, in preventing their arming against this colony, and in neutralizing the effect of their manoeuvres near the American government, and with Agents of Foreign powers in the United States." This pronouncement was humiliating enough for the white refugees, but on the basis of the decision in Paris, Sonthonax declared that the exiles were "forever banished" from Saint-Domingue: Adet was to issue no passports to refugees in the United States to return to the colony. Sonthonax noted that exiles could petition the French government for pardons on a case-by-case basis and admitted that some women, children, and old men had been, through no fault of their own, forced to flee; nevertheless, the new commission in Saint-Domingue would work to thwart the exiles' return in order to "guarantee this portion of the Republic, from the pestilential influence of their principles."[111]

The decree was a blow to white refugees in the United States: not only were they publicly disgraced, but all possible avenues of influence seemed shut to them. The *débats* had debilitated rather than strengthened their position, yet they were not—as the Colonial Commission and Sonthonax had hoped—the last word. The political sincerity of the exiles came under official scrutiny again in 1797, when Sonthonax was encouraged to leave Saint-Domingue by the black republican general Toussaint Louverture. The two leaders had increasingly clashed over, among other things, Louverture's willingness to welcome former planters in an attempt to reinvigorate the plantation economy.[112] Sonthonax's departure in the late summer of 1797, along with the almost complete withdrawal of the British army by that time, provided the refugees an opening to press the French government to reconsider their position. For its part the government looked for a new way to reassert control (preferably cheaply) over the divided colony, and some members of the Council of Five Hundred, the lower house of the French legislature during this era, proposed a measure to bankroll the refugees' return to the island and to underwrite the revitalization of their plantations. Most likely, the proponents of this plan had colonial economic interests or thought that emancipation had gone too far—or both. To win over their colleagues, advocates of this scheme needed to establish the worthiness of the exiles, and they tried to do so by formalizing distinctions among the white Saint-Dominguans. They argued that there were two kinds of exiles: "refugees" and "émigrés." According to their reports, the term "refugee" referred to a blameless victim of the war, while "émigré" was reserved for a person whose migration was motivated by opposition to the French Revolution and who subsequently, conspired against it.

Having heard about the wretched fates of French continental exiles accused of dissension, white Saint-Dominguans in the United States feared the "émigré" label. Émigré status eliminated all possibilities of reclaiming or receiving compensation for property in Saint-Domingue and France, and the category usually meant the guillotine for those caught on French soil. Some exiles turned their dread of émigré status into an argument for their own innocence. Years before, Page and Brulley had emphasized, in their appeals to the National Assembly, that they and those they represented had suffered because counterrevolutionary émigrés residing in England had encouraged the British assault on Saint-Domingue in 1793.[113] Unlike those in Britain, they claimed, the exiles in the United States were simply running for their lives and seeking refuge in a nearby republic.[114]

In 1797–98, the colonists' supporters in the Council of Five Hundred picked up on previous themes as they attempted to illustrate that the Saint-Dominguan exiles in the United States (and those in France) were indeed refugees. Much of the rhetoric was reminiscent of the white Saint-Dominguans' own interpretations of events. They detailed the perils of the slave rebellion, railed against "hypocritical philanthropy," denounced the "atrocious soul of Sonthonax," and lamented the persecution endured by the colonists. They pointed to the exiles' eagerness to return to Saint-Domingue and their willingness to resuscitate its economy.[115] The proposal that the government subsidize the exiles' return met with stiff resistance, however. Some council members disagreed with the plan because it did not extend amnesty far enough: one member wanted the council to excuse some of those who stayed during the British occupation. In the "horrible confusion" that reigned during the war, he maintained, sectors still loyal to the revolution were forced to wave the white flag to the British.[116] At the other end of the spectrum, another member rejected the plan because it failed to ensure the end of slavery, leaving vulnerable the "men who, before the revolution, knew only the iron rod, the weight of their labors and those of their chains." He thought deportation a fitting punishment for the white exiles who, he hoped, would "rest . . . [in] the hell of remorse."[117] Others cited years of reports from the French consuls in the United States griping about the exiles' scheming. If they were innocent, some wondered, why had more of them not returned to France even when offered passage by the minister?[118]

The arrival of eleven deputies from Saint-Domingue, including several free men of color as well as Sonthonax, halted whatever momentum the white Saint-Dominguans' cause had gained. The deputies' scathing testimony saw to it that the plans for a state-sponsored return of exiles were scrapped, as was any kind of categorical decision about the status of the white Saint-Dominguans.[119] There was no collective amnesty; instead, status—whether "refugee" or "émigré"—was, for the moment, determined on an individual basis, with petitioners having to go before government authorities with the appropriate documentation in hand.[120] This was a dicey proposition for those exiles who sought to return to France during this period. Given the long history of suspicion about the colonists, it was by no means certain that a white Saint-Dominguan exile would receive the required paperwork, and even those who did faced aggression. On his arrival in France from Philadelphia in 1798, Moreau de St. Méry was accused of being an émigré. He denied the allegation and scrambled around Paris to acquire the proper "identity cards" to secure his neck.[121] Some preferred to gamble with their fates in Saint-Domingue, heading back to the island in response to encouragement from Toussaint Louverture.

Refugees followed these developments carefully because many wished to leave the United States. Although several factors contributed to this desire, the hostile political climate was a significant reason. During Washington's two presidential administrations, the United States had managed to remain neutral in the war between Britain and France, but France became frustrated by the American refusal to join the war on the side of the revolution and was angered by the Jay Treaty of 1795, an agreement between Britain and the United States which established terms of trade. France interpreted the treaty as aiding the British war effort, and during Adams's presidency a neutral course became untenable, as French foreign policy took more erratic and antagonistic turns. Tensions between the two countries mounted, and American public opinion of the French plummeted to a nadir in 1798 when the story broke that French officials had refused to consult with American ministers until bribed, an incident that became known as the XYZ Affair. Anti-French sentiment reached a fever pitch; the most zealous Francophobes called for war. What they got instead was the so-called "Quasi War," two years of naval skirmishes between American and French vessels, mostly in the Caribbean.

In a xenophobic frenzy, the Federalist-dominated Congress passed the Alien Enemies Act of 1798. The law permitted President John Adams to deport any alien in the United States whom he judged a menace to the nation, and while Adams, no doubt, had several people on his wish list of deportees, the French were seen as the most likely "alien enemies."[122] Relations with France worsened, and supporters of the Alien Enemies Act cautioned that French saboteurs had destroyed the Dutch, Swiss, and Batavian republics from within. Given this precedent, advocates insisted, French immigrants in the United States, including Saint-Dominguans, should be monitored and their citizenship delayed.[123] Secretary of State Timothy Pickering wrote to Robert Liston, the British minister to the United States, in reference to a group of refugees who arrived at Philadelphia in the summer of 1798, "it seems proper to remark (what must have occurred to the passengers themselves since their arrival) that the actual state of things between the United States and France, induced by the violence, intrigues and real hostilities of the latter, may render their residence here less eligible than at any former period." He went on to observe that if Franco-American relations continued to decline, the United States might "prescribe regulations and measures, in regard to French citizens, not before contemplated, but which the public security may require."[124]

As Pickering's comments made clear, white Saint-Dominguans could have faced draconian consequences, but few, if any, did. Perhaps their acerbic criticism of the French Republican regime as well as their inability to convince Americans beyond a doubt of their republican sentiments saved the refugees from scrutiny: during this period Americans were more concerned about "Jacobins" in their midst. In fact, the exiles' arguments about corrupt republicans in Saint-Domingue, Sonthonax in particular, crept back into the American press in the late 1790s. Accounts from Boston alleged that several ministers in Paris shared in Sonthonax's "plunder" as payment for "having suppressed information of the attrocities of that tyrant of St. Domingo." Others pointed out that Sonthonax's second recall in 1797 proved his "criminality"—a criminality that, incidentally, was not limited to the French colony.[125] In September 1797 the *Pennsylvania Gazette* ran an extract of a story from a London newspaper, stating, "Sonthonax hired a number of persons to go into the United States, and set fire to the populous towns. That some had returned, received their reward, and had gone thence again."[126]

In some measure, the salacious rumors about Sonthonax seemed to confirm what the white refugees had been contending since 1793—that the republican commissioner was not republican at all. Yet the anxious anti-French climate at the end of the decade worked against refugees, especially recent arrivals, as Americans were wary that they might be Sonthonax's handmaidens. In 1798 the British withdrawal from Port-au-Prince sent thousands of its residents looking for refuge, and that summer, hundreds of them turned up in Charleston and Philadelphia, where they were barred entry by each state's governor. While American officials were concerned about the potential negative influence of the black passengers, they were also suspicious of the white Saint-Dominguans. The episodes prompted William Bingham, a Federalist senator from Pennsylvania, to propose a bill allowing the president to authorize screening of the landing of all "French passengers" (as well as other foreigners) to determine whether they should be permitted to disembark or not. The bill passed the Senate but failed in the House after merchants complained that such a measure would imperil trade and after the refugees proclaimed that they were "all peaceable people and of good character." With the bill's demise the Saint-Dominguans in Philadelphia were allowed to land, but those in Charleston were sent on to St. Augustine.[127]

As the debates in the United States and the *débats* in France demonstrate, the white Saint-Dominguan refugees were on uncertain political ground at the end of the 1790s. Neither national legislature could come to a lasting decision about the character of the exiles, leaving them prone to capricious and antagonistic migration policies. The refugees existed in a kind of political no man's land, to some extent representative of the refugees' position throughout the decade. Whereas other groups, like the Girondins and Jacobins, rode a revolutionary wave until it crested and finally broke, the Saint-Dominguans were constantly treading the tumultuous political waters of the Atlantic. Aristocratic associations dogged them, yet the competing and ever changing visions of republicanism both in France and the United States made the exiles difficult to discount completely. As one group rose and another fell out of favor, the refugees found themselves and their politics up for reappraisal.

This story of indecision is significant in the American context. When the emancipation decrees of 1793–94 in Saint-Domingue tested the correlation between counterrevolutionary politics and the slave insurrection, white Americans were forced to consider other political influences that might promote the instability and even collapse of governments. In light of the stormy arguments between Genet and commissioners, on the one hand, and between Galbaud and the white exiles, on the other, American observers drew conclusions about the perils of faction that shaped each proto-party's approaches to political participation and immigration. Discussions about the politics of the white refugees, in other words, contributed to Federalist and Democratic Republican approaches to sustaining the early republic in the face of challenges from the Francophone Atlantic.

By focusing on the allegiances of white Saint Dominguans, white Americans sought to ignore, if not deny, the political motivations of black and colored Saint-Dominguans and to evade the issue of slavery. But try as they might, white Americans could not avoid talking about slavery. Since the question about the relationship between politics and slave rebellion was still unresolved, white Americans could not be confident that their particular brand of republicanism (either Federalist or Democratic Republican) would deliver them from Saint-Domingue's fate. And the thousands of black and colored refugees arriving in the United States made it impossible for American residents not to consider whether their republic might be prone to insurrection—either imported or inspired from within.

CHAPTER FOUR

THE CONTAGION OF REBELLION

Among slaveholders in the Atlantic world, one of the common tropes used in describing slave revolts was "contagion." The term likened an insurrection of the enslaved to an unpredictable and voracious malady, spreading quickly and striking the innocent without warning. In the eighteenth century, the causes of epidemic diseases were often unknown, and the methods of treatment were debated. Anticipating the next round of illness, experts and their adherents experimented with preventive measures—inoculations, quarantines, and stop-gap solutions. News of an outbreak would send waves of panic throughout a population: some fled, a few worked to check its spread, and still others succumbed to its vagaries, usually in very gruesome ways. As accounts of smallpox and yellow fever epidemics attest, contagion was, from the perspective of its victims, a nasty and frightening business.

The figurative equation of contagious diseases with slave rebellions, including the Haitian Revolution, has many implications. On the one hand, it served as yet another means to deny the ideological motivations of the enslaved: disease did not have a political agenda, nor did it control its own actions. As in the portrayal of the Haitian Revolution as a "volcano," insurrection was seen as a malevolent force of nature—a reading that played into the hands of the master class.[1] On the other hand, the metaphor of contagion provides an interesting point of entry for considering how populations reacted to slave rebellion. Present-day appraisals of the effects of the Haitian Revolution typically emphasize the fear that it evoked among Atlantic slaveholders: the violent and "successful" resistance of the enslaved in Saint-Domingue brought death to slaveowners and the demise of their insidious institution. But extending the metaphor of contagion produces a more nuanced interpretation of fear in action, one that includes not only terror and flight but also efforts to control or mitigate the potential dangers of exposure to rebellion. Slaveowners were reactive and proactive during the Haitian Revolution, and the United States provides a test case to examine this dynamic in practice.

For residents of the early American republic, the Haitian Revolution, perceived as contagion, presented both ideological and practical challenges. White Americans sought to account for the uprising in the French colony in ways that exempted the United States from a similar destiny, attributing the insurrection to conditions specific to slavery as practiced on the island. Opponents of slavery refuted this interpretation of events and argued that Saint-Domingue proved that the American republic was vulnerable to a slave rebellion. In response, most abolitionists proposed cautious cures for American slavery, ones that shirked the bold French decision for universal emancipation and black citizenship. Both of these assessments were contested by black and colored Saint-Dominguan refugees in the United States. Although the reasons for this population's migration were diverse, white Americans saw black and colored exiles as potential carriers of the contagion of rebellion who could easily corrupt susceptible African Americans, free and enslaved, and encourage them to turn on local white residents. Throughout the 1790s white southerners and northerners identified signs of the exiles' malign influence. Some took steps to neutralize the threat, but white Americans also exhibited enormous confidence in the health and stability of their society. At times, they brazenly disregarded the prospect of insurrection in the United States, as they continued to trade with the island and receive its migrants. Just how far white Americans were willing to court this danger came up for official debate at the end of the decade, when the Adams administration considered formalizing trade relations with Saint-Domingue under Toussaint Louverture. Supporters contended that a treaty with Louverture would protect the United States from a slave uprising, and their arguments triumphed—at least for a few years, until Jefferson's "revolution of 1800" altered the nature of U.S. ties with Saint-Domingue. Motivated by fears of an uprising at home, the new president opted for a complete quarantine of the second republic in the Americas.

As white Americans worried it might, the example of the Haitian Revolution did spread ideas among African Americans. From their perspective, the Haitian Revolution represented not a deadly disease but, a possible cure for the ills of enslavement and racism. The arrival of black and colored refugees had ideologi-cal and practical consequences for black locals. Few African Americans consid-ered the methods of their Saint-Dominguan peers viable in the American con-text; the climate of white fear, in all of its manifestations, limited what black residents could achieve. Nevertheless, they adapted and appropriated aspects of the Haitian Revolution and the opportunities afforded by the exiles' presence in order to defy slavery and racism. This resistance ranged from guarded declara-tions of support to protests on the streets, and their responses demonstrate how the ethos of the revolutionary Atlantic did—and did not—resonate among black Americans.

"THAT HELL OF THE NEGROES, THE WEST-INDIA ISLANDS"

When white Americans first learned about the rebellion in Saint-Domingue, they looked for reasons to explain why slaves were so quick to revolt, and initial reports in U.S. newspapers ascribed black Saint-Dominguans' enthusiasm for insur-rection to the viciousness of the Caribbean slave system. According to observers, living in "that hell of the negroes, the West-India islands" conditioned "miserable slaves" to rise up against their masters.[2] This rationalization served two purposes: it provided an apolitical justification for the revolt (denying the political motiva-tions of enslaved rebels), and it particularized the rebellion, making it unique to circumstances on the island. This line of argument had its detractors, among them abolitionists who maintained that events in Saint-Domingue were the result of the institution itself, no matter its specific application. Yet even their accounts show a tendency to avoid seeing how much similarity there was between the United States and the French colony. More often than not, they backed away from the radical calls for emancipation and black citizenship that the Haitian Revolu-tion eventually embraced and instead advocated measured, gradual, and still deeply racist solutions to the problem of slavery at home.

Since the colonial period, white Americans, along with their British and French continental counterparts, had cultivated the opinion that slavery in the Caribbean was harsher than its U.S. equivalent, and this belief became even more popular during the Haitian Revolution. As Moreau de St. Méry carped, "Since the misfor-tunes of the French colonies, it has been the habit in France to praise the attitude of the United States toward slaves."[3] Some writers claimed that the sultry climate of the West Indies "enfeeble[d] and destroy[ed]" newly arrived Africans, but others fingered Caribbean masters and mistresses as the culprits.[4] Poems, anecdotes, and articles lamented the cruelty of West Indian slaveowners and overseers and the suffering of their slaves. In the eyes of some commentators, brutal behavior was inculcated in Caribbean colonists at a very early age: "The Creole child is trained up to be a tyrant; he domineers over a troop of little slaves, from whom he will bear no contradiction."[5] Adulthood only hardened this penchant for despotism; one poem, published in a Baltimore paper, elaborated on the sadistic creativity of West Indian masters: "*One,* with a gibbet [gallows] wakes his negroe's fear, / One to the wind-mill nails him by the ears; / *One* keeps his slave in dismal dens unfed, / One puts the wretch in pickle ere he's dead; / *This,* to a tree suspends him by the thumbs, / That from his table grudges even the crumbs!"[6] Even by the low standards of the day, Caribbean slavery was popularly considered to be beyond the pale.

While these descriptions referred to the the West Indies in general, Saint-Domingue was singled out as a place with particularly barbarous master-slave relations. A story titled "The negro equalled by few Europeans," published serially in an American magazine in 1791, highlighted the severity of slavery in Saint-Domingue as told from the perspective of an African recently enslaved and arrived in the colony. Throughout the tale, the African, named Itanoko, commented on the effects of slavery on white, black, and colored people. He witnessed, "A young, beautiful, elegant, European woman, with rage in her eyes, and a large stick on fire in her hand, pursuing a female negro. The unfortunate creature was naked to her waist. The lady overtook her; threw her down; loaded her with outrages; struck her; and tore her breast in several places with the infernal fire-brand. . . . And what was [the slave's] offence? She had forgotten to serve the favorite cat with its breakfast."[7] Itanoko's as well as the reader's repulsion derives not only from the horrific punishment meted out on a slave for a trivial infraction but also from the corruption of the white woman. Caribbean slavery transformed otherwise demure and refined women—those supposed repositories of virtue and feeling—into wrathful and irrational fiends.

The suggestion from this episode and others like it was that slaves could not bear such ruthlessness for long, and evidence soon appeared that merciless Saint-Dominguan masters drove their slaves to reckless acts. In 1789 word circulated about an anonymous slave in Saint-Domingue who was "tortured for a slight offense, of which he was not even guilty." "Stung by resentment," he carried the children of "his cruel and unfeeling oppressor" to the roof of the house, and then as the master watched, the slave threw each child and finally himself to the ground.[8] The sensational death of another black Saint-Dominguan named Romain inspired the publication of an antislavery tract in Philadelphia in 1803. The title page of the work proclaimed that the "melancholy death" of the "French

Suicide of a Desperate Saint-Dominguan Slave. Edward Darlington, *Reflections on Slavery; with Recent evidence of its Inhumanity Occasioned by the Melancholy Death of Romain, A French Negro* (1803). As aghast observers look on, Romain, a "French negro," slits his throat on the street rather than be taken back to slavery in Saint-Domingue. Note the black woman at the far left of the image who turns to take in the scene. Courtesy Library Company of Philadelphia.

negro" offered new proof of the "inhumanity" of slavery. According to the exposé, Romain's owner, Anthony Salaignac, a refugee from Saint-Domingue, decided to end his exile in Trenton, New Jersey, and return to the colony with his slaves in tow. Romain, however, "well knew the cruelties inflicted on slaves in the West Indies, of which he probably bore visible marks. . . . he was determined not to return; as he had experienced here more humanity than he was before accustomed to." Concerned white residents appealed to the local authorities on behalf of Romain, but when the mayor of Trenton determined that Salaignac was legally entitled to remove his slaves from the state, Romain despaired. As he was led to a carriage hired to take him to the ship bound for Saint-Domingue, he took out a pruning-knife from his pocket, slit his throat three times, and fell dead on the pavement. The jury at the inquest pronounced a verdict of "suicide, occasioned by the dread of slavery."[9]

These dramatic deaths exemplified the desperate straits to which Saint-Dominguan bondsmen were driven, that they would prefer suicide to continued slavery. While chilling and sympathetic, both accounts shied away from more radical conclusions. The first incident was an act of personal rather than collective resistance: the murders were targeted, and the threat of future rebellion was cut short by the slave's own death. Romain is another case of individual and short-lived protest. Certainly, the writer of the tract hoped that the slave's death would not have been in vain but would move citizens "to exert their influence in procuring a repeal of laws, so fraught with cruelty, foreign to the principles of humanity, and inimical to the Spirit of the Constitution."[10] Yet, at the same time, the author emphasized that Romain feared "the catalogue of cruelties that *awaited him*" in Saint-Domingue, after having enjoyed more "humanity" in the United States than on the island.[11] Even as this pamphlet advocates the end of slavery (importantly, through the actions of the white population), the author implies that Romain would not have been driven to such a dire act had he stayed a slave in New Jersey.

That sentiment was typical of Americans in this period. White Americans frequently congratulated themselves on their "humane" treatment of slaves, and as a remedy for the revolt in Saint-Domingue, they prescribed a compromise "by which the servitude of those unfortunate and miserable Africans is rendered more tolerable."[12] This idea was shared by some in the colony. At the outbreak of the rebellion in August 1791, black leaders made limited demands: a reduction in days worked, better provisions, alleviation from certain types of punishments, and the emancipation of rebel leaders.[13] When Sonthonax and Polverel disembarked on the island in 1792, they promised to mitigate the wretched conditions of the slaves.[14] By that point, however, the insurgents' goal had gone beyond improved conditions to freedom; but Sonthonax and Polverel's presence, according to early reports, calmed the storm of insurrection, at least temporarily. Shortly after the commissioners' arrival, American newspapers noted that many slaves had put down their weapons and headed back to the plantations. It also seemed that slaveowners in Saint-Domingue had learned their lesson: "they . . . have thought it proper to alter their mode of treatment towards their slaves . . . [who] have now a good allowance of beef and pork every day, and are clothed with frocks and trowsers, instead of being exposed naked to the burning ray of the sun, with a scanty allowance of homoney, and sometimes no allowance whatever."[15] If bondsmen experienced a modicum of decency, the reasoning went, they could continue to endure their enslavement; they would be content.

These readings of rebellion in Saint-Domingue provided American slave masters with a means to explain away the insurrection as an event born out of singular circumstances that had little similarity to slavery as practiced in the United States. As an article in the *National Gazette* summed it up, the revolt in the French colony stemmed from the "tyrannies and cruelties . . . inflicted by the whites" that "def[ied] a parallel in all history, ancient or modern."[16] In other words, slavery in Saint-Domingue was a uniquely diabolical manifestation of the institution that had no comparison to any other time or place, including the United States. Because American masters had some regard for their slaves, white society could find solace in the notion that the uprising was an isolated case that did not herald disaster for North America.

A few American writers took this carefully constructed fiction to task and argued for the justness of black Saint-Dominguans' actions and aspirations. Authors in this vein fell into two camps. The first were those who saw the rebellion as an inevitable outgrowth of the African slave trade: the enslavement and force migration of hundreds of thousands of formerly free Africans bred a deep resentment among them that, these writers maintained, was sure to explode into insurrection at the first opportunity. The second camp blamed the institution of slavery itself. In their view, masters could not evade the inherent cruelty of enslavement, no matter how "humanely" it was practiced. The very institution cultivated rebellion among its oppressed. While these critiques are significant and even radical for this period, they also reveal a reticence to embrace the universalist vision that the Haitian Revolution advocated, namely that all men are free, equal, and entitled to the rights of citizens. Most U.S. abolitionists looked to adapt the lessons of Saint-Domingue in ways that would avoid such tremendous change in the young republic.

Some commentaries made a clear link between the evils of the slave trade and the rebellion in Saint-Domingue. A poem featured in the Philadelphia magazine the *American Museum* in 1792 interpreted the insurrection as God's retribution for the heinous crime of selling and buying people. The anonymous author of "Lines on the devastation of St. Domingo" opened his work with descriptions of destruction on the island: billowing smoke from burning plantations filling the skies, and the frantic cries of mothers, fathers, and children pleading for mercy with their last breaths. He then asked who or what was responsible for these scenes and replied, "'tis the Afric, home-bred foe" who "Arm'd with judgments, his right hand / Whelms at once a guilty land: / Now's repaid the trade in blood: / Now is loos'd the scourge of God." According to the author, the hand of God was working through slaves to exact justice in Saint-Domingue and would do so in other slaveholding colonies and nations as well: "learn this truth divine, / Hand to hand as one may join, / In oppression's horrid trade, / But the wrong shall be repaid . . . Soon or late shall surely come, / And all the *Indies* share one doom."[17] Some areas might ward off their downfall temporarily, yet the day was imminent as long as Caribbean colonies continued to trade in slaves. God would not let this sin go unpunished.

Another writer looked to revolutionary ideology rather than divine retribution to validate the rebellion. The U.S. press picked up an editorial by Thomas Clarkson, one of the leaders of the British anti–slave trade movement. Clarkson refuted accusations made by white colonists that his group was responsible for the insurrection in Saint-Domingue and instead blamed the African slave trade. Because of this traffic, he wrote, "thousands are annually poured into the islands who have been fraudulently and forcibly deprived of the rights of men. All these come into them, of course, with dissatisfied and exasperated minds."[18] His view is in keeping with historians' accounts of slave resistance. As several scholars have demonstrated, the African slave trade to Saint-Domingue reached its peak in the years just prior to the rebellion; and more generally, historians have pointed to the influence of recently enslaved Africans in animating revolts throughout the Atlantic world.[19] Clarkson, however, used his appraisal to proffer a solution that would maintain slave societies. He concluded that opponents of the African slave trade needed to redouble their exertions "if we have any value for our own islands, or any wish that the present proprietors of them may preserve their estates to themselves, and perpetuate them to their posterity."[20] For Clarkson, ending the slave trade from Africa was a means to preserve the plantation economies of the Caribbean. He anticipated that once the primary evil (the slave trade) was eliminated, its abolition would usher in the need for the better treatment of slaves, which would in turn prepare slaves for *eventual* freedom. He envisioned emancipation as a slow process, and one that would ensure the economic viability of empire.[21]

Both of these pieces reflect British concern with the future of slavery in the Caribbean, but the emerging abolition movement was an Atlantic phenomenon. Societies throughout the Atlantic basin corresponded and shared strategies which no doubt were food for thought for white Americans. Perhaps one of the most provocative—and indigenous—interventions was an anonymous editorial printed in a couple of northern newspapers and addressed to slaveholding Saint-Dominguan refugees in the fall of 1793. The author, a self-identified "northerner," lamented the exiles' current predicament but suggested that their displacement presented an opportunity "to press a lesson of humanity and justice." The writer then launched into an eloquent comparison of the migratory experiences of white Saint-Dominguan exiles and African slaves that is worth quoting at some length:

> Have you not seen cargoes of poor Africans cast upon your coasts in vastly more distressing circumstances than yours at present? You have escaped the hands of your enemies, they were not so fortunate. Your enemies were open and known; theirs were secret, unnatural, perjured kidnappers. You had time to anticipate, consider and prepare for the worst; they were surprised in the midst of domestic tranquility, and snatched away in a moment. You were able to bring off your wives, your children and some of your property: They were torn away from partners, from parents, from children, never to see them more. . . . You were treated well on your passage; they were manacled, stowed into holds, whipped, starved. You have the consoling hopes of one day returning to enjoy your friends and estates; they have to bid eternal adieu to such prospects, and anticipate nothing but a life of toils, and fatigues, and hunger, with fetters of iron, whips and insults. Decide now—Whose situation is the most pitiable?[22]

Playing on the sympathetic rhetoric surrounding the white refugees, the author argued that Africans enslaved and transported through the transatlantic trade to Saint-Domingue deserved more pity than their oppressors. He went on to contrast the reception of enslaved Africans arriving at the French colony with that of white Saint-Dominguans coming to the United States: whereas Americans bestowed a multitude of kindnesses on the refugees, Saint-Dominguan masters administered many abuses to *their* new immigrants, Africans. He queried the audience, "Now seriously ask yourselves, why we did not treat you in the same manner when you arrived on our coasts? What makes you to differ from the

Africans?" This question set off another long comparison of the white exiles and Africans—in this instance, of their characteristics. As the author ran through each population's traits, including everything from intellectual and emotional capacities to physical characteristics and language, he found similarity after similarity. In the end, he deduced, "There is not the least absolute difference between you and them, except superior wretchedness on their part."[23]

This was a frank indictment of Saint-Dominguan masters and their racism. Beginning with a denunciation of the African slave trade, it developed to challenge fundamental stereotypes that underpinned the institution of slavery throughout the Atlantic world. But for all its allusions to equality, the article stopped short of advising white Americans to reform their ways. Instead, the closing paragraph urged the refugees to take a cue from their U.S. hosts: "Go home, then, and learn to commiserate and assist the wretched who arrive upon your own coasts. Remember, that we did not drive you from the ships into pens and stables, and doom you to perpetual bondage, but liberally provided for your wants. We would have done the same to strangers from Africa. We cannot see them to be brutes, no more than yourselves."[24] These final remarks could have been meant to jar local readers to consider whether they would, indeed, give refuge to Africans, yet the overwhelmingly assured tone of the article—its willingness to indict the exiles so straightforwardly—indicates a desire to assert difference between white Americans and white Saint-Dominguans. As in other accounts of Saint-Dominguan slavery, the island and its masters were a foil on which white Americans could convince themselves their society was immune from rebellion.

Although the connection between the Haitian Revolution and the African slave trade yielded some powerful critiques, the emphasis on the trade was the softer side of the attack on slavery. In fact, slave trade abolition was often interpreted as a means to bolster slave societies, and in the case of the United States, it was presented as if it were a *fait accompli*. Although as many as 170,000 slaves entered the early republic between the American Revolution and 1810, white observers, like the "northerner" who addressed the refugees, saw the end of the slave trade to the United States as inevitable.[25] Several states had banned the entrance of foreign slaves, and masters, even in the South, were less inclined to see the importation of Africans as necessary for their local economies. Although the Constitution prohibited Congress from ending the importation of slaves until 1808, the date stood out, in the minds of many, as the moment when the African slave trade would be abolished. The lessons of the Haitian Revolution strengthened this belief, and during the 1790s it offered relief to white Americans. They were convinced that since they were already committed to ending the trade, then rebellion would be averted.

Other white American commentators found in the early moments of the Haitian Revolution a less comforting message for the United States. Instead of highlighting the differences between the French colony and the new republic, these observers concluded that circumstances in Saint-Domingue presaged the U.S. future unless something was done about slavery at home. In their view the United States was becoming a "hell"—not for "Negroes," but for their masters, and the uprising in Saint-Domingue spurred these observers to think seriously and quickly about possible plans for emancipation in the United States.

Within days of the slave insurrection outside Cap Français in late summer 1791, Sylvanus Bourne, the U.S. consul in Saint-Domingue, wrote to his superior, Secretary of State Thomas Jefferson. After describing how the northern plain had been laid to waste, Bourne mused on the import of recent events. "Here we have a lively instance of the baneful effects of Slavery, and I wish that America might add another laurel to her wreath of Fame, by leading the way to a general emancipation."[26] In Bourne's reading, the insurrection was quite simply the result of slavery—without any qualifications. Slavery bred rebellion, and although he spoke in terms of America's "fame" rather than its self-preservation, the two were clearly intertwined. In order to dodge the "baneful effects of Slavery," emancipation was the only answer.

Bourne's observation was incisive, but he kept it private. A few men of similar mind in the early 1790s made their trailblazing opinions public, and the boldest among them was Abraham Bishop. Adopting the alias "J. P. Martin," Bishop, a Connecticut radical, penned "The Rights of Black Men," an article that appeared in several northern newspapers between 1791 and 1793.[27] The piece contended not only that the enslaved of Saint-Domingue were justified in their actions but that republican principles animated their endeavor. To drive his point home, Bishop compared the position of the rebels with that of American and French revolutionaries. In his view the cause of black Saint-Dominguans was even more righteous than that of the French: "Can we believe that the French people were ever [as] oppressed as the blacks have been?"[28] Bishop drew on America's own recent past to defend the rebel slaves: "We fought with bravery, and prayed earnestly for success upon our righteous cause when we drew the sword and shed the blood of Englishmen—for what! Not to gain freedom; for we were never slaves; but to rid ourselves of taxes imposed without our consent, and from the growing evils of usurpation." He drew a distinction between slavery as a metaphor for the situation of the colonists on the eve of the American Revolution and slavery as an everyday reality for the black insurgents in Saint-Domingue. Bishop implored his readers to consider that "freedom is the natural right of all rational beings, and we know that the blacks have never voluntarily resigned that freedom. Then is not their cause as just as ours?"[29] To reason otherwise smacked of hypocrisy—the double standard of race prejudice. Bishop encouraged his readers to live up to their ideals and to endorse the rebels in Saint-Domingue.

Bishop's argument was sure to raise eyebrows, for he dared to articulate what many African Americans no doubt felt and what many white Americans refused to conclude. Most daringly, "The Rights of Black Men" defended the means by which Saint-Dominguan slaves were seeking their freedom, namely armed revolution. Bishop bid his readers to "review the history of their [the slaves'] past sufferings, be but a moment in their situation, and judge whether, in a climate as warm as theirs, your blood would flow coolly."[30] Although Bishop regretted "that the blood of white men is spilling," he believed that the slaves had no choice. Had black Saint-Dominguans pursued freedom through peaceful measures, they would have been annihilated, he conjectured.[31] For most abolitionists, let alone the general white public, this was an outrageous statement. Most late-eighteenth-century antislavery activists wanted to eradicate slavery through moderate measures. They advocated gradual manumission and achieved legislation to that effect by working within the political and legal systems. They sent petitions, published tracts and articles, and prayed for the peaceful end of slavery. In places where emancipation laws were already implemented, abolition societies took violators to court, arguing on the behalf of wrongly enslaved black people. Antislavery advocates' efforts yielded success, especially in the north. By 1784 every northern state except New York and New Jersey had passed bills that provided for gradual emancipation, and by 1804 those two states had joined the effort to eradicate slavery; but until the rest of the American states adopted similar measures, abolitionists advised slaves to remain submissive to their masters in order to receive better treatment and to persuade slaveowners gently of the injustice of the institution.[32]

The forceful affirmation of "the rights of black men" through arms ran counter to the tactics and sensibilities of American abolitionists. They, too, wanted to avoid a Saint-Domingue in the United States. Bishop was frustrated by the feeble response of white abolitionists to the Haitian Revolution: "If, at this time, the liberating societies do not come forward, how ridiculous must appear their orations, their publications, their record; their addresses to the passions, and to the reason, in favor of the poor black."[33] Yet for all his irritation with antislavery advocates and for all of his championing of "the rights of black men," he did not conclude his essay with a rallying cry to black Americans to take up arms or to members of "liberating societies" to press for immediate emancipation. Despite his sympathetic reading of the slave insurrection, Bishop stopped short of endorsing the use of Saint-Dominguan methods in the United States. While he may have wanted abolitionists to become more emphatic in their calls for freedom, and while he may have seen the cause of black Saint-Dominguans as just and universal, he did not see the methods being used in the colony as a template for achieving black freedom and equality in the United States. Bishop's rousing validation included the caveat: "I wish success to their arms, with all my heart, and lament, that it is not in my power to afford them effectual assistance."[34] For all its transnational implications, Bishop still saw the fight as particular to Saint-Domingue—and one to which he could offer no aid.

Bourne, Bishop, and others (such as Theodore Dwight of Connecticut and David Rice of Kentucky) were writing in the earliest phases of the Haitian Revolution—before the emancipation decrees of 1793 and 1794. In the aftermath of the new laws, a few white observers continued to lend qualified support to immediate emancipation in the French West Indies, yet most rejected its universalist rhetoric.[35] This dismissal promoted the consideration of an American variation of emancipation, one that would avoid what commentators saw as the pitfalls of Saint-Domingue.

One of the most elaborated considerations of an American emancipation came from the pen of St. George Tucker, a professor of law at the College of William and Mary, a judge of the Virginia General Court (the highest tribunal in the state), and a corresponding member of the Pennsylvania Abolition Society. In his 1796 *A Dissertation on Slavery* Tucker contended that the Haitian Revolution demonstrated that after the end of slavery, black and white people could not live side by side. Fifteen years earlier, in *Notes on the State of Virginia*, Thomas Jefferson had predicted that emancipation would lead to "the extermination of the one or the other race," and to Tucker, Saint-Domingue proved the sagacity of Jefferson's prophecy.[36] In Tucker's highly selective reading, the protracted war in Saint-Domingue was the result of an emancipation that he saw as foolishly attempting "to smother those prejudices which have been cherished for a period of almost two centuries."[37] The United States should learn from Saint-Domingue that "the early impressions of obedience and submission, which slaves have received among us, and the no less habitual arrogance and assumption of superiority, among the whites, contribute, equally, to unfit the former for *freedom*, and the latter for *equality*."[38] Neither white nor black Americans were ready for the end of slavery.

The general message of the Haitian Revolution after 1793, Tucker believed, was the impossibility of a harmonious multiracial and free society. Nevertheless, he determined that emancipation was necessary. He wanted to eradicate "the evil, before it becomes impossible to do it, without tearing up the roots of civil society with it."[39] Tucker proposed the gradual manumission of American slaves, but after liberty, freedmen would not gain the full rights of citizens. They would be excluded from holding office, bearing arms, and owning property in the hopes that these indignities would encourage them to migrate elsewhere.[40] Jefferson echoed Tucker's sentiments and vision when he read the pamphlet the following year, at which time he was vice president. His response is shot through with urgency, for he saw Saint-Domingue as part of the "revolutionary storm now sweeping the globe [that] will be upon us." "From the present state of things in Europe and America," he continued in a letter to Tucker, "the day which begins our combustion must be near at hand, and only a single spark is wanting to make that day tomorrow." Jefferson held out hope that the right emancipation plan, speedily enacted, would give the firestorm of liberation "an easy passage over our land"; but he desired a scheme that stipulated, rather than simply urged, the removal of former slaves from the United States. The answer to the question, as he put it, "Whither shall the coloured emigrants go?" eluded him—and continued to do so for years to come.[41]

Colonization schemes for resettling emanicipated slaves developed more fully in the late 1810s, as both African Americans and their supporters became despondent about the pace of change in the United States; but for the purposes of this discussion, plans like Tucker's and Jefferson's are important for how, in the face of the Haitian Revolution, they tried to navigate a course that would sidestep the perils of slave rebellion and emancipation. They were looking for a way to rein in the implications and demands of the Haitian Revolution with a homegrown cure. This inclination did not just reflect the ideological flailing of tormented southerners; northern abolitionists wrestled with similar problems. While the Pennsylvania Abolition Society rejected Tucker's proposal, it retreated from earlier calls for universal liberty, and focused on cultivating a plan that was specific to its population and state. In the eyes of Pennsylvania abolitionists, the radicalism of the Haitian Revolution placed it outside the purview of their efforts.[42]

This outlook seeped into the popular press as well. In a 1797 poem from the New York *Time Piece*, a literary magazine, a writer signed "Caroline" mused on the situation in Saint-Domingue, where, in the aftermath of immediate emancipation, "licentious liberty reigns uncontroul'd" because of "the madning croud from bondage free." The author proposed that such ghastly scenes could have been checked had the colony's masters "gently relax'd the ever galling chain," an allusion perhaps to better treatment or even gradual emancipation. Then, considering a "nearer scene of horror," the writer called specifically on George Washington to free his slaves, arguing that in order for the revolutionary leader and former president to fit the model of Cincinnatus, "who *his* country sav'd," he must "till . . . his own ground and keep no man enslav'd."[43] As in the interpretations by Tucker, Jefferson, and others, this author saw immediate emancipation in Saint-Domingue as a disaster and advocated a measured process for ending slavery, whereby the founders would encourage others through their example. In this scheme, there would be no government intervention. Rather, individual slave-owners would see the error of their ways—how their practice was incongruous with the ideals of the revolution—and they would eventually release their slaves from bondage. This, in the author's view, would prove sufficient to thwart slave rebellion at home.

While the poem is naïve in comparison to the other interpretations of the consequences of the revolution, what all of the readings share—whether in observations about treatment, calls for ending the African slave trade, or approaches to gradual manumission—is an impulse to particularize the Haitian Revolution in order to stave off its consequences. Each looked for a means to dismiss it as prophecy by suggesting how circumstances in the United States were or could be different. This tendency to read the Haitian Revolution as unique encouraged responses ranging from smug self-satisfaction to frantic worry about the viability of the American republic. In all of these cases, white Americans were determined to keep this West Indian "hell" from invading their shores, but this resolve was tested as thousands of black and colored Saint-Dominguans landed in U.S. seaports.

EXPORTING INSURRECTION

A commentator writing from Cap Français in May 1792 hoped that "the ocean which surrounds Hispaniola will check the extension of the spirit of revolt; for, if it should become general through the islands, it will require almost half Europe to subdue it."[44] This hope was dashed. Soon after the uprising began, reports circulated about defiant activity throughout the Atlantic basin, as black and colored Saint-Dominguans used the sea as a highway to export rebellion abroad. The Caribbean, as the observer from Le Cap had fretted, was the first to witness signs of discontent. In the early 1790s, U.S. newspapers carried articles about slave plots uncovered in Jamaica, Martinique, and Cuba.[45]

The association of migrating black Saint-Dominguans and the appearance— or more accurately in some instances, the insinuation—of rebellion elsewhere had important consequences for the United States. The migration of thousands of black and colored Saint-Dominguans to North American cities caused many white Americans to wonder whether they were opening their society to discord and ultimately revolution. Time and again white residents saw evidence of the insurrectionary power of black refugees in their midst, yet they just as readily disregarded their own warnings about "French negroes" (as they were called) and seemed confident, if not downright cocky, about the stability of their own slave society. This bravado did not stem from complaisance among African Americans, for they were inspired by their Saint-Dominguan peers. However, this inspiration took on a variety of forms that underscore the limitations and possibilities for this population at this critical juncture.

White refugees were well aware of the bad press surrounding black and col- ored Saint-Dominguans. They had helped to perpetuate it: in order to garner support, white exiles inundated American audiences with harrowing accounts that played up the savagery of their black and colored foes. Such tales put the white refugees in a predicament; when they brought their chattel into the United States, they were forced to delineate more carefully among the members of the enslaved Saint-Dominguan population. They argued that *their* slaves—the ones who migrated with them—were different from the rebellious ones on the island.[46] Whereas mutinous slaves generally stayed in the colony, faithful ones, the white exiles contended, followed their masters to the United States. As proof of this loyalty, white refugees recalled the brave actions of devoted slaves who had facilitated their escape. John Thomas Carré recollected his terrifying flight from Saint-Domingue in a letter to his American patron, Charles Willson Peale. He described how he and his family were able to fend off an attack from rebel slaves, thanks to "my Negroes making a wall with their own bodies all around me, [and] threaten[ing] of an instant death whomsoever Should do me the least harm." While Carré attributed his deliverance to "God Almighty," he readily acknowl- edged that his slaves had been instrumental in protecting the family and per- suading the rebels to desist. In the aftermath of the episode, Carré recounted how his slaves comforted him and his family, telling them "that they would die rather than to Suffer anything bad Should happen to us; and they indeed performed their promises" by helping the Carrés to find safety in a seaside town near the northern parish of Le Borgne.[47]

These types of narratives abound in the history of the Haitian Revolution. The most famous one is that of Toussaint Louverture, who, the story went, ensured the safety of his former master and family before joining the insurgents. Certainly, some slaves were loyal to their masters or at least preferred not to see them killed. As scholars of the revolution have documented, some bondsmen fought on the side of antirepublican, proslavery forces. In the 1790s, however, these acts were milked for propagandistic purposes. White Saint-Dominguans trotted out examples of fidelity as they campaigned for reconquering the colony. They reasoned that if some slaves remained faithful to their masters, then all was not lost in Saint-Domingue.[48] Such stories also justified the entry of enslaved refugees into the United States.

The masters' language of loyalty masked more complicated relationships between white exiles and black and colored ones. Enslaved refugees were not blindly doing their owners' bidding by migrating to the United States. White residents often coerced black and colored Saint-Dominguans to flee the island, yet many slaves elected to leave the war-torn colony. In some cases, black and colored refugees traveled with white exiles as part of family units, being acknowledged as the sons, daughters, or lovers of (usually) white men. Refugee wills reveal that several women of color relocated with the white men who had fathered their children. Every instance was a story of its own. In 1797 Pierre Toussaint moved to New York City with his master, Jean-Jacques Bérard. In doing so he was able to stay with his sister, Rosalie, although they were parted from their parents, who did not emigrate. One researcher speculates that the parents orchestrated this solution to spare their children, aged fifteen and ten, from being endangered by the bitter fighting near their home on the Artibonite plain in western Saint-Domingue.[49] Many black and colored exiles migrated in an attempt either to keep their families together or to promote their survival.

Evidence also shows that the migration of black and colored refugees with white Saint-Dominguans reflected a bargain. In his final will and testament, John Davis urged his executors to honor the agreement he had made with "his black Domestic" to be paid "at the rate of ten Dollars a Month and to provide for his passage for his return to the Cape."[50] The wording suggests that the unnamed servant had struck a deal with Davis, making his journey to Baltimore contingent on his receiving wages while there and a free return passage. Perhaps the servant had economic motivations for moving to the United States, calculating that he had better prospects of secure earnings abroad than in Saint-Domingue—monies that could eventually prove helpful back in the French colony. Finally, some black Saint-Dominguans migrated to the United States to secure their freedom. In 1801, the New York Manumission Society considered the case of several black refugees from Port-au-Prince who had left the island years earlier during the British invasion in order to avoid reenslavement and had traveled to New York under the protection of a white exile. While they attracted the notice of the committee because they were under threat of being sold south into slavery, the story of their migration provides another example of black and colored Saint-Dominguans strategizing to make the best of difficult circumstances.[51]

It bears remembering that black and colored Saint-Dominguans' moves to the United States were not necessarily permanent, for considerable numbers went back to the island. Several white refugees included provisions in their wills to bankroll return passage to the colony for their slaves and servants, many of whom took advantage of the offer to rejoin their families and friends still in Saint-Domingue. Other black and colored Saint-Dominguans sailed back and forth between the island and the United States during the revolution, on business either of their own or for their owners. Pierre Toussaint's fellow slave in the Bérard household, Marie Bouquement, voyaged from New York to Saint-Domingue in order to locate her daughter Adèle.[52] Whether she intended to stay with Adèle or return with her to New York is unclear; in the end, Marie Bouquement came back to the United States alone, having been unable to find her daughter. Regardless, this kind of movement was not uncommon among enslaved and freed refugees.

The circulation of black and colored exiles followed a range of motivations and paths characteristic of movement throughout the Atlantic world. In fact, white refugees and white Americans sometimes relied on the networks that the migration by black and colored people facilitated. The exile mouthpiece, the *American Star*, ran an update on the latest maneuvers of André Rigaud, a free colored leader in southern Saint-Domingue; the news came from, in the words of the article, "a trusty negro of Mr. Dacher, inhabitant of Du Bas de la Cote, who sailed from here [Philadelphia] in the month of October by order of his master, in a vessel which carried him first to Monte Christ, then to the Mole, afterwards to Jeremie, and lastly to Cayemette," before finally arriving in New York.[53] The "trusty negro's" peripatetic route is testimony not only to the amount of traveling by some slaves between and within the United States and Saint-Domingue but also to the fact that, in this privileged capacity, these slaves provided information for black and white alike. The black and white Atlantics intertwined in many ways.

Finally, the experiences of black and colored exiles indicate that they were not a united community. Some free people of color had been slaveowners in Saint-Domingue, in some cases, quite prominent ones; and they, too, sought to bring their bondsmen to the United States. In 1808 in New York, two "coloured" boys approached members of the local abolition society and reported that in 1802 they had been brought from Cap Français to New York City by Madame Hositt, "a Yellow [mulatto] woman" to whom they had belonged. After the woman's death two years later, the boys were bequeathed to her mother, who owned them for a year before selling them to Madame Bardie, a "French coloured woman."[54] In another case that the society considered, a "French black man," in league with two white French men, was accused of "enticing" two free local black men (one of whom bore the significant name "Samuel African") into slavery.[55] Both of these episodes suggest that black and colored refugees could at times have competing interests as well as interests at odds with the local African American community. In this regard, black and colored Saint-Dominguans were as diverse—and as human—as any other population.

White Americans had their own take on the black and colored Saint-Dominguans, and while it usually failed to match the actual circumstances of enslaved refugees, it was not monolithic. White locals sometimes toed the white Atlantic line that black and colored exiles were the harbingers of insurrection, and at other moments they seemed unfazed by the population who had come into their midst. The variety of responses reveals the complicated dynamics of fear—how it waxed and waned as white Americans considered other issues in conjunction with the revolution. Although potent, the fear of slave uprisings did not automatically trump all other concerns.

The first allusions to the contagion of rebellion appeared in the United States shortly after the revolution in Saint-Domingue began. As early as 1792 white Americans identified in their communities the "insidious" work of "French negroes," and concern grew as the numbers of refugees swelled during 1793. Charleston, in particular, emerged as a hotbed of insurrectionary activity. Early in the 1790s, a white Charlestonian expressed anxiety about his city's tenuous circumstances: "The negroes who have come here with the French people, have said so much about the insurrections at *St. Domingo*, that we have every reason to apprehend one here."[56] His trepidation seemed legitimized by the detection of the so-called Secret Keeper Plot in the fall of 1793. A white resident reported, "Two letters have been intercepted, by which it appears that the negroes and mulattoes intended to serve us as the inhabitants of Cape-Francois were served: They had heard so much from the French negroes about it, and [about] liberty and equality."

According to the captured correspondence, black and colored Charlestonians had formed alliances with those in Virginia and North Carolina, and they planned to revolt simultaneously.[57] An article in the *Boston Gazette* stated that "emissaries were expected from St. Domingo, to assist and even to take the lead in this infernal business," a general insurrection in the southern states.[58] While this plot was narrowly averted, another came to light in Charleston just a few years later—again led by black Saint-Dominguans. In 1797 the *Pennsylvania Gazette* informed its readers that "seventeen French negroes intended to set fire to the town in different places, kill the whites, and probably take possession of the powder magazine and the arms."[59] At least two "French negroes" involved in the plan were executed, and another two were expelled from the state.[60]

Both plans were daring and required coordination throughout Charleston and across state lines—designs reminiscent of the carefully orchestrated uprising in Saint-Domingue. There was no doubt in the minds of white Charlestonians and their fellow southerners that the conspirators sought to strike at the heart of slavery and that "French negroes" were instrumental in showing the way to local bondsmen. Such episodes were not limited to areas below the Mason-Dixon line. Although the plots were more dramatic in southern slave states, white northerners linked rebellious activity among local African American communities to the presence of "French negroes." Hearsay alleged that several fires in New York City in the mid-1790s had been set by black Saint-Dominguans. In a conversation overheard on the street, a few "French negroes" told their American counterparts: "Ah, you Americans are animals; you do not know how to set fire—we at the Cape know better."[61] This rumored comment shows how white Americans perceived the presence of "French negroes" as a dual threat: black Saint-Dominguans would not only instigate insurrectionary action but they would also corrupt the "good character" of African Americans. The exchange implied that black New Yorkers did not know how to plan a large-scale attack and would not have thought of doing so, were it not for pressure from "French negroes."

In accounts of the Haitian Revolution white Charlestonians and New Yorkers may have seen the slaves as pawns of warring white factions, but in assigning responsibility for the conspiracies in their own communities, they laid the blame directly at the feet of black Saint-Dominguans. Not all, however, were comfortable with this attribution. Some observers claimed that four white Frenchmen with revolutionary sympathies had had a hand in the Secret Keeper Plot of 1793. The accused Frenchmen, in turn, blamed white refugees, who, they argued, had "dared to arm their slaves, and to plunge their country into anarchy." They claimed that the Secret Keeper conspiracy demonstrated that the refugees planned to do the same in the American South.[62] A few years later, accounts of Gabriel's Rebellion reiterated the alleged connections between French republicans and black rebelliousness. During the spring and summer of 1800, slaves in and around Richmond, Virginia, prepared to fight for their freedom. Heavy rains and militia patrols delayed the execution of the plan until late August, and then the plot unraveled when magistrates, acting on a tip from a slave, interrogated and charged one of the conspirators. At the trial, two slaves testified that "two white French Men were the first instigators of the Insurrection." A contributor to a Fredericksburg newspaper maintained that the conspiracy stemmed from "some vile French Jacobins, aided and abetted by some of our own profligate and abandoned democrats."[63] As a result of this affair, "French" men—both white and black—were subjects of derision and distrust.

These charges against white Frenchmen reflected the tense political climate of the 1790s and the bitter political infighting among the French community, but it is surprising how infrequently white Americans accused white Frenchmen of fomenting rebellion in the United States. Perhaps doing so threatened transnational racial solidarity in ways that made many white Americans uncomfortable. Instead, "French negroes" provided the preferred excuse—a means to account for and explain away—any real or perceived rebellious activity among black Americans. As their critiques of West Indian slavery illustrated, white Americans prided themselves on the "good" slaves that their supposedly beneficent version of slavery produced. In their myopic view, only the introduction of a foreign element, like the "French negroes," could spoil American slaves.[64] Of course, many black Americans *were* inspired by events in Saint-Domingue and by the tales told by newly arrived black Saint-Dominguans. However, African Americans were not, as white Americans implied, incapable of conceiving and carrying out defiant gestures without "French negroes."

In addition, when white Americans invoked the influence of Saint-Domingue, they did so histrionically—fires, ambitious conspiracies, and mass murders—in scenes that subscribed to white versions of events on the island. On the one hand, black and colored refugees may have engaged in such actions in the United States, although decisive evidence is wanting. On the other hand, these theories about the cause of slave unrest whipped up fear among the white population (in both North and South) that was useful to proslavery interests. This self-serving correlation demands reappraisal. Most accounts about the impact of "French negroes" grew out of overheard conversations and rumor and featured ambiguous plots, but there is documentation, although slim, of revolutionary sentiment among African Americans. This support for the Haitian Revolution was expressed in more prosaic but still powerful ways.

Black Americans found the Haitian Revolution ideologically compelling, and this sympathy was most manifest in northern cities.[65] In the mid-1790s, for example, a group of "citizens of color of Philadelphia" drafted a letter to the French National Assembly, thanking the legislators for passing the "immortal decree" that ended slavery in the French Caribbean. The writers made no mention of the rebellion in Saint-Domingue, but they referred to the slaves in French possessions as "our brothers."[66] Given the extensive newspaper coverage of both revolutions and the swarms of refugees in the city, black Philadelphians knew what was happening in France and Saint-Domingue. Some adopted the revolutionary appellation "citizen," and as their letter indicates, they saw their interests as tied to those of French Caribbean slaves.[67] Nevertheless, aware of the maelstrom of negative opinion surrounding the insurrection, the authors emphasized the decree of the National Assembly, an act that complemented the achievements of the Pennsylvania state legislature. The colored citizens were treading a fine line between expressing their enthusiasm for the Haitian Revolution and steering clear of its more radical—and from the perspective of white locals, more threatening—implications for American society.

As the decade wore on, some leading African Americans made more daring ideological connections between Saint-Domingue and the United States. In a 1797 address to the Boston African Masonic Lodge, black leader Prince Hall encouraged his audience—both at the lodge and those who read his text later in print—to take heart from the example of their peers in Saint-Domingue. Listing the "insults" that African Americans faced "daily . . . in the streets of Boston," Hall reminded them of the adage, "the darkest is before the break of day," and turned to the French colony to prove it: "My brethren, let us remember what a dark day it was with our African brethren six years ago in the French West Indies."[68] Hall may have been counseling perseverance among local African Americans, but by dating the moment of Saint-Domingue's liberation to 1791—the year the slave rebellion began—he also was celebrating the achievements of ordinary black men and women (rather than of members of the French National Assembly or an American state legislature). For Hall, the Haitian Revolution proved that change for people of African descent was possible and that it was in their own hands.

Like his Philadelphia counterparts, however, Hall steered clear of advocating armed revolution. Frankly, to have done so in the viciously racist climate that prevailed even in "free" cities would have been suicidal. But African Americans did become more confrontational in ways that evoked the Haitian Revolution, especially in the early 1800s, when they took their ideological inspiration to the streets. In New York City, "French negroes" joined local African Americans in a riot in 1801. Word had spread that a white refugee from Saint-Domingue, Madame Jeanne Mathusine Droibillan Volunbrun, had arranged to send her twenty slaves south in an attempt to evade New York's recently passed gradual emancipation law. Volunbrun was well-known among members of the New York Manumission Society for her "wanton cruelty" toward these slaves: "she has not only shaved many of their Heads, but has put them in Irons and beats them inhumanely." According to the society's report, her slaves had been gathered up by a "number of Frenchmen & constables, who now guard the House, in order to defeat any measures that may be taken for their liberation."[69] Livid at Volunbrun's audacity and by the inability of the manumission society to stop her from executing her plan, a crowd of about 250 black Saint-Dominguans and African Americans met in front of Volunbrun's house until they were dispersed by the town watch.[70] This is a fascinating instance of African American and black Saint-Dominguan collective action, and its implication—that the two groups (one supposedly trained in the arts of insurrection) were willing to band together publicly to defend emancipation—would not have been lost on white New Yorkers. A few years later in Philadelphia, several hundred African Americans expressed their frustration with persistent racism by marching through the city in military formation armed with bludgeons. The following day, the group reconvened and proclaimed to white passersby that "they would shew them St. Domingo." The march happened in 1804, the year Haiti achieved independence, and on July 4 and 5, during celebrations of American independence.[71] The significance of these pregnant dates is hard to miss: black Philadelphians were calling for a U.S. republic that looked more like Haiti, which granted black men the full rights of citizens.

Responses to the Haitian Revolution among African Americans would intensify in the early nineteenth century, as an independent Haiti became a lodestar in the campaign for emancipation and citizenship at home. But during the 1790s, the resistance sparked by the Haitian Revolution occurred more often at the individual level, as Saint-Dominguans and African Americans alike turned to one of the longstanding weapons in the arsenal of slaves: running away. The presence of Saint-Dominguan slaves on the runaway rolls was noticeable and novel in this era. In the fourteen years between 1791 and 1805, New York City newspapers issued at least forty-seven advertisements for French-speaking runaways, whereas only nine had appeared during the preceding twenty years.[72] Other cities experienced a similar phenomenon as "French negroes" sought to escape their enslavement. Their stories exhibit a range of motivations. For some, a personal affront compelled their flight, while others left to reunite with family. In December 1794 three teenage slaves absconded from a farm in Rahway, New Jersey, in order to rejoin their mother in New York City. Some enslaved Saint-Dominguans resented being sold to American masters and fled.[73] In some cases, exiled masters claimed that their slaves had not willfully left their service but had been "enticed" by cunning agents—an explanation that was frequently invoked by masters throughout the Atlantic world.[74] Finally, black refugees ran away in a desperate bid for individual liberty. A Saint-Dominguan slave named Anthony fled from Philadelphia after petitions for his freedom failed, while one runaway, whom his master had named François but who referred to himself as Prince Coyaux, posed as a freeman in an attempt to gain employment—and a means of escape—as a sailor.[75]

The patterns of flight of Saint-Dominguan slaves fit the trends among enslaved persons in the United States and elsewhere in the Americas. For centuries, slaves had been running away for similar reasons and for similar ends. While not assaulting the institution of slavery in as dramatic a fashion as armed rebellion, these incidents disrupted the system, reminding masters of the discontent of their bondsmen. A Saint-Dominguan runaway was alarming to white Americans, as was any slave unmoored from the purview of his or her master. Moreover, "French negroes" sometimes traveled with and abetted American runaways. Several U.S. slaveowners reported that their bondsmen had taken off with "French negroes"; in a noteworthy case from Charleston, owner David Haig explained that his slave Lando "speaks French tolerable well, and is too fond of the French Negroes; it is supposed that he is harbored by some of them."[76] In such instances Saint-Dominguan slaves were (again) interpreted as a malevolent influence on otherwise obedient American slaves.

The very arrival of black Saint-Dominguans could inspire individual local bondsmen to action. In September 1793 slaveowner David Harris submitted to the *Baltimore Evening Post* an advertisement for his runaway slave Tower, who, he conjectured, was on the road to Philadelphia, already a common destination for enslaved southerners in search of freedom. Harris postulated that Tower would endeavor to elude detection on his way north: "as he speaks a little French, and is known to have put a striped ribbon round his hat, it is probable he will attempt to pass as one who lately came in the fleet from Cape-Francois." Clearly, Tower was aware of events in France and its colonies: he purposefully wore a "striped ribbon"—probably representing the French tricolor—to illustrate his support of the French Revolution. Also, living in Baltimore, Tower had most likely witnessed the landing of some of the hundreds of refugees who had arrived that summer. He realized that many colored exiles were free, and so, having acquired this knowledge and a little French, Tower took advantage of the circumstances and fled.[77]

The case of a runaway indentured servant reveals even more vividly how the slave insurrection in Saint-Domingue affected the resident colored community. In November 1794 Crispin, a sixteen-year-old indentured to the prominent merchant Stephen Girard, disappeared from Philadelphia.[78] Crispin was from Malabar, a coastal region of southwest India, and although sources offer no insight about how exactly he ended up bound to Girard, the merchant had connections with French firms in southern India and hoped to expand his enterprise into the Indian Ocean, in particular to Isle de France, east of Madagascar.[79] Crispin spoke French much better than he did English, and when in Philadelphia, he chose to underscore his French affiliations with his clothing. Girard noted that his servant "usually wears a national cockade made of ribbons cut out in the shape of a carnation."[80] Like Tower's "striped ribbon," Crispin's cockade indicated his endorsement of events in France, and, it turned out, those in Saint-Domingue. As Girard discovered a year later, Crispin posed as the slave of a Spaniard traveling to the Caribbean in order to abscond to Port de Paix, a seaport in the northwestern region of the colony. On learning of Crispin's whereabouts, Girard appealed to French revolutionary leaders in Saint-Domingue to return him to Philadelphia, but Etienne Laveaux, the governor-general of the colony between 1793 and 1796, rejected Girard's request with indignation: "You must know very little of me to dare to hope that in defiance of our Glorious Constitution, I would consent to force a man against his own will to leave the land of liberty where he has taken refuge. . . . In coming to Port de Paix [Crispin] has come to enjoy liberty. In Philadelphia he was a slave. Have I the right to order him to take up his chains again? Assuredly not."[81] In Laveaux's estimation—and in Crispin's as well—Saint-Domingue, not Philadelphia, was the "land of liberty." Laveaux overstated the certainty of freedom for Crispin in the colony; the end of slavery in Saint-Domingue was still very much contested in the mid-1790s. He spoke with such conviction because he felt that the French revolutionary regime was committed to making freedom and racial equality a reality in Saint-Domingue. According to the governor-general, the colony promised to become a haven from slavery (if it was not quite so already), and so he attributed Crispin's actions to a desire for freedom.[82] Crispin understood the meaning of the cockade he wore and believed that he would be a free citizen in revolutionary Saint-Domingue.[83]

While Crispin's flight is remarkable—both for its trajectory and for the survival of evidence surrounding the case—it is typical in its reflection of the impact of the Haitian Revolution on people of color living in the United States. Events in Saint-Domingue stirred African Americans—more often individually, but also sometimes collectively—to find freedom and mitigate racism in the early republic. The black refugees provided cover and aid for individual rebellion, and the presence of the black exiles threw into sharp relief the promises of Haiti and the shortcomings of the United States. However, for all the insurrectionary power of black and colored refugees (in the white imagination and in reality), white Americans took few steps to stem the tide of their immigration. Individual states barred their entry, but most white Americans, even with these bans, seemed to expect— and at times, court—their arrival.

Citing the power of "French negroes" to corrupt local African Americans, some state governments tried to banish them. In October 1793 William Moultrie, the governor of South Carolina, mandated that all free black and colored Saint-Dominguans leave the state within ten days of the posting of his decree.[84] In addition, all incoming nonwhite migrants, whether free or enslaved, were to be held at Fort Johnson until they could be deported.[85] The same year, Georgia forbade entry to slaves from the West Indies, and in 1795 North Carolina prohibited the admission of Caribbean slaves over the age of fifteen. Early in the decade, Maryland had permitted French subjects to bring their personal slaves, but outlawed that concession in 1797. A few northern states passed similar laws. In 1798 Governor Thomas Mifflin of Pennsylvania heard that shiploads of Saint-Dominguans had arrived in Philadelphia's harbor, having evacuated Port-au-Prince when British troops that had been stationed there withdrew. Dreading another influx of black Saint-Dominguans, Mifflin issued a proclamation that disallowed "French negroes" from landing in Pennsylvania. He encouraged President Adams to urge other states to adopt analogous measures, but to no avail.[86]

State governments met with some success in the enforcement of these laws. South Carolina, which was the most assertive in its actions to bar "French negroes," reported a few incidents in which black Saint-Dominguans were hunted down and expelled from the state. In May 1794 a committee of citizens notified the public that a privateer had recently landed a cargo of sixty-five slaves. Most of them were "from the island of St. Domingo and of bad character," and so the committee sought to locate and export them "to some foreign port."[87] Several months later, twenty-two "French negroes" were detained when they attempted to disembark in Charleston. Seventeen were placed in the workhouse; the other five, "consisting of two free women and their children," were in the custody of a ship captain who promised to sail within the week.[88]

Although these accounts point to a degree of vigilance on the part of U.S. residents, in general, the exclusionary laws were impossible to implement effectively. The unpredictable nature of the refugees' migration made their entry difficult to monitor. Saint-Dominguans sometimes disembarked in sizable numbers but more often landed sporadically in small groups. Even in Charleston, the governor complained about shoddy barriers: "A number of vessels from the West Indies . . . are daily bringing into this state, negroes and people of color, bond and free, in violation of an act passed . . . and often pass Fort Johnson without reporting them, and when they come to the city, suffer them to go on shore, by which means they elude the law."[89] In this manner thousands of black and colored Saint-Dominguans came into the United States. More tellingly, the refugees' ability to evade the laws indicates that white Americans were willing, on occasion, to look the other way. In the early stages of the rebellion, this leniency derived from the belief that the exiles' stay was temporary. White residents may have tolerated the entry of Saint-Dominguan slaves with the assurance that they would depart as soon as possible. The sympathy that many U.S. residents felt for the white refugees also contributed to lax enforcement of the exclusionary laws. In slaveholding areas, the plea for allowing "French negroes" to enter sometimes proved persuasive despite standing laws against it: the Norfolk police admitted that, "from motives of humanity," they had suspended state laws that prohibited the entry of slaves and freemen from the West Indies.[90] White Americans saw as a right the ability of white Saint-Dominguans to travel with their human property.

Between the British invasion of the French colony in the fall of 1793 and the signing of the Jay Treaty in 1795, American newspapers issued numerous reports of British privateers' abducting Saint-Dominguan slaves and free people of color from ships en route to the United States and selling them into slavery. These articles cast the refugee slaveowners (rather than the black and colored victims) in an empathetic light, pointing out the cruel cost of these seizures for those who had already lost so much. Not surprisingly, there was an American political component to this rhetoric: white American observers were incensed that hundreds of their ships were being subjected to devastating privateer attacks, and this indignation encouraged many to refer to the plight of the white refugees in order to gain the moral high ground against their British adversaries.[91] Thomas Jefferson characterized British privateers as particularly unscrupulous because they preyed on the exiles, and this sentiment permeated the ranks of everyday citizens, who expressed their sympathy in similar terms.[92] As a group of Charleston residents explained, "Those who thought themselves happy escaping with the small remnants of their property, have been insulted and plundered on the high seas by the most hard hearted monsters that ever avarice created, and have been brought to our coasts destitute of everything, except their miserable existence."[93]

These characterizations of the refugees abetted the interests of Americans who sought to whip up vitriol against the British and to push the federal government to take a tougher stand against the former mother country. But for the exiles, this rhetoric meant a tacit acknowledgment of their right to keep slaves. While Jefferson avoided alluding to slaves as part of the "small remnants of their property," other accounts recognized the importance of bondsmen to the white refugees. When privateers boarded the ship of a Captain Doane, bound for New London, Connecticut, with several Saint-Dominguans, "they took with them seven negro servants, but the tears and supplications of their owners, induced capt. Doane to redeem six of them with his own money, at two hundred dollars each."[94] During these years several newspapers ran appeals from exiles listing the property they had lost to privateers. Slaves dominated the rolls, and individual refugees turned to American and Caribbean contacts to help them recover seized bondsmen and freedmen who had been in their employ.

The reports about deprivations by privateers illustrate that, notwithstanding the inflammatory language about and exclusionary laws against black and colored Saint-Dominguans, many white Americans expected their arrival: importing them was a master's prerogative. In a few northern states, however, the status of enslaved black and colored exiles was challenged—at the expense of their white owners. In late 1792 a group of white Saint-Dominguans petitioned the Pennsylvania General Assembly for exemption from its law stipulating that all slaves (unless owned by members of Congress from other states or foreign ministers) were considered free six months after their entry into the state. The reporting committee of representatives ruled in early 1793 that, although they understood the refugees' distress, the Saint-Dominguans would have to withdraw their request. The legislators did not feel "justified in recommending . . . a dispensation with a law which appears to have originated . . . from the sacred and immutable obligations of justice and natural right. The committee are of opinion that slavery is obviously contrary to the laws of nature, the dictates of justice, and the constitution of this state."[95] Their decision elicited praise from their New England peers, "the real friends of liberty," and they wished that "the Federal legislature influenced by an example so brilliant, so worthy and conspicuous, may be induced to 'Go and do likewise.'"[96] As a result of the legislature's ruling, officers of the Pennsylvania Abolition Society registered 456 free black Saint-Dominguans between 1793 and 1796 alone, but the U.S. Congress made no such move.[97]

Despite general wariness about "French negroes," both free and slave states anticipated and accepted their presence. Some white Americans actually sought to *increase* the numbers of enslaved Saint-Dominguans in the United States. To borrow from historian David Brion Davis's keen observation, greed often trumped fear during the Haitian Revolution, and throughout the 1790s slaveowners and slave traders found a ready market in the United States for Saint-Dominguan slaves.[98] The scores of advertisements for the services of and occasional sale of "French negroes" attest to the willingness of white Americans to have them work in their homes, on their plantations, and in their industries. Some traders went even further to slake the white American thirst for French slaves, traveling to Saint-Domingue, capturing black and colored people, and selling them to eager U.S. buyers. In 1792 Jefferson, in his capacity as secretary of state, received complaints that a certain Captain Hickman had sailed to Cap Français and "enticed some Negroes on board his vessel, under pretext of employment." He had then sold them into slavery in Georgia, a crime for which the French minister, Jean-Baptist de Ternant, demanded satisfaction—not on behalf of the slaves but of their former owners.[99] It seems that this practice continued throughout the decade, for in 1801 Toussaint Louverture issued a proclamation (translated and printed in U.S. newspapers) regarding the kidnapping of black citizens from the colony. He cited two recent instances when American captains had carried away black Saint-Dominguans and reduced them to slavery in the United States. Louverture denounced the practice and required that civil and military officers search vessels for passengers held against their will and prosecute the offending captains.[100] No matter the stage of revolution in the French colony, there were Americans eager to import and enslave the island's residents.

White Americans' readiness to ignore their own exclusionary laws, to admit, hire, buy, or trade enslaved Saint-Dominguans—in short, to accept their presence in the United States—points to a kind of confidence in American slave society. Indeed, throughout the 1790s white U.S. residents downplayed and even dismissed rumors about slave rebellion in their own communities. In the summer of 1792, inhabitants of Newbern, North Carolina, worried that their slaves were "in contemplation to rise against their masters, and to procure themselves their liberty." Although the white residents increased their watch over the black community, they doubted the plot would come to fruition: "It is very absurd of the blacks, to suppose they could accomplish their views; and from the precautions that are taken to guard against a surprise, little danger is to be apprehended."[101] When two black men in Newark, New Jersey, danced around the American flag while wearing liberty caps in celebration of recent French military victories, white locals stopped them. Instead of becoming alarmed and fomenting frenzy among white residents about the spread of revolutionary sentiment to black people, these white locals chalked up the black men's actions to "drunkenness and complexion."[102] Even in the aftermath of Gabriel's Rebellion in 1800, white Virginians quickly relegated the conspiracy to the category of "nothing formidable."[103] In 1801 a Boston newspaper chided these lackadaisical southerners to "Remember ere too late / The tale of St. Domingo's fate. / Tho' Gabriel dies, host remain / Oppress'd with slavery's falling chain / And soon or late the hour will come / Mark'd with Virginia's dreadful doom."[104] But this allusion to Saint-Domingue failed to resonate. In the view of white Virginians, they had successfully rooted out and quashed the rebellion before it had begun, and having attributed the seed of insurrection to outside agitators (the French), they saw little need to revamp their society.

Such confidence was exuded in other contexts as well, including the popular arts. In 1798 John Murdock, a Philadelphia hairdresser turned playwright, wrote *The Politicians; or A State of Things*, in which he used the notion of black people as citizens as a vehicle for humor. The play featured a scene in which three black men—with the stereotypical names of Caesar, Pompey, and Sambo—met on the street. They addressed one another using the French revolutionary title of "citizen," as was fashionable among many white Philadelphians, and mimicked the politesse of gentlemen in a vulgar dialect that Murdock employed for comic effect.[105] The three men conversed about the "trong talke [of] French war." One professed himself in favor of France, the other for Britain, and the third for the United States. Murdock made clear, though, that their opinions were formed not by themselves but rather in accordance with those of their masters. Pompey, who backed the French, declared, "France for eber! France git liberty to slabe liberty," yet this alone did not explain his support. "My massa for France—so I."[106]

Murdock utilized the exchange to plug a position of American neutrality in international affairs; by placing the discussion in the mouths of black people, a formally depoliticized population, he could tread lightly around a contentious topic. In so doing, Murdock worked from his audience's denigrating assumptions about the nature of black Americans. Such prejudices were not necessarily incongruous with abolitionist sentiment, however. Murdock's works sometimes embraced an antislavery position. His 1795 play *The Triumphs of Love, or Happy Reconciliation*, involved a Quaker character, George Friendly, who was so moved by an "untutored" speech given by his slave Sambo that Friendly manumitted him. Friendly elaborated, though, that Sambo's life as a slave was better than that of his white counterparts: there were "many thousands of the poorer class of white . . . whose actual situation are vastly inferior to [Sambo's]: he has no anxious cares for to-morrow, no family looking up to him for protection—no duns at his doors." In the end, Friendly finds that "there is something wanting. It is cruel. It is unjust, for one creature to hold another in a state of bondage for life."[107] Sambo, now calling himself "Citizen Sambo," celebrates his freedom by promptly getting drunk and singing a bastardized version of the anthem popular during the Reign of Terror, the *Carmagnole*, "Dans sons carmagnole, &c. &c. Liberty and equality for eber and eber."[108] The former slave associated his emancipation with the French Revolution (with its most violent moment, no less), yet, as Murdock showed, Sambo had no idea what the revolution or citizenship meant. There was therefore no need to fear that the *Carmagnole*—and the bloodshed that accompanied it—would appear in the United States.[109]

Although fears did persist in the 1790s that the Haitian Revolution would spread to the United States, and although some white U.S. residents saw evidence of this possibility everywhere, many denied such threats. They dismissed what could be interpreted as rebellious activity among African Americans or attributed it to the presence of black and colored refugees—a convenient excuse that helped maintain the fiction about the beneficence of U.S. slavery. African Americans were, indeed, inspired by news of the Haitian Revolution and by their exiled peers, and their inspiration translated to a range of individual and collective action, from guardedly supportive statements to running away to protests on the streets. For all their ingenuity in this regard, African Americans were deeply circumscribed by the racist society in which they found themselves. But white Americans' willingness to ignore their own warnings provoked official debate when Governor-General Toussaint Louverture sent a letter to President John Adams requesting the establishment of formal trade relations between the United States and Saint-Domingue.

TRADING IN REVOLUTION

White Americans were at times unabashed in their discounting of the specter of revolution, but a trade agreement with Louverture's administration in Saint-Domingue would make such disregard government policy. There was a difference between flouting laws and changing them to reflect actual circumstances, and white residents feared that a formal accord would undercut slavery. The deal with Louverture would endorse the legitimacy of a black leader and abet his cause in Saint-Domingue, which was under threat from Bonaparte's government; in so doing, it would whittle away at the racial underpinnings of slavery in the

United States. It would also encourage even more traffic to and from the island and hence increase the flow of information, inspiration, and perhaps rebellion to slaves in the United States. Americans would be trading in revolution abroad and at home.

In the 1790s, many American merchants overcame the fears they had harbored about importing insurrection from Saint-Domingue, and rumors circulated that they were trading with black rebels. In 1794, American newspapers printed a report from Bermuda that lauded the activities of British privateers in the Caribbean. The author hoped that their ships would hound U.S. vessels and thereby "totally exclude" American merchants "from carrying on their infamous and illicit trade to St. Domingo, with the revolted negroes."[110] This accusation of illegal trafficking could have been British posturing—part of their attempt to justify the seizure of neutral American ships during this period. But the comment is revealing for its failure to admit that many of the "revolted negroes" were by this point emancipated French citizens, fighting in the name of the republic with which the United States had an official trade agreement. White British West Indians struggled to accept this recent turn of events, and they were banking on the fact that many white Americans felt the same.

The Jay Treaty of 1795 eased trade relations between the United States and Great Britain, and that year, more than six hundred American ships pulled into Saint-Domingue, many of them into the British-held western part. However, individual merchants also cultivated commercial ties with Toussaint Louverture's army. A general of the French army journeyed to the United States in late 1795 and early 1796 to drum up interest in and cultivate trade connections to support the, by then largely black, republican army on Saint-Domingue. In February 1796 Stephen Girard sent a boat laden with goods to Gonaïves, a port in the northwestern region of the island (maybe in an effort to sway officials to hasten his escaped servant Crispin's return). To protect the cargo, the French general wrote a letter to Louverture explaining that the vessel belonged "to a good French citizen, good patriot, named Gerard . . . owner of one of the best commercial houses in this city and in the best condition to come to the aid of the Republic of St. Domingo. . . . I beg you, General, to give every satisfaction possible to this merchant, to expedite the return of his ship, that it may continue to go to your relief."[111] (One wonders if Crispin would have agreed with this glowing account of Girard.) Other U.S. merchants followed Girard's example and took advantage of privileges proffered by the French republican administration on the island as it sought to court American business. While the volume of trade with Saint-Domingue did not approach its prerevolutionary heights and there were persistent complaints about ship security, devalued payments, and the like, U.S. merchants still relied on the colony as an important site of exchange throughout the 1790s.

The fact that American ships were staffed with black seamen made this trade especially audacious. Scholars estimate that thousands of black sailors, most of them free men, voyaged to Saint-Domingue/Haiti between 1790 and 1830, and they were vital links in the information networks that crisscrossed the Atlantic, collecting news on their travels and distributing it to black Americans along their routes.[112] In the age of revolution, the French and Haitian Revolutions were the hottest topics. White citizens recognized the role of black seamen as informants and possible catalysts of rebellious activity, yet in the 1790s states passed little, if any, legislation that restricted the mobility of black sailors.[113] Although wary, white Americans remained confident enough not to act on their concerns.

Trade with Saint-Domingue became much more difficult in the early days of John Adams's presidency. As the French government grew irritated with the United States in the second half of the decade, French sea captains interpreted this displeasure as carte blanche to attack U.S. ships, and they did so, seizing at least three hundred ships in one year alone. By June 1798 the situation had reached a point of crisis, and the federal government suspended trade with France and its colonies. Anxious about the effects of the embargo on the campaign in Saint-Domingue, officials there took matters into their own hands, much to the consternation of the mother country. They quickly issued two declarations aimed at curbing French designs on American ships, and at the end of the year, Governor-General Toussaint Louverture petitioned President Adams to reopen trade between the island and the United States.[114] The timing of his request was important, for the American embargo of France and its colonies was due to expire, and Congress was scheduled to decide whether to renew the embargo or not at its next session, in early 1799. Louverture's appeal instigated a fiery debate in Congress about the terms of the so-called Intercourse Act and the potential consequences of a formal trade agreement with Saint-Domingue without France.

In the 1790s Louverture was not unknown to U.S. government officials or to the general American public. As observers followed the course of the Haitian Revolution, it was hard to miss the meteoric rise of Louverture. The press covered his achievements avidly. In fact, the earliest published mention of Louverture anywhere in the Atlantic world appeared in Mr. Gros's *An Historick Recital* published in Baltimore (and France and Saint-Domingue) in 1792–93. Known only by his last name, Gros had been a lawyer of some standing in the parish of Vallière, Saint-Domingue, and had been taken prisoner by rebel forces in the fall of

1791. In the first-person narrative of his captivity, Gros cast Louverture in a some-what positive light when describing an incident in which Gros and his fellow white colonists faced execution by Georges Biassou, one of the leading insur-gents: "*Toussaint, of Breda,* . . . braving all Danger, attempted to save us, though he might have been himself the Victim of this Monster's Rage." Louverture emerged as courageous in Gros's estimation not only because he intervened to protect the lives of white colonists but also because he insisted on the rule of law, demanding that Gros and the others be tried and found guilty before any punish-ment took place. Later on in Gros's tale, Louverture had "tears in his eyes" as he lamented the renewal of war between the black rebels and white colonists.[115] As Louverture moved from the wings to center stage in the theater of war in Saint-Domingue, his coverage in American print grew; readers followed reports of his military victories and read translated versions of his official pronouncements. White observers greeted with a tentative approval his determination to reinstitute the plantation economy and his invitation for white exiles to return to the island to aid in that endeavor. Even his ousting of Sonthonax was judged favorably.[116]

Although Louverture was spared the more denigrating and racist appellations doled out to black revolutionary leaders by white American observers, his trade proposal to Adams still sparked concern. Several issues were at work in the debates over, as Jefferson termed it, "Toussaint's clause" to the Intercourse Act, not the least of which was its possible economic payoff.[117] Despite the years of upheaval and destruction on the island, many merchants—and their congres-sional representatives—viewed Saint-Domingue as a "mine of gold," waiting to be reopened for American exploitation.[118] Most pertinent for our discussion was the question of whether trade with Saint-Domingue would promote or quaran-tine black rebelliousness. For adversaries of the bill, doing business with Saint-Domingue would abet an insurrection (for they still saw it as a revolt rather than a legitimate arena of the French Revolution) whose aims and actions they found reprehensible. They argued that renewed trade would compromise the remaining white population in the colony. A February 1799 article in the *Pennsylvania Ga-zette* illustrates the logic of their view. According to an island resident, provisions were scarce and fetched good prices. Aware of American qualms about safety, the author assured readers that, even though "the brigands are determined to mas-sacre all the whites," they nevertheless "offered a free and unmolested commerce on their part to all nations that will trade with them [the "brigands"]."[119] To those opposed to the proposal, these kinds of reports provided proof that American products supported actions against white inhabitants—a consequence that some congressmen found unconscionable.

"Toussaint Louverture Chef des Noirs Insurgés de Saint Domingue" (Paris, ca. 1800, artist unknown). This portrait of Toussaint Louverture was part of a series of images of French revolutionary generals. Like his white peers, Louverture is featured with all the honorific trappings of a distinguished military leader. Courtesy John Carter Brown Library at Brown University.

Foes of "Toussaint's clause" doubted that Louverture had the authority to enter into an agreement with the United States, and they took umbrage at the fourth section of the proposed Intercourse Bill which, they claimed, legitimated his power. In the eyes of the bill's detractors, the rider favored Louverture's rule over that of the French government and encouraged Saint-Dominguan independence. The problems of Saint-Dominguan independence were manifold, but the bill's opponents dreaded, in particular, the impact that a nearby nation of former slaves might have on the United States. Albert Gallatin, the Swiss-born representative from Pennsylvania and leader of the Democratic Republicans in Congress, was the most blunt in this regard. Although Gallatin professed his hatred of slavery, he worried that, if independent, Saint-Domingue's "interest will be wholly black," and part of that "black" agenda would be to "visit the States of South Carolina and Georgia, and spread their views among the negro people there, and excite dangerous insurrections among them."[120] Drawing on the rhetoric that white refugees employed about the Haitian Revolution, Gallatin described the perils of "throw[ing] so many wild tigers on society."[121] An independent Saint-Domingue provided an opening, he maintained, for transatlantic black radicalism—a radicalism that would pit savagery against civilization.

Proponents of an agreement with Louverture interpreted the bill differently. They focused on the legitimacy of Louverture's authority and denied that the bill fostered Saint-Dominguan independence. Because the French government had appointed Louverture governor-general of the colony, he possessed the power to enter into negotiations with the United States. They pointed to several precedents.[122] Federalist Harrison Gray Otis of Massachusetts drew his colleagues' attention to American policy toward the French governments of the 1790s: "Have we not uniformly adhered to the principle that those who exercise power *de facto* are the only persons that we are bound to recognize? From the first dawn of the [French] Revolution, we have . . . never questioned the legitimacy of the power exercised in France; to us it seemed indifferent whether Jacobins or Girondists were at the helm of affairs. . . . It is now too late to change this system."[123] Fellow party member Thomas Pinckney of South Carolina recalled how neutral nations had traded with the United States during its war for independence from Great Britain, and at that time, "we saw no moral turpitude in this."[124] While Pinckney's comment is revealing for the way it casts Saint-Domingue in a position similar to that of the United States during the American Revolution, both Otis and Pinckney depicted Louverture as a leader like any other and Saint-Domingue as a political entity like any other. In some sense they attempted to draw the conversation away from "blackness" and onto colorblind ground.

Nevertheless, supporters recognized the unique situation in Saint-Domingue, especially the intertwined issues of independence and the spread of slave rebellion. On the question of independence, advocates like Samuel Smith of Maryland reminded members that the bill would be void should Saint-Domingue declare independence; in this way, he contended, it deterred Toussaint Louverture from repudiating French oversight.[125] In other words, trade was one way to hold the island in check and keep it a colony. Saint-Domingue's very survival, Smith intimated, demanded it. Yet, some supporters, like Pinckney (a South Carolinian no less), insisted that Saint-Dominguan independence was nothing to fear, that such an event would protect southern states from French invasion. Pinckney reasoned that if the colony were independent, an increasingly confrontational France would lose a critical base from which to launch reprisals against the United States.[126] Regardless of their specific take on Saint-Dominguan autonomy, promoters of the bill affirmed that friendly commercial terms would quarantine rebellion: "Refuse to these people our commerce, and the provisions of which they stand in need, and you compel them to become pirates and dangerous neighbors to the Southern States; but so long as you supply them, they will turn their attention to the cultivation of their plantations."[127] Banning trade would only excite animosity from the island's residents. According to Smith, Pinckney, and other proponents, trade was essential to promoting peace and the plantation economy, to maintaining the status quo that the bill's opponents were so afraid of losing.

As the variety of voices indicates, the debate about the bill was not split strictly along the Mason-Dixon line, with southerners fighting an agreement with Louverture and northerners supporting it. Party politics more than regional interests shaped the discussion. Federalists, in general, backed the measure, while Democratic Republicans usually countered it. Democratic Republicans thought that a trade agreement with Saint-Domingue would provoke war with France, yet Federalists viewed it as a means to cope with what they perceived as a very real threat from the continent. From the latter's standpoint, France seemed unwilling to deal fairly with the United States, and the American republic had to look out for its best interests, in this case renewed trade with Saint-Domingue and the profits and security it offered. The triumph of party politics over racial solidarity galled Jefferson, who lamented in a letter to James Madison that "even South Carolinians in the H[ouse] of R[epresentatives]" had voted for "Toussaint's clause." Thanks to their shortsightedness, the vice president warned, "we may expect . . . black crew, supercargoes & missionaries thence into the Southern states."[128] In Jefferson's estimation, the South would pay the price for this political folly and failure to realize its common, racialized interest.

Much to Jefferson's relief, Congress voted to renew the embargo against France and its colonies, but his relief was short-lived, for the revised embargo act of February 1799 included a proviso that permitted the president to reopen traffic with Saint-Domingue at his own discretion. A few months later, urged by another letter from Toussaint Louverture, Adams did just that. Edward Stevens, the U.S. consul in Saint-Domingue, brokered a three-way deal among Louverture, Adams, and General Thomas Maitland, a representative for Great Britain, which, despite its recent military defeat in the island, still had economic and political interests there. As part of the negotiation, Adams and Stevens required the termination of island-sponsored privateering and a promise that Saint-Domingue would not export rebellion elsewhere; in return, Louverture guaranteed free trade with the ports under his control, namely Cap Français and Port Républicain, formerly Port-au-Prince.[129]

Adams's course of action toward Saint-Domingue stands out as a unique moment in early American foreign policy when economic interest trumped racism.[130] But it must be remembered that the treaty with the black governor-general was just one aspect of Adams's attempt to find a peaceable solution to the Quasi War. While pursuing trade in Saint-Domingue, he initiated talks with France—a strategy that sat uneasily with Louverture, given his tense relations with Napoleon Bonaparte. In addition, the U.S. deal was as much a recognition of the ineffectiveness of the previous embargo as a diplomatic move. As Edward Stevens observed in a dispatch, "the Flag of the United States is seen as frequently in every part of this Colony, as it was before the prohibiting Act was passed," thanks to the lively clandestine trade carried out by numerous American merchants.[131] With or without official sanction, merchants were determined to flood into the colony's ports. Soon after the final agreement went into effect on August 1, 1799, more than thirty "richly laden" U.S. ships pulled into Port Républicain within two weeks. Louverture was keeping up his end of the bargain; as a colonist reported to his contact in Philadelphia, "American vessels are usually treated with consideration by our government, which has given up issuing commissions for privateers."[132] Viewed in this context, Adams's negotiations with Saint-Domingue represent a practical response to a sticky diplomatic and economic situation.

As Jefferson and his party suspected, however, trade with Saint-Domingue had consequences that went beyond exchange. The pact with Louverture gave the U.S. government an interest in keeping him happy, and this had ramifications at home and in the colony. The agreement made a significant impact on refugees in American cities. In response to a query from white exiles, Secretary of State Timothy Pickering noted that, in light of "Toussaint's clause," refugees could travel to the island, yet their return would depend "on the conditions which General Toussaint shall prescribe."[133] The United States would follow Louverture's rules—not the other way around—and this assertion must have been galling for a population disgruntled with the revolution in Saint-Domingue. Even though Louverture had, in September 1798, appealed to white exiles in the United States to reclaim their plantations, some white Saint-Dominguans found life under a black leader hard to swallow and held on to their own designs for the future of the colony.[134] Pickering's message intimated his distrust of their motives: "All quiet well disposed Frenchmen may expect permission to return to their habitations; while he [Louverture] may deem it necessary to exclude or even to banish intriguers, who shall be inclined to subvert that order of things."[135] In this configuration it was the white exiles who threatened the "order of things"—an order with a black man at its apex.

By late in the decade, American officials had grown wary of letting Saint-Dominguans into the United States. In June 1799 Oliver Wolcott, of the U.S. Treasury, warned, "No persons, excepting citizens of the United States, are to be brought from the island of St. Domingo, unless they produce the written passports of the general in chief of the army of St. Domingo [Toussaint Louverture], authorising their departure, and also separate passports from the consul general of the United States."[136] American authorities feared that they would rankle Louverture if their vessels facilitated the departure of the very people whom the general wanted to remain on the island, but from the white exiles' perspective, the United States was denying them asylum.

Edward Stevens advised that it would be to the advantage of the United States to do more than tailor its migration policies to please Louverture; the American government needed to assist in his efforts to consolidate control over the colony. Although Louverture ruled the north and west, André Rigaud, a free colored leader with his own plan for the colony, dominated the south. The outcome of the battle between the two men affected American commerce. As Stevens made clear in a letter to Timothy Pickering in June 1799, "if Toussaint should prove unsuccessful [in his campaign against Rigaud], all the Arrangements we have made respecting Commerce must fall to the Ground. The most solemn Treaty would have little Weight with a Man of Rigaud's capricious and tyrannical Temper. This Circumstance points out the absolute Necessity of supporting Toussaint by every legal measure."[137] Stevens, perhaps aware of the racial implications of his request, went on to emphasize that support for Louverture aided the local white population. He concluded that both black and white Saint-Dominguans backed Louverture: "His humane and mild Conduct has render'd him respectable to the latter, and they now look up to him as their only Shield against the cruel Tyranny of Rigaud."[138] In Stevens's calculated reading, Louverture was the only possible guarantor of a peaceful multiracial society in Saint-Domingue—and of American trade.

With Adams's consent, Stevens authorized the delivery of a shipment of stores for Louverture's army which provided critical support for the campaign against his rival. Even more significantly, the U.S. frigate *General Greene* cut off Rigaud's supply vessels near Jacmel and bombarded his forts during the final attack; and when the mulatto leader fled the island in October 1800, the American schooner *Experiment* captured him.[139] While Louverture's forces deserve the credit for routing Rigaud, the U.S. government and American merchants were instrumental in hastening the governor-general's victory. In order to preserve the trade agreement, white Americans had become complicit in the Haitian Revolution, actively intervening in the course of war in the colony and doing so in the name of its black leader.

The implications of these actions were too much for men like Jefferson. When he was elected president—part of what became known as the "revolution of 1800"—he wanted to change the tenor of U.S.–Saint-Dominguan relations. Always concerned about the consequences of the slave revolution, Jefferson in the summer of 1801 had assured the French chargé d'affaires, Louis A. Pichon, that the United States would support a French invasion of the island: "Nothing would be easier than to furnish your army and fleet with everything, and to reduce Toussaint to starvation."[140] Nevertheless, six months later Jefferson was aghast at the enormous size of the Leclerc expedition sent to reconquer Saint-Domingue, and he worried that, should the French recover the island, Bonaparte would use it as a launching pad from which to reclaim the Louisiana territory, which Jefferson desperately wanted to obtain in order to fulfill his vision of an agrarian republic. Reconsidering, Jefferson declined to make good on his promise to Pichon, allowing trade to continue between the United States and the colony. As public opinion turned against the French in 1802 because of rumors about Bonaparte's designs in Louisiana, American merchants refused to enter French-held Saint-Dominguan ports, docking instead at those secured by Louverture. Pichon repeatedly complained to Jefferson that Boston merchants were supplying the black armies with arms, ammunition, and provisions, but his objections fell on deaf ears.[141] Within three months of their arrival, Leclerc and his army were the ones being starved out.

Jefferson's policy contributed significantly to the demise of the Leclerc expedition, which in turn forced Bonaparte to give up his Louisiana scheme and sell the territory to the United States. As Alexander Hamilton noted perceptively in an editorial in the *New-York Evening Post*, "To the deadly climate of St. Domingo, and to the courage and obstinate resistance made by its black inhabitants, we are indebted for the obstacles which delayed the colonization of Louisiana, till the auspicious moment, when a rupture between England and France gave a new turn to the projects of the latter, and destroyed at once all her schemes as to this favorite object of her ambition."[142] While Hamilton recognized the U.S. debt to Haiti for Louisiana, President Jefferson preferred to forget it; and as American merchants celebrated the French evacuation and traded briskly with the island, Jefferson promptly moved to sever ties with Haiti.

Motivated by panic that black rebellion would spread to the United States and by the tantalizing possibility of attaining Florida from France, the president urged Congress to act against the new republic.[143] In 1804, just months after the declaration of Haitian independence, Jefferson asked Congress to ban U.S. merchants from arming their vessels—a precaution that they thought necessary to navigating the privateer-infested waters en route to Haiti. William Plumer, a Federalist senator from New Hampshire, declared that the text was "more empty & vapid, & wrapt in greater obscurity than any of his [Jefferson's] preceding messages"; but with it Jefferson took his first step toward restraining commerce with the new republic, for, as he well knew, few merchants would hazard such a risky trip without their cannons.[144] Debate in Congress was fierce, and the vitriol spilled out into the public sphere. Democratic Republican newspapers, such as the *Aurora*, decried that "commerce with a horde of uncivilized and bloodthirsty revolters . . . would devastate the West Indies and even threaten us with domestic danger."[145] In retaliation, merchants openly flouted the law; in one instance, a New York convoy celebrated its successful mission to Haiti with a public banquet, including toasts that lauded free American trade as well as "the government of Haiti, founded on the only legitimate basis of all authority . . . the people's choice. May it be as durable as its principles are pure."[146] The lines were drawn.

Recognizing the ineffectiveness of this first measure, Jefferson's party pushed through a bill the following year that prohibited all trade with the black nation. Yet again, the discussion was bitter. Federalists accused Democratic Republicans of catering to Bonaparte, while Democratic Republicans retorted that Federalists endorsed a trade that violated the laws of nations and ran counter to the interests of the United States, specifically the preservation of slavery and the averting of war with France.[147] Democratic Republicans raised the specter of rebellion repeatedly, deploying the racist rhetoric surrounding the Haitian Revolution to allege that associating with such "brigands" would wreak havoc on southern states.

Federalists countered that the Haitians were free men who fought only to preserve their liberty, but their arguments were overwhelmed by the tide of terror unleashed by southern Democratic Republicans—and the willingness of their northern counterparts in the party to go along with them. The embargo against Haiti passed.[148]

In the end, Jefferson and his supporters seemed to have gotten what they wanted regarding Saint-Domingue/Haiti, namely a total quarantine, but it had taken them over a decade to do so. Throughout the 1790s and early 1800s Americans—both white and black—had various responses to the potential contagion of rebellion, as each population sought to interpret the lessons of and opportunities afforded by the Haitian Revolution and its refugees to suit circumstances in the United States. African Americans worked within their precarious position in a deeply racist society to take advantage of the possibilities for change that Saint-Domingue and its exiles offered. For the moment, they could not lay claim to the boldest assertions of the revolution—demands for emancipation and citizenship—but they drew ideological inspiration from Haitian accomplishments and continued to employ the usual forms of individual and collective resistance.

As for white residents, on the one hand, many feared the prospect of a slave revolution on U.S. shores and saw the disturbing imprint of black and colored refugees, it seems, almost everywhere. On the other hand, their fear was often tempered by other concerns—be they economic, political, or social—that led them to ignore their own warnings and, at times, to provide qualified support to the very revolution they professed to revile. Nevertheless, few white Americans—even the most abolitionist-minded among them—went so far as to endorse the version of liberty, equality, and fraternity that Haitian revolutionaries espoused, and none endorsed the methods they employed to realize their vision. The goal throughout was to cope with the contagion of rebellion in a way that would strengthen rather than debilitate the American body politic.

For Jefferson, once his prized Louisiana Purchase was secured, the goal became to isolate the source of corruption—the newly independent Haiti—from the United States. But his remedy proved temporary, for in 1809 a new wave of refugees arrived consisting of thousands of slaves and free people of color. They came from Cuba, and most of them headed to New Orleans, the premier port in Jefferson's crowning, if still controversial, achievement. As Hamilton had pointed out, Haitian revolutionaries made the acquisition of the territory possible, and now the ten thousand exiles who flooded into the region threatened to undermine Jefferson and his followers' plan for the area—its swift incorporation into the United States.

CHAPTER FIVE

"THE HORRORS OF ST. DOMINGO"
—A REPRISE

In 1808 newspapers along the eastern seaboard announced the publication of a new novel called *Secret History; or, the Horrors of St. Domingo*. Written, so the title page explained, by an American woman in Cap Français during the last phase of the Haitian Revolution, the story unfolded in a series of letters addressed to the former U.S. vice president and *persona non grata*, Aaron Burr. The author was Leonora Sansay, the daughter of a Philadelphia innkeeper, who in 1800 married a refugee from Saint-Domingue (on the recommendation of her on-again-off-again lover, Burr), and traveled with him to the island in 1802 to reclaim his plantation. Dissatisfied with her marriage and with her status in American society, Sansay wrote *Secret History* in an attempt to craft her public image. The loosely autobiographical account provides unique insight into the final years of the French regime in Saint-Domingue.[1]

The novel follows the trials and tribulations of two American sisters as they are caught in the crossfire between one sister's loveless marriage and the war for independence in the colony. Fleeing both, the two women seek refuge in Cuba and Jamaica before returning to the United States. Along the way, the narrator comments on the situation in Saint-Domingue—on the diverse actors and their roles in the war, the latest turns of events, and the vagaries of life there and in exile. She identifies "horrors" ranging from the "savagery" of black rebels and the cowardice of French forces to the sexual exploits of Caribbean women and the follies of white creole men. Although she gestures to worthy exceptions to these generalizations, especially among women, every sector of the population falls under Sansay's critical gaze, and all are seen as complicit in the demise of the colony. Continental French soldiers, former slaves, and white and colored residents share responsibility for the—in Sansay's view, lamentable—transformation of Saint-Domingue into Haiti.[2]

Secret History revisited many issues concerning the Haitian Revolution and its refugees that had first surfaced in the 1790s but in 1808 sparked renewed interest among Americans, for the time of the book's publication closely corresponded with another migration of Saint-Dominguans. Only a year after the novel appeared in bookshops, at least 10,000 exiles who, like Sansay, had in 1803 sought asylum in Cuba turned up in American cities. The refugees of 1809 provoked the same debates as had those who arrived during the previous decade: considerations of social and cultural fitness, philanthropy, politics, and slave rebellion.

However, two additional, more recent developments shaped reactions to this latest wave of exiles. First, although some refugees sailed to ports along the eastern seaboard, the majority landed in New Orleans. Acquired by the United States in 1803, the city and the surrounding territory were undergoing an uneasy transition to American rule. U.S. officials struggled to assert authority among a multiracial and largely Francophone population that was none too happy about its new national allegiance, and authorities also faced scathing criticism from white American migrants who clashed with locals and were frustrated by territorial policies. The refugees complicated this already fraught venture. Whereas in the 1790s Saint-Dominguans represented a minority of urban residents on the Atlantic coast (albeit a vocal and visible one), their numbers amounted to a significant demographic change in New Orleans and its vicinity. In the early 1800s, Orleans Parish (the area in and around New Orleans) had only 17,000 people, and the arrival of the Saint-Dominguans contributed dramatically to the population. American officials were eager that the area should be settled, in order to establish U.S. dominion as quickly as possible, yet they had a specific type of migrant in mind to carry out this enterprise—an image that the exiles did not fit. Consisting of more than 3,000 slaves and more than 3,000 free people of color who had been exposed to revolutionary ideals, and thousands of white colonists of questionable character and loyalties, this wave of refugees bolstered the very sectors of the community of which authorities were already wary. The Saint-Dominguans' presence had the power to delay even longer, if not thwart altogether, the successful integration of the territory into the United States.

The second influence on responses to the exiles was the timing of their arrival.

They sought asylum just a year after passage of landmark federal legislation that banned the importation of foreign slaves to the United States. By bringing thousands of bondsmen with them, the refugees tested U.S. commitment to the law on two fronts. Abolition of the foreign slave trade was motivated not only by humanitarian rhetoric but also by the fear that introducing too many slaves from Africa and the Caribbean would result in a slave rebellion like Saint-Domingue's. In other words, ending the trade was as much about the preservation of American society (and, for many southerners, the institution of slavery) as it was about philanthropic ideals, and therefore both slaveowners and opponents of slavery rallied to the cause. Given the overwhelming support for the law's passage, the reaction to the exiles should have been straightforward: they affronted the moral underpinnings of the law, and they came from the very site of insurrection that white Americans most dreaded. The Atlantic states, for the most part, toed one of these lines. Northern states applied state manumission laws to enslaved refugees (in accordance with the moral rationale), while southern states enforced the ban against enslaved exiles and invoked it also to bar the entry of free people of color (following the self-preservationist approach). In the case of southern states, this reflected a change from white approaches to enslaved refugees in the 1790s, a change that was informed by their particular understanding of Haitian independence.

New Orleans was a different situation. Although Congress had abolished the importation of foreign slaves as of January 1, 1808, it had been unable to decide how to punish violators and so had left the law's enforcement in the hands of individual states. The legislature for the Territory of Orleans had not made the provisions required to put the foreign slave trade abolition law into practice, which meant that the federal government had to figure out how to apply the legislation to the Saint-Dominguan exiles. After much foot-dragging, U.S. representatives voted almost unanimously to exempt the refugees from the slave trade ban. In so doing they went against all justifications for abolition, against eastern states' approaches to the crisis, and against a longstanding prohibition on admission of Saint-Dominguan slaves to Louisiana. Fears about slave rebellion were set aside as congressmen and territorial authorities looked to avoid what, from their perspective, was a more difficult predicament: how to put federal law into effect in an area saddled with political and social strife.

The Haitian Revolution made the Louisiana Purchase and the abolition of the foreign slave trade possible, yet the 1809 migration of Saint-Dominguan refugees imperiled both of these accomplishments. In the already unstable Orleans Territory, the exiles had the power to reproduce the fractious and incendiary conditions that Sansay had witnessed in colonial Saint-Domingue. Together, the white refugees with their Francophone sensibilities and mores, the discontented and dangerous free people of color, and slaves fresh from years of revolutionary rhetoric and bloodshed, could transplant the "horrors of St. Domingo" to Louisiana and jeopardize the very area on which Jefferson staked the future of republic. However, officials were able to turn the refugees' presence to advantage—to tame the "horrors of St. Domingo" to serve, once again, American ends.

FROM SAINT-DOMINGUE TO CUBA TO THE ATLANTIC STATES

The tipping point for Leonora Sansay, and for many white Saint-Dominguans still on the island, came in 1803. General Donatien-Marie-Joseph de Vimeur, vicomte de Rochambeau (son of the famous infantry officer who had fought in the American Revolution) conceded the failure of the French invasion of the colony and capitulated to the black army led by Jean-Jacques Dessalines. Dessalines's determination to rid the island of slavery, racism, and the French colonialism that had perpetuated both sent thousands of residents into exile, and most, like Sansay, ended up in nearby Cuba. But their time in the Spanish colony was only a brief interlude before international tumult compelled them to the United States in 1809. Nevertheless, their experiences in Cuba and the popular discussion surrounding them influenced American reactions to the refugees. Some U.S. responses continued trends from the previous decade, but the slave trade abolition law created, particularly in the South, new conditions for exiled slaves and free people of color.

In the early years of the Haitian Revolution, Cuba was not a destination of choice for refugees. Although the exiles were not explicit about their decision in this regard, the historical context indicates a few explanations. When France declared war on Spain in 1793, Spanish colonial forces almost immediately invaded Saint-Domingue via Santo Domingo, which occupied the eastern two-thirds of Hispaniola, but Spain ended up ceding Santo Domingo to France in the Treaty of Bâle in 1795. Not much love was lost on either side, as each accused the other of using slaves to further its cause, and this acrimony prevented white Saint-Dominguans from seeking relief in the lands of their rivals.[3] More specifically, the volatile political situation in Cuba dissuaded exiles from settling there. The controversial policies of Governor Luis de Las Casas split Cuban society into competing camps, and in 1796 the discord reached such a frightful pitch that crown officials recalled the governor at the end of year, hoping to avoid rebellion in the colony.[4] From the exiles' point of view, these circumstances resembled all too closely their own recent past, and so throughout the 1790s they turned to places with seem-ingly greater stability, such as Jamaica and the United States.[5]

Not until 1803 did Cuba see a large influx of Saint-Dominguan refugees, who came mostly from the southern and western regions of the island. (At this point France had lost Santo Domingo to black forces, so Spain and France could com-miserate over their Caribbean losses.) Spanish authorities in Cuba went out of their way to welcome the French newcomers, "with a view," as officials explained, "to the encouragement of agriculture and the arts," and their exertions paid off.[6] Historians estimate that by 1804 at least 10,000 Saint-Dominguans were living in the Spanish colony, and they energized its economy. Since Cuba lacked the precious metals that had made Peru and New Spain famous, it had been consid-ered for centuries an economic backwater on Spain's colonial map. Small farms, mostly of tobacco, but also of sugar and coffee, dotted the eighteenth-century Cuban landscape. At the turn of the nineteenth century, though, a new dynamism invigorated the island, even with its political difficulties. Between 1770 and 1820, its economy flourished as the result of expanded trade, diversified agriculture, internal investments, and immigration. The disruption of Saint-Dominguan sugar and coffee production during the Haitian Revolution provided other oppor-tunities on which Cubans capitalized.[7]

The exiles tapped into these economic currents and helped accelerate their pace. In the words of one refugee, "French industriousness" was apparent every-where, but it was most striking in and around Santiago de Cuba, a town on the eastern end of the colony. In this relatively undeveloped area, the Saint-Domin-guans applied their experience and skill at plantation agriculture, and Cuban authorities promoted their efforts by selling and leasing land to them on afford-able terms. As more exiles settled near Santiago, production skyrocketed. Before their arrival, a typical coffee harvest had yielded no more than 8,000 *arrobes* (approximately 4,894 tons); by 1805, the total had climbed to 80,000 *arrobes*, and it went to 300,000 *arrobes* in the following year.[8]

Not all refugees were able to excel in plantation agriculture: they either lacked the financial wherewithal or were reticent to commit to new lives in Cuba, and so they contributed to fulfilling Spanish officials' other hope for the colony—the cultivation of the arts. As they did in North American cities, white Saint-Domin-guans in Cuba marketed their refinement, designing gardens, building ball-rooms, and staging theatrical and musical performances. Single and widowed women were assiduous in mining their "talents" in order to keep destitution at bay, but their attempts met with mixed success.[9] According to the refugees, indi-gence marked almost every sphere of Cuban society. They were appalled by the rawness of eastern Cuban towns, with their muddy streets, makeshift domestic architecture, and crude furnishings. The conditions were all the more galling because, with so many exiles flooding into the area, such houses commanded ever higher prices. In this context the lavishness of the Catholic churches highlighted the destitution that surrounded them, and, to make matters worse, religion seemed to fail to inculcate proper morals in parishioners. In sum, the refugees saw the locals as wanting in taste, education, and principle.[10] One exile in Cuba wrote to a friend in New Orleans: "My nine-month stay on this island [has] only confirmed the repugnance that I had about going to the Spanish possessions; besides all the problems they try to give to the French, there is the regime and the Spanish subject you have to give in to, add to that superstition and the lowest form of ignorance possible and you will have a good idea of my plight."[11] While Cubans were fellow Caribbean creoles and fellow Catholics, white Saint-Dominguans felt that their counterparts were markedly inferior.

Their disdain for Cuban society aside, Saint-Dominguan refugees found viable asylum in the Spanish colony during the years immediately following Haitian independence, but when the continental political situation exploded toward the end of the decade, the refugees' position in Cuba grew tenuous. In 1808 one hundred thousand troops sent by Napoleon Bonaparte to annex Spain ousted King Ferdinand VII from the throne and replaced him with the French leader's own brother. The reverberations of this metropolitan uproar were soon felt in the Spanish colonies. In South America the overthrow brought about a series of crises that sparked wars for independence. While Cuba would remain part of the empire for another eighty or so years, it, too, smarted under Spanish indignities on the Continent, and Cubans took out their frustrations against the resident French. Initially, Cuban authorities expelled all Frenchmen who failed to take an oath of allegiance to the deposed Spanish king. By the spring of 1809, however, pledges offered little protection for Frenchmen, and riots swept the colony. In stories that recalled the Haitian Revolution, American newspapers reported that white Saint-Dominguans, "without regard to age or sex, or the length of time they have been [in Cuba], or station in life," had "sustained total loss—and some of them lost their lives." Witnesses described how "negroes rose and plundered all the French houses . . . and committed some murders."[12] As they had with black Saint-Dominguans, white observers attributed black Cubans' actions to "actors behind the scene" who had goaded them to violence.[13] Often the instigators were depicted as lower-class rabble-rousers who, through their machinations, sought to drive the Saint-Dominguans off the island and compel them "to sell [their] large property for almost nothing."[14] According to the U.S. press, the white refugees were once again subject to racialized violence that led to the loss of life and property.

The initial bloodshed was staunched when more than two hundred rioters were imprisoned, and throughout the spring, the militia pursued the rest of the "flying negroes."[15] This show of force did not signal a change of heart regarding the Saint-Dominguan refugees; rather, it reflected authorities' desire to flex their muscle in the matter. After the unrest subsided, officials in Santiago and Havana ordered all "Frenchmen" to leave; in Santiago, Cubans were encouraged to "assist those comprised in the proclamation, to facilitate their departure."[16] Perhaps residents took these words too much to heart, for rumors circulated that the populace had killed those exiles who had not left by the mandated departure date.[17] As Saint-Dominguans evacuated, the Spanish government confiscated their property. In the view of white American audiences, the specter of the Haitian Revolution seemed to follow the white exiles like a dark cloud.

American newspapers anticipated that Saint-Dominguans would escape the colony on U.S. vessels. In spite of sporadic metropolitan attempts to apply strict mercantilist policies to Cuba, trade between the United States and the Spanish island had flourished. Colonists shipped tropical produce, and Americans supplied provisions and, often, slaves. Between 1800 and 1805 more Philadelphian ships sailed to Cuba than to any European or Asian destination, and in 1806–7 the value of North American imports reached $12 million. The troubles in the colony in 1809 threatened to disrupt this commerce, and there was widespread apprehension that "the fate of the Island of Cuba may be as wretched, as has been that of St. Domingo."[18] Given the U.S. embargo against Haiti, Americans could ill afford to lose another valuable trading partner, let alone witness another site in the Caribbean erupt into racialized war.

Even with the brisk traffic between the United States and Cuba, the refugees' need for passage outstripped supply. The scenes resembled the colonists' flight from Saint-Domingue a few years before. In mid-June a captain who had just returned from the town of Baracoa reported, "There is great distress among the French—thousands endeavoring to get away, but vessels not to be had."[19] Port officials in Havana searched American ships, looking for French property, "political incendiaries," and "suspicious letters."[20] Not surprisingly, merchants and passengers resented this interference, but it was only one of a number of perils. Once Saint-Dominguans gained berths, the journey was especially dangerous because of the privateer activity promoted by the Napoleonic Wars, and slaves and people of color were, as usual, at unique risk. A vessel traveling from Santiago to Baltimore in May 1809, for instance, lost three slaves to a privateer.[21] In addition, many ships were unprepared to accommodate so many passengers. Captain Wilson Jacobs rescued a schooner on the high seas that had "about 300 unfortunate Frenchmen heaped one upon another, without water or any provisions of any kind." The *Louisiana Courier* asserted that without Jacobs's intervention, the exiles would have met "the most cruel and certain death."[22]

The parallels of the 1809 migration with that of the 1790s—the searches, seizures, and overall difficult circumstances—would not have been lost on passengers, captains, or the American reading public, and these reports conditioned the reception of the refugees as they arrived by the hundreds at cities along the East Coast of the United States. As in the previous decade, the white exiles (not the free people of color or the enslaved) were portrayed as "unfortunate fugitives" who had "saved nothing but their lives."[23] The *Enquirer*, in Richmond, Virginia, lamented the devastating impact on the refugees of their eviction from Cuba, considering the Saint-Dominguans' stormy past: "This measure reduces to beggary several thousands of the most industrious planters, who, after being expelled by revolutions from St. Domingo, carried their experience and industry to Cuba, which they had cultivated into a rivalship with the former riches of St. Domingo."[24] Exiles stressed this double displacement in their appeals to individuals and to Americans generally. In a letter to Thomas Jefferson, a Madame Deshay described her situation in Baltimore thus: "Forced to abandon my properties in Saint Domingue, obliged to leave the island of Cuba where I had taken refuge and where I could provide for my existence, I am now here in a country that is foreign to me; stripped of everything, very elderly, without relatives, without friends."[25] Like her predecessors in the 1790s, Deshay emphasized not only her coerced migration and subsequent dislocation in the United States, but also her capabilities in Saint-Domingue and in Cuba. She had been a productive member of society, and this, coupled with her pitiful situation, made her—she tacitly argued— worthy of aid.

The white refugees had again fallen on hard times, and their dramatic stories moved locals to action on their behalf. City residents organized charity campaigns, borrowing from conventions employed in the 1790s. A few days after the arrival of the ship *Speedwell*, which brought 153 refugees to Philadelphia, inhabitants of the Lower Delaware Ward called a meeting, established a relief committee, and sent out volunteers to canvass the neighborhoods for donations.[26] According to one report, they received pledges for at least $3,000 within a matter of days. The article went on to celebrate the generosity of Philadelphians: "It evinces strongly that their benevolence is universal in its offices, to all the distressed children of men, without regard to country or clime."[27] George Slessman, the chairman of the Philadelphia fundraiser, saw the outpouring of support as indicative of the charity not only of that city's residents but of the nation as well. In an address to the public, he declared that the campaign showed how the United States was "the asylum for the oppressed of all nations."[28] By aiding the refugees in 1809, Americans hoped to realize their revolutionary promise to welcome the world's downtrodden.

But, as in the 1790s, asylum—and the philanthropy that supposedly went along it—were not as transparent as Slessman and his contemporaries believed. The charity campaign in Philadelphia was inspired by sympathy for the white refugees and by strict laws regarding migrants. In order to enter the city, the exiles from Cuba had to promise that they would not become burdens on the community; and, as a writer to *Poulson's American Daily Advertiser* made clear, "this many of them cannot do, as they are in a state of extreme suffering." He warned his neighbors, "Let not the stigma rest on the citizens of Philadelphia, of permitting human beings to perish for want of the common necessaries of life."[29] Officially, asylum was limited to the financially viable, and the article in *Poulson's* suggests that, when it came to the refugees, locals had reservations about this restriction.

Although the charity was, once more, only for white Saint-Dominguans, permission to enter various American cities did pertain to enslaved exiles, and on this score, the slave trade abolition law created a new context. The law was supposed to bar the admission of any foreign slave to the United States, including those from the West Indies, but in some northern cities enslaved refugees entered and were freed. In New York City, for example, several exiled Saint-Dominguan slaves from Cuba sought the assistance of the local manumission society to gain their freedom.[30] When confronted with the enslaved refugees, northern states applied their manumission laws, in part because state legislation outlined what authorities should do with illegally imported slaves, namely, free them through the legal processes and institutions already in place. Manumission also reflected the moral impulse behind abolishing the trade—an ethical high ground that white northerners felt they could afford given the small numbers of enslaved exiles.

Southern states took a more aggressive stance in enforcing the federal law, especially compared to the slipshod measures enacted in the 1790s. Consider three cases—one from Georgia, one from South Carolina, and a final example from Virginia. In May 1809 the brig *Nancy White* docked in Savannah with 141 French passengers from Santiago de Cuba; at least 44 of these exiles were enslaved or free people of color.[31] The ship captain appealed to the collector of the port and then to the mayor and city council for permission to land the enslaved and free colored migrants, but his request was denied. When notified about the refusal, the American consul in Santiago pleaded for leniency for the refugees, yet Savannah officials replied that the *Nancy White* was not a case for city or state law, but for federal authority. A writer for the *Republican and Savannah Evening Ledger* attested, "We believe it not in the power of the [state] executive to grant indulgence in such cases, the admission of people of colour from abroad, being now prohibited by the constitution of the United States."[32] Interestingly, the 1807 federal law was referenced to justify the exclusion of foreign slaves *and* free people of color. In 1803 Congress had passed a bill that forbade the entry of any foreign people of color to states where they were already refused admittance.[33] Rather than cite this 1803 legislation, though, authorities in Georgia linked their exclusion of Saint-Dominguan free people of color to the ban on the imporation of foreign slaves. These Georgians imbued the 1807 law with wider powers than it held, seeing it as a new means for bolstering state measures.

According to one New York newspaper, Savannah officials merely allowed the vessel in question to restock its supplies and then sent it on its way with the slaves still on board. However, local records and newspaper accounts indicate that authorities in Savannah pursued the case further.[34] Militia officers took the Saint-Dominguan slaves and free people of color into custody and, after justices investigated the case, city officials demanded that the ship's owners cover the expense of holding and eventually transporting the detainees out of the state. The district attorney for Georgia, William B. Bulloch, prosecuted the captain and owners of the *Nancy White* for the illegal importation of slaves. All property on board the ship was seized, including the slaves, and those with interest in the vessel and its cargo were required to attend a special court of admiralty.[35]

Georgia's neighbor to the east applied the 1807 law to Saint-Dominguans with rigor as well. In May 1809 the governor of South Carolina issued an executive order in which he acknowledged that several foreign slaves had been permitted to land in the state "contrary to law," but "from principles of compassion to the distressed owners, orders have not been given to prosecute for the same." As was true in the 1790s, sympathy for slaveowners prompted officials to turn a blind eye, yet the governor warned ship captains not to expect "similar indulgences" in the future, since such leniency would lead to "extensive abuses and ultimately be of injurious nature."[36] Coming from the only state that had permitted the foreign slave trade until the day before its federal abolition, this commitment to enforcing the law of 1807 shows that white South Carolinians saw the enslaved refugees (unlike the approximately forty thousand Africans they had imported between 1803 and 1807) as a distinctly undesirable population, and this undesirability stemmed from the exiles' ties to the Haitian Revolution.[37]

As white refugees started to arrive in Norfolk, Virginia, in the late spring of 1809, officials were unsure how to proceed within state and federal laws. In keeping with the rhetoric of the 1790s, some white Virginians, like Governor John Tyler, reasoned that "the great laws of humanity and hospitality seemed to us superior to the rigid policy which forbids any slave to be brought into the United States; which policy could not embrace a subject so extraordinary and distressing." But white Virginians were unwilling to act on this impulse without direction from the federal government.[38] One example suggests that the abolition of the foreign slave trade encouraged retroactive action against resident enslaved Saint-Dominguans and their owners. In October 1809 a white refugee named Alexander Burot wrote to Thomas Jefferson complaining of harsh treatment at the hands of local officials. Burot had migrated to Virginia in 1796 with his wife, two children, and nine "negro and mulatto domestics, whom [he] chose from [his] plantations in Saint Domingue to serve his family." They bought and settled on a plantation in Chesterfield County, but on learning of the Leclerc expedition, Burot decided to try his luck again in the French colony, leaving his family behind. In 1803, after the failure of the French invasion, Burot left for Cuba, and then in 1809, he evacuated the island with the rest of the Saint-Dominguan exiles. When he returned to his plantation in Chesterfield, he was astonished to find "all my Negroes had been freed, my wife evicted from her plantation, having not been able to pay a mortgage in the absence of her laborers who had been freed, in a word, my family and myself reduced to beggary." He wanted to know why he was suddenly subject to "this law," which, as far as he knew, had not been enforced anywhere else in the state previously. By "this law" Burot most likely referred to a longstanding but much revised statute that prohibited bringing slaves into Virginia. In the 1790s the penalty for violation of the law had been freedom for the contraband slaves, but in 1806 the punishment had been changed to a fine and sale of the slaves to benefit the overseers of the poor. Burot questioned the law's application to Saint-Dominguan refugees, who, in his estimation, were "thrown into this hospitable land by infamous misfortunes" and hence deserved an exemption from the statute. While Jefferson's response is unknown, the case indicates that in the early 1800s white Virginians, like their Lowcountry counterparts, were reconsidering the consequences of black and colored Saint-Dominguans in their midst and taking more assertive measures to neutralize their impact, regardless of the cost to white exiles.[39]

In barring the entry of black and colored refugees in 1809, southern states were responding to fears that slave rebellion would be imported from Haiti. Whereas, a decade before, white Americans, even southerners, had set aside their reservations either in the name of "humanity" or out of self-interest, this became harder to do after Haitian independence. These qualms were key to the abolition of the slave trade. To be sure, part of the impetus behind the federal decision to end the foreign slave trade was the growing condemnation of the traffic in moral terms. Like their British contemporaries (who also instituted a ban in 1808), many Americans found the slave trade reprehensible, citing the kidnapping of Africans and the Middle Passage as evidence of its heinousness.[40] But in the wake of events in Saint-Domingue, many American (and British) observers saw slave importation as a threat to national and social self-preservation. The argument went that the greater the number of slaves introduced into an area, the more prone that place would be to rebellion. If the ratio of slave to free was grossly skewed in favor of the enslaved, then, the theory was, it was only a matter of time until slaves used the power of their numbers to rise up and overwhelm the master class. Additionally, the arrival of new slaves, unaccustomed to their status and disaffected, could excite discontent among resident bondsmen and encourage them to rebel. Caribbean slaves, in particular those from Saint-Domingue, were seen as tainted by their experiences during the Haitian Revolution and likely to bring insurrection to the United States. In the eyes of many white southerners, abolishing the foreign slave trade was critical to safeguarding American slavery.[41]

These points had been bandied about in the 1790s, but they became even clearer to white observers with the declaration of Haitian independence. Americans followed avidly the early moments of Haitian nationhood, especially the deeds and proclamations of its first leader, Jean-Jacques Dessalines. Reports characterized Dessalines—who eventually took the title "Emperor"—as "ferocious, ignorant, and savage"; and this savagery was, at least for white Americans, evident in his treatment of the white population.[42] Throughout 1804 newspapers listed the names and numbers of those slain at the hands of Dessalines's army and recounted episodes of violence in grisly detail: white residents "hacked down with swords and plunged with bayonets," bodies left to rot in city streets, Frenchmen of all ages and both sexes "held in the most abject slavery, . . . daily expire from hardship and fatigue," and so on.[43] One author avowed that Haiti was the site of "one of the most horrid acts which has occurred in modern times."[44] It was a world turned upside down, where, as Leonora Sansay put it, white Saint-Dominguans' "colour alone [was] deemed sufficient to make them hated and to devote them to destruction."[45] This, according to white observers, was reverse racism,

Dessalines from *Vida de J. J. Dessalines, gefe de los Negros de Santo Domingo* (Mexico, 1806). This plate is from a Mexican biography of Jean-Jacques Dessalines, but white Americans shared the view it expresses. Dessalines wields his sword in one hand and the severed head of a white woman in the other, making clear the upshot of Dessalines's reign—and of the Haitian Revolution more generally, in the mind of white audiences. The impression of Dessalines contrasts starkly with images of his predecessor, Toussaint Louverture. Courtesy John Carter Brown Library at Brown University.

whereby the regime, punishments, and pretexts for the enslavement of people of African descent were applied to the former master class.

The unnerving message resonated with white Americans. A writer to the New York *Bee* warned in the summer of 1804, "When we look into some parts of our own country, we are pained with the reflections which irresistibly strike the mind. O South Carolina! Heaven defend thee from all evil."[46] The author singled out South Carolina because of its continued participation in the slave trade, and in this reading, events in Haiti proved that South Carolina's slave masters were flirting with disaster by trafficking in foreign slaves. This interpretation sidestepped any consideration of the institution of slavery, but Dessalines refused to let white Americans evade the issue so easily. In a famous proclamation that was reprinted in U.S. newspapers, he justified the violence in Haiti with these stirring lines: "Yes, we have rendered to these true cannibals, war for war, crime for crime, outrage for outrage; Yes, I have saved my country; I have avenged America."[47] White Americans figured that the Haitian leader's desire for vengeance would lead him to seek retribution on other shores, and reports hinted that he intended to do just that. Rumors circulated that Dessalines's army pursued fleeing white residents to Cuba, intending to spark insurrection among the enslaved there, while in his own proclamations, Dessalines called on bondsmen in Martinique and elsewhere in the Caribbean to rise up and join his struggle.[48] Evidence intimated that the United States was not impervious to Dessalines's designs. Observing that "a great number of native blacks and men of color are suffering in the United States of America," Dessalines offered ship captains forty dollars for each black person given transportation to Haiti.[49] And it seemed that some African Americans were inspired by the news from the island. *The Spectator* in New York ran a letter addressed to Dessalines in which "An injured Man of Color" praised the general for his actions, which he hoped would "prove to your enemies and to the world, that an attempt to subvert your independence, and enslave your fellow-citizens, will terminate in the disgrace and ruin of your adversaries—and that a united and valiant people, who are fully sensible of their right to the blessings of liberty, are an unconquerable bulwark against an empire of treachery, violence and unrelenting ambition."[50] White Americans needed to create a bulwark to prevent another Haiti in their own backyard.

While there is no doubt that Dessalines's regime was marked by violence against the white population, accounts in the U.S. press relished this hostility, playing up its ferocity and cruelty to self-serving ends. In one of the few critiques from this period, the British activist James Stephen, in his 1804 work *The Opportunity*, noted that Americans were unreliable in their reports about the final days of the Haitian Revolution and the early era of the country's independence—even more so than were the French (a damning indictment, indeed, from an Englishman). According to Stephen, this flagrant misrepresentation could be chalked up to two reasons: first, the "apprehension of slave owners, that the state [of slavery] will be wholly abolished"; and second, the greed of American merchants who "spread false . . . highly exaggerated accounts of horrors supposed to have been witnessed by them in St. Domingo . . . to deter other merchants from sending cargoes to the same port to which they themselves have been recently trading, or to which they mean to return." In Stephen's view, slave masters and merchants spun news about Dessalines's regime to suit their base interests.[51]

Skeptical voices like Stephen's were rare, however, and the ghastly images persisted and were renewed for white audiences with works about the Haitian Revolution (such as Sansay's) in subsequent years. Although Dessalines's regime fell in October 1808, the negative depictions of Haiti from this era became emblematic—even making their way into school texts.[52] Importantly for the white refugees of 1809, these narratives were fodder for white Americans' sympathy, yet these tales also led to a way of seeing the consequences of the Haitian Revolution that made the entry of vast numbers of black and colored refugees untenable. The self-preservationist impulses behind the abolition of the slave trade, combined with the moral rhetoric enforced in the North, discouraged Saint-Dominguan exiles from Cuba from settling in the Atlantic states. Free people of color and white exiles who wanted to keep their slaves had to look elsewhere for refuge. In the words of one Saint-Dominguan, had it not been for his bondsmen, he would have chosen Charleston. Instead he ended up in Louisiana, which, he lamented, was "the most wretched country known to man."[53] His view of the territory was shared, not only by some fellow exiles, but also by large swaths of the American population. While Jefferson and his followers lauded the acquisition of the Orleans Territory as a great achievement that would secure the future of the republic, others were not so sure. Since its purchase six years earlier, the region and its resident populations had proved unwieldy and controversial, and the refugees had the potential to exacerbate rather than ameliorate this discord.

TERRITORIAL TROUBLES

A few years before the refugees' arrival in 1809, American authorities worried about the weak hold that the United States had on Louisiana, and one solution was to promote migration into the region in order to secure U.S. sovereignty and to start turning a profit. On the face of it, an influx of almost ten thousand Saint-

Dominguans would seem to offer a quick fix to this problem, particularly in light of their economic accomplishments in Cuba; but their presence gave U.S. officials pause, for in the eyes of many Americans, the Saint-Dominguans were not desirable migrants. The Louisiana Purchase was a keystone in Jefferson's "empire for liberty," which would be held together by likeminded republicans (preferably white freeholding farmers and planters) whose interests, sensibilities, and virtues corresponded to those of the union. Although this vision acknowledged the presence of slavery, it also argued that the territory would diffuse the practice into oblivion as slaves were spread ever more thinly across the vast expanse. This notion of decentralized empire relied on homogeneity in the character of citizens to sustain it, and, in the view of both advocates and detractors of this scheme, Louisiana was already wanting in this respect.[54] It harbored a white French population who chafed at American rule, a prominent class of free people of color who sought to assert their rights, and slaves who, if recent events were any indication, roiled with discontent. With their Franco-Caribbean and revolutionary background as well as their multiracial profile, the refugees threatened to make Louisiana even more intractable and to subvert American endeavors in the area altogether.

The huge influx of Saint-Dominguans to New Orleans in 1809 was a novelty, not just from an American perspective, but from that of the locals as well. During the Haitian Revolution, Louisiana had not been favored as a destination for exiles because it was considered, at that point, too far away from Saint-Domingue, and because it was under Spanish rule. Only about 1,100 refugees made their way into the territory between 1791 and 1804. By 1809, however, many white Saint-Dominguans had resigned themselves to the loss of Saint-Domingue; and as a place to resettle permanently, Louisiana offered several benefits. Some exiles had connections to the area, many of which had been established through trade. While eighteenth-century Louisiana did not yield the tropical products that France craved, the region had provided Saint-Domingue with a crucial commodity: lumber. Louisiana supplied the boards and beams that built everything from houses to sugar casks. When France ceded Louisiana to Spain in 1762, Spanish authorities disrupted trade with the French colony, but by the 1770s they were encouraging exchange. Trade ebbed and flowed with the tides of war, depending on whether France and Spain were allies or enemies; nevertheless, ties persisted that refugees took advantage of when they arrived.[55]

In addition, despite four decades of Spanish presence and heavy American immigration on the heels of the Louisiana Purchase, New Orleans remained culturally familiar to Saint-Dominguans. Spain had exerted its influence institutionally, introducing new military and judicial structures, but by and large the Spanish colonial regime tried to appeal to rather than shun the French population. As a result, Louisiana in 1809 bore the unmistakable signs of French influence in its language, mores, and overall disposition. Pierre Collette, a self-described "poor colonist," explained his preference for the Louisiana territory over Cuba: "First of all, they [the Louisianans] speak the same language. . . . Moreover, one finds there the same habits, as well as Frenchmen who . . . share more or less the same culture."[56] Refugees complained that the level of cultural sophistication of New Orleans did not match that of Cap Français: the Crescent City lacked the theaters, scientific societies, and other arenas of civility and education for which Le Cap was famous. New Orleans had a rougher quality, but the refugees felt that its largely Francophone population (unlike that of Santiago de Cuba) was poised to appreciate the refinement tendered by Saint-Dominguans.

As in Saint-Domingue, however, the Frenchness of Louisiana reflected a colonial character, and this was most starkly seen in its demography. Like the port towns of Cap Français and Port-au Prince, and unlike most American cities along the East Coast, New Orleans was a tri-caste society, and the incoming refugees reinforced this order. Of the 9,059 emigrants who disembarked between May 1809 and January of the following year, only 2,731 (much to territorial officials' chagrin) were white colonists, and there were 3,102 free people of color and 3,226 slaves. The local New Orleans free people of color, in particular, benefited from the migration; with the arrival of the exiles, their population more than doubled, fortifying the community most under threat of being overwhelmed by American migrants.[57]

While the exiles found much about New Orleans familiar, American officials saw the very sources of this similitude—cultural and social parity with French colonialism—as some of the most stubborn obstacles stymieing the integration of the territory into the United States. Whereas Cuban authorities initially welcomed the Saint-Dominguans with an eye to fostering economic and social progress, white Americans questioned whether the refugees would bring the appropriate type of advancement to the area, for the demographic distribution of the exiles bolstered the very sectors of Louisiana society that U.S. officials deemed troublesome, if not dangerous. Well before the exiles disembarked, authorities had surveyed the inhabitants of the United States' latest possession and come to the conclusion that the slaves were among the most problematic. In Louisiana, under Spanish rule between 1769 and 1803, slavery had developed differently than in the eastern states. The disparities resulted from the respective material conditions of the areas and because the legal culture of Spanish slavery contrasted conspicuously with its American counterpart. Spanish law granted and guaranteed to slaves certain rights that U.S. and French legal systems did not; for example, a slave could petition authorities about mistreatment as well as demand that an owner set a price for a slave so that the slave could purchase his or her freedom. By the end of the Spanish period, almost 1,500 people in bondage had been awarded their liberty through cash payments—an impressive figure given that in 1806 the New Orleans slave population totaled about 8,000.[58]

Even with these mollifying provisions, slavery in Spanish-era Louisiana was no less brutal than it was in other areas of the Atlantic world, and bondsmen lashed out at the system. This, too, was cause for concern for the new U.S. administration. During 1795 and 1796 alone, white Louisianans uncovered at least four slave conspiracies. Like Americans on the East Coast, white residents in the territory attributed the insurrectionary activity to the influence of the Haitian Revolution; and as a result, they prohibited the importation of foreign, specifically Saint-Dominguan, slaves.[59] In fact, Louisiana had a long history of wariness toward slaves from the French West Indian colony. As early as 1763, a decree barred the entry of black Saint-Dominguans because "Negro poisoners" were allegedly rampant on the island. The Spanish strengthened these bans as word about new plots spread, and in the 1790s white Louisianans pressed for additional safeguards because of the revolutions in France and Saint-Domingue. In 1796 authorities outlawed the foreign slave trade altogether, yet at the turn of the century, revitalized agricultural prospects convinced lawmakers to reconsider this decision.[60] The Spanish Cabildo voted, by a narrow margin, to reopen the trade in 1800, but they continued to exclude Saint-Dominguan slaves, and this prohibition persisted after the retrocession of Louisiana to France. In 1803 the leading French official in the area, Pierre Clément de Laussat, commented: "The colony is quiet. Greedy types have tried to introduce here Negroes from Saint-Domingue. I have formal orders to oppose this with the utmost vigilance."[61] Even the voracious desire for slaves could not persuade the French to permit the entry of those they deemed incendiary. Concern about the importation of slave rebellion to Louisiana grew after Haiti declared independence in 1804. White residents of New Orleans complained about the presence of black Saint-Dominguans with their "torches still smoking" and their bodies "still smeared with the blood of our unhappy compatriots [white Saint-Dominguans]."[62] The "horrors of St. Domingo" were fresh in the minds of white Louisianans of every heritage, and the entry of more than 3,000 slaves in 1809 from the site of this revolution promised to heighten these fears.

The large and outspoken free colored population in Louisiana further impeded white Americans' attempts to master the area's enslaved. As scholars have repeatedly pointed out, free people of color undercut the neat correlation between white and free, black and enslaved, jeopardizing the racist underpinnings of U.S. slave society. Officials wrestled with ways to rein in the influence of free people of color in Louisiana, for they enjoyed privileges unthinkable in the eastern United States. The participation of free people of color in the militia especially bothered territorial authorities. As General James Wilkinson, the commander of the nation's western army, wrote to his superiors in Washington in 1803, "the formidable aspect of the armed Blacks & Malattoes, officered and organized, is painful and perplexing."[63] The Haitian Revolution had demonstrated the risks to the white master class of a fighting force of black and colored men. It seemed to some observers that the danger had already been borne out in Louisiana, for several free people of color in New Orleans had been linked to slave conspiracies during the 1790s, and rumors circulated that there were plans for similar cooperative actions when Americans took over the territory.[64]

In the early years of U.S. control, territorial legislators passed laws designed to check the free black and colored population. These measures included laws common in some eastern states, such as exacting weekly fees from free black migrants, requiring residency permits, and prohibiting interracial marriage.[65] Often, historians interpret these laws as the imposition of an American racist regime on Louisiana, and this is to some extent true; yet these measures were enacted by the territorial legislature, a body not exclusively made up of Americans. During the colonial era, white French residents of Louisiana had complained to Spanish authorities about the slackness of laws regarding free people of color and slaves. The new U.S. administration provided the opportunity, not necessarily the impulse, to pursue more restrictive measures.[66]

These laws to curb the disruptive power of free men of color have also been attributed to the white backlash against the Haitian Revolution. Examples suggest, however, that American authorities were sometimes conciliatory, rather than hostile, in their relations with free people of color precisely *because of* the lessons of Saint-Domingue. For instance, in 1804 when a free man of color in New Orleans organized his contemporaries to petition Congress for rights as citizens, the governor of Louisiana chose, against the counsel of New Orleans municipal leaders, not to prosecute the man. The governor explained to Secretary of State James Madison, "I remembered that the events which have Spread blood and desolation in St. Domingo, originated in a dispute between the white and Mulatto inhabitants, and that the too rigid treatment of the former, induced the Latter to seek the support & assistance of the Negroes."[67] Afraid of fostering a dangerous alliance between enslaved and free colored residents *à la* Saint-Domingue, the governor chose not to bring legal action against the organizer of the petition, in the hope of maintaining the delicate social balance.

Even in occasional moments of leniency, Louisiana's leaders (French and American alike) agreed that one of the best ways to avoid the "horrors of St. Domingo" was to prevent the migration of free men of color into the territory. In 1806 the first Louisiana legislature prohibited the entry of French West Indian men of color, with specific reference to those from Saint-Domingue. The following year, representatives passed a more comprehensive measure that barred any free black or colored man from entering the territory. A person found in violation of the law was fined and warned out, and if he failed to pay and leave, he was then jailed and indentured, to recoup the initial fee and the court costs. Gaps in the local records prevent determination of whether the law was strictly enforced, but it is clear that the Saint-Dominguan free people of color tested white Louisianans' commitment to the exclusionary act.[68] The migration of 1809 presented the logistical problem of denying thousands of free people of color entry at the same time. How could a small cadre of officials block so many people? Moreover, the free colored Saint-Dominguans were, in general, richer, more powerful, and had more political and military experience than their New Orleans counterparts; if mismanaged by American authorities, this group could translate their dissatisfaction into armed resistance that would spread to slaves. This interpretation assumed an affinity between enslaved and free people of color—an empathy that was not necessarily present. After all, some colored exiles, like white Saint-Dominguans, had fled the Haitian Revolution and all that it represented.[69] Nevertheless, the mere suggestion of a possible alliance with local enslaved and free colored people was enough to put the U.S. administration on its guard.

Perhaps Americans would have felt more confident in their control over the resident enslaved and free colored populations had they been more comfortable with the white ruling class in Louisiana, but here, too, officials faced a disparate, and in their view unstable, group. Wrote one administrator, "Make a tour throughout that city, and in every street you will encounter native Americans, native Louisianians, Frenchmen, Spaniards, Englishmen, Germans, Italians &ᶜ &ᶜ."[70] Such diversity was evident in some East Coast cities as well, but in New Orleans this variety was seen as hindering the establishment of U.S. government. Residents preferred their "ancient laws and usages" to American ones, and U.S. officials worried that some of the "foreigners" in the territory might serve as agents for their home countries.[71] The region did have a history of international intrigue: the 1790s were marked by rumors that French revolutionaries planned to take over the area, fears that Spain was persuading Tennessee and Kentucky to secede from the United States, and incessant badgering by Britain and its Indian allies. America's relationship with France was most unstable, oscillating as it did between celebrations of mutual republicanism and quasi war. Although this ardor (in both love and hate) had cooled during the Napoleonic era, Americans remained suspicious of French designs. They were concerned that Frenchmen in Louisiana might seek to subvert U.S. authority in the region—with or without the aid of the metropole—and that the white Saint-Dominguan exiles, with their concrete and cultural ties to the French locals, might abet these plans.

Officials deemed almost every sector of the extant population of Louisiana untrustworthy, and authorities struggled to find a means to bring them all successfully (and peacefully) under American control. According to some observers, the surest cure to the ills that plagued the territory was migration; but in the view of statistician and slavery opponent Samuel Blodgett, only "useful emigration" into the territory would secure it from foreign invasion and slave rebellion. By "useful," Blodgett meant white settlers who would establish farms and exert a stronger white presence in the region. Contemporaries credited the "rapid emigration from the different states, and also from Europe" with having turned Ohio from a "wilderness into a *fruitful field*"; and, following Jefferson's vision, many onlookers hoped for the same success in Louisiana.[72] Despite the economic achievements some of them had known in the Caribbean, the Saint-Dominguans failed to fit this model, given their multiracial, Francophone, and revolutionary background, but so, too, did most of the white Americans who had migrated to the region in the early years of its acquisition.[73] Officials grumbled constantly about the dubious agendas of relocating easterners, whose escapades attracted national attention. The Louisiana Purchase had been touted as the future of the republic, and Congress had taken a tremendous chance (and elicited a good bit of criticism) when it appropriated an enormous sum to fund this venture. Americans of all stripes—doubters, devotees, and potential migrants to the region, among others—were curious to see how this future was unfolding, and very quickly the Orleans Territory had earned a reputation as a breeding ground for scandal.

The year 1809 was an especially fertile one for corruption. The Burr conspiracy had been exposed in 1806, and its ramifications were still being felt when the refugees arrived. What exactly Aaron Burr planned as he lit out west in 1805 remains unclear: some speculated that he intended to foment secession of the area from the United States, and others hypothesized that he wanted to invade

Mexico. Even his web of contacts (including Sansay, who couriered messages for him) was unsure what was afoot.[74] Whatever the goal, Burr's western adventure was a fiasco for the Jefferson administration: as if killing (and martyring) Alexander Hamilton in 1804 was not enough, the former vice president was possibly plotting to sabotage the young republic. Finally chased down in 1807, Sansay's lover was brought up on charges of treason. Although he was acquitted and shortly thereafter ran away to Europe, observers continued to invoke his name any time they caught wind of scandal in Louisiana. The governor complained about "a faction in New Orleans, (the remnants of Burrism) whose sole object is, to embarrass the administration, & to excite discontent," mainly through their "libellous publications."[75] The decision to send General James Wilkinson to the territory in 1809 provoked additional controversy along these lines. Wilkinson had been one of Burr's confidantes, and while a federal inquiry had exonerated him of all charges in 1808, some still maintained that he was "the soul of the conspiracy." When Wilkinson returned to New Orleans, the press once more rehashed his relationship with Burr.[76] Scandal dogged other appointees as well. In the winter of 1809, the New Orleans port collector purportedly absconded with over $100,000 of public funds.[77] At the moment when the exiles disembarked, the area seemed plagued by vice and intrigue.

In part, these reports from and about Orleans Territory were influenced by a resurgence in party politics around 1809. The Federalists had suffered a crushing defeat with Jefferson's election in 1800, yet in 1808 his party, now known simply as Republicans, came under fire when the embargo of the previous year crippled the national economy. Garnering support from people unhappy with the president's economic policies, the Federalists attacked the Republican administration without mercy, and they played up the debacles in Louisiana as more proof of the ineptitude of Jefferson's government. Occasionally, party labels were directly connected to notorious incidents in Louisiana. In the case of the port collector, the *Baltimore Whig* claimed that he was a Federalist while the *Massachusetts Spy*, a Federalist mouthpiece, affirmed that he was "a true Jeffersonian Jacobin."[78] But the controversies in the Orleans Territory were not simply used as pawns in a political chess game between party operatives. Problems in Louisiana carried national import because their resolution often fell under the purview of the federal government. Congress limited the powers of territorial legislatures during this era in an effort to usher new areas into statehood gradually. Such precedents had been in place since the 1780s, when Congress outlined the procedure for incorporating the Northwest Territory, yet Louisiana presented a unique problem.

Unlike in other regions slated for integration, residents of Orleans Territory were accustomed to civil (either French or Spanish), not common, law, which presented concerns in the early days of American control.[79]

Several legal issues came up for debate in the first years of American governance, but the question of whether to admit the Saint-Dominguan refugees was one of the most controversial. Not only did the exiles, with their French affiliations, have the potential to bolster the civil law proponents in the resident population, but the migration of foreign slaves and free people of color challenged extant federal and territorial laws. However, there is a difference between law and its enforcement, and in 1809 the federal administration, knee-deep in a political quagmire, searched for a compromise that would appease all involved. This was no easy feat, given the antagonistic local population with its divergent agendas. Perhaps more troubling, the one point of consensus between the French and American master classes—that the presence of free people of color and slaves from Saint-Domingue in the territory should be checked—gave way because of the 1809 migration. French residents pressed the governor to permit their entry, while most white American locals used the language of self-preservation to oppose the disembarkation. Crossing either population could have severe consequences, and in navigating these treacherous political waters, the governor had to go it alone, receiving no direction from Congress (the ultimate arbiter of the affair) until after circumstances had forced his hand.

RESOLVING THE REFUGEE CRISIS

Governor William Claiborne found himself in the proverbial hot seat over the admission of Saint-Dominguan refugees. A lawyer from Virginia and a loyal Republican, Claiborne had some experience in government before his posting to the Orleans Territory. He had served in Congress as a representative from Tennessee for two terms and as the governor of the Mississippi Territory from 1801 to 1803. Jefferson initially saw Claiborne, despite his credentials, as a temporary solution to the need for American leadership in Louisiana. The president had hoped to convince someone with a French background (he was keen on the Marquis de Lafayette)—or at least with knowledge of the language (such as James Monroe)—to take the governorship; but his preferred choices had fallen through, and Claiborne, who spoke neither French nor Spanish, received the gubernatorial appointment.[80]

Well before the refugees pulled into New Orleans harbor in 1809, Claiborne's administration had been having a difficult time reining in the local population. Like the Spanish before him, Claiborne adopted a conciliatory stance toward the white Francophone community, trying to persuade them through good will to embrace, or at least grudgingly submit to, U.S. rule; but he faced a French resentment toward Americans that predated the Louisiana Purchase. As early as the 1780s, Spanish authorities detected an almost rabid desire among Americans to press west across the continent. In the words of one official, "their method of spreading themselves and their policy are so much to be feared by Spain as are their arms," and no doubt, French locals in Louisiana shared the Spanish authorities' worries that Americans would overrun their land and lives. In an attempt to overcome decades of suspicion, Claiborne honored residents' land claims and appointed several prominent Frenchmen to important posts. These overtures, however, could not cloak the drastic and threatening changes—legal, political, demographic, cultural, social—that the U.S. takeover heralded.[81] In the early years of American rule, white French locals were far from satisfied.

Incoming white Americans were none too pleased either. Newly arrived easterners on both sides of the political fence protested territorial policies, especially what detractors saw as Claiborne's French favoritism.[82] His critics averred that the governor, "doubtless with a view of showing the wisdom and popularity of his administration," had "grossly misrepresented the disaffection of the people of this country" in his communications with authorities in Washington. From their perspective, the French residents of Louisiana were not friendly to the U.S. government, as Claiborne insisted; rather they were on the verge of rebelling against the imposition of American laws and customs. Claiborne's detractors were irked that Frenchmen received coveted civilian and military posts, thereby infecting the American government, so they contended, with French ways.[83]

The arrival of the Saint-Dominguan refugees fueled the acrimony between local Frenchmen and Americans, and both pressed their claims on Claiborne. Most of the debates took place in New Orleans's lively print culture. Several newspapers (some published in both English and French, and a few, incidentally, established by Saint-Dominguan exiles in the 1790s) thrived, and each editor staked out a stance in local politics. The *Moniteur* and the *Louisiana Courier* generally supported the governor, while the *Orleans Gazette*, the *Louisiana Gazette*, and the *Lanterne Majicale* were the vehicles for the most severe criticism of Claiborne's administration, even though among these last three newspapers, the first sympathized with the Republicans, the second with the Federalists, and the third with France.[84] Newspapers along the East Coast also picked up reports, as Louisiana residents, frustrated with Claiborne's response, appealed to a national forum to air their views.

The crisis began in May 1809. At that point, only forty refugees had reached New Orleans but the governor anticipated many more. He shared privately with the secretary of state his reservations about the character of the migrants: "I fear there will also be many, who can alone be ranked among the worthless class of community. Of that class, New Orleans had already its full complement."[85] Claiborne's worries were dispelled for the moment by reports that the white exiles were "industrious planters and mechanics."[86] Not all New Orleans residents were as confident as Claiborne in the industry of the exiles. Opponents of their immigration highlighted the destitution of the Saint-Dominguans and the ensuing hardship they spelled for the community at large, which would have to foot the bill for their sustenance. Sensitive to this concern, Claiborne staggered the refugees' disembarkations.[87] For their part, local Frenchmen solicited subscriptions of support, and by August they had collected $5,000 and launched a second campaign. The relief committee worked to find employment for incoming refugees, and several planters offered to lease land to exiles in exchange for improvements.[88] Their efforts on behalf of their Saint-Dominguan peers not only eased the refugees' transition to life in New Orleans but checked a line of protest from white Americans.

The entrance of white refugees was legal, and so, try as they might, white Americans could make only limited objections to their arrival. The real controversy emerged over the exiled slaves and free people of color. Given their approaches to Saint-Dominguan bondsmen in the recent past, New Orleans's white residents seemed committed to barring this population, but French Louisianans overcame their misgivings when faced with black Saint-Dominguans in 1809. French locals came to the (as it turned out, correct) conclusion that the white exiles would stay in Louisiana only if their slaves were allowed entry and remained enslaved. In their view, the benefits of the white refugees' presence outweighed the risks: they were more concerned about being overwhelmed by white Americans than by rebellious slaves. To this end, as white refugees petitioned territorial and federal authorities, several French-language newspapers ran articles throughout the month of May that supported an exemption from the federal slave trade law.[89] Advocates for the exiles contended that the law did not apply to the Saint-Dominguans—that it was subordinate to "divine law, the law of humanity [that] dictates to us the duty not to repulse these unfortunates from our shores."[90] The "law of humanity" had been cited to endorse the ban on foreign slaves, but the refugees' supporters appealed to universal sympathy in hopes of exempting Saint-

Dominguans from the federal law. In the latter interpretation of the two groups' plights, the masters were suffering more than their slaves.

Despite the persistent lobbying of the white French community, Governor Claiborne was not initially swayed. When the refugees first appeared in New Orleans harbor, his actions resembled those of officials in Georgia and South Carolina: slaves and free people of color had to remain on board. White exiles protested the arrangement as soon as they set foot on shore. Claiborne wrote, in a letter marked "private" to Julien Poydras, the territory's delegate to the U.S. House of Representatives, "I am assailed every day with entreaties to interfere in their favour; A Father of a family will assure me, that one & sometimes two or three faithful slaves constitute his only means of support — & a Lady will pray me to have pity on her Infant Child whose nurse is not permitted to leave the Vessel." As they had in the 1790s, the white exiles emphasized the loyalty of their slaves (in contrast to the image of black Saint-Dominguans as bloodthirsty rebels), and argued, as did resident Frenchmen, for the necessity of their slaves to their survival. These testimonies may have alleviated Claiborne's concerns about the character of the incoming slaves; nevertheless he lacked the authority to make an outright exemption to the law. As he put it, "Congress can alone give them relief, as related to their slaves."[91]

By June, Claiborne had still not received guidance from his federal superiors, and the pressure proved too great. Ships filled with slaves and free people of color clogged the harbor, while the white refugees, who Claiborne thought would disperse quickly into the countryside, refused to leave New Orleans without their slaves. He started releasing exiled bondsmen to their masters as long as the owners posted bonds and promised to turn their slaves over to authorities if so demanded.[92] Not all white refugees could afford the fees, so the charity campaign, supported mostly by local white Frenchmen, fronted them the money.[93] The governor also decided to permit the entry of the free people of color, but he ordered males over the age of fifteen post bond and prepare to leave the territory. Although Claiborne did not explain the motivations behind this decision, circumstances in New Orleans offer a few plausible reasons. Perhaps local free people of color urged the governor to allow colored Saint-Dominguans to disembark. Like their white, French-speaking counterparts in New Orleans, resident free people of color welcomed the colored exiles as a way to boost their numbers among the increasingly Anglicized population. Claiborne's acquiescence may have been in service of his attempts to avoid "too rigid treatment" of the free colored community of New Orleans. In addition, some of the colored women and children (who made up a significant proportion of the incoming colored exiles) were partners or offspring of white refugees, who would have advocated authorization for their family members to enter the city. The fact that Claiborne warned out only the men of color reveals his sensitivity to this possibility.

As the summer continued, so, too, did the arrival of refugees. What Claiborne hoped would be a lone episode developed into a steady stream of migrants. In his July 1809 report on the exiles, Mayor James Mather tried to assuage Claiborne's anticipated "astonishment." He stressed that the size of the slave population was not a result of Claiborne's indulgent policy but of the "great mass of the french population" fleeing Cuba.[94] (The declaration of the bitter Frenchman who could not get his slaves into Charleston and so went to New Orleans suggests the contrary.) Mather did state that he was having little success enforcing Claiborne's order regarding free men of color. Only 64 of a total of 271 men had come forward to post bond, and the mayor admitted that he knew of few who had left the territory. The administration simply lacked the wherewithal to enforce its policies, yet Mather attempted to reassure the governor: "I have however reason to believe that several of them have sailed for the Atlantic States, and that others will endeavor to return to St. Domingo if they find a chance to do it."[95] On what this belief was based, he failed to elaborate.

Mather's optimism did not persuade Claiborne, and he looked for ways to minimize the exiles' impact. In August 1809 Claiborne sought to curtail the tide of refugees at the source by writing to Maurice Rogers, the U.S. consul in Santiago de Cuba. Griping about the burdens Louisiana citizens suffered because of the exiles, he asked Rogers to advise Saint-Dominguans "to seek an Asylum in some other District of the U. States." The governor singled out free people of color for special discouragement: "We have already a much greater proportion of that population, than comports with the general Interest."[96] Claiborne sent similar letters to contacts in Jamaica and Santo Domingo, trying to divert the refugees' course before it even began.[97] In light of the policies regarding slaves and free people of color elsewhere in the United States, it seemed wishful thinking that refugees would divert their path, especially as word of Claiborne's exemption circulated throughout the Caribbean.

Perhaps realizing the futility of his requests, the governor tried to transform the refugees—at least rhetorically—into migrants who were well-suited to the needs of the area. In particular he encouraged them to disperse throughout the surrounding countryside, which, in Claiborne's view, would be beneficial in two respects. First, the white exiles and their slaves would cultivate the land; in a petition to President James Madison for permission to disembark their slaves in New Orleans, the white refugees had made this argument themselves, by expressing their willingness to "occupy uncultivated lands" and presumably transform them, with the labor of their slaves, into valuable plantations.[98] Although this strategy did not follow the yeoman model that Jefferson had envisioned, it did reflect more accurately what was already occurring on the ground in the territory. Between 1807 and 1812, public land sales favored wealthy planters rather than small farmers, as the government sought to generate revenue. To Congressmen, it seemed only logical that the very acquisition that had deepened the national debt should help to pay for that debt's alleviation. But as affluent eastern planters scooped up more and more land, it became clear that plantation agriculture, specifically cotton and sugar, with all of the trappings that accompanied it, would dictate the economy and society of the Deep South.[99] The Saint-Dominguans are frequently credited with developing the sugar industry in Louisiana, but historians have shown that the exiles' impact on agriculture was less dramatic than previously assumed. As early as 1803, southern Louisiana annually yielded 4.5 million pounds of sugar, valued at $750,000.[100] Nevertheless, the experienced refugees could contribute to the growth of large-scale plantation agriculture in the area.

Second, the governor thought that the Saint-Dominguans' dispersal into the interior of the territory would neutralize the threat of slave rebellion. Some commentators reasoned that the expansion of slavery into the west would distribute slaves over a greater area, thinning out their numbers until they became insignificant. With slaves scattered across the vast territory (rather than concentrated in a small area like the city of New Orleans), the likelihood of insurrection would diminish, they concluded.[101] This logic rested on the dubious assumptions that the slave population would not increase significantly and that the white population would. However, in the late summer of 1809, Claiborne asked Mather to assess the possibility of the refugees' settlement in rural areas, and this time, Mather's report was not so positive. The mayor enumerated several obstacles that hindered the Saint-Dominguans' migration inland. Many lacked the resources to purchase plantations, and unless the government acted swiftly to offer exiles land at advantageous prices, Mather argued, another impediment—the approaching winter—would keep the refugees in New Orleans until the spring. Also, since Saint-Dominguan masters were obligated to turn over their bondsmen if the government required, Mather asked, "How can they under such circumstance consider any extensive plans of establishment?"[102] While Claiborne anticipated that the Saint-Dominguans would serve a similar function as they had in Cuba, he—unlike Cuban officials—was not yet ready to appropriate funds to promote that transformation. He trusted that permitting entry to enslaved exiles would be enough assistance.

Disappointed in how the situation was unfolding, Claiborne banked on the prospect that some refugees had no intention of staying in Louisiana but would seek permanent refuge elsewhere or return to the Caribbean. Here again, Claiborne's hopes were foiled—this time by the Non-Intercourse Act of 1809, which forbade American ships from directly entering French territories and, therefore, impeded a potential mass exodus of exiles. A few refugees made the attempt. One group of exiles requested permission from President James Madison to leave for Nantes or Bordeaux, and in March 1810 thirty-four people, "whereof more than one half are men of Color," sought passage to St. Bartholomew because "they could find in [Louisiana] no means to subsist."[103] Other exiles considered resuming their lives in Cuba once the Napoleonic Wars blew over, while some dreamed of returning to Saint-Domingue. In 1812 an observer in New Orleans described the refugees as those who "await here the circumstances that will permit them to return to Saint-Domingue."[104] Well into the 1810s, several white exiles continued to list their holdings in the former colony, anticipating the moment "when the French [would] regain their property" there.[105]

Few of these schemes came to pass, and most refugees remained in the Orleans Territory—more than Claiborne had expected. Writing to an associate in Washington, D.C., he mulled over his decision: "As relates to the slaves, I am not certain, that I took the correct course; . . . I had alone to consult my own discretion, for neither the Laws of the United States, or of the Territory had made express provision on this point." Claiborne rehearsed the logic behind his choice: the territorial government could not bear the expense of either imprisoning the slaves or sending them out of the area. On the latter point, the governor pointed out that the Non-Intercourse Act and the recent wars made relocation to "a proper place" difficult, if not impossible. Lastly, Claiborne maintained that releasing the slaves to their owners spared city residents from supporting the newcomers.[106] Noticeably absent from Claiborne's list of considerations was concern over slave rebellion.

If Claiborne had doubts about the correctness of his actions, many Americans were openly critical. His policy on the Saint-Dominguan exiles was greeted with "more Newspaper abuse than I ever before experienced," he noted to a correspondent.[107] To American residents of New Orleans, his handling of the refugee influx represented another example of Claiborne's misguided, French-influenced policy, and his opponents denigrated the white exiles in articles published throughout the nation. The *Alexandria Gazette* in Virginia stated that "the whites have among them about a dozen respectable families; the remainder are privateersmen, with mulatto mistresses," while the *Connecticut Courant* claimed, "there are among them several of the most notorious cannibals of the revolution, the bloody co-adjutors of Robespierre."[108] Such reports cast aspersions on the moral and political make-up of the exiles, arguing that their values were anathema to those espoused by Americans. In the words of one critic, because of the governor's decision regarding the refugees, Louisiana bore "more the appearance of a *French colony* than an American territory" and, if the refugees' supposed plans were realized, would become a French dominion again. Tapping into apprehensions about the frail security of the Orleans Territory, detractors posited that the Saint-Dominguan exiles would join forces with Napoleon's "spies and agents" and take control of the area in the name of "their imperial master."[109]

The refugees did not treat derision lightly. According to James M. Bradford, the printer of the *Orleans Gazette* and a man strident in his contempt for the exiles, a group of emigrants barged into his office and demanded to know who had written disparaging articles about them. Bradford refused to name his source and threatened to use the law against the refugees: "They replied that they disregarded the law, and they would have satisfaction." For Bradford, the incident offered proof of the subversion of American liberties to French tyrannies; he wondered, "If the liberty of the press is to be regulated by St. Jago patriots, what has become of your boasted constitution?"[110] As he saw it, the refugees challenged the very bedrock of the nation and in so doing imperiled the republic.

Ultimately, critics blamed Claiborne for the situation. After all, they pointed out, he had led the way by disregarding U.S. law himself. How could the exiles help but follow in his footsteps? An inhabitant of New Orleans complained to the *Freeman's Journal*, "This motley collection has reached New-Orleans, and our *common father* has permitted them all to land, regardless of the law of the United States, prohibiting the importation of slaves, and the statute law of this territory, forbidding the landing of free negroes or people of color." The author went on to lambaste the governor for refusing to enforce American jurisprudence in favor of "the most odious features of the old Spanish system."[111] In his critics' view, Claiborne's decisions not only flew in the face of American law but also left New Orleans vulnerable to opportunists. In December 1809 the *New-York Evening Post* ran an article that pointed to the "evil . . . from shewing too much lenity." The paper reported that vessels in New Orleans harbor claimed falsely that their enslaved and colored passengers were from Saint-Domingue. Taking the moral high ground, the author concluded that "a trade is no doubt carried on this way—Slaves are purchased and covered as the property of the unfortunate French."[112] The exemption, the author implied, made a mockery of the American republic in principle and practice.

According to these critics, although Claiborne purported to act in the name of humanity, he compromised the humanitarian ideals that had motivated the abolition of the slave trade in the first place. Americans also again employed the language of self-preservation to convince officials to deny asylum to the refugees. They summoned the demeaning stereotypes of black and colored Saint-Dominguans that were typical of white accounts of the revolution and Haiti's early independence. Reports in East Coast newspapers attested that among the exiles was "a due proportion of negroes—St. Domingo blacks, some of whom acted a conspicuous part in the different massacres on the island."[113] The free colored Saint-Dominguans were accused of similar atrocities: they were "the refuse of St. Domingo," and "the bloody-thirsty miscreants, whose hands are yet red with the blood of their [the whites'] families."[114] Detractors implicated some white refugees in the events that shook Saint-Domingue, contending that they had abetted enslaved and free colored exiles. Back in 1805, a white exile known as Grand Jean had been arrested in Louisiana for plotting to incite insurrection among local slaves and free people of color; and with the migration of 1809, the governor's foes swore that residents would bear witness to more of these schemes.[115] In this scenario, all members of the incoming population—black, white, and colored—would wreak havoc on New Orleans. One author asked, "When the whole of these half starved, cutthroat robbers shall be landed, what security will there be for person or property in the Orleans territory?"[116] To add insult to injury, Claiborne's opponents insisted that his appointees had direct links to the Haitian Revolution. Monsieur Domereau, the parish judge of Point Coupée, was allegedly "an assassin of St Domingo," while Moreau de Lislet, the interpreter of the court, was "a great favorite of Toussaint in St. Domingo, and head of a free-mason lodge comprised of negroes" which, a report in a New York newspaper sarcastically remarked, "certainly ought to be a great recommendation to hold an office in a country where slavery is authorized."[117] To Claiborne's detractors, his exemption of the ban on black and colored immigrants was assisting a conspiracy to ruin Louisiana—to reproduce the "horrors of St. Domingo" on American soil.

In his public addresses Claiborne ignored all criticism based on the possible importation of slave rebellion. Instead he highlighted the benefits of his policy. Claiborne's decision to permit entry to the exiled slaves and free people of color was, as his critics asserted and he admitted, a political maneuver to gain the favor of the white Saint-Dominguans and French-speaking locals. In a speech to the Orleans legislature, Claiborne was adamant that, with the white refugees, "motives of gratitude (the strongest incentive to virtuous minds) must create an attachment for a country, that has so generally received them, and will also I trust, secure their fidelity to a government."[118] Permitting their slaves to land would cement the white Saint-Dominguans' loyalty—as well as that of local French-speaking residents—to his administration and by extension, to the United States. Economic motives also spurred Claiborne's decision. By renting out or selling their bondsmen, the white exiles could avoid burdening the community, for the French locals could provide support for so many for only so long. In his view his actions promoted stability in the territory.

Claiborne's authority, however, was not absolute in this regard, and his detractors knew it. By indicting the governor so forcefully and using the rationale for slave trade abolition to do so, they wanted to spur national relief from their perceived grievances. Such relief was not forthcoming, for the same month that the governor granted a dispensation to the refugees, Congress—unbeknownst to Claiborne—deliberated very briefly over an official exemption for the Saint-Dominguans. Application of the slave trade ban to the Saint-Dominguans should have been clear at the federal level; the refugees offended moral imperatives as well as jeopardized American security. But supporters of the exemption bill, while attesting to their abhorrence of the slave trade generally, pointed to the "singular circumstances" of this migration and played up the troubles of the white refugees: their traumatic experiences in Saint-Domingue and Cuba, their loss of property, and their limited options for asylum.[119] Tragic tales of displacement were rehearsed yet again in an effort to cast the white exiles as more worthy of sympathy than were forcibly enslaved and transported Africans. Other supporters, employing a line of reasoning similar to Claiborne's about slave dispersal, insisted that the bill was necessary to "get rid of the immense number of slaves brought into New Orleans." This argument treated the enslaved refugees' entrance as a *fait accompli* rather than as an issue up for debate, and yet the actual bill lacked a provision for moving the slaves out of New Orleans. As John Ross of Pennsylvania, the only outspoken opponent of the exemption on record, retorted, "it was strange that the House should have a bill before it contemplating the removal of a certain description of persons out of the country, when nothing of the kind appeared" within the bill.[120]

The logical gymnastics employed in favor of an exemption circumvented the real problem at hand: if Congress held the refugees accountable to the law, how would federal officials enforce it? During the debates over abolishing the foreign slave trade, representatives had divided sharply over how to implement the act. With other types of contraband, the federal government seized the goods and sold them for the profit of the U.S. Treasury. Some members of Congress balked at this approach to illegally imported slaves because the federal government would become, in essence, a slave broker.[121] As Timothy Pitkin, Jr., a representative from Connecticut, thundered on the floor of Congress, "Shall we, in a law made for the express purpose of preventing the slave trade, declare that these unfortunate blacks, brought into this country, not only against their own will, but against the express provisions of the law itself, shall be sold as slaves for the benefit of the United States, and the price of their slavery be lodged in the public coffers? I trust not."[122] Such a mode of enforcement was too hypocritical in the minds of too many representatives.

Congressmen discussed numerous other ways to carry out the ban. Options included sending the slaves back to Africa, indenturing them for life, freeing them altogether, and various combinations of these proposals.[123] Few, if any, approved of the emancipation of these contraband slaves; as Joseph Quincy of Masachusetts pointed out, "the policy of those [southern] States, the first duty of self-preservation, forbids it."[124] Northerners, too, worried about an influx of "vaga-bonds" to their states, who were "ignorant of our language, our climate, our laws, our character, and our manners."[125] Such persons had the potential to disrupt northern communities where the transition from slavery to freedom was an un-easy process.[126]

Barnabas Bidwell of Massachusetts tendered a compromise that relieved the federal government of responsibility. He recommended that each state determine how to implement the new law. Some congressmen objected to this plan because they saw it as a lost opportunity for the federal government to "civilize" incoming Africans.[127] But most representatives were not concerned with the "rehabilitation" of Africans; they simply did not want any more foreign black people introduced into American society. In the end Bidwell's bill passed, and the onus of enforce-ment fell on the individual states. Application of the law was inconsistent, in part because until about 1820 the federal government did not appropriate funds to assist states in enforcing the law. Also, no single branch of government coordi-nated the activities of the diverse actors involved—federal judges, marshals, and district attorneys, state and territorial authorities, private citizens, and the U.S. Navy, among others. The 1807 law did suggest penalties for violation, but at the state level actual punishments varied widely. For example, a federal judge in Maryland imposed a fine of $10 and one day in jail for a man convicted of partici-pating in the foreign slave trade—a small price indeed for a crime commonly seen as morally reprehensible and a threat to social stability.[128]

Congressional representatives realized that the case of the 1809 refugees in New Orleans could reopen the seemingly irreconcilable debates over enforcing the foreign slave trade ban. If U.S. authorities treated the Saint-Dominguan slaves as contraband—an option that had not been ruled out in the wording of the 1807 law—then the federal government would become a slave dealer, which was an outcome that Congress wanted to steer clear of. Alternatives to sale were implausible. Representatives could not free the slaves, in light of the "self-preservation" argument made by many states; and, as Claiborne pointed out, sending the Saint-Dominguan slaves elsewhere (if a destination could be decided upon) would be difficult because of the Non-Importation Act and the Napoleonic Wars. Perhaps establishing a system of indentures, as a kind of gradual manumission program, seemed too costly and cumbersome to organize and sustain. Maybe some congressmen, despite the protests of white Americans in New Orleans, were persuaded by the prediction of slave dispersal and its power to mitigate an explosive situation.

In the end, allusions to the "horrors of St. Domingo" failed to convince Congress to prevent thousands of black and colored refugees from entering the Orleans Territory. Concerns about involving the federal government in enforcing the slave trade ban prevailed over fears of a reoccurrence of the Haitian Revolution in the southern United States. Congressmen preferred to overlook the principles behind the law and to wrap up their involvement in the affair in the quickest way—whatever the consequences—to avoid confronting the federal commitment to ending the slave trade. In June 1809, Congress voted almost unanimously to exempt the Saint-Dominguans from the slave trade ban. The federal decision bolstered Claiborne's response at the local level. He, too, had set aside qualms about slave rebellion, in his case in an effort to shore up political support among a disparate and disaffected local population. In his mind they were potentially more dangerous than the slaves and free people of color from Saint-Domingue. As a result of both federal and territorial initiatives, more than three thousand foreign slaves entered New Orleans during 1809 and 1810.

Ironically, only a few months after the federal bill exempting the Saint-Dominguan refugees passed, people of color in New York celebrated the anniversary of the foreign slave trade's demise in the United States. By all accounts it was a noteworthy affair. In the eyes of the New York Manumission Society, it was too noteworthy, and members tried to persuade black locals of the "evil consequences" of a public commemoration. Black New Yorkers refused to be deterred and responded to the committee that "they had incurred considerable expense in providing their Standards and other things, and that they could not think of relinquishing their proposed method of celebrating the day."[129] As part of their festivities, they made several toasts, one of which *Poulson's American Daily Advertiser* called "well pointed": "*France* has not *abolished*, but *extended* the *slave trade!*" France's failure to ban the foreign slave trade was seen not only as immoral but also as un-republican. One couplet encapsulated the sentiment: "Slaves fight for what were better cast away; / A chain that binds them—and a tyrant's sway."[130]

While quick to denigrate France, the celebrants remained silent about the American government's cowardly violation of its own slave trade ban. The silence is not surprising. Given the tenuous position of free African Americans in most communities, an outright condemnation of the government would have excited white ire and backlash. After all, black Americans were supposed to be grateful to the U.S. government for its progressive measure—whatever its numerous compromises—and African Americans tried, as much as possible, to use this expectation of appreciation to spur white citizens to further action. The loudest cries of discontent regarding the exiles and their exemption came from white Americans in New Orleans. They continued to complain about the strain that the Saint-Dominguan refugees placed on city resources and infrastructure, and they launched new attacks on the exiles, describing their shady business dealings in Louisiana's black market.[131] In scathing criticism of the refugees as slave masters, their opponents rebuked white Saint-Dominguans for cruel treatment of slaves. In a September 1809 letter published in a Philadelphia newspaper, a New Orleans writer identifying himself only as "H" made "allowance for the prejudice of education and custom" of exile masters, but he pleaded for the federal government to do something to ameliorate the condition of the slaves: "How much soever the government of the United States might commiserate their [the white exiles'] flight from persecution, pass laws and remit fines for the reception of slaves, it is a sorrowful reflection for the progress of humanity, daily to witness thousands of these poor creatures, used much worse than your cart horses." He described slaves working "like brute beasts" while "their masters are rolling at Billiard Tables, or such like amusement," and asserted that this callous treatment put the entire territory at risk.[132] It was only a matter of time, he surmised, before these slaves rose up against their cruel masters.

He may have been right. A slave revolt often cited as the largest ever to have occurred on American soil would take place in January 1811, when slaves in St. Charles and St. John Parishes, just north of New Orleans, rose up against their masters. Reports claimed that a Saint-Dominguan man of color and slave driver named Charles Deslondes led the rebellion, and some observers pointed to Deslondes's background to prove that "French emissaries" had organized the revolt. Others laid the blame at the feet of local French planters. In an account that echoed early explanations for the Haitian Revolution, one commentator noted:

"The ill treatment of the slaves is said to be the cause of their late rising. Americans, who have negroes, are under no fear . . . But the foreigners allow a negro but a peck of corn for a month; some have blankets, and some have none. . . . They [the French] are unfriendly and inhuman."[133] As their East Coast counterparts had in the 1790s, American slave masters in Louisiana saw themselves as above reproach and found in the white refugees—and their slave management—a convenient scapegoat to explain away the rebellion. But, implicit in this line of reasoning was a critique of the government. It had permitted the entry of both incendiary slaves and brutal masters who, through their ruthlessness, stoked the fires of insurrection. By not asserting American values more forcefully, the administration jeopardized the entire territory.

Neither Claiborne—nor the federal government for that matter—responded to any of these allegations. In 1810 the territorial legislature voted to return the bonds that white Saint-Dominguans had posted for their slaves and restored full dominion of refugee slaveowners over their bondsmen. Saint-Dominguan masters could treat, rent, sell, and buy their slaves as they saw fit—a decision that further ingratiated the governor to the Francophone community.[134] Despite this overture to the exiles, Claiborne and other local officials did pursue violators of the foreign slave trade ban. As early as September 1809, the governor prosecuted two vessels from Jamaica that attempted to unload slaves.[135] In March 1810, the legislature passed laws that effected the prohibition of the slave trade, yet, apparently lacking Congress's misgivings about government's benefiting from the illegal activity, representatives stipulated that imported slaves would be seized and sold to the benefit of the territorial treasury.[136] Enforcement, however, was spotty; not until the late 1810s did the legislature go after violators with vigor, prodded by a renewed federal commitment to halting the trade.[137]

As for the refugees, they soon set about establishing themselves in New Orleans. They founded gazettes and schools, ran theaters and ballets, filled the pews of Catholic churches, and engaged in trade, crafts, and plantation agriculture. In short order, the exiles—black, white, and colored—fell into step with the rhythms of life in Louisiana.[138] And the white exiles did, indeed, feel indebted to the governor. Claiborne's political gamble paid off. He was elected governor in 1812, thanks largely to the support of the French-speaking population. The refugees also proved their allegiance to the United States, or at least their contempt for Britain, during the War of 1812; both white and colored exiles joined battalions that fought alongside Americans in the Battle of New Orleans.[139] As George Washington Cable reminisced in his late-nineteenth-century work, *The Creoles of Louisiana*, "Creoles, Americans, and San Domingans, swords and muskets in hand, poured in upon the Place d'Armes from every direction and sought their places in the ranks."[140] At last, it seemed that the divided master class had found a common, if temporary, cause.

The 1809 migration of Saint-Dominguan exiles led white Americans to deliberate once more what the "horrors of St. Domingo" portended for the future of the early republic—in this instance, quite literally as the refugees arrived by the thousands to the area on which the prospects and viability of the nation were staked. This reconsideration involved not only black and colored refugees, with their damning (if somewhat erroneous) reputations for rebellion, but also the white exiles, who were not above suspicion for their role in the Haitian Revolution and for their Francophone background. In an attempt to resist the migration, white Americans in Louisiana invoked the atrocities which Sansay and others made so vivid, but their calls were disregarded, and in the end the refugees in Orleans Territory helped to secure the region for the republic—and for slavery, a legacy that continued to trouble the nation deep into the antebellum era.

CONCLUSION

S oon after arriving at Charleston, South Carolina, in 1804, a group of Saint-Dominguan exiles hosted a benefit concert to raise money for their own support. A local newspaper urged residents to attend the event to demonstrate the philanthropy that was a hallmark of an enlightened republic: "Sons of Freedom! Souls of bounty and benevolence, open, we conjure you, open wide your arms to them! let not the fruitful issues of the kindly heart, be obstructed by a close niggard hand." Crucially, the anonymous writer went on to elaborate why the refugees merited generosity, using terms that, given the past decade of debate, were by then familiar. He assured his readers that the exiles were "amiable" and "harmless"; they were the victims, not the handmaidens, of "the hell-born revolutionists of France." Of course, he referred only to the white refugees, and this became evident when he reminded his largely white readership, "you are stretching forth your hands to your equals, not *Rights of Man* equals, but your equals in the true sense of equality."[1] As his audience well knew, the most radical application of the "rights of man" had been in Saint-Domingue and it had caused the white colonists—the very subjects of the appeal—to flee.

No doubt some readers of the *Charleston Daily Courier* objected to this view of the exiles. A fervent denunciation of the French Revolution and its architects conditioned the author's message, and such a damning declaration would not have sat well with Republicans. Politics aside, some people preferred to hold their purse strings more tightly than the writer demanded, or doubted that the Francophone refugees were as innocuous as their champion averred. For other Charlestonians, especially African Americans, the Haitian version of freedom and equality was cause for celebration rather than denigration.

Whatever their opinion, residents of Charleston recognized the issues at stake. Time and again, the exiles—and the revolution that motivated them to emigrate— tried central tenets of American nationhood. While slavery was a key component of the debate, so, too, as the newspaper article reiterated, were concerns over U.S. national character, the parameters of asylum, and republican politics. These controversies were most prominent during the 1790s, when Saint-Domingue was a site of heated and uncertain contest and when the exiles first disembarked in American cities in substantial numbers. The ramifications of the revolution did not end with the declaration of Haitian independence in 1804. Another wave of refugees, in 1809, compelled Americans to revisit disputes of the previous decade and to meet the new test of territorial expansion.

The arrival of the exiles from revolution in Saint-Domingue called into question for Americans whether a slaveholding republic was viable. For all their achievements, the American Revolution and the Constitution left a host of ambiguities. Slavery and the slave trade were the most glaring contradictions in a nation purportedly founded on liberty, and residents of the early republic struggled to translate other facets of the ideal republic into practice: how to maintain a virtuous citizenry, how to run (not just establish) an enlightened government, and how to ensure the perpetuation of the "noble" experiment. The presence of the Saint-Dominguan refugees exacerbated the already contentious debates on these subjects, challenging Americans of varied backgrounds to reappraise their nation.

In coming to grips with the Saint-Dominguans, Americans articulated, in both word and deed, competing visions of their republic. These notions were unstable; the latest turn of revolution brought new trials and new responses. Nevertheless, the Haitian Revolution helped to forge this crucial moment in U.S. nation building. Despite the ambivalence that marked U.S. attitudes toward the revolution, the result was a bolstering of the slaveholding republic, as white Americans used the exiles as a foil in arguing for their nation's exceptionalism. Because they differed from their Saint-Dominguan counterparts, the reasoning went, white Americans could prevent a similar fate in the United States, or at least had time to find another, more acceptable solution to the national paradox. In their selective reading of events, white Americans were of sounder character and were better republicans than the French creoles and black Americans were content under a more benign version of slavery. As best they could, African Americans (and a few white abolitionists) invoked the Haitian Revolution to fight the status quo, yet not until shortly before the Civil War would their rhetoric resonate and lead to decisive action.

This book has focused on the moment of the Haitian Revolution's immediate impact, but debates continued after the exiles blended into the resident population. Allusions to the refugees appeared repeatedly in the public sphere throughout the nineteenth century, as Americans continued to grapple with what Haiti's experience portended for the United States. While references to the exiles were numerous and diverse, three issues in particular had their roots in the 1790s—national character, asylum, and slavery—and they suggest that the age of revolutions marked the beginning of a long process of American nation making vis-à-vis Haiti.

Well into the 1800s, Americans relied on the cultural novelty of the refugees to reinforce distinctions between the French colony and the United States. Antebellum writers identified the perfect ingredients for melodrama in the Haitian Revolution and the lives of the white colonists. Dozens of popular tales, many likely penned by the "scribbling women" whom Nathaniel Hawthorne derided, were shot through with romance: pampered damsels escaped from the clutches of predatory black men thanks to the gallant actions of dashing creole or American men; beautiful free women of color sacrificed their lives to save French soldiers; and stoic white men and women endured woeful reversals of fortune but received sympathy as they made do in the United States.[2] As the authors set the scene for their fanciful plots, they played up the exoticism of Saint-Domingue—its lush, tropical landscape and its Francophone and multiracial population, with special attention to free women of color. White readers enjoyed the thrill and titillation of these stories; perhaps the knowledge that Saint-Domingue was (or had been) real, not fictional, and that its revolution had indeed occurred heightened such sensations. But the audience also took comfort in these portrayals that cast Saint-Domingue as patently distinct from the United States. These stories presented the colony as a land so foreign that its history had few lessons for white Americans. Thus white Americans robbed the Haitian Revolution of its political power yet again and rendered it merely entertaining and exotic.

Nineteenth-century accounts of migration to America incorporated the experiences of Saint-Dominguan exiles in telling ways. As white Americans evaluated their recent past, they retooled the history of the white refugees to suit an idealized vision of the United States as a place of asylum. Articles remarked on the exiles' contributions to U.S. communities—how they invigorated everything from theater in Charleston and markets in Baltimore to sugar cultivation in New Orleans and Georgia and education in New York—not to mention the personal fortunes of merchants like Stephen Girard.[3] Chronicles by urban boosters celebrated locals' relief campaigns on behalf of the refugees; in the 1820s a northern periodical presented Duncan McIntosh, whom the refugees had feted years before, as a model of Christian charity for his efforts to save white Saint-Dominguan colonists from black "demons."[4] On the floor of the House of Representatives in 1827 one member cited federal generosity toward the exiles in the 1790s as a precedent, in the hope of securing aid for Greek revolutionaries in their struggle for independence.[5]

Through these references Americans made the exiles' experiences conform to a romanticized model of asylum in the United States: as the beneficiaries of American generosity and hospitality, the refugees eventually achieved economic independence that stimulated the larger community. In the words of one author, "on these happy shores," the Saint-Dominguans discovered that "its fields were green, its skies clear, its waters pure; its freedom was peaceful: open doors welcomed the exiles, and warm hearts received, cherished, and essayed to comfort."[6] In the antebellum reflection on events, fears that the refugees would transform U.S. cities into "new Capes" evaporated, as did controversies over financial support and over the exiles' potentially detrimental impact on the western territories. The United States was a new Eden, and the white Saint-Dominguans confirmed the idyllic narrative of American immigration. The ambiguity and debate of the earlier period gave way to a self-congratulatory story about the promise of America.[7]

Fiery antebellum debates over slavery, however, made this rosy image hard to maintain. Even with all the explanatory gymnastics of the 1790s, the question of slaveholder responsibility for the Haitian Revolution still plagued Americans, and the answer became pressing as the lines between anti- and pro-slavery camps were drawn ever more emphatically and politicized. This was no longer the politics of the first decades of the early republic, with Federalists and Democratic Republicans decrying the dangers of faction. In subsequent years the political landscape had changed dramatically, becoming at once more democratic, as more white men participated in political life, and more sectional, as southerners and northerners (and westerners) split over the role of slavery in the United States. The Haitian Revolution and its exiles figured notably in these disputes. Pro-slavery writers luxuriated in grisly portrayals of the revolution, adopting the language that white refugees had employed in the 1790s: the rebel slaves were like "unchained tigers," "a long slumbering volcano," and "assassins," and their deeds included the standard litany of heinous abuses.[8] Slavery's supporters attributed these harrowing scenes to emancipation, not slavery. Echoing the rhetoric of the white exiles, they contended that "massacre . . . will ever be the consequence of that foolish philanthropy"—a philanthropy prompted by none other than William Wilberforce.[9] Slavery advocates argued that northern U.S. abolition societies were "the Jacobin clubs" of their age. These new *amis des noirs* were goading "three million raging blacks" to arms, and the result would be "a terrible tragedy, to which the experience of St. Domingo is but a prelude."[10]

In this vein slavery's defenders ascribed rebellious activity among antebellum slaves to the rash interference of outsiders. Southern historians maintained that Gabriel's Rebellion was motivated by "religious fanaticism, that frequent instrument used by designing men," by the French Revolution, and by "the success of the efforts of the same race in Hispaniola in overcoming and slaughtering the whites."[11] White southerners trotted out similar excuses in accounting for Denmark Vesey's conspiracy in Charleston in 1822 and for Nat Turner's rebellion in Southampton, Virginia, in 1831.[12] On the eve of the Civil War, they asserted that "no attempt at insurrection in the South has ever originated from the domestic negro; but such nefarious designs have always been fomented from other sources—such as Vesey, of St. Domingo, and Northern incendiaries."[13] For them, the Haitian Revolution continued to provide a justification for sustaining what nineteenth-century Southerners called "our peculiar institution."

Abolitionists had the burden of refuting the purported link between emancipation and race war associated with Haiti. As in the 1790s, ambivalence laced their appraisals; but in the nineteenth century, both black and white antislavery activists became bolder in their defenses of the black republic and its history. One of the thorniest aspects of this task was justifying the violence of the Haitian Revolution. As an editorial in the *Philanthropist* complained, "All have something to tell you of the 'horrors of St. Domingo.' The true history of that interesting Island has been kept in the dark. . . . This impression has been received from the party-colored statements of the exiles from the Island, and from the false accounts of pro-slavery writers."[14] Whether the wordplay about being "party-colored" and "kept in the dark" was intentional or not, the stories that white refugees had propagated were a powerful weapon for the pro-slavery camp. To overturn these "false accounts," American abolitionists recounted—in much greater detail than did their foes—the actors, events, and chronology of the revolution in order to prove that immediate emancipation had not caused the war. They dissected the

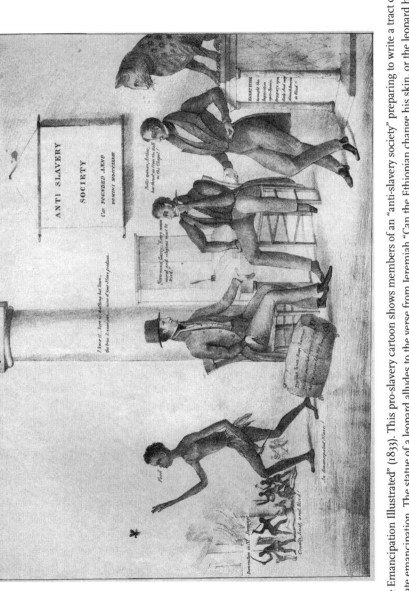

"Immediate Emancipation Illustrated" (1833). This pro-slavery cartoon shows members of an "anti-slavery society" preparing to write a tract calling for immediate emancipation. The statue of a leopard alludes to the verse from Jeremiah "Can the Ethiopian change his skin, or the leopard his spots?" which was invoked by many white Southerners to question the ability of black people to make the transition from slaves to freemen. The inscription below the leopard states that the "fanaticism" of abolition will "drench America in blood," and for proof of this assertion, the artist turns to the example of the Haitian Revolution. In the background, barely clothed black men kill a white child, woman, and man while their house burns. Just in case the viewer had any doubts about the meaning of the scene, the captions around the background vignette proclaim: "Insurrection in St.

decisions of key players, analyzed the responses of black and colored Saint-Dominguans, and weighed the distinctive traits of the colony's northern, southern, and western regions.

Their close scrutiny mirrored the complicated assessments of the 1790s. In fact, nineteenth-century abolitionists drew on some of the same sources and lines of reasoning as their predecessors, for example, blaming the white colonists for the fate of Saint-Domingue. According to their reading, white royalists had provoked the slave rebellion on the northern plain in 1791 and the destruction of Cap Français in 1793, and Sonthonax and the National Assembly's emancipation declarations had brought peace and even prosperity to the island: "We find that the liberated negroes . . . continued to work upon their *old plantations*, and for their *old masters*; so that there was also a *spirit of industry* among them, and that they gave no uneasiness to their employers; for they are described as continuing to work *as quietly as before*."[15] This situation persisted, antislavery writers asserted, until Napoleon Bonaparte, egged on by the machinations of white planters, decided to renege on black freedom and citizenship and reinstitute slavery. The "treachery of the whites" yielded the "bitter fruit" of war, and the "barbarities" of the former slaves paled in comparison to those carried out by the invading French army and by colonists.[16] After securing their liberty in 1804, the freedmen—like so many farmer-soldier Cincinnati—laid down their swords and took up their plows to cultivate the land.[17]

This "true history" of the Haitian Revolution established that emancipation had not led to insurrection and war and, more importantly, that immediate abolition was, as one commentary put it, "safe" to apply elsewhere (in other words, in the United States).[18] For some proponents of emancipation, part of this "safety" involved preserving the plantation economy, while other supporters insisted that emancipation was "safe" because black men and women had the capacity to exercise freedom responsibly. Here again, they located an example in Haiti with Toussaint Louverture. Antebellum biographies and novels about Louverture charted his rise from humble slave to savvy general, touting his mental and physical capacities, impeccable morals, and judicious restraint. He was the black George Washington: after all, "each was the leader of an oppressed and outraged people, each had a powerful enemy to contend with, and each succeeded in founding a government in the New World." A few even declared Louverture the superior, in that the black man, unlike his white counterpart, fought to free slaves and to build a nation truly based on liberty for all.[19]

Before the Civil War, some African Americans, impatient with the slow pace and half-hearted nature of reform in the United States, made their way to Haiti.

Like other black resettlement efforts, to Africa and even within the United States, difficulties plagued the project in Haiti almost from the start. Small numbers of African Americans migrated in the early 1820s, and, encouraged by positive reports, thousands followed. A high point of this emigration was 1824, when between six thousand and seven thousand black Americans relocated to the island.[20] The movement coincided with France's official recognition of Haitian independence, a development which the abolitionist periodical *Genius of Universal Emancipation* hailed as an "advancement of the whole African cause, and by a mighty stride," even though Haiti paid 150 million francs in indemnities to exiled white planters in return for official French acknowledgment and subsequently sank into a crippling cycle of debt.[21] Despite the high tide of enthusiasm, the resettlement scheme soon faltered, and participants rushed to deflect criticism of the endeavor. When a shipload of migrants sailed back to the United States (on a vessel named, incidentally, the *Stephen Girard*), supporters of the venture chalked it up to the homesickness typical of any emigrant.[22] But deeper problems became harder to disguise, as the undertaking suffered from logistical setbacks and Haitian President Jean Pierre Boyer rethought the wisdom of filling the nation with people who might alter its political make-up. Many African Americans chose to depart because they found the linguistic, religious, and social differences between themselves and their Haitian neighbors too great to surmount.[23]

In the 1850s, a group of black Americans, led by a former slave, Reverend James T. Holly, renewed the campaign for emigration to Haiti, but this latest appeal included an explicit missionary element. Holly and others planned to bring Protestantism as well as economic and social uplift to Haitians. Their attitude toward the black republic reflected a mix of admiration for its past and condescension to the shortcomings of its present. Instead of accepting the nation, its people, and its revolution on their own terms, these African Americans wanted to transplant the United States—albeit free from slavery and racism—to the Caribbean.[24] Failing to find an America in the West Indies, however, many of these migrants returned home, ready to fight in the next decade to transform the United States into what they felt Haiti could have been.

Even after the Civil War made clear that a slaveholding republic could not stand, Haiti and its revolution persisted as a presence in American life. As African Americans confronted deep-seated racism in the late nineteenth and twentieth centuries, they turned to the black republic and its history for inspiration. Over the course of the last century, the U.S. government's relations with Haiti have remained controversial. The American occupation from 1915 to 1934, the repeated interventions in Haitian politics, and the notorious treatment of recent refugees to American cities have all again provoked debate about what kind of nation the United States is and about its relationship to the wider world. In many ways, the United States still wrestles with the contradictions brought into sharp relief by the Haitian Revolution and its exiles in the early republic; via U.S. interaction with Haiti, questions about American racism, asylum, democracy, and dominion endure.

The Haitian Revolution continues to resonate for historians, too, as they look to events in Saint-Domingue in order to understand the age from which sprang some of the most celebrated legacies of the West, including democracy and human rights. In a sense, scholars are returning to the ethos of the 1790s, shedding the provincialism that has all too often characterized studies of the early republic to appraise the nation's early years as contemporaries did, in the context of revolutions elsewhere in the Atlantic world. Just as the Saint-Dominguan refugees prompted Americans to reassess the successes and shortcomings of their republic, considering Haiti puts the early United States in a new light for scholars. While the approach may be similar, the results, we hope, are different. An Atlantic frame of reference provides us with the opportunity to discover possibilities in the U.S. republic that disrupt the narratives of self-satisfying exceptionalism perpetuated by past actors and their histories. Perhaps this more expansive vision of the early United States will enable us to redress more fully the ambiguities and injustices that linger.

NOTES

INTRODUCTION

1. Thomas Jefferson to James Monroe, July 14, 1793, *The Papers of Thomas Jefferson*, ed. John Catanzariti (Princeton: Princeton University Press, 1995), 26:503.

2. Michel-Rolph Trouillot, *Silencing the Past: Power and the Production of History* (Boston: Beacon Press, 1995).

3. Laurent Dubois, "An Enslaved Enlightenment: Rethinking the Intellectual History of the French Atlantic," *Social History* 31, no. 1 (February 2006): 1–14.

4. Laurent Dubois, *Avengers of the New World: The Story of the Haitian Revolution* (Cambridge: Harvard University Press, 2004); Carolyn Fick, *The Making of Haiti: The Saint Domingue Revolution from Below* (Knoxville: University of Tennessee Press, 1990); John D. Garrigus, *Before Haiti: Race and Citizenship in French Saint-Domingue* (New York: Palgrave Macmillan, 2006); David Geggus, *Haitian Revolutionary Studies* (Bloomington: Indiana University Press, 2002); and idem, *Slavery, War, and Revolution: The British Occupation of Saint-Domingue, 1793–1798* (New York: Oxford University Press, 1982).

5. James Alexander Dun, "Dangerous Intelligence: Slavery, Race, and St. Domingue in the Early American Republic" (Ph.D. diss., Princeton University, 2004), chapters 2–4.

6. Julius Scott, "The Common Wind: Currents of Afro-American Communication in the Era of the Haitian Revolution" (Ph.D. diss., Duke University, 1986).

7. Dubois, *Avengers of the New World*, 7.

8. Examples taken from April Lee Hatfield, *Atlantic Virginia* (Philadelphia: University of Pennsylvania Press, 2004); Jorge Cañizares-Esguerra, *Puritan Conquistadors: Iberianizing the Atlantic, 1550–1700* (Stanford: Stanford University Press, 2006); Ira Berlin, *Many Thousands Gone: The First Two Centuries of Slavery in North America* (Cambridge: Harvard University Press, 1998).

9. Joyce Chaplin, "Expansion and Exceptionalism in Early American History," *Journal of American History* 89, no. 4 (March 2003): 1431–55; Cañizares-Esguerra, 222–23.

10. William O'Reilly, "Genealogies of Atlantic History," *Atlantic Studies* 1, no. 1 (2004): 68. Interestingly, the landmark book for black Atlantic studies also begins in the modern era: Paul Gilroy, *The Black Atlantic: Modernity and Double Consciousness* (Cambridge: Harvard University Press, 1993).

11. The unevenness of comparison between the colonial and revolutionary periods is

evident, for example, in Bernard Bailyn's *Atlantic History: Concept and Contours* (Cambridge: Harvard University Press, 2005).

12. Linda Colley, "The Sea Around Us," *New York Review of Books*, June 22, 2006; Alison Games, "Atlantic History: Definitions, Challenges, and Opportunities," *American Historical Review* 111, no. 3 (June 2006): 752.

13. Innovative approaches to the age of revolution include David Brion Davis, *The Problem of Slavery in the Age of Revolution, 1770–1823*, 2nd ed. (New York: Oxford University Press, 1999); Peter Linebaugh and Marcus Rediker, *The Many-Headed Hydra: Sailors, Slaves, Commoners, and the Hidden History of the Revolutionary Atlantic* (Boston: Beacon Press, 2000); and Scott, "The Common Wind." Recently, some scholars have tempered the stark divide between the colonial and national eras by highlighting the continued influence of imperial structures on definitions of sovereignty and nationhood on both sides of the Atlantic. See Jeremy Adelman, "An Age of Imperial Revolution," *American Historical Review* 113, no. 2 (April 2008): 319–40, and idem, *Sovereignty and Revolution in the Iberian Atlantic* (Princeton: Princeton University Press, 2006), 1–12.

14. Historians of the early republic have acknowledged the impact of the French Revolution on the United States, but the subject warrants further scrutiny. They have considered only affairs in Europe—the storming of the Bastille, the execution of Louis XVI, and the rise of Bonaparte, among others—neglecting the colonial arena of revolution. On nation making as an Atlantic process, see Peter S. Onuf, "Nations, Revolutions, and the End of History," in *Revolutionary Currents: Nation Building in the Transatlantic World*, ed. Michael A. Morrison and Melinda Zook (Lanham, MD: Rowman & Littlefield, 2004), 184–86.

15. Recent groundbreaking works on refugees who affected North America include John Mack Faragher, *A Great and Noble Scheme: The Tragic Story of the Expulsion of the French Acadians from Their American Homeland* (New York: W. W. Norton, 2005); Christopher Hodson, "Refugees: Acadians and the Social History of Empire, 1755–1785" (Ph.D. diss., Northwestern University, 2004); Maya Jasanoff, "The Other Side of Revolution: Loyalists in the British Empire," *William and Mary Quarterly* 65, no. 2 (April 2008): 205–32; Neil Kamil, *Fortress of the Soul: Violence, Metaphysics, and Material Life in the Huguenot's New World, 1517–1751* (Baltimore: Johns Hopkins University Press, 2005); Cassandra Pybus, *Epic Journeys of Freedom: Runaway Slaves of the American Revolution and Their Global Quest for Liberty* (Boston: Beacon Press, 2006); and Bertrand Van Ruymbeke, *From New Babylon to Eden: The Huguenots and Their Migration to Colonial South Carolina* (Columbia: University of South Carolina Press, 2005).

16. The Essay on Sources has a complete list of studies of Saint-Dominguan refugees, but the latest works are Susan Branson and Leslie Patrick, "Étrangers dans un Pays Étrange: Saint Dominguan Refugees of Color in Philadelphia," in *The Impact of the Haitian Revolution in the Atlantic World*, ed. David P. Geggus (Columbia: University of South Carolina Press, 2001); Nathalie Dessens, *From Saint-Domingue to New Orleans: Migration and Influences* (Gainesville: University Press of Florida, 2007); R. Darrell Meadows, "Engineering Exile: Social Networks and the French Atlantic Community, 1789–1809," *French Historical Studies* 23, no. 1 (Winter 2000): 67–102; idem, "The Planters of Saint-Domingue, 1750–1804" (Ph.D. diss., Carnegie Mellon University, 2004); Gary Nash, "Reverberations of Haiti in the American North: Black Saint Dominguans in Philadelphia," *Explorations in*

Early American Culture: A Special Supplemental Issue of Pennsylvania History 65 (1998): 44–73; and Jennifer J. Pierce, "Discourses of the Dispossessed: Saint-Domingue Colonists on Race, Revolution, and Empire, 1789–1825" (Ph.D. diss., Binghamton University, 2005).

CHAPTER I: THE "NEW CAPE"

1. Charles Laurent Aîné, June 13, 1798. Landing Reports of Aliens, 1798–1807. Eastern District of Pennsylvania. Hereafter cited as Alien Reports.

2. Mr. Fortier to Stephen Girard, October 4, 1792. Correspondence of Stephen Girard. Microfilm Collection, Stephen Girard papers, American Philosophical Society, Philadelphia, PA. Collection hereafter abbreviated as SGP.

3. David Geggus, "The Major Port Towns of Saint Domingue in the Later Eighteenth Century," in *Atlantic Port Cities: Economy, Culture, and Society in the Atlantic World, 1650–1850*, ed. Franklin W. Knight and Peggy K. Liss (Knoxville: University of Tennessee Press, 1991), 95; James Roger Sharp, *American Politics in the Early Republic: The New Nation in Crisis* (New Haven: Yale University Press, 1993), 76; Stanley Elkins and Eric McKitrick, *The Age of Federalism: The Early American Republic, 1788–1800* (New York: Oxford University Press, 1993), 333; James Alexander Dun, "'What avenues of commerce, will you, Americans, not explore!': Commercial Philadelphia's Vantage onto the Early Haitian Revolution," *William and Mary Quarterly* 62, no. 3 (July 2005): 473–504.

4. Aaron Fogelman, "From Slaves, Convicts, and Servants to Free Passengers: The Transformation of Immigration in the Revolutionary Era," *Journal of American History* 85, no. 1 (June 1998): 64. For more on the Huguenot migration to North America, see Jon Butler, *The Huguenots in America: A Refugee People in New World Society* (Cambridge: Harvard University Press, 1983); Neil Kamil, *Fortress of the Soul: Violence, Metaphysics, and Material Life in the Huguenot's New World, 1517–1751* (Baltimore: Johns Hopkins University Press, 2005); and Bertrand Van Ruymbeke, *From New Babylon to Eden: The Huguenots and Their Migration to Colonial South Carolina* (Columbia: University of South Carolina Press, 2005). On American contact with frontier Frenchmen, see Edward Watts, *In This Remote Country: French Colonial Culture in the Anglo-American Imagination, 1780–1860* (Chapel Hill: University of North Carolina Press, 2006).

5. *Courrier National de Saint-Domingue*, April 24 and May 1, 1791.

6. *Baltimore Evening Post*, July 13, 1792.

7. Philippe Séguy, "Costume in the Age of Napoleon," in *The Age of Napoleon: Costume from Revolution to Empire, 1789–1815*, ed. Katell le Bourhis (New York: Metropolitan Museum of Art / Harry N. Abrams, 1989), 56–59.

8. John D. Garrigus, *Before Haiti: Race and Citizenship in French Saint-Domingue* (New York: Palgrave Macmillan, 2006), chapter 1; Laurent Dubois, *Avengers of the New World: The Story of the Haitian Revolution* (Cambridge: Harvard University Press, 2004), 26.

9. Geggus, "Major Port Towns," 89–91.

10. Médéric-Louis-Elie Moreau de St. Méry, *A Civilization that Perished: The Last Years of White Colonial Rule in Haiti*, trans., abr., and ed. by Ivor D. Spencer (New York: University Press of America, 1985), 96. Hereafter cited as Moreau, *Civilization*; Geggus, "Major Port Towns," 96–97.

11. Garrigus, 2.

12. Ibid., chapter 2.

13. Ira Berlin, *Many Thousands Gone: The First Two Centuries of Slavery in North America* (Cambridge: Harvard University Press, 1998), 228, 282–84, 320–24.

14. For a critique of scholars' neglect of urban areas in the Caribbean, see Anne Pérotin-Dumon, "Cabtoage, Contraband, and Corsairs: The Port Cities of Guadeloupe and Their Inhabitants, 1650–1800," in Knight and Liss, *Atlantic Port Cities,* 58.

15. José Moya, "A Continent of Immigrants: Postcolonial Shifts in the Western Hemisphere," *Hispanic American Historical Review* 86, no. 1 (February 2006): 14–15.

16. Geggus, "Major Port Towns," 107.

17. Ibid., 108; Dubois, 22.

18. Berlin, 241–42.

19. Ibid., 273–74.

20. Sue Peabody, *"There Are No Slaves in France": The Political Culture of Race and Slavery in the Ancien Régime* (New York: Oxford University Press, 1996), introduction.

21. David N. Gellman, *Emancipating New York: The Politics of Slavery and Freedom, 1777–1827* (Baton Rouge: Louisiana State University Press, 2006); Joanne Pope Melish, *Disowning Slavery: Gradual Emancipation and "Race" in New England, 1780–1860* (Ithaca: Cornell University Press, 1998); Gary Nash, *Forging Freedom: The Formation of Philadelphia's Black Community, 1720–1840* (Cambridge: Harvard University Press, 1988); and Shane White, *Somewhat More Independent: The End of Slavery in New York City, 1770–1810* (Athens: University of Georgia Press, 1991).

22. Geggus, "Major Port Towns," 106; Carole Shammas, "The Space Problem in Early United States Cities," *William and Mary Quarterly* 57, no. 3 (July 2000): 506.

23. Moreau, *Civilization,* 112.

24. Richard Bushman, *The Refinement of America: Persons, Houses, Cities* (New York: Alfred A. Knopf, 1992), 140–50; James D. Kornwolf, *Architecture and Town Planning in Colonial North America* (Baltimore: Johns Hopkins University Press, 2002) 2: 1170–77; for a contemporary comparison of Philadelphia and Le Cap , see Leonora Sansay (a.k.a. Mary Hassal), *Secret History; or the Horrors of St. Domingo,* ed. Michael J. Drexler (Peterborough, Ontario: Broadview Editions, 2007), 95. Sansay's *Secret History* was originally published in 1808 in Philadelphia by Bradford & Inskeep and printed by R. Carr. (The publications are differentiated below as "Drexler ed." and "1808 ed.".)

25. Shammas, 526; Geggus, "Major Port Towns," 88, 106.

26. Bushman, 151–60; Geggus, "Major Port Towns," 106.

27. Moreau, *Civilization,* 113, 145; James E. McClellan III, *Colonialism and Science: Saint Domingue in the Old Regime* (Baltimore: Johns Hopkins University Press, 1992); Bushman, 160–68.

28. Moreau, *Civilization,* 131–32. On French plays performed in the Cap Français theater, see Christopher L. Miller, *The French Atlantic Triangle: Literature and Culture of the Slave Trade* (Durham: Duke University Press, 2008), 78.

29. Dubois, 24.

30. Moreau, *Civilization,* 149, 133.

31. For meanings of "creole" in the North American and Spanish American contexts,

see J. H. Elliott, *Empires of the Atlantic World: Britain and Spain in America, 1492–1830* (New Haven: Yale University Press, 2006), 234–45.

32. Doris Garraway, *The Libertine Colony: Creolization in the Early French Caribbean* (Durham: Duke University Press, 2005), 260–75; Joan Dayan, *Haiti, History, and the Gods* (Berkeley: University of California Press, 1995), 117–18, 229–37; Joyce E. Chaplin, *The First Scientific American: Benjamin Franklin and the Pursuit of Genius* (New York: Basic Books, 2006); and David Waldstreicher, *Runaway America: Benjamin Franklin, Slavery, and the American Revolution* (New York: Hill & Wang, 2004). On laws, see Garrigus, introduction; Berlin, 239, 319–20, 322; and Whittington B. Johnson, *Black Savannah, 1788–1864* (Fayetteville: University of Arkansas Press, 1996), 38, 44.

33. Moreau, *Civilization*, 12–13.

34. Garraway, 250–52.

35. McClellan, 195–97, 226–27.

36. Moreau, *Civilization*, 110; Dubois, 24.

37. Quotation from Julius Scott, "The Common Wind: Currents of Afro-American Communication in the Era of the Haitian Revolution" (Ph.D. diss., Duke University, 1986), 26; on black Atlantic oral culture, see idem, "The Common Wind," chapter 3; W. Jeffrey Bolster, *Black Jacks: African American Seamen in the Age of Sail* (Cambridge: Harvard University Press, 1997); Peter Linebaugh and Marcus Rediker, *The Many-Headed Hydra: The Hidden History of the Revolutionary Atlantic* (Boston: Beacon Press, 2000); and Deborah Gray White, "'Yes,' There Is a Black Atlantic," *Itinerario* 23, no. 2 (1999): 127–40.

38. Gabriel Debien, "Les colons de Saint-Domingue réfugiés à Cuba, 1793–1815," *Revista de Indias* 13–14 (1953–54): 559–605; 11–36; Philip Wright and Gabriel Debien, "Les colons de Saint-Domingue passés à la Jamaïque (1792–1835)," *Bulletin de la Société d'histoire de la Guadeloupe* 26 (4e trimestre 1975): 3–216.

39. R. Darrell Meadows, "Engineering Exile: Social Networks and the French Atlantic Community, 1789–1809," *French Historical Studies* 23, no. 1 (Winter 2000), 74.

40. Ashli White, "'A Flood of Impure Lava': Saint-Dominguan Refugees in the United States, 1791–1820" (Ph.D. diss., Columbia University, 2003), chapter 1.

41. Médéric-Louis-Elie Moreau de St. Méry, *Description topographique, physique, civile, politique et historique de la partie française de l'isle Saint-Domingue* (1797; reprint, Paris: Société de l'histoire des colonies françaises, 1958) 1:299–300; idem, *Civilization*, 99.

42. Bernard Herman, *Town House: Architecture and Material Life in the Early American City, 1780–1830* (Chapel Hill: University of North Carolina Press, 2005), 3–4.

43. Jean Louis Polony, Will, September 9, 1805. Will Book D, Charleston, SC. At the time of his death, however, his plantation was mortgaged to another refugee, Marie Laurent Therese Leaumont de Lomenie. Madame Marie Laurent Therese Leaumont de Lomenie, Inventory, October 6, 1806. Charleston, SC.

44. Jean Baptiste Collas, Will, November 8, 1806. Will Book E, Charleston, SC.

45. Pierre Andre François Thebaudieres, September 22, 1798. Alien Reports.

46. On boardinghouses and taverns in this era, see Herman, chapter 7.

47. Althéa de Puech Parham, ed. and trans., *My Odyssey: Experiences of a Young Refugee from Two Revolutions by a Creole of Saint Domingue* (Baton Rouge: Louisiana State University Press, 1959), 99. Hereafter cited as *My Odyssey*.

48. Shammas, 505–42.

49. Kenneth Roberts and Anna M. Roberts, trans. and eds., *Moreau de St. Méry's American Journey [1793–1798]* (New York: Doubleday, 1947), 54–55, 317. (Hereafter cited as *Moreau's Journey*.) James Pongaudin, Will, September 1, 1792. Will Book B, Charleston, SC.

50. Pierre Bonnell, Will, October 14, 1796. Philadelphia, PA.

51. Aubert to Stephen Girard, July 18, 1793, SGP. For examples of refugees moving to less expensive neighborhoods of Philadelphia, see François Quentin, James Aubin, and Jean Guerin, Wills, September 5, 1795; September 21, 1793; and October 19, 1797, resp., Philadelphia, PA; Mary M. Schweitzer, "The Spatial Organization of Federalist Philadelphia, 1790," *Journal of Interdisciplinary History* 24, no. 1 (Summer 1993): 51.

52. François Hyacinth Brocas, Will, 1794. Philadelphia, PA.

53. On North American houses, see Herman, chapter 4; Shammas, 512, 521; and for those in Saint-Domingue, see Moreau, *Civilization*, 99.

54. François Testas, Will, July 1795. Philadelphia, PA.

55. David Geggus, "Slave and Free Colored Women in Saint Domingue," in *More Than Chattel: Black Women and Slavery in the Americas*, ed. David Barry Gaspar and Darlene Clark Hine (Bloomington: Indiana University Press, 1996), 262; Herman, chapter 4; Kornwolf, 1:477–81, 486.

56. Jonathan Prude, "To Look upon the 'Lower Sort': Runaway Ads and the Appearance of Unfree Laborers in America, 1750–1800," *Journal of American History* 78, no. 1 (June 1991), 147.

57. Jean Aubin, Will, 1793. Philadelphia, PA. On American slaves and their investment in clothing, see Shane White and Graham White, "Slave Clothing and African-American Culture in the Eighteenth and Nineteenth Centuries," *Past and Present* no. 148 (August 1995): 149–86.

58. Jean Mares, Account of Estate, 1798. Philadelphia, PA. These goods made more at auction than their estimated value on the inventory. Jean Mares, Inventory, January 23, 1798.

59. L'Anglois to Stephen Girard, July 22, 1793, SGP.

60. George Dupirct, Inventory, March 31, 1817. Charleston, SC.

61. Susan Branson and Leslie Patrick, "Étrangers dans un Pays Étrange: Saint Domingan Refugees of Color in Philadelphia," in *The Impact of the Haitian Revolution in the Atlantic World*, ed. David P. Geggus (Columbia: University of South Carolina Press, 2001), 200.

62. Quoted in Howard Mumford Jones, *America and French Culture, 1750–1848* (Chapel Hill: University of North Carolina Press, 1927), 145.

63. Berlin, 317.

64. Lewis John Baptist Grand, Inventory, November 8, 1809. Charleston, SC.

65. Danse Fabre, Inventory, September 26, 1798. Baltimore, MD.

66. Geggus, "Slave and Free Colored Women," 262.

67. *Gazette française et américaine* (New York), September 9, 1795.

68. At Mares's estate sale, for example, two gold snuffboxes sold for $58.50 and $80. Jean Mares, Account of Estate, 1798. The snuffboxes also earned more at auction than on the inventory.

69. For example, Jean Herault, Will, n.d. Philadelphia, PA; John Magdeleine-Louis Felix Polony, Inventory, November 28, 1808, Charleston, SC.

70. General de Rouvray, Inventory, July 23, 1798. Philadelphia, PA; *City Gazette and Daily Advertiser* (Charleston), September 19, 1793.

71. On Atlantic travelers and their objects, see Herman, chapter 7.

72. Peter Benjamin Maingault, Inventory, January 18, 1795. Philadelphia, PA.

73. *Moreau's Journey*, 35; John Peter Guichard, Will, August 24, 1797 [but not proved until December 9, 1806]. Baltimore, MD.

74. Pierre Jaronay, Will, January 7, 1796. New York, NY.

75. Dayan; Leslie G. Desmangles, *The Faces of the Gods: Vodou and Roman Catholicism in Haiti* (Chapel Hill: University of North Carolina Press, 1992).

76. F. X. Reuss, "Baptismal Records from Holy Trinity Church, Philadelphia," *Records of the American Catholic Historical Society* 22, no. 1 (March 1911), 1–20; idem, "Marriage Registers for Holy Trinity Church, Philadelphia," *Records of the American Catholic Historical Society* 24, no. 2 (June 1913), 140–61; idem, "Marriage Registers for St. Joseph's Church," *Records of the American Catholic Historical Society* 20, no. 1 (March 1909), 22–48; idem, "Sacramental Registers of St. Joseph's Church, Philadelphia," *Records of the American Catholic Historical Society* 15–17 (September 1904–September 1906).

77. Reuss, "Sacramental Registers for St. Joseph's," 16, no. 1 (March 1905), 56; Reuss, "Marriage Registers for St. Joseph's," 20, no. 1 (March 1909), 31.

78. Johnson, 16–17.

79. Walton Charlton Hartridge, "The Refugees from the Island of St. Domingo in Maryland," *Maryland Historical Magazine* 38, no. 2 (June 1943), 121.

80. Diane Batts Morrow, "Francophone Residents of Antebellum Baltimore and the Origins of the Oblate Sisters of Providence" in *Slavery in the Caribbean Francophone World: Distant Voices, Forgotten Acts, Forged Identities*, ed. Doris Y. Kadish (Athens: University of Georgia Press, 2000), 123, 125.

81. Hartridge, 120–21; Reuss, "Sacramental Registers of St. Joseph's," 15, no. 4 (December 1904), 455; Baptismal Register, Church of St. Peter, Wilmington, DE (April 1796 to May 1834), transcribed by Rev. Fr. Carley (February 1985); Frances Sergeant Childs, *French Refugee Life in the United States, 1790–1800: An American Chapter of the French Revolution* (Baltimore: Johns Hopkins Press, 1940), 41; and *Columbian Herald* (Charleston), September 22, 1794.

82. Craig Wilder, *In the Company of Black Men: The African Influence on African American Culture in New York City* (New York: New York University Press, 2001), 91.

83. Edmond Suire, Will, December 11, 1798, and Widow Leroi, Will, July 26, 1799. Baltimore, MD.

84. *Moreau's Journey*, 339.

85. Nathalie Dessens, *From Saint-Domingue to New Orleans: Migration and Influences* (Gainesville: University Press of Florida, 2007), 68.

86. *Moreau's Journey*, 339, 49.

87. Garraway, 248–49; Dubois, 8–11.

88. *Moreau's Journey*, 203–4, 225, 206, 176–78.

89. Saint-Dominguan refugees founded newspapers while in exile in other Caribbean islands as well. Scott, "The Common Wind," 190–92.

90. Most of these jobs are cited by refugees in Philadelphia in their alien reports. See Alien Reports, 1798–1807.

91. Johnson, 61–62.

92. Jean Henri Roberjot to Stephen Girard, November 17, 1794, SGP; and *City Gazette and Daily Advertiser* (Charleston), February 8, 1794.

93. Maurice Parfait Daligny, May 11, 1804. Alien Reports.

94. John Henry Roberjot, December 18, 1798, and John Baptiste Porée, December 22, 1798. Alien Reports; F. X. Reuss, "Sacramental Registers of St. Joseph's Church," *Records of the American Catholic Historical Society* 17, no. 1 (March 1906), 20.

95. *City Gazette and Daily Advertiser* (Charleston), October 8, 1793.

96. *My Odyssey*, 110; Hartridge, 111.

97. Charles Laurent, June 13, 1798. Alien Reports.

98. R. Darrell Meadows, "The Planters of Saint-Domingue, 1750–1804: Migration and Exile in the French Revolutionary Atlantic" (Ph.D. diss., Carnegie Mellon University, 2004), 83–84, 91–92; Susan Socolow, "Economic Roles of the Free Women of Color of Cap Français," in Gaspar and Hine, *More Than Chattel*, 282.

99. Andre Anthony Charles Lechais, Will, May 20, 1811. Will Book E, Charleston, SC; Johnson, 73. Another example of a white businesswoman is in *City Gazette and Daily Advertiser* (Charleston), October 24, 1793 (milliner and "tayloress").

100. *City Gazette and Daily Advertiser* (Charleston), December 28, 1793; *Daily Advertiser* (New York), May 20, 1794.

101. *My Odyssey*, 190–91.

102. Caroline Weber, *Queen of Fashion: What Marie Antoinette Wore to the Revolution* (New York: Henry Holt, 2006), 131–63.

103. *Gazette française et américaine* (New York), November 13, 1795, and January 25, 1796; *City Gazette and Daily Advertiser* (Charleston), September 6, 1793.

104. *Gazette française et américaine* (New York), September 4, 1795, and January 25, 1796.

105. Alexandre Heguy, Will, April 3, 1800. Philadelphia, PA.

106. *Baltimore Daily Intelligencer*, December 24, 1793.

107. *City Gazette and Daily Advertiser* (Charleston), September 14, 1793.

108. Jones, 191–96; Susan Branson, *"These Fiery Frenchified Dames": Women and Political Culture in Early National Philadelphia* (Philadelphia: University of Pennsylvania Press, 2001), 68; and Wendy Cooper, *Classical Taste in America, 1800–1840* (New York: Abbeville Press and Baltimore Museum of Art, 1993). On Francophilia in Britain, see Robin Eagles, *Francophilia in English Society, 1748–1815* (London: Macmillan Press, 2000).

109. *Daily Advertiser* (New York), August 26 and October 16, 1794.

110. *Daily Advertiser* (New York), April 9, 1794.

111. Garraway, 250–52. On "creoleness" across the races in Jamaica, see Erin Skye Mackie, "Cultural Cross-Dressing: The Colorful Case of the Caribbean Creole," in *The Clothes that Wear Us: Essays on Dressing and Transgressing in Eighteenth-Century Culture*, ed. Jessica Munns and Penny Richards (Newark: University of Delaware Press, 1999), 265–68.

112. *Baltimore Evening Post*, July 13, 1792.

113. For statistics on the languages spoken by runaway slaves in New York and New Jersey during the colonial and revolutionary era, see Graham Russell Hodges and Alan Edward Brown, eds., *"Pretends to be Free": Runaway Slave Advertisements from Colonial and Revolutionary New York and New Jersey* (New York: Garland Publishing, 1994), appendix 1, table 8.

114. Stephen Girard to Mr. Duplessis, November 15, 1805, SGP.

115. *Baltimore Daily Intelligencer*, April 2, 1794.

116. Carolyn Fick, *The Making of Haiti: The Saint Domingue Revolution from Below* (Knoxville: University of Tennessee Press, 1990), 22, 25. *Gazette française et américaine* (New York), September 16, 1795, and October 30, 1795 (slaves from the Congo nation); *Gazette française et américaine* (New York), January 1, 1796 (slave from "Mozonbie"); *Baltimore Daily Intelligencer*, December 3, 1793 (slave from nation Nago); *City Gazette and Daily Advertiser* (Charleston), September 6, 1793 (slaves from Congo, Ebo, and Arada).

117. Moreau, *Civilization*, 67–71.

118. "Character of the Creoles of St. Domingo," *American Museum* (November 1789), 359.

119. *Moreau's Journey*, 265.

120. Bushman, 68–69.

121. "Character of the Creoles of St. Domingo," *American Museum* (November and December, 1789), 359, 466.

122. Bushman, 63–69.

123. *Moreau's Journey*, 281–83.

124. *Claypoole's American Daily Advertiser* (Philadelphia), March 21, 1799.

125. *City Gazette and Daily Advertiser* (Charleston), July 15, 1799.

126. Moreau, *Civilization*, 71.

127. Jean Girard to Stephen Girard, December 25, 1786, SGP. Many thanks to Billy Smith for this reference.

128. Prude, 146–47; Bushman, 70; Munns and Richards, introduction, 15.

129. *My Odyssey*, 109.

130. Ibid., 95.

131. Jean Charles Joyeux, Will, November 15, 1800. Will Book D, Charleston, SC. François Testas, Inventory, 1795, Philadelphia, PA.

132. "Character of the Creoles of St. Domingo," *American Museum* (December 1789), 467.

133. Aileen Ribeiro, *Fashion in the French Revolution* (New York: Holmes & Meier, 1988), 127.

134. *Moreau's Journey*, 283; Michele Majer, "American Women and French Fashion," in le Bourhis, *The Age of Napoleon*, 217–37; Edward Warwick, Henry C. Pitz, and Alexander Wyckoff, *Early American Dress: The Colonial and Revolutionary Periods* (New York: Benjamin Blom, 1965), 225–27.

135. *Federal Gazette* (Philadelphia), August 30, 1792.

136. Handkerchiefs: *Federal Gazette* (Philadelphia), July 24 and August 30, 1792; *Federal Gazette* (Baltimore), April 18, 1797; *Daily Advertiser* (New York), April 14, 1795 and April

19, 1798. Earrings: *Federal Gazette* (Philadelphia), August 30, 1792; *Baltimore Daily Intelligencer*, April 2, 1794; *American Star* (Philadelphia), May 1, 1794; *Claypoole's American Daily Advertiser* (Philadelphia), March 21 and August 24, 1799. Shoes with ribbons: *Federal Intelligencer* (Baltimore), July 21, 1795; *Dunlap's American Daily Advertiser* (Philadelphia), August 13, 1795. On American slaves and handkerchiefs, see Shane White and Graham White, "Slave Hair and African American Culture in the Eighteenth and Nineteenth Centuries," *Journal of Southern History* 61, no. 1 (February 1995): 70–75. For an example of a white American woman with "her head generally dressed in the French West-India style," see *City Gazette and Daily Advertiser* (Charleston), March 20, 1793.

137. Warwick, Pitz, and Wyckoff, 218, 227; Ribeiro, 89, 124; Philippe Séguy, "Costume in the Age of Napoleon," 49. In fact, now, in French slang a hoop earring is called a "creole." Thanks to Yvie Fabella for this information.

138. Garraway, 196–97, 229–39; Sansay (Drexler ed.), 65, 95–96; and Mackie, 260–61.

139. *Moreau's Journey*, 311.

140. Ibid., 309.

141. *Baltimore Daily Intelligencer*, February 8, 1794. Original French: "L'on prévient Mess. Les Etrangers qui se proposent d'y assister, qu'on ne danse qu'à l'anglose, et chacun á son tour, selon les usages du pays."

142. *Dunlap's American Daily Advertiser* (Philadelphia), January 26, 1793; Joseph George Rosengarten, *French Colonists and Exiles in the United States* (Philadelphia: J. B. Lippincott, 1907), chapter 17; Childs, 112–14, 119–20; and Hartridge, 112.

143. *Baltimore Evening Post*, January 11, 1793; Joseph Aubaye, December 17, 1798. Alien Reports.

144. *My Odyssey*, 112.

145. Quoted in Childs, 60.

146. *My Odyssey*, 187, 175.

147. *Columbian Herald* (Charleston), November 26, 1795.

148. Baltimore City Archives, 1817, RG 16 s1, box 14, #253. Baltimore, MD. Many thanks to Seth Rockman for this reference. In Saint-Domingue, washerwomen had gained "an erotic reputation" among the white population. Moreau, *Description de l'isle Saint-Domingue* 2:585.

149. Quoted in Branson and Patrick, 197.

150. *Moreau's Journey*, 311, 60. On how local complaints about sexual intimacy between white men and enslaved women were linked to the attire of enslaved women, see S. White and G. White, "Slave Clothing," 161.

151. Other scholars have considered the resonance of Saint-Domingue (and its refugees) in Charles Brockden Brown's *Arthur Mervyn* as well as Leonora Sansay's *Secret History*. Sean Goudie, *Creole America: The West Indies and the Formation of Literature and Culture in the New Republic* (Philadelphia: University of Pennsylvania Press, 2006), chapter 5 and afterword; Drexler, editor's introduction to Sansay, *Secret History*; and Dayan. Here I am looking beyond the realm of the novel to other popular amusements that were informed by the Haitian Revolution.

152. *Dunlap's American Daily Advertiser* (Philadelphia), September 26, 1795.

153. Kevin Salatino, *Incendiary Art: The Representation of Fireworks in Early Modern Eu-*

rope (Los Angeles: Getty Research Institute for the History of Art and the Humanities, 1997).

154. On an exile actress, see *Gazette française et américaine* (New York), September 9, 1795.

155. John Murdock, preface to *The Beau Metamorphized, or the Generous Maid* (Philadelphia, 1800), iv. For a class interpretation of Murdock's plays, see Heather S. Nathans, "Trampling Native Genius: John Murdock versus the Chestnut Street Theatre," *Journal of American Drama and Theatre* 14 (Winter 2002): 29–43.

156. John Murdock, *The Triumphs of Love; or Happy Reconciliation* (Philadelphia, 1795), 70.

157. Murdock, *Triumphs*, 19.

158. Ibid., 20.

159. *My Odyssey*, 195.

160. *Moreau's Journey*, 59–60.

161. Durand Echeverria, *Mirage in the West: A History of the French Image of American Society to 1815* (Princeton: Princeton University Press, 1957), chapters 2 and 4; Doina Pasca Harsanyi, "The Burdens of a Moderate Revolutionary in a Revolutionary Land: The Duc de Liancourt's Exile in America (1794–1797)" in *National Stereotypes in Perspective: Americans in France, Frenchmen in America*, ed. William L. Chew III (Amsterdam: Editions Rodopi B.V., 2001).

162. *My Odyssey*, 179.

163. Reported in *City Gazette and Daily Advertiser* (Charleston), September 20, 1793.

164. As quoted in Thomas Fiehrer, "From La Tortue to La Louisiane: An Unfathomed Legacy" in *The Road to Louisiana: The Saint-Domingue Refugees, 1792–1809*, ed. Carl A. Brasseaux and Glenn R. Conrad (Lafayette: University of Southwestern Louisiana Press, 1992), 21.

CHAPTER 2: THE DANGERS OF PHILANTHROPY

1. Lynn Hunt, *Politics, Culture, and Class in the French Revolution* (Berkeley: University of California Press, 1984), 45; Elizabeth Barnes, *States of Sympathy: Seduction and Democracy in the American Novel* (New York: Columbia University Press, 1997), ix–x.

2. Conrad Wright, *The Transformation of Charity in Postrevolutionary New England* (Boston: Northeastern University Press, 1992), 7.

3. Marilyn Baseler, *"Asylum for Mankind": America, 1607–1800* (Ithaca: Cornell University Press, 1998), 130–34.

4. Wright, 120–21. For similar trends in altruism in Europe, see Hugh Cunningham and Joanna Innes, eds., *Charity, Philanthropy, and Reform: From the 1690s to 1850* (New York: St. Martin's Press, 1998).

5. The tension between sympathy and democracy was apparent in American novels of the era. See Julia Stern, *The Plight of Feeling: Sympathy and Dissent in the Early American Novel* (Chicago: University of Chicago Press, 1997).

6. Gordon S. Brown, *Toussaint's Clause: The Founding Fathers and the Haitian Revolution* (Jackson: University Press of Mississippi, 2005), 52–55.

7. *Virginia Herald and Fredericksburg Advertiser,* August 23, 1792.

8. Stephen Girard to Mr. Pille, April 2, 1793. Correspondence of Stephen Girard, Microfilm Collection, Stephen Girard papers, American Philosophical Society, Philadelphia, PA. Collection hereafter abbreviated SGP.

9. *Virginia Herald and Fredericksburg Daily Advertiser,* January 24, 1793.

10. *National Gazette,* May 7, 1792, quoted in Brown, *Toussaint's Clause,* 60.

11. Quoted in Laurent Dubois, *A Colony of Citizens: Revolution and Slave Emancipation in the French Caribbean, 1787–1804* (Chapel Hill: University of North Carolina Press, 2004), 177. Similar accusations were leveled at British West Indian creoles by their metropolitan peers.

12. *American Museum* (Philadelphia: printed by Mathew Carey, November 1789); on negative accounts of white West Indian men in early republican literature, see Leonard Tennenhouse, "Caribbean Degeneracy and the Problem of Masculinity in Charles Brockden Brown's *Ormond*" in *Finding Colonial Americas: Essays Honoring J. A. Leo Lemay,* ed. Carla Mulford and David Shields (Newark: University of Delaware Press, 2001).

13. Barnes, 44.

14. David Bell, *The Cult of the Nation in France: Inventing Nationalism, 1680–1800* (Cambridge: Harvard University Press, 2001), 125–28, 149–54.

15. *New-York Journal,* January 4, 1792.

16. *Columbian Centinel* (Boston), July 24, 1793.

17. *Columbian Herald* (Charleston), August 17, 1793.

18. *Dunlap's American Daily Advertiser* (Philadelphia), July 12, 1793.

19. Dubois, *A Colony of Citizens,* 150 (quotation), 162, 167, 226.

20. Althéa de Puech Parham, ed. and trans., *My Odyssey: Experiences of a Young Refugee from Two Revolutions by a Creole of Saint Domingue* (Baton Rouge: Louisiana State University Press, 1959), 30–31. Hereafter cited as *My Odyssey.*

21. François Furstenberg, "Beyond Freedom and Slavery: Autonomy, Virtue, and Resistance in Early American Political Discourse," *Journal of American History* 89, no. 4 (March 2003): 1295–1330.

22. Denigrating terms for black and colored soldiers appeared in newspapers as well as other published and private sources. See, for example, Leonora Sansay (a.k.a. Mary Hassal), *Secret History; or the Horrors of St. Domingo* (Philadelphia: Bradford & Inskeep, publr.; R. Carr, printer; 1808), 147; *My Odyssey,* 40, 42; and John Thomas Carré to Charles Willson Peale, ca. 1792, Sellers Family Papers, American Philosophical Society, Philadelphia, PA. (Hereafter, Sellers Family Papers.) This vocabulary was also invoked in France to criticize the Jacobin regime. Lynn Hunt, *The Family Romance of the French Revolution* (Berkeley: University of California Press, 1992).

23. *Augusta Chronicle and Gazette of the State* (Georgia), November 12, 1791.

24. Laurent Dubois, *Avengers of the New World: The Story of the Haitian Revolution* (Cambridge: Harvard University Press, 2004), 110–11.

25. In her analysis of appeals for aid in eighteenth-century London newspapers, Donna Andrew notes that petitioners consistently asserted that they were not morally responsible for their poverty. Andrew, "'To the Charitable and Humane': Appeals for Assistance in the Eighteenth-Century London Press" in Cunningham and Innes, *Charity, Philanthropy, and*

Reform, 95. On the language of misfortune and sentimental narratives in eighteenth-century France, see David J. Denby, *Sentimental Narrative and the Social Order in France, 1760–1820* (New York: Cambridge University Press, 1994).

26. *Dunlap's American Daily Advertiser* (Philadelphia), September 11, 1793; *Charleston Daily Courier,* February 11, 1804.

27. *The Philadelphia Minerva,* May 23, 1795.

28. Julie Ellison, *Cato's Tears and the Making of Anglo-American Emotion* (Chicago: University of Chicago Press, 1999).

29. Reported in the *Baltimore Evening Post,* September 18, 1793, and *Virginia Chronicle* (Norfolk), July 13, 1793. See also John Thomas Carré to Charles Willson Peale, ca. 1792. Sellers Family Papers.

30. James E. McClellan III, *Colonialism and Science: Saint-Domingue in the Old Regime* (Baltimore: Johns Hopkins University Press, 1992), 91–92; Médéric-Louis-Elie Moreau de St. Méry, *A Civilization that Perished: The Last Years of White Colonial Rule in Haiti,* trans., abr., and ed. by Ivor D. Spencer (Boston: University Press of America, 1985), 125–26; Alfred Hunt, *Haiti's Influence on Antebellum America: Slumbering Volcano in the Caribbean* (Baton Rouge: Louisiana State University Press, 1988), 43.

31. *Columbian Herald* (Charleston), September 10, 1793.

32. Ibid.

33. Amit S. Rai, *Rule of Sympathy: Sentiment, Race, and Power, 1750–1850* (New York: Palgrave, 2002), xviii–xix; see also Michelle Burnham, *Captivity and Sentiment: Cultural Exchange in American Literature, 1682–1861* (Hanover: University Press of New England, 1997).

34. Reported in the *City Gazette and Daily Advertiser* (Charleston), September 18, 1793; for additional examples of this kind of sympathetic appeal, see *Columbian Centinel* (Boston), July 31, 1793; *Pennsylvania Gazette* (Philadelphia), December 24, 1793; and *Columbian Herald* (Charleston), August 13, 1793.

35. *Virginia Chronicle* (Norfolk), July 13, 1793.

36. Karin Wulf, *Not All Wives: Women of Colonial Philadelphia* (Ithaca: Cornell University Press, 2000), 153–54; quotation in John K. Alexander, *Render Them Submissive: Responses to Poverty in Philadelphia, 1760–1800* (Amherst: University of Massachusetts Press, 1980), 117–18.

37. Robert E. Cray, Jr., *Paupers and Poor Relief in New York City and Its Rural Environs, 1700–1830* (Philadelphia: Temple University Press, 1988), 73.

38. Billy G. Smith, *The "Lower Sort": Philadelphia's Laboring People, 1750–1800* (Ithaca: Cornell University Press, 1990), 149.

39. John Alexander, *Render Them Submissive,* 86–87.

40. Ibid., 122–41.

41. On French support for the refugees, see *Virginia Chronicle* (Norfolk), August 21, 1794; *Daily Advertiser* (New York), August 26, 1794; *Baltimore Daily Intelligencer,* October 2, 1794; *Dunlap and Claypoole's American Daily Advertiser* (Philadelphia), November 24, 1794; Eliot to Stephen Girard, June 19, 1801, SGP; and R. Darrell Meadows, "The Planters of Saint-Domingue, 1750–1804: Migration and Exile in the French Revolutionary Atlantic" (Ph.D. diss., Carnegie Mellon University, 2004).

42. The best-documented illustration of this process of selecting relief leaders is for Charleston, where citizens elected by ballot three committee members, who in turn, appointed additional members to aid with the solicitation and distribution of funds. Reported in the *Baltimore Evening Post*, September 18, 1793.

43. *Dunlap's American Daily Advertiser* (Philadelphia), July 12 and 15, 1793.

44. *New-York Journal and Patriotic Register*, August 3 and 7, 1793; *Columbian Herald* (Charleston), July 30, 1793.

45. Quotation from James Robinson, *The Philadelphia Directory, City and County Register for 1802* (Philadelphia: printed by William W. Woodward, 1802), xxiii. Evidence from other societies from *An Account of the Philadelphia Dispensary, Instituted for the Medical Relief of the Poor, April 12, 1786* (Philadelphia: printed by Budd & Bartram, 1802); John F. Jones, *Jones's New-York Mercantile and General Directory . . . 1805–6* (New York: printed for the editor and for sale at the bookstore of Samuel Stansbury, 1805); *A Brief Account of the Female Humane Association Charity School, of the City of Baltimore* (Baltimore: printed by Warner and Hanna, 1803).

46. *An Account of the Philadelphia Dispensary.*

47. Smith, 117 fn 78. This figure is derived from Smith's example of the 1799 wages of Job Harrison, a journeyman shoemaker.

48. Thomas M. Doerflinger, *A Vigorous Spirit of Enterprise: Merchants and Economic Development in Revolutionary Philadelphia* (Chapel Hill: University of North Carolina Press, 1986), 15–17.

49. *Votes and Proceedings of the House of Delegates of the State of Maryland* (November, 1793), 19.

50. *Dunlap's American Daily Advertiser* (Philadelphia), July 20, 1793.

51. Ibid.

52. *Columbian Herald* (Charleston), July 23, 1793.

53. *Columbian Centinel* (Boston), July 31, 1793; *Baltimore Daily Intelligencer*, January 9, 1794.

54. An exception is Norfolk, where donors were asked to sign up at the post office. *Virginia Chronicle* (Norfolk), July 13, 1793.

55. *Baltimore Evening Post*, July 19, 1793.

56. Reported in the *Baltimore Evening Post*, September 18, 1793.

57. *City Gazette and Daily Advertiser* (Charleston), August 5, 1793; *Boston Gazette*, July 22, 1793; *Dunlap's American Daily Advertiser* (Philadelphia), July 15, 1793.

58. Reported in *Dunlap's American Daily Advertiser* (Philadelphia), July 27, 1793.

59. In Williamsburg alone, subscriptions totaled $1,075. *Virginia Herald and Fredericksburg Advertiser*, August 8, 1793; *Dunlap's American Daily Advertiser* (Philadelphia), July 20 and 26, 1793. For similar campaigns in small towns on the Eastern Shore, see Walter Charlton Hartridge, "The Refugees from the Island of St. Domingo in Maryland," *Maryland Historical Magazine* 38, no. 2 (June 1943): 105.

60. *Columbian Centinel* (Boston), August 3, 1793.

61. *Baltimore Evening Post*, July 18, 1793.

62. Ibid.

63. *Dunlap's American Daily Advertiser* (Philadelphia), August 9, 1793; *Pennsylvania Gazette* (Philadelphia), August 14, 1793.

64. *City Gazette and Daily Advertiser* (Charleston), October 10, 17, 26, 28, and November 1, 1793.

65. *Virginia Chronicle* (Norfolk), August 3, 1793.

66. *Columbian Herald* (Charleston), October 1, 1793.

67. *Baltimore Evening Post,* July 19, 1793; quotation from a report in the *Boston Gazette,* July 22, 1793; *City Gazette and Daily Advertiser* (Charleston), November 28, 1793.

68. *Columbian Herald* (Charleston), September 10, 1793. On the role of women in charitable organizations, see Margaret Morris Haviland, "Beyond Women's Sphere: Young Quaker Women and the Veil of Charity in Philadelphia, 1790–1810," *William and Mary Quarterly* 51, no. 3 (July 1994): 419–46.

69. *City Gazette and Daily Advertiser* (Charleston), July 19, 1793.

70. Reported in the *New-York Journal and Patriotic Register,* August 13, 1793. For praise for Baltimore residents, see the *Baltimore Evening Post,* July 19, 1793.

71. *Columbian Centinel* (Boston), August 3, 1793.

72. *Votes and Proceedings of the House of Delegates of the State of Maryland* (November 1793), 94.

73. Alfred Hunt, *Haiti's Influence on Antebellum America,* 43.

74. Kenneth Roberts and Anna M. Roberts, trans. and eds., *Moreau de St. Méry's American Journey [1793–1798]* (New York: Doubleday, 1947), 42.

75. Wulf, chapter 5. On the question of the deserving poor among the Saint-Dominguan refugees from the French perspective, see Meadows, chapter 3.

76. *Columbian Centinel* (Boston), March 26, 1794.

77. *City Gazette and Daily Advertiser* (Charleston), January 9 and 10, 1794. Italics in original.

78. Quotations from Philadelphia case, *Dunlap's American Daily Advertiser* (Philadelphia), August 9, 1793. On aid distribution schemes in Baltimore, see ibid., July 31, 1793, and *Votes and Proceedings of the House of Delegates of the State of Maryland* (November, 1793), 18–19.

79. *Dunlap's American Daily Advertiser* (Philadelphia), August 9, 1793.

80. René Lambert to Stephen Girard, May 7, 1794, SGP.

81. *Virginia Chronicle* (Norfolk), August 31, 1793.

82. For the example of Baltimore, see *Baltimore Evening Post,* July 19, 1793; for New York, see *New-York Journal and Patriotic Register,* August 17, 1793 and September 23, 1794. For an example of contract bidding, see *Columbian Herald* (Charleston), October 1, 1793.

83. *Virginia Chronicle* (Norfolk), August 3, 1793.

84. *New-York Journal and Patriotic Register,* August 7, 1793.

85. *Dunlap's American Daily Advertiser* (Philadelphia), July 15, 1793. See also the *Baltimore Evening Post,* August 17, 1792, and *New-York Journal and Patriotic Register,* August 3, 1793.

86. Thomas Hart Benton, *Abridgment of the Debates of Congress, from 1789 to 1856* (reprint, New York: AMS Press 1970), 1:462. Hereafter cited as *Abridgment of Debates.*

87. Thomas Jefferson to James Monroe, July 14, 1793, *The Papers of Thomas Jefferson,*

ed. John Catanzariti (Princeton: Princeton University Press, 1995) 26:503. Jefferson made a similar comment in a letter to James Wood, July 17, 1793, ibid., 26:20.

88. Reported in the *Columbian Herald* (Charleston), December 10, 1793.

89. Reported in the ibid., December 27, 1793.

90. *Acts and Resolutions of the General Assembly of the State of South Carolina, passed in December 1793* (Charleston, 1794), 31.

91. *Votes and Proceedings of the House of Delegates of the State of Maryland* (November 1793), 19.

92. *Abridgment of Debates,* 1:462.

93. Ibid., 1:463, 474–75.

94. Ibid., 1:463.

95. Ibid., 1:474.

96. Ibid.

97. Ibid., 1:475.

98. For the refugees' appeal for the remission of tonnage duties, see Thomas Jefferson to George Washington, December 15, 1793, *The Papers of Thomas Jefferson,* ed. John Catanzariti (Princeton: Princeton University Press, 1997) 27:525; Minutes from Cabinet Meeting, Opinions on Relations with France and Great Britain, December 7, 1793 in *The Papers of Alexander Hamilton,* ed. Harold C. Syrett, 27 vols. (New York: Columbia University Press, 1961–87) 15:446 n.5.

99. George Washington to Alexander Hamilton, March 21 and 31, 1794, *The Papers of Alexander Hamilton* 16:189, 223.

100. *Virginia Chronicle* (Norfolk), April 11, 1794.

101. *City Gazette and Daily Advertiser* (Charleston), April 17, 1794.

102. Cabinet Meeting, Opinion on the Application of Money Given by Law to the Indigent of Santo Domingo, April 22, 1794, *The Papers of Alexander Hamilton* 16:309; George Washington to Alexander Hamilton, April 24, 1794, ibid., 16:335–36.

103. George Washington to Alexander Hamilton, March 4, 1794, ibid., 16:117 n.1.

104. *Abridgment of Debates,* 2:41.

105. *American Star* (Philadelphia), February 13, 1794.

106. *Abridgment of Debates,* 1:474.

107. Enclosure, November 23, 1793, *The Papers of Alexander Hamilton,* 15:407.

108. *Abridgment of Debates,* 2:40–41.

109. Ibid., 2:41.

110. Ibid.

111. Ibid., 2:43.

112. Ibid., 2:41.

113. *Baltimore Daily Intelligencer,* March 11, 1794. For New York, see *New-York Journal and Daily Advertiser,* September 23, 1794.

114. *American Star* (Philadelphia), April 10, 1794.

115. Smith, 167; John Alexander, *Render Them Submissive,* 125.

116. Mathew Carey, *A Short Account of the Malignant Fever; Lately Prevalent in Philadelphia: with a Statement of the Proceedings that took place on the Subject in Different Parts of the United States. To Which are Added, Accounts of the Plague in London and Marseilles; and a List*

of the Dead, from August 1, to the middle of December, 1793, 4th ed. (Philadelphia: printed by the author, January 16, 1794), 11.

117. *City Gazette and Daily Advertiser* (Charleston), March 29, 1794.

118. Reprinted in *Dunlap's American Daily Advertiser* (Philadelphia), December 27, 1793.

119. *Dunlap's American Daily Advertiser* (Philadelphia), December 30, 1793.

120. Julie Winch, *Philadelphia's Black Elite: Activism, Accommodation, and the Struggle for Autonomy, 1787–1848* (Philadelphia: Temple University Press, 1988), 10.

121. Reported in the *Pennsylvania Gazette* (Philadelphia), January 13, 1796; Thompson Westcott, *A History of Philadelphia, from the time of the first settlements on the Delaware to the consolidation of the city and districts in 1854* (Philadelphia: Pewson & Nicolson for Brinton Coxe, 1886), 3:608.

122. *Acts and Resolutions of the General Assembly of the State of South Carolina, passed in December 1796* (Charleston, 1797), 119.

123. *Charleston Daily Courier*, February 27, March 5 and 31, April 2 and 11, and June 5, 1804.

124. *Charleston Daily Courier*, February 29, 1804.

125. *Minutes of the Common Council of the City of New York, 1784–1831* (New York: City of New York, 1917), 2:306, 436, 438, 440, 442, 454, 466, 473, 478, 576, 607, 629, 650, 691, and 742; 3:476, 487, 557, 629, 662, 655, and 665. Names of Saint-Dominguan exiles punctuated New York City's almshouse admissions lists well into the 1820s. As late as 1822, two women from "St. Domingo" entered the institution because one was pregnant and the other was ill. Like their American counterparts, Saint-Dominguans came and went from the almshouse, with stays lasting from a few days to a couple of years. Typically, Saint-Dominguan refugees resided at the almshouse for a month or two. (List of Admissions, Discharges, and Deaths, Almshouse Records. Municipal Archives, New York, NY).

126. *New-York Journal and Patriotic Register*, August 21, 1793.

127. *City Gazette and Daily Advertiser* (Charleston), January 8, 1794. Original French: "un paix pour azile, un peuple genereux, / Qui peut seul adoucir, notre sort malhereux."

128. Andrew, 89.

129. Magnan Cabeuil to Stephen Girard, November 7, 1793, SGP.

130. *Pennsylvania Gazette* (Philadelphia), October 12, 1791.

131. Quoted in Rai, 126.

132. *New-York Journal and Patriotic Register*, February 11, 1792.

133. On Wilberforce and the Amis des Noirs, see David Brion Davis, *The Problem of Slavery in the Age of Revolution, 1770–1823,* 2nd ed. (New York: Oxford University Press, 1999), 94 n.10, 95, 138–46; Robin Blackburn, *The Overthrow of Colonial Slavery, 1776–1848* (London: Verso, 1988), 146–53. On the ambiguities and limitations of French abolitionism, see Christopher L. Miller, *The French Atlantic Triangle: Literature and Culture of the Slave Trade* (Durham: Duke University Press, 2008).

134. *American Star* (Philadelphia), February 6, 1794. On the island, the argument about the Amis' responsibility emerged in the immediate aftermath of the slave rebellion. See Jeremy D. Popkin, *Facing Racial Revolution: Eyewitness Accounts of the Haitian Insurrection* (Chicago: University of Chicago Press, 2007), 7–9.

135. Bernard-Barnabe B. O'Shiell, "Introduction à un Ouvrage relatif aux Hommes de couleur et nègres libres des Antilles" (Philadelphia, n.d.), 5–6. On O'Shiell's family background, see Frances Sergeant Childs, *French Refugee Life in the United States, 1790–1800: An American Chapter of the French Revolution* (Baltimore: Johns Hopkins Press, 1940), 50. Advertisement for O'Shiell's work in *Gazette française* (New York), April 23, 1798.

136. M. E. McIntosh and B. C. Weber, eds., *Une correspondence familiale au temps des troubles de Saint-Domingue: Lettres du Marquis et de la Marquise de Rouvray a leur fille, Saint-Domingue—États-Unis (1791–1796)* (Paris: Société de l'histoire des colonies françaises et Librairie Larose, 1959), 40. Hereafter cited as Rouvray correspondence. Original French: "Les Amis des Noirs ont sans doubte été la cause première de nos malheurs, ma chère enfant. Il m'est évident qu'ils nous ont envoyé beaucoup de leurs émissaires et on en a pendu deux qui ont été convaincus d'avoir prêché leurs dogmes parmi nos esclaves."

137. Rouvray correspondence, 109. Original French: "Vous rappelez-vous, ma fille, toutes mes prédictions annoncées dans mes trois pamphlets contre les Amis des Noirs et les Jacobins? C'était au mois de juin 1789 que j'écrivais que la secte des Amis des noirs méditait la destruction de tous les trônes, de toutes les formes de gouvernement, de toutes les religions, du globe."

138. Chôtard, "Précis de la révolution de Saint Domingue, depuis la fin de 1789, jusqu'au 18 juin 1794" (Philadelphia: printed by Parent, 1795), ii, vii. Original French: "Le vrai philanthrope est ami de sa patrie; sa patrie est l'universe." On the Jacobin preoccupation with unmasking, see Lynn Hunt, *Politics, Culture, and Class in the French Revolution,* 39–41, 44.

139. *Columbian Centinel* (Boston), December 11, 1793.

140. *My Odyssey,* 40–41.

141. *Gazette française* (New York), March 23, 1796. Original French: "elles pouvaient persuader le pretendu philosophe qui a cre render un important service à l'humanité, en lâchant sur la race blanche 500 mille tigres noirs & jaunes."

142. Quoted in Dubois, *A Colony of Citizens,* 370.

143. See, for example, Depositions of Henry Troup and Joseph Hudson, January 14, 1809, Duncan McIntosh Papers, Maryland Historical Society, Baltimore, MD; *Tribute of Public Gratitude. Some Account of an Entertainment Given in Honor of Mr. Duncan M'Intosh, in Baltimore, on the 9th January, 1809. With a Collection of the Pieces Delivered on that Occasion* (printed for Coale and Thomas, by John W. Butler, 1809).

144. George C. Grove and Daniel H. Wallace, *The New-York Historical Society's Dictionary of Artists in America, 1564–1860* (New Haven: Yale University Press, 1957), 263; Robert Alexander, *The Architecture of Maximilian Godefroy* (Baltimore: Johns Hopkins University Press, 1974); and idem, "The Drawings and Allegories of Maximilian Godefroy," *Maryland Historical Magazine* 53 (1958): 17–34.

145. *Tribute of Public Gratitude . . . in Honor of Mr. Duncan M'Intosh,* 35.

146. Eliza Boudinot to Sarah Colt, January 20, 1810. Vertical File, Maryland Historical Society, Baltimore, MD.

147. *Tribute of Public Gratitude . . . in Honor of Mr. Duncan M'Intosh,* 46.

148. Ibid., 33, 45.

149. Ibid., 43.

150. Mr. Gros, *An Historick Recital, of the Different Occurrences in the Camps of Grand-Reviere, Dondon, Sainte-Suzanne, and others, from the 26th of October, 1791, to the 24th of December, of the same year* (Baltimore: Samuel and John Adams, n.d.), 27–28. For more on Gros's account, see Jeremy Popkin, "Facing Racial Revolution: Captivity Narratives and Identity in the Saint-Domingue Insurrection," *Eighteenth-Century Studies* 36, no. 4 (2003): 511–33.

151. This poem is printed on white silk and mounted with string to a board. Poem, ca. 1808, Duncan McIntosh Papers, Maryland Historical Society, Baltimore, MD.

152. *New-York Journal and Patriotic Register*, August 7, 1793. See also *Dunlap's American Daily Advertiser* (Philadelphia), July 15, 1793.

CHAPTER 3: REPUBLICAN REFUGEES?

1. Stephen Girard to Aubert, Chauveau & Bacon, July 7, 1793. Correspondence of Stephen Girard, Microfilm Collection, Stephen Girard papers, American Philosophical Society, Philadelphia, PA. Collection hereafter abbreviated SGP.

2. Michel-Rolph Trouillot, *Silencing the Past: Power and the Production of History* (Boston: Beacon Press, 1995).

3. Aid appeal dated from Philadelphia, July 12, 1793, and reprinted in the *City Gazette and Daily Advertiser* (Charleston), August 5, 1793.

4. Laurent Dubois, *Avengers of the New World: The Story of the Haitian Revolution* (Cambridge: Harvard University Press, 2004), 102–9.

5. "Discours de J. P. Brissot, Député, Sur les causes des troubles de Saint-Domingue" (Paris: printed by order of the National Assembly, December 1, 1791), 51–53. On Brissot's views of the white colonists, see Jennifer J. Pierce, "Discourses of the Dispossessed: Saint-Domingue Colonists on Race, Revolution and Empire, 1789–1825" (Ph.D. diss., Binghamton University, 2005), 38–43.

6. *New-York Journal and Patriotic Register*, May 23, 1792.

7. Nathaniel Cutting to Thomas Jefferson, December 28, 1791, *The Papers of Thomas Jefferson*, ed. Charles T. Cullen (Princeton: Princeton University Press, 1986), 22:460–61.

8. Rayford W. Logan, *The Diplomatic Relations of the United States with Haiti, 1776–1891* (Chapel Hill: University of North Carolina Press, 1941), 33–36, 40; William Doyle, *The Oxford History of the French Revolution* (New York: Oxford University Press, 1989), 188.

9. David Waldstreicher, *"In the Midst of Perpetual Fetes": The Making of American Nationalism, 1776–1820* (Chapel Hill: University of North Carolina Press, 1997), chapter 3; David Brion Davis, *Revolutions: Reflections on American Equality and Foreign Liberations* (Cambridge: Harvard University Press, 1990), 30–31.

10. Thomas Jefferson to Martha Jefferson Randolph, May 26, 1793, *The Papers of Thomas Jefferson*, ed. John Catanzariti (Princeton: Princeton University Press, 1995), 26:122.

11. *Virginia Chronicle* (Norfolk), November 17, 1794.

12. For an in-depth analysis that tries to ascertain if the white colonists were in favor of independence, British rule, or neither, see David Geggus, *Slavery, War, and Revolution: The British Occupation of Saint-Domingue, 1793–1798* (New York: Oxford University Press, 1982), chapter 3.

13. *Columbian Centinel* (Boston), November 20, 1793. On oaths of allegiance to the British king by residents of Môle Saint-Nicolas, see *Dunlap's American Daily Advertiser* (Philadelphia), December 5, 1793.

14. *Columbian Herald* (Charleston), December 5, 1793.

15. For an example of a complaint about the British presence, see *Baltimore Daily Intelligencer*, August 7, 1794; quotation from *Pennsylvania Gazette* (Philadelphia), December 4, 1793.

16. Letter to ministers from Gaspard Monge, French minister of the navy, and Pierre LeBrun, French minister of foreign affairs, January 17, 1793, in *Correspondence entre le Citoyen Genet, Ministre Plenipotentiaire de la Republique Française pres les Etats-Unis, et les membres du gouvernement fédéral, precedee des instructions données à ce ministre par les autorités constituées de la France* (Philadelphia: printed by Benjamin Franklin Bache, 1794), 11; see also *New-York Journal and Patriotic Register*, June 8, 1793.

17. *American Minerva* (New York), January 2, 1794.

18. Marie-Dominique-Jacques D'Orlic Esquire, January 14, 1799. Professions of loyalty to the French king were also recorded by the following: Guillaume Pecholier, December 6, 1798; Jeane Marine Chovot, December 8, 1798; Jules Le Fer, December 15, 1798; Joseph Marie Thomas, December 17, 1798; John Vincent Marie Robineau de Bougon, January 18, 1799; John Baptiste Seneraud, August 18, 1815; Rosalie Lezelle Demonterclan, May 16, 1816 [one of the few women making a testament in her own name]; Ann Golbert Marc Anotine Frenayem October 21, 1816; John Charles Nicholas Leplicher, August 18, 1818; and François Cinq, March 14, 1823. Allegiance to the "emperor of France," in other words, Napoleon Bonaparte, were made by John Audubon, September 5, 1806, and Peter H. Duquesney, January 12, 1811. Participation in the British army in Saint-Domingue was affirmed by Jean Baptiste Thiry, December 18, 1798. All attestations appear in the Landing Reports of Aliens, 1798–1807. Eastern District of Pennsylvania. Hereafter cited as Alien Reports.

19. Pierre Andre François Thebaudieres, September 22, 1798. Alien Reports.

20. On white colonists' views of what their citizenship should be, see Pierce, 57.

21. John de la Fond, December 15, 1798. Alien Reports.

22. Robert Louis Stein, *Léger Félicité Sonthonax: The Lost Sentinel of the Republic* (London: Associated University Presses, 1985), 27.

23. Untitled address from inhabitants of the Quarter of Petit-Goave to the National Assembly (printed in Port-au-Prince, October 1789), in vol. 1 of *Révolutions de St. Domingue*, John Carter Brown Library, Providence, RI.

24. Dubois, *Avengers of the New World*, 84–87.

25. March 23, 1791, open letter by Chôtard published in *Suite des lettres adressées par différentes municipalités de la colonie, à celle du Port-au-Prince*, vol. 2 of *Révolutions de St. Domingue*, John Carter Brown Library, Providence, RI. Original French: "La colonie entière ayant reconnu la souveraineté de l'assemblée nationale, l'emploi despotique de la force publique, la seduction, & les menées sourdes des mal-intentionnés."

26. Thomas Jefferson to Edmond Charles Genet, November 24, 1793, *The Papers of Thomas Jefferson*, ed. John Catanzariti (Princeton: Princeton University Press, 1997) 27: 430.

27. *Baltimore Evening Post*, September 27, 1793; Pierce, 241; Claude-Corentin Tanguy de la Boissière, "Proposals for Printing a Journal of the Revolutions in the French Part of St. Domingo" (n.p., 1793), 10–11.

28. Dubois, *Avengers of the New World*, 82–83; Frances Sergeant Childs, *French Refugee Life in the United States, 1790–1800: An American Chapter of the French Revolution* (Baltimore: Johns Hopkins Press, 1940), 51–56.

29. Tanguy, 1.

30. Bertrand Van Ruymbeke, "*Refugiés* or *Émigrés?* Early Modern French Migrations to British North America and the United States (c. 1680–c. 1820)," *Itinerario* 30, no. 2 (2006): 11.

31. Jon Butler, *Awash in a Sea of Faith: Christianizing the American People* (Cambridge: Harvard University Press, 1990), 198–99, 269.

32. Tanguy, 1.

33. Ibid., 2.

34. James Alexander Dun, "'What avenues of commerce, will you, Americans, not explore!': Commercial Philadelphia's Vantage onto the Early Haitian Revolution," *William and Mary Quarterly* 62, no. 3 (July 2005): 473–504.

35. For Sonthonax's accusations of white Saint-Dominguans as "independentists," see Stein, 47.

36. Tanguy, 3.

37. Pierre François Page, *Conspirations, trahisons et calomnies: dévoilées et dénoncées par plus de dix mille français réfugiés au continent de l'Amérique* (Paris: L'imprimerie de la citoyenne Fotronge, Jardin Egalité, no. 71, 1794), 10.

38. On the background of Chôtard, see letter dated March 13, 1791 in *Suite des lettres adressées par différentes municipalités de la colonie, à celle du Port-au-Prince*, vol. 2 of *Révolutions de St. Domingue Collection*, John Carter Brown Library, Providence, RI.

39. Announcements of these celebrations: "Procés Verbal de la fête qui a eu lieu le 2 Pluviose (21 Janvier v. st.)" (Philadelphia: printed by Parent, 1795); "Procés Verbal de celebration de la fête du 23 Thermidor (10 Août v. st.)" (Philadelphia: printed by Parent, 1794); "Relation de l'Anniversaire de la Fèdération du 14 Juillet 1789, Célebrée à C[h]arleston, le Sextidi 26 Messidor, l'An 3e. de la Republique Française, Une & Indivisible, 14 Juillet 1795 (V.S.)" (Charleston: printed by Béleurgey, 1795). On refugee celebrations see Jean-Charles Benzaken, "Le refus de l'abolition: les colons français réfugiés aux États-Unis et l'organisation des fêtes révolutionnaires et contre-révolutionnaires" in *Esclavage, résistances et abolitions*, published by the Comité des travaux historiques et scientifiques, 123e Congrès des sociétés historiques et scientifiques, Fort-de-France-Schoelcher, 6–10 avril 1998 (Editions du CTHS, 1999), 235–51. Simon P. Newman, *Parades and the Politics of the Street: Festive Culture in the Early American Republic* (Philadelphia: University of Pennsylvania Press, 1997), chapter 4.

40. Pierre François Page and Augustin Jean Brulley, *Developpement des Cases des Troubles et Désastres des Colonies Françaises, présenté a la Convention Nationale, par les Commissaires de Saint-Domingue, sur la demande des comites de Marine & Des Colonies, réunis, après en avoir donné communication aux Colons résidens à Paris, & convoqués, à cet effet, le 11 juin*

1793, l'an 2e. de la République (Paris[?], 1793), 10, 67. As noted in idem, "Calomniateurs Dénoncés a la Convention Nationale" (Paris: le 8 Fructidor, l'an 2), 3.

41. "Protestions des Colons Patriotes de Saint-Domingue, Réfugiés à Philadelphie, Contre un Encrit intitulé Service Funebre de Louis XVI, &c" (1794), 1.

42. *Notes fournies au Comité de Salut Public par les Commissaires de Saint-Domingue, Page & Brulley* (Paris, 1794), 71. Original French: "Les colons qui se sont réfugiés à l'Amérique du Nord, sont divisés en deux classes: les democrats ou les amis de la république; les contre-révolutionnaires ou les partisans de la royauté."; see also Pierre François Page, Augustin Jean Brulley, and Jean-Baptiste-Bernard Legrand, "Adresse a la Convention Nationale" (Paris: le 2 fructidor, an 2), 1.

43. Tanguy, 2.

44. Carolyn Fick, *The Making of Haiti: The Saint-Domingue Revolution from Below* (Knoxville: University of Tennessee Press, 1990), chapter 3; Geggus, "Racial Equality, Slavery, and Colonial Secession," 1290–1308; and Stein, 27–33.

45. Stein, 38–48.

46. Ibid., 22, 47.

47. Ibid., 69–70.

48. Ibid., 71–77; Fick, 158–59.

49. Stanley Elkins and Eric McKitrick, *The Age of Federalism: The Early American Republic, 1788–1800* (New York: Oxford University Press, 1993), 328–29; Thomas Paine, "Reasons for Preserving the Life of Louis Capet," in Michael Foot and Isaac Kramnick, eds., *The Thomas Paine Reader* (New York: Penguin, 1987), 394–98.

50. Quotation from *New-York Journal and Patriotic Register*, August 10, 1793. Elkins and McKitrick, 335–36; Newman, *Parades and the Politics of the Street*, 139–40; and Waldstreicher, 133–36.

51. *Dunlap's American Daily Advertiser* (Philadelphia), July 4, 1793.

52. Elkins and McKitrick, 391.

53. James Roger Sharp, *American Politics in the Early Republic: The New Nation in Crisis* (New Haven: Yale University Press, 1993), 8–13.

54. *Dunlap's American Daily Advertiser* (Philadelphia), September 13, 1793; *Baltimore Daily Intelligencer*, January 4, 1794.

55. *Baltimore Daily Intelligencer*, November 4, 1793.

56. *Dunlap's American Daily Advertiser* (Philadelphia), September 13, 1793.

57. Genet to Jefferson, September 19 and 25, 1793, *The Papers of Thomas Jefferson* 27: 404–6, 436–39.

58. *Dunlap's American Daily Advertiser* (Philadelphia), August 14, 1793.

59. Reprinted from the *New-York Daily Gazette* in the *Columbian Centinel* (Boston), July 13, 1793.

60. Childs, 53.

61. "Extrait du Mémoire justificatif de Citoyen Larchevesque-Thibaud, déporté de Saint-Domingue" (Paris, 1793); Pierce, 82–85.

62. *Conspirations*, vii–viii; see also Page, Brulley, and Legrand, 3.

63. J. Marie de Bordes, *Défense des Colons de Saint-Domingue; ou Examen Rapide de la*

Nouvelle Déclaration des Droits de l'Homme, en ce qu'elle a particulièrement de relatif aux Colonies (Philadelphia?, 1796), 35.

64. "Rencontre d'un Colon avec un des Egorgeurs de son Pays" signed by Therou, "a colonist from Saint-Domingue" (Paris: le 8 fructidor l'an 2e).

65. *Columbian Herald* (Charleston), December 27, 1793.

66. *Virginia Chronicle* (Norfolk), November 23, 1793; *Baltimore Daily Intelligencer*, account dated April 20, 1794, but printed on May 31, 1794; *Columbian Centinel* (Boston), November 27, 1793; and *American Minerva* (New York), December 14, 1793.

67. Tanguy, 4.

68. Etienne Bellumeau Delavincendiere, Will, January 1801, Will Book D. Charleston, SC. See also Jean Baptiste Collas, Will, March 31, 1805. Charleston, SC.

69. Gabriel Jean-Baptiste Larchevesque-Thibaud, *Mémoire et pieces justificatives adressés a la Convention nationale, par le Citoyen Larchevesque-Thibaud, ancien procureur de la commune du Cap François* (Paris: L'imprimerie de Testu, 1793).

70. On Ternant's frustrations with the refugees during his tenure, see Gordon S. Brown, *Toussaint's Clause: The Founding Fathers and the Haitian Revolution* (Jackson: University Press of Mississippi, 2005), 52–58; Ternant to Armand Marc, comte de Montmorin, September 28 and October 24, 1791, in "Correspondence of the French Ministers to the United States, 1791–1797," ed. Frederick J. Turner, *Annual Report of the American Historical Association for the Year 1903* (Washington, DC: Government Printing Office, 1904) 2:45–47, 60–65.

71. Edmond Charles Genet to Thomas Jefferson, August 4, 1793, *The Papers of Thomas Jefferson* 26:612.

72. Elkins and McKitrick, 333, 335–36, 345–54.

73. Brown, 87.

74. *Conspirations*, 14.

75. *Conspirations*, 37, 75; *Courrier politique de la France et de ses Colonies*, no. 40, December 1793, 158.

76. The circular letter appeared in *The Baltimore Daily Intelligencer*, December 2, 1793; *Pennsylvania Gazette* (Philadelphia), December 4, 1794; *Columbian Centinel* (Boston), December 7, 1793; and *Columbian Herald* (Charleston), December 17, 1793.

77. *City Gazette and Daily Advertiser* (Charleston), November 26, 1793.

78. Ibid., December 2, 1793.

79. *Virginia Chronicle* (Norfolk), February 8, 1794.

80. *Columbian Centinel* (Boston), July 20, 1793.

81. Elkins and McKitrick, 263–70.

82. *The American Museum* (Philadelphia: from the press of Mathew Carey, 1792), 288.

83. *New-York Journal and Patriotic Register*, June 27, 1792.

84. *Baltimore Evening Post*, November 12, 1792.

85. Quotation from Cutting to Jefferson, December 28, 1791, *The Papers of Thomas Jefferson* 22:463. For additional commentary from Cutting on faction, see his dispatches to Jefferson dated November 29, 1791, 22:349–51; March 1 and April 13, 1792, 23:177–79, 414.

86. Quotation from Elkins and McKitrick, 360; Matthew Schoenbachler, "Republicanism in the Age of Democratic Revolution: The Democratic-Republican Societies of the 1790s" *Journal of the Early Republic* 18, no. 2 (Summer 1998), 245–46; and Todd Estes, "Shaping the Politics of Public Opinion: Federalists and the Jay Treaty Debate," *Journal of the Early Republic* 20, no. 3 (Fall 2000), 408–9.

87. *Southern Centinel and Universal Gazette* (Augusta, GA), September 12, 1793.

88. *City Gazette and Daily Advertiser* (Charleston), January 9, 1794.

89. Kenneth Roberts and Anna M. Roberts, trans. and eds., *Moreau de St. Méry's American Journey [1793–1798]* (New York: Doubleday, 1947), 144. Hereafter cited as *Moreau's Journey*. Italics in original. See also Althéa de Puech Parham, ed. and trans., *My Odyssey: Experiences of a Young Refugee from Two Revolutions by a Creole of Saint Domingue* (Baton Rouge: Louisiana State University Press, 1959), 181. This sentiment was shared by French continental exiles as well.

90. *Virginia Herald and Fredericksburg Advertiser*, August 8, 1793; *Columbian Centinel* (Boston), July 20, 1793.

91. Elkins and McKitrick, 451–61.

92. Robin Blackburn, "Haiti, Slavery, and the Age of Democratic Revolution," *William and Mary Quarterly* 63, no. 4 (October 2006): 643–74; Simon P. Newman, "American Political Culture and the French and Haitian Revolutions: Nathaniel Cutting and the Jeffersonian Republicans" in David Geggus, ed., *The Impact of the Haitian Revolution on the Atlantic World* (Columbia: University of South Carolina Press, 2001), 72–85.

93. *Baltimore Daily Intelligencer*, November 13, 1793.

94. Laurent Dubois, *A Colony of Citizens: Revolution and Slave Emancipation in the French Caribbean, 1787–1804* (Chapel Hill: University of North Carolina Press, 2004).

95. Marilyn Baseler, *"Asylum for Mankind": America, 1607–1800* (Ithaca: Cornell University Press, 1998), 264.

96. *The Debates and Proceedings in the Congress of the United States* (Washington, DC: Gales and Seaton, 1834–56) 4:1034. Hereafter cited as *Annals of Congress*.

97. *Annals of Congress* 4:1038.

98. Thomas Hart Benton, *Abridgment of the Debates of Congress, from 1789 to 1856* (reprint; New York: AMS Press, 1970), 1:559. Hereafter cited as *Abridgment of Debates*.

99. Ibid., 1:556, 561.

100. *Annals of Congress*, 4:1042–43; *Abridgment of Debates*, 1:559–60; on the 1790s naturalization debates, see Baseler, chapter 7.

101. Pierce, 211–13.

102. Stein, 116; R. Darrell Meadows, "The Planters of Saint-Domingue, 1750–1804: Migration and Exile in the French Revolutionary Atlantic" (Ph.D. diss., Carnegie Mellon University, 2004), 207–8; on connections with refugees in the United States, see *Débats entre les Accusateurs et les Accusés, dans l'Affaire des Colonies, Imprimés en Exécution de la Loi du 4 Pluviose* (Paris, Pluviôse an 3), 1:6–7.

103. *Gazette française et américaine* (New York), July 17, 1795. In October the paper did publish a list of the charges against Sonthonax and Polverel (see October 19, 1795).

104. Stein, 117.

105. Pierce, 236–37.

106. On Jefferson, see *Débats* 9:71; on Genet, see 1:14–16 and 4:136; on Galbaud, see 4:125–47.

107. On conspiracy, see *Débats* 1:11; on Tanguy, see 3:342–45 and 9:121; on the funeral service, see 4:86–87; on the cockade, see 3:342; and on the British, see 4:79.

108. Pierce, 227.

109. Ibid., 269.

110. Stein, 117–19.

111. *New York Journal and Patriotic Register*, June 14, 1796.

112. Dubois, *Avengers of the New World*, 206–7.

113. During the earliest days of the French Revolution, London had emerged as a hub of counter-revolutionary activity. On French émigrés in London, see Kirsty Carpenter, *Refugees of the French Revolution: Émigrés in London, 1789–1802* (London: Macmillan, 1999); on French émigrés throughout Europe, see Kirsty Carpenter and Philip Mansel, eds., *The French Émigrés in Europe and the Struggle against Revolution, 1789–1814* (London: Macmillan, 1999).

114. Pierce, 300.

115. (Following all from L'imprimerie nationale, Paris.) On philanthropy see Vincent Marie Viénot, comte de Vaublanc, "Opinion de Vienot-Vaublanc, sur la pétition des déportés de Saint-Domingue, détenus à Rochefort, sur la competence des conseils militaries" (1797, 22 germinal, an 5); on Sonthonax and suffering see François Louis Bourdon, "Rapport fait par Bourdon (de l'Oise) au nom de la commission des colonies, composée des représentans du peuple Vaublanc, Tarbé, Hélot, Villaret-Joyeuse" (1797, 3 Messidor, an 5); and on deportation see Louis Antoine Esprit Rallier, "Opinion de Rallier, sur la resolution du 24 Messidor, an 5, relative aux déportés & réfugiés des colonies" (1798, 6 vendémiaire, an 6); (first name unknown) Leconte-Puiraveau, "Rapport fait par Leconite-Puiraveau, au nom de la Commission des Colonies Occidentales, sur les déportés & réfugiés de Saint-Domingue, soit en France, soit en continent Américain" (1797, 4 Germinal, an 5); and Pierce, 300–313.

116. Rallier, 4, 6.

117. P. Bordas, "Rapport fait par P. Bordas, depute de la Haute-Vienne, au nom de la commission composée des représentans Lecouteulx, Lacoste, Dupuch, Comberousse & Bordas, chargée d'examiner la résolution du 24 messidor, concernant les réfugiés & déportés des colonies" (Paris: L'imprimerie nationale, 1797) (complémentaire, an 5), 3, 16.

118. Pierce, 287, 302–5, 311.

119. Ibid., 313–26.

120. As Darrell Meadows points out, however, the lack of collective political amnesty did not mean that the Saint-Dominguan exiles were not seen as worthy recipients of aid from the French state. Throughout the decade many petitioned the government successfully for financial support and aid in kind—despite their politics. Meadows, 185–99, 212–14, 229–44.

121. *Moreau's Journey*, 369–72.

122. *Abridgment of Debates*, 2:283.

123. Baseler, 272–73.

124. Timothy Pickering to Robert Liston, July 3, 1798. *Naval Documents related to the*

Quasi-War between the United States and France, 7 vols. (Washington, DC: U.S. Government Printing Office, 1935), 1:162.

125. Reported in *Pennsylvania Gazette* (Philadelphia), October 18, 1797; Reported in *Pennsylvania Gazette* (Philadelphia), August 23, 1797.

126. *Pennsylvania Gazette* (Philadelphia), September 6, 1797.

127. Baseler, 289–90.

CHAPTER 4: THE CONTAGION OF REBELLION

1. On the depoliticization of accounts of the Haitian Revolution, see Michel-Rolph Trouillot, *Silencing the Past: Power and the Production of History* (Boston: Beacon Press, 1995).

2. *The Universal Asylum, and Columbian Magazine* (Philadelphia: from the Press of M. Carey, September 1792), 214. Slaveowners in Cuba also depicted Saint-Dominguan slavery as extraordinarily harsh, to differentiate Cuban from Saint-Dominguan slavery and to discount the possibility of a rebellion in Cuba. See Matt Childs, "A Black French General Arrived to Conquer the Island: Images of the Haitian Revolution in Cuba's 1812 Aponte Rebellion," in *The Impact of the Haitian Revolution in the Atlantic World*, ed. David P. Geggus (Columbia: University of South Carolina Press, 2001).

3. Kenneth Roberts and Anna M. Roberts, trans. and eds., *Moreau de St. Méry's American Journey [1793–1798]* (New York: Doubleday, 1947), 303. Hereafter cited as *Moreau's Journey*.

4. *New-York Journal*, January 2, 1792.

5. "Character of the Creoles of St. Domingo," *The American Museum* (Philadelphia: from the Press of M. Cary, November 1789), 360. For accusations against Caribbean slaveholders in the French and British press, see David Brion Davis, *The Problem of Slavery in the Age of Revolution, 1770–1823*, 2nd ed. (New York: Oxford University Press, 1999); Robin Blackburn, *The Overthrow of Colonial Slavery, 1776–1848* (London: Verso, 1988); and idem, *The Making of New World Slavery: From the Baroque to the Modern* (London: Verso, 1997).

6. *Baltimore Evening Post*, July 27, 1792.

7. Joseph Lavallée, "The negro equalled by few Europeans," *The American Museum* (April 1791), 211n.

8. "Revenge," *The American Museum* (November 1789), 406.

9. [Edward Darlington], *Reflections on Slavery; with Recent Evidence of its Inhumanity. Occasioned by the Melancholy Death of Romain, a French Negro. By Humanitas.* (Philadelphia: printed for the author by R. Cochran, 1803), 13–14, 17.

10. Ibid., 17.

11. Ibid., 15. Italics mine.

12. *New-York Journal and Patriotic Register*, February 20, 1793. A similarly phrased report about the treatment of Saint-Dominguan slaves appeared in the *Augusta Chronicle and Gazette of the State* (Georgia), March 9, 1793.

13. Carolyn Fick, *The Making of Haiti: The Saint-Domingue Revolution from Below* (Knoxville: University of Tennessee Press, 1990), 116–17.

14. *New-York Journal and Patriotic Register*, August 17, 1793.

15. *Virginia Herald and Fredericksburg Advertiser*, November 8, 1792; also reported in *Pennsylvania Gazette* (Philadelphia), October 31, 1792.

16. *National Gazette* (Philadelphia), July 31, 1793.

17. "Lines on the devastations of St. Domingo," *The American Museum* (Appendix, July–December 1792), 13.

18. Thomas Clarkson, "West Indian Insurrections," *The American Museum* (June 1792), 298.

19. On the importance of an African presence to slave rebellions, see Eugene Genovese, *From Rebellion to Revolution: Afro-American Slave Revolts in the Making of the Modern World* (Baton Rouge: Louisiana State University, 1979).

20. Clarkson, 300.

21. On Clarkson's views of emancipation, see Davis, *The Problem of Slavery*, 311.

22. *United States Chronicle* (Providence, RI), September 26, 1793; also printed in *American Apollo* (Boston), September 20, 1793.

23. Ibid.

24. Ibid.

25. On slave import figures for this era, see James A. McMillin, *The Final Victims: Foreign Slave Trade to North America, 1783–1810* (Columbia, SC: University of South Carolina Press, 2004).

26. Sylvanus Bourne to Thomas Jefferson, *The Papers of Thomas Jefferson*, ed. Charles T. Cullen (Princeton: Princeton University Press, 1986) 22:133.

27. J. P. Martin [Abraham Bishop], "Rights of Black Men," *The American Museum* (November 1792). On Bishop and his circle, see Davis, *The Problem of Slavery*, 327; Franklin B. Dexter, "Abraham Bishop, of Connecticut, and his Writings," *Proceedings of the Massachusetts Historical Society*, 2nd ser., 19 (1905), 190–99; James Alexander Dun, "Dangerous Intelligence: Slavery, Race, and St. Domingue in the Early American Republic," (Ph.D. diss., Princeton University, 2004), 200–208; Tim Matthewson, "Abraham Bishop, 'The Rights of Black Men,' and the American Reaction to the Haitian Revolution," *Journal of Negro History* 67, no. 2 (Summer 1982): 148–54; and David Waldstreicher and Stephen R. Grossbart, "Abraham Bishop's Vocation; or, the Mediation of Jeffersonian Politics," *Journal of the Early Republic* 18, no. 4 (Winter 1998): 617–57. According to Davis, Waldstreicher, and Grossbart, Bishop's article was also published in the *National Gazette*, July 31, 1793; *Columbian Centinel* (Boston), September 21, 1791; *The Argus* (Boston), November 22 and 25 and December 5, 1791; and in the *Cumberland Gazette* (Falmouth, MA), December 5 and 12, 1791; and according to Dun, the article also appeared in the *Federal Gazette* (Philadelphia), December 3, 7, and 17, 1791.

28. [Bishop], 300.

29. Ibid., 299.

30. Ibid., 300.

31. Ibid.

32. See James Brewer Stewart, *Holy Warriors: The Abolitionists and American Slavery*, rev. ed. (New York: Hill & Wang, 1996), chapter 1; Davis, *The Problem of Slavery*, 317. On legal efforts to enforce the gradual manumission laws in Philadelphia, see Gary Nash, *Forging Freedom: The Formation of Philadelphia's Black Community, 1720–1840* (Cambridge:

Harvard University Press, 1988), 108, 140–42. On the difficulties of gradual manumission in New England, see Joanne Pope Melish, *Disowning Slavery: Gradual Emancipation and "Race" in New England, 1780–1860* (Ithaca: Cornell University Press, 1998).

33. Quoted in Matthewson, "Abraham Bishop," 153.

34. Ibid., 152.

35. On the tenor of support for emancipation in the French West Indies in Philadelphia newspapers, especially those of Bache and Freneau, see Dun, "Dangerous Intelligence," 224–37.

36. Thomas Jefferson, *Notes on the State of Virginia*, ed. Frank Shuffelton (New York: Penguin Books, 1999), Query XIV, 145. For more about Jefferson's views on the aftermath of abolition, see Peter S. Onuf, "'To Declare Them a Free and Independent People': Race, Slavery, and National Identity in Jefferson's Thought," *Journal of the Early Republic* 18, no. 1 (Spring 1998): 1–46.

37. St. George Tucker, *A Dissertation on Slavery: with a Proposal for the Gradual Abolition of it, in the State of Virginia* (Philadelphia: printed for Mathew Carey, 1796), 88.

38. Ibid., 77.

39. Ibid., 68.

40. Ibid., 95–96.

41. Thomas Jefferson to St. George Tucker, August 28, 1797, *The Papers of Thomas Jefferson*, ed. Barbara B. Oberg (Princeton: Princeton University Press, 2001) 29:519.

42. Dun, "Dangerous Intelligence," chapter 5; Richard S. Newman, *The Transformation of American Abolitionism: Fighting Slavery in the Early Republic* (Chapel Hill: University of North Carolina Press, 2002), 26–28.

43. *Time Piece* (New York), June 23, 1797.

44. *Pennsylvania Gazette* (Philadelphia), May 16, 1792.

45. On the possibility of slave revolts in Jamaica see *Pennsylvania Gazette* (Philadelphia), June 27, 1792, but the article was dated May 19; and *Virginia Herald and Fredericksburg Advertiser*, July 5, 1792, but account within article dated from May. For an excellent explanation of why the slaves in Jamaica (who had a long history of rebellion) did not revolt during the Haitian Revolution, see David Geggus, "The Enigma of Jamaica in the 1790s: New Light on the Causes of Slave Rebellions," *William and Mary Quarterly* 44, no. 2 (April 1987): 274–99; on Martinique, see *Pennsylvania Gazette* (Philadelphia), January 27, 1796; and on Cuba see José Morales, "The Hispaniola Diaspora, 1791–1850: Puerto Rico, Cuba, Louisiana, and Other Host Societies" (Ph.D. diss., University of Connecticut, 1986), 54. Rumors of slave revolts circulated throughout Latin America and the Caribbean. See Jeremy Adelman, *Sovereignty and Revolution in the Iberian Atlantic* (Princeton: Princeton University Press, 2006), 91–96; and Julius Scott, "The Common Wind: Currents of Afro-American Communication in the Era of the Haitian Revolution" (Ph.D. diss., Duke University, 1986), chapter 4.

46. Exiles in Jamaica made the same case about the loyalty of their slaves. See Peter M. Voelz, *Slave and Soldier: The Military Impact of Blacks in the Colonial Americas* (New York: Garland Publishing, 1993), 170.

47. John Thomas Carré to Charles Willson Peale, ca. 1792. Sellers Family Papers, American Philosophical Society, Philadelphia, PA.

48. David Geggus, "Slave, Soldier, Rebel: The Strange Career of Jean Kina," in *Haitian Revolutionary Studies*, ed. David Geggus (Bloomington: Indiana University Press, 2002); and Ashli White, "The Saint-Dominguan Refugees and American Distinctiveness in the Early Years of the Haitian Revolution" in *The World of the Haitian Revolution*, ed. David Geggus and Norman Fiering (Bloomington: Indiana University Press, 2009).

49. Arthur Jones, *Pierre Toussaint* (New York: Doubleday, 2003), 97.

50. Joseph Davis, Will, August 4, 1798. Will Book 1797–1802. Baltimore County, MD.

51. Standing Committee Minutes, August 11, 1801. New York Manumission Society Papers. New-York Historical Society, New York, NY. Hereafter abbreviated NYMS Papers.

52. Jones, *Pierre Toussaint*, 97.

53. *American Star* (Philadelphia), February 4, 1794. On black networks of information throughout the Caribbean, see Scott, "The Common Wind," 244, 281.

54. Standing Committee Minutes, November 5, 1808. NYMS Papers.

55. Society Minutes, Report of the Standing Committee, April 12, 1808. NYMS Papers.

56. *Columbian Centinel* (Boston), October 19, 1793.

57. *Virginia Chronicle* (Norfolk), October 19, 1793. For more on the Secret Keeper Plot, see Douglas Egerton, "The Tricolor in Black and White: The French Revolution in Gabriel's Virginia" in *Slavery in the Caribbean Francophone World: Distant Voices, Forgotten Acts, Forged Identities*, ed. Doris Y. Kadish (Athens: University of Georgia Press, 2000), 96–98; Sylvia R. Frey, *Water from the Rock: Black Resistance in a Revolutionary Age* (Princeton: Princeton University Press, 1991), 230–31; and James Sidbury, "Saint-Domingue in Virginia: Ideology, Local Meanings, and Resistance to Slavery, 1790–1800," *Journal of Southern History* 63, no. 3 (August 1997): 531–52.

58. *Boston Gazette*, November 11, 1793.

59. *Pennsylvania Gazette* (Philadelphia), December 13, 1797; for more detail on the Charleston plots, see George D. Terry, "A Study of the Impact of the French Revolution and the Insurrections in Saint-Domingue upon South Carolina: 1790–1805" (M.A. thesis, University of South Carolina, 1973), 46–131.

60. *Pennsylvania Gazette* (Philadelphia), December 13, 1797.

61. Quoted in Shane White, *Somewhat More Independent: The End of Slavery in New York City, 1770–1810* (Athens: University of Georgia Press, 1991), 65.

62. Quotation from *Baltimore Daily Intelligencer*, December 4, 1793; additional commentary appeared in the *Columbian Centinel* (Boston), December 4, 1793. For a consideration of the white politics behind the Secret Keeper Plot, especially as it concerned Federalists and Democratic Republicans in South Carolina, see Robert Alderson, "Charleston's Rumored Slave Revolt of 1793" in Geggus, *Impact of the Haitian Revolution*. Jefferson sent word to Governor Moultrie of South Carolina about a "Brissotin" plot to incite insurrection in his state. Letter quoted in Gordon S. Brown, *Toussaint's Clause: The Founding Fathers and the Haitian Revolution* (Jackson: University Press of Mississippi, 2005), 102.

63. Quoted in James Sidbury, *Ploughshares into Swords: Race, Rebellion, and Identity in Gabriel's Virginia, 1730–1810* (Cambridge: Cambridge University Press, 1997), 129. On the Frenchmen involved in Gabriel's Rebellion, see Douglas R. Egerton, *Gabriel's Rebellion: The Virginia Slave Conspiracies of 1800 and 1802* (Chapel Hill: University of North Carolina Press, 1993), 182–85.

64. Cuban planters blamed black and colored Saint-Dominguans in their assessment of the Aponte Rebellion in 1812. See Childs, "A Black French General."

65. For the case that the Haitian Revolution informed black ideology in Virginia, see Sidbury, "Saint-Domingue in Virginia."

66. Draft of a letter by "Les Citoyens de couleur de Philadelphie à L'Assemblée Nationale,"1793. Révolutions de St. Domingue Collection. John Carter Brown Library, Providence, RI. Although dated 1793, this letter—because of its reference to the abolition decree of February 1794—must be later. There is no indication as to whether this letter was actually sent or who wrote it.

67. On the depth of newspaper coverage of the Haitian Revolution in Philadelphia, see Dun, "Dangerous Intelligence," chapters 2–4.

68. Prince Hall, *A Charge, Delivered to the African Lodge, June 24, 1797, at Menotomy* (Boston, 1797), 10–11; on Hall, see Sara C. Fanning, "The Roots of Early Black Nationalism: Northern African Americans' Invocations of Haiti in the Early Nineteenth Century," *Slavery and Abolition* 28, no. 1 (2007): 64.

69. Standing Committee Minutes, October 6, 1801. NYMS Papers.

70. Shane White, *Somewhat More Independent*, 144–45.

71. Fanning, 65; Shane White, "'It Was a Proud Day': African Americans, Festivals, and Parades in the North, 1741–1834," *Journal of American History* 81, no. 1 (June 1994), 34.

72. Shane White, *Somewhat More Independent*, 191.

73. *Daily Advertiser* (New York), December 16, 1794; *City Gazette and Daily Advertiser* (Charleston), June 5, 1794.

74. *Daily Advertiser* (New York), August 12, 1794; *Baltimore Daily Intelligencer*, November 1, 1793. On "enticement" as a trope in explaining slaves' rebellious behavior, see John Hope Franklin and Loren Schweninger, *Runaway Slaves: Rebels on the Plantation* (New York: Oxford University Press, 1999), 250.

75. *Daily Advertiser* (New York), August 2, 1794; *Baltimore Daily Intelligencer*, February 27, 1794. On "French negroes" posing as free, see also *City Gazette and Daily Advertiser* (Charleston), May 28, 1793.

76. On French and American slaves running away together, see *Daily Advertiser* (New York), November 11 and December 24, 1793, and February 19, 1802. On the case of Lando, see *City Gazette and Daily Advertiser* (Charleston), July 15, 1797.

77. *Baltimore Evening Post*, September 18, 1793; on cockades and who wore them in the United States, see Simon P. Newman, *Parades and the Politics of the Street: Festive Culture in the Early American Republic* (Philadelphia: University of Pennsylvania Press, 1997), chapters 4 and 5.

78. For a longer discussion of Crispin and Girard, see Ashli White, "Crispin's Flight: Master and Servant in an Age of Revolutions," in "Early America and the Haitian Revolution," ed. Michael Drexler and Elizabeth Maddock Dillon (unpublished manuscript).

79. John Bach McMaster, *The Life and Times of Stephen Girard: Mariner and Merchant* (Philadelphia: J. B. Lippincott, 1918), 1:275. On European presence in eighteenth-century India, see Ranbir Vohra, *The Making of India: A Historical Survey*, 2nd ed. (Armonk, NY: M. E. Sharpe, 2001); on American involvement in India, see Susan S. Bean, *Yankee India: American Commercial and Cultural Encounters with India in the Age of Sail, 1784–1860* (Salem, MA: Peabody Essex Museum, 2001), 17.

80. On Crispin's language, J. H. Roberjot to Stephen Girard, March 7, 1795; on his clothing, Jean Girard to Mr. Adam, November 21, 1794. Correspondence of Stephen Girard, Microfilm Collection, Stephen Girard papers, American Philosophical Society, Philadelphia, PA. Hereafter cited as SGP.

81. Etienne Laveaux to Genty Lavaud, September 9, 1795, SGP.

82. On Laveaux's views on slavery and racial equality, see Bernard Gainot, "Le Général Laveaux, Gouverneur de Saint-Domingue deputé Jacobin," in *Esclavage, colonization, libérations nationales de 1789 à nos jours* (Paris: Editions L'Hartmattan, 1990); and idem, "La constitutionnalisation de la liberté générale sous le directoire," in *Les abolitions de l'esclavage 1793 1794 1848 de L. F. Sonthonax à V. Schoelcher*, ed. Marcel Dorigny (Paris: Éditions UNESCO, 1995).

83. For cases of African Americans heading to Haiti during the revolution, see Scott, "The Common Wind," 284–89, and Julius Scott, "Afro-American Sailors and the International Network: The Case of Newport Bowers," in *Jack Tar in History: Essays in the History of Maritime Life and Labour*, ed. Colin D. Howell and Richard J. Twomey (Fredericton, N.B.: Acadiensis Press, 1991): 37–52.

84. *Columbian Herald* (Charleston), October 19, 1793.

85. *City Gazette and Daily Advertiser* (Charleston), October 9, 1793.

86. Davis, *The Problem of Slavery*, 120; Frey, 232; Alfred Hunt, *Haiti's Influence on Antebellum America: Slumbering Volcano in the Caribbean* (Baton Rouge: Louisiana State University Press, 1988), 109; Nash, *Forging Freedom*, 175; Thompson Westcott, *A History of Philadelphia, from the time of the first settlements on the Delaware to the consolidation of the city and districts in 1854* (Philadelphia: mounted and bound by Pewson & Nicolson for Brinton Coxe, 1886) 3:637. Laws barring the entrance of slaves were also passed in France well before the revolution. See Sue Peabody, *"There Are No Slaves in France": The Political Culture of Race and Slavery in the Ancien Regime* (New York: Oxford University Press, 1996).

87. *City Gazette and Daily Advertiser* (Charleston), May 12, 1794.

88. *Columbian Herald* (Charleston), September 8, 1794.

89. *City Gazette and Daily Advertiser* (Charleston), January 5, 1798.

90. Tommy L. Bogger, *Free Blacks in Norfolk, Virginia, 1790–1860: The Darker Side of Freedom* (Charlottesville: University Press of Virginia, 1997), 27.

91. By the spring of 1794, 250 American vessels had fallen into British hands. Stanley Elkins and Eric McKitrick, *The Age of Federalism: The Early American Republic, 1788–1800* (New York: Oxford University Press, 1993), 391.

92. For Jefferson's take on British privateers, see his letter printed in the *Pennsylvania Gazette* (Philadelphia), December 24, 1793.

93. Reported in *Dunlap's American Daily Advertiser* (Philadelphia), September 11, 1793.

94. Reported in *City Gazette and Daily Advertiser* (Charleston), September 17, 1793. For another example of Saint-Dominguan slaves being "redeemed," see *Virginia Chronicle* (Norfolk), August 24, 1793.

95. *Dunlap's American Daily Advertiser* (Philadelphia), January 1, 1793.

96. Ibid., March 20, 1793.

97. Nash, *Forging Freedom*, 142. For the case of a white refugee who continued to pro-

test the manumission law, see Susan Branson and Leslie Patrick, "Étrangers dans un Pays Étrange: Saint Domingan Refugees of Color in Philadelphia" in Geggus, ed. *The Impact of the Haitian Revolution*, 194–95.

98. David Brion Davis, "Impact of the French and Haitian Revolutions" in Geggus, ed. *The Impact of the Haitian Revolution on the Atlantic World*. The slave trade also grew quickly in Latin America after 1790. See Adelman, *Sovereignty and Revolution*, chapter 2.

99. *The Papers of Thomas Jefferson*, ed. John Catanzariti (Princeton: Princeton University Press, 1990) 24:599, 603, 693–95. Quotation from 693–94. Evidence suggests that American captains were smuggling slaves out of Martinique as well. *Dunlap's American Daily Advertiser* (Philadelphia), July 2, 1792.

100. *Gazette of the United States* (Philadelphia), October 27, 1801.

101. Reported in *Pennsylvania Gazette* (Philadelphia), August 15, 1792.

102. Account and quotation from Newman, *Parades and the Politics of the Street*, 157–58.

103. Sidbury, *Ploughshares*, 133–34.

104. Quoted in Alfred Hunt, 118.

105. John Murdock, *The Politicians; or, a State of Things. A Dramatic Piece* (Philadelphia: printed for the author, 1798), 19. On racism and representations of dialect, see Melish, 169–83.

106. Murdock, *The Politicians*, 20.

107. Idem, *The Triumphs of Love; or Happy Reconciliation. A Comedy. In Four Acts. Written by an American, and a Citizen of Philadelphia* (Philadelphia: printed by R. Folwell, September 10, 1795), 52.

108. Ibid., 67.

109. On the Democratic Republican impulse behind Murdock's writings, see Heather S. Nathans, *Early American Theatre from the Revolution to Thomas Jefferson: Into the Hands of the People* (New York: Cambridge University Press, 2003), 92–101.

110. *Pennsylvania Gazette* (Philadelphia), March 26, 1794.

111. February 19, 1796, Pageot, General of the Brigade [writing from Philadelphia], to Toussaint Louverture. Copied in the correspondence of Stephen Girard, SGP. Alfred Hunt argues that only Federalist merchants were keen on cultivating relations with Toussaint Louverture, but Stephen Girard was an ardent Democratic Republican (Hunt, 33).

112. W. Jeffrey Bolster, *Black Jacks: African American Seamen in the Age of Sail* (Cambridge: Harvard University Press, 1997), 145; Peter Linebaugh and Marcus Rediker, *The Many-Headed Hydra: Sailors, Slaves, Commoners, and the Hidden History of the Revolutionary Atlantic* (Boston: Beacon Press, 2000); Scott, "The Common Wind"; and Sidbury, "Saint-Domingue in Virginia."

113. Bolster, 147.

114. *Pennsylvania Gazette* (Philadelphia), August 8, 1798. See Mats Lundahl, "Toussaint L'Ouverture and the War Economy of Saint-Domingue," *Slavery and Abolition* 6, no. 2 (September 1985): 123; and "Letters of Toussaint Louverture and of Edward Stevens, 1798–1800," *American Historical Review* (in Documents) 16, no. 1 (October 1910): 64–101.

115. Quotations from Mr. Gros, *An Historick Recital of the Different Occurrences in the Camps of Grande-Reviere, Dondon, Saine-Suzanne, and others from the 26th of October, 1791,*

to the 24th of December, of the same Year (Baltimore: printed by Samuel and John Adams, 1792–93), 62, 67. On the publication history of Gros's account and his presentation of Toussaint Louverture, see Jeremy D. Popkin, "Facing Racial Revolution: Captivity Narratives and Identity in the Saint-Domingue Insurrection," *Eighteenth-Century Studies* 36, no. 4 (2003): 515–17, 519; and idem, *Facing Racial Revolution: Eyewitness Accounts of the Haitian Revolution* (Chicago: University of Chicago Press, 2007), 105–55. On the growing rift between Louverture and Biassou, see Laurent Dubois, *Avengers of the New World: The Story of the Haitian Revolution* (Cambridge: Harvard University Press, 2004), 178, 183.

116. On the memory and image of Toussaint Louverture during the antebellum era and the Civil War, see Alfred Hunt, 84–101; and Matthew Clavin, "'Men of Color, To Arms!': Remembering Toussaint Louverture and the Haitian Revolution in the American Civil War" (Ph.D. diss., American University, 2005). For early laudatory accounts from a British pen but addressed to American as well as British audiences, see Samuel Whitchurch, "Hispaniola, A Poem; with Appropriate Notes. To Which are Added, Lines on the Crucifixion; and Other Poetical Pieces" (Bath: printed by W. Meyler, 1804); and anon., *Life and Military Achievements of Toussaint Louverture, late General in Chief of the Armies of St. Domingo,* 2nd ed. (printed for the author, 1805).

117. Thomas Jefferson to James Madison, February 12, 1799, *The Papers of Thomas Jefferson,* ed. Barbara B. Oberg (Princeton: Princeton University Press, 2004) 31:29–30.

118. Thomas Hart Benton, *Abridgment of the Debates of Congress, from 1789 to 1856* (reprint; New York: AMS Press, 1970), 2:340. Hereafter cited as *Abridgment of Debates.*

119. Reported in *Pennsylvania Gazette* (Philadelphia), February 6, 1799.

120. *Abridgment of Debates,* 2:339.

121. Ibid.

122. Ibid., 2:336.

123. Ibid.

124. Ibid., 2:342.

125. Ibid., 2:340.

126. Ibid., 2:343.

127. Ibid., 2:340.

128. Thomas Jefferson to James Madison, February 12, 1799, *The Papers of Thomas Jefferson* 31:29–30.

129. On Britain's economic interests in Saint-Domingue, see Carl Ludwig Lokke, "London Merchant Interest in the St. Domingue Plantations of the Émigrés, 1793–1798," *American Historical Review* 43 (July 1938), 795–802.

130. On the effect of "Toussaint's Clause" on our reinterpretation of Federalists (versus Democratic Republicans), see Michael Zuckerman, *Almost Chosen People: Oblique Biographies in the American Grain* (Berkeley: University of California Press, 1993), 175–218.

131. "Letters of Toussaint Louverture and of Edward Stevens," 72.

132. A. Morin to Stephen Girard, August 12, 1799; and Cassarrouy to Stephen Girard, August 14, 1799, SGP.

133. Timothy Pickering to Major General Charles C. Pinckney, May 16, 1799. *Naval Documents related to the Quasi-War between the United States and France,* 7 vols. (Washington, DC: U.S. Government Printing Office, 1935), 3:193.

134. Dubois, *Avengers of the New World*, 227.

135. Timothy Pickering to Major General Charles C. Pinckney, May 16, 1799. *Naval Documents* 3:193.

136. Reported in *Pennsylvania Gazette* (Philadelphia), July 10, 1799.

137. "Letters of Toussaint Louverture and of Edward Stevens," 80.

138. Ibid., 77.

139. Elkins and McKitrick, 659; David Brion Davis, *Revolutions: Reflections on American Equality and Foreign Liberations* (Cambridge: Harvard University Press, 1990), 25–26.

140. Quoted in Elkins and McKitrick, 661. On Jefferson, racism, and the Haitian Revolution, see Zuckerman.

141. Donald Hickey, "America's Response to the Slave Revolt in Haiti, 1791–1806," *Journal of the Early Republic* 2, no. 4 (Winter 1982), 365, 367; Tim Matthewson, "Jefferson and Haiti," *Journal of Southern History* 61, no. 2 (May 1995), 228; and David Brion Davis, "Impact of the French and Haitian Revolutions" in Geggus, *The Impact of the Haitian Revolution.* For a consideration of what might have happened had Adams won in 1800, see Douglas Egerton, "The Empire of Liberty Reconsidered," in *The Revolution of 1800: Democracy, Race, and the New Republic,* ed. James Horn, Jan Ellen Lewis, and Peter S. Onuf (Charlottesville: University of Virginia Press, 2002), 309–30.

142. Quoted in (anon.), "Hamilton on the Louisiana Purchase: A Newly-Identified Editorial from the New York Evening Post," *William and Mary Quarterly* 12, no. 4 (1955): 274. On Hamilton's general view toward the Haitian Revolution, see Daniel G. Lang, "Hamilton and Haiti," in *The Many Faces of Alexander Hamilton: The Life and Legacy of America's Most Elusive Founding Father,* ed. Douglas Ambrose and Robert W. T. Martin (New York: New York University Press, 2006), 238–42.

143. Matthewson, "Jefferson and Haiti."

144. *William Plumer's Memorandum of Proceedings in the United States Senate, 1803–1807,* ed. Everett S. Brown (New York: Da Capo Press, 1969), 186–87, 210.

145. Quoted in Gordon Brown, *Toussaint's Clause,* 258.

146. Quoted in ibid., 264.

147. On Federalists, see *Plumer's Memorandum,* 387, 435, 540–41. On Democratic Republicans, see *Abridgment of Debates,* 3:349–50.

148. On the embargo generally, see Gordon Brown, *Toussaint's Clause,* 263–91.

CHAPTER 5: "THE HORRORS OF ST. DOMINGO"——A REPRISE

1. For Leonora Sansay's biography, see Michael J. Drexler's introduction to *Secret History; Or, the Horrors of St. Domingo* and *Laura* (Peterborough, Ontario, Canada: Broadview Editions, 2007), 27–29.

2. For literary analyses of Sansay's *Secret History,* see ibid., introduction; Joan Dayan, *Haiti, History, and the Gods* (Berkeley: University of California Press, 1995); Elizabeth Maddock Dillon, "Caribbean Revolution and Print Publics: Leonora Sansay and 'The Secret History of the Haitian Revolution,'" *Proceedings of the American Antiquarian Society* 116, part 2 (2006): 353–73; and Jeremy D. Popkin, *Facing Racial Revolution: Eyewitness Accounts of the Haitian Insurrection* (Chicago: University of Chicago Press, 2007).

3. C. L. R. James, *The Black Jacobins: Toussaint L'Ouverture and the San Domingo Revolution* (1938; 2nd ed., New York: Vintage Books, 1989), 124, 160; Laurent Dubois, *Avengers of the New World: The Story of the Haitian Revolution* (Cambridge: Harvard University Press, 2004), 152–53.

4. Sherry Johnson, *The Social Transformation of Eighteenth-Century Cuba* (Gainesville: University Press of Florida, 2001), 161–66.

5. David Geggus, "The Enigma of Jamaica in the 1790s: New Light on the Causes of Slave Rebellions," *William and Mary Quarterly* 44, no. 2 (April 1987): 274–99.

6. As reported in the *Alexandria Gazette* (Virginia), May 13, 1809.

7. Franklin Knight, "Origins of Wealth and the Sugar Revolution in Cuba, 1740–1850," *Hispanic American Historical Review* 57, 2 (May 1977): 243.

8. Gabriel Debien, "The Saint-Domingue Refugees in Cuba, 1793–1815," in *The Road to Louisiana: The Saint-Domingue Refugees, 1792–1809*, ed. Carl A. Brasseaux and Glenn R. Conrad (Lafayette: Center for Louisiana Studies, University of Southwestern Louisiana, 1992), 53, 72–73, 86. One *arroba* is equal to 555 kg.

9. Debien, "The Saint-Domingue Refugees in Cuba," 53–54; Sansay, *Secret History* (Drexler ed.), 118.

10. Sansay, *Secret History* (Drexler ed.), 107–8.

11. Quoted in Debien, "The Saint-Domingue Refugees in Cuba," 85.

12. *Aurora* (Philadelphia), April 13, 1809.

13. *National Intelligencer* (Washington, DC), April 14, 1809.

14. *New-York Gazette and General Advertiser*, June 5, 1809. On the respectability (or lack thereof) of the instigators, see *National Intelligencer* (Washington, DC), April 26, 1809, and Sherry Johnson, 174–75.

15. *Aurora* (Philadelphia), April 14, 1809.

16. *Republican and Savannah Evening Ledger* (Georgia), May 25, 1809; *Boston Gazette*, July 3, 1809.

17. *Alexandria Gazette* (Virginia), June 1, 1809.

18. Knight, "Origins of Wealth," 249; Linda Salvucci, "Supply, Demand, and the Making of a Market: Philadelphia and Havana at the Beginning of the Nineteenth Century," in Franklin Knight and Peggy Liss, eds., *Atlantic Port Cities: Economy, Culture, and Society in the Atlantic World, 1650–1850* (Knoxville: University of Tennessee Press, 1991), 40–52; Louis A. Pérez, Jr., *Cuba and the United States: Ties of Singular Intimacy* (2nd ed., Athens: University of Georgia Press, 1997), chapter 1; D. C. Corbitt, "Shipment of Slaves from the United States to Cuba, 1789–1807," *Journal of Southern History* 7, no. 4 (November 1941): 540–49; and *Official Letter Books of W. C. C. Claiborne, 1801–1816*, ed. Dunbar Rowland (New York: AMS Press, 1972), 4:352. Hereafter cited as *Claiborne Letter Books*. On how Cuba and Haiti were often linked in the minds of white Americans, especially southerners, see Don E. Fehrenbacher, completed and edited by Ward M. McAfee, *The Slaveholding Republic: An Account of the United States Government's Relations to Slavery* (New York: Oxford University Press, 2001), 126.

19. *Alexandria Gazette* (Virginia), June 24, 1809.

20. *Aurora* (Philadelphia), April 28, 1809; *Republican and Savannah Evening Ledger* (Georgia), March 17, 1810.

21. *New-York Gazette and General Advertiser*, May 27, 1809.

22. Recalled in the *Louisiana Courier* (New Orleans), August 26, 1811.

23. *Poulson's American Daily Advertiser* (Philadelphia), June 26, 1809.

24. *The Enquirer* (Richmond), July 14, 1809. On the riots in Cuba generally, see Debien, "The Saint-Domingue Refugees in Cuba," 89–92, 97–99.

25. Madame Deshay to Thomas Jefferson, August 18, 1809, *The Papers of Thomas Jefferson, Retirement Series*, ed. J. Jefferson Looney (Princeton: Princeton University Press, 2004), 1:450. Hereafter cited as *Papers of Thomas Jefferson, Retirement Series*.

26. *Poulson's American Daily Advertiser* (Philadelphia), June 24 and 26, 1809.

27. *New-York Evening Post*, June 27, 1809.

28. *Poulson's American Daily Advertiser* (Philadelphia), June 24, 1809.

29. Ibid.

30. Standing Committee Minutes, April 4 and 8, May 3, 1811. New York Manumission Society Papers. New-York Historical Society. New York, NY. Hereafter cited as NYMS Papers.

31. Other reports cite arrival of a larger number of black and colored exiles at Savannah. One estimated 52, another 82. See *Republican and Savannah Evening Ledger* (Georgia), June 20 and July 27, 1809, respectively.

32. *Republican and Savannah Evening Ledger* (Georgia), May 23, 1809.

33. The bill was enforced by customs and revenue officers, adding federal muscle to state law. "Bill to prevent the importation of certain Persons into certain States, where, by the laws thereof, their admission is prohibited," February 10, 1803. Early American Imprint Series, nos. 5268–69. See also Fehrenbacher, 141–42.

34. *New-York Evening Post*, June 7, 1809.

35. Savannah City Council Minutes, May 22 and 26, August 7, 1809. Office of the Clerk of City Council, Research Library and Municipal Archives, City Hall, Savannah, GA. Many thanks to Richard Demirjian for sharing this source. See also *Republican and Savannah Evening Ledger* (Georgia), July 27, 1809.

36. *Republican and Savannah Evening Ledger* (Georgia), May 25, 1809.

37. Many of the slaves imported to South Carolina between 1803 and 1807 were transported to markets throughout the South. Fehrenbacher, 142. Significantly, even when South Carolina reopened the slave trade, the legislation expressly forbade the importation of slaves from the French West Indies. See *Acts and Resolutions of the General Assembly of the State of South-Carolina, passed in December 1803* (Columbia: Daniel & J. J. Faust Printers, 1804), 49.

38. John Tyler to James Madison, June 1, 1809. *The Papers of James Madison, Presidential Series,* ed. Robert A. Rutland, et al. (Charlottesville: University Press of Virginia, 1984), 1:219–20. Hereafter cited as *The Papers of James Madison.*

39. Alexander Burot to Thomas Jefferson, October 23, 1809, *Papers of Thomas Jefferson, Retirement Series,* 623–24.

40. See, for example, David Brion Davis, *The Problem of Slavery in the Age of Revolution, 1770–1823,* 2nd ed. (New York: Oxford University Press, 1999), 311–12. On how the moral rhetoric against the slave trade was compromised in actual practice, see W. E. B. Du Bois,

The Suppression of the African Slave-Trade to the United States of America, 1638–1870 (1896; reprint, New York: Social Science Press, 1954).

41. Davis, *The Problem of Slavery*; Fehrenbacher, *The Slaveholding Republic*; and Peter Onuf, "'To Declare Them a Free and Independant People': Race, Slavery, and National Identity in Jefferson's Thought," *Journal of the Early Republic* 18 (Spring 1998): 1–46.

42. *Philadelphia Evening Post*, March 19, 1804.

43. *Mercantile Advertister* (New York), April 17, 1804; *The Hive* (Northampton, MA), May 15, 1804, *Philadelphia Evening Post*, June 5, 1804; *Maryland Herald* (Elizabethtown), June 13, 1804.

44. *Republican Watch-Tower* (New York), June 6, 1804.

45. Sansay, *Secret History* (Drexler ed.), 121.

46. *The Bee* (Hudson, NY), June 12, 1804.

47. *Philadelphia Evening Post*, June 5, 1804. This proclamation was reprinted in several American newspapers.

48. *Vermont Gazette* (Bennington), July 10, 1804; *Daily Advertiser* (New York), June 5, 1804.

49. *The Courier* (Norwich, CT), April 11, 1804; *The Bee* (Hudson, NY), April 10, 1804.

50. *The Spectator* (New York), June 13, 1804.

51. James Stephen, *The Opportunity* (London, 1804), 125–26. For another example of a public defense of Dessalines, see *Life and Military Achievements of Toussaint Louverture* (2nd edition, printed for the [anon.] author, 1805), 25.

52. See the entry for "St. Domingo" in *Geographical compilation for the use of schools being an accurate description of all the empires, kingdoms, republics and states in the known world . . . compiled from the best American, English and French authors* (1806), 901–4.

53. Quoted in Debien, "The Saint-Domingue Refugees in Cuba," 96–97.

54. Peter S. Onuf, *Jefferson's Empire: The Language of American Nationhood* (Charlottesville: University Press of Virginia, 2000), 53–79; Adam Rothman, *Slave Country: American Expansion and the Origins of the Deep South* (Cambridge: Harvard University Press, 2005), 24–34; and James Sidbury, "Thomas Jefferson in Gabriel's Virginia," in *The Revolution of 1800: Democracy, Race, and the New Republic*, ed. James Horn, Jan Ellen Lewis, and Peter S. Onuf (Charlottesville: University of Virginia Press, 2002), 199–219.

55. Gabriel Debien and René Le Gardeur, "The Saint-Domingue Refugees in Louisiana, 1792–1804" in Brasseaux and Conrad, *The Road to Louisiana*, 118–19, 123–41.

56. Quoted in Debien, "The Saint-Domingue Refugees in Cuba," 86; Nathalie Dessens, *From Saint-Domingue to New Orleans: Migration and Influences* (Gainesville: University Press of Florida, 2007), 35–40.

57. In 1806 there were 2,312 free people of color in New Orleans. Paul Lachance, "The 1809 Immigration of Saint-Domingue Refugees to New Orleans: Reception, Integration and Impact," in Brasseaux and Conrad, *The Road to Louisiana*, 247–48; Paul Lachance, "Repercussions of the Haitian Revolution in Louisiana," in *The Impact of the Haitian Revolution in the Atlantic World*, ed. David P. Geggus (Columbia: University of South Carolina Press, 2001), 213; Thomas Fiehrer, "From La Tortue to La Louisiane: An Unfathomed Legacy," in Brasseaux and Conrad, *The Road to Louisiana*, 23. In his discussion about Louisiana society, Lachance draws a distinction between the first and second phases of the

formation of a three-caste society: the first phase includes the growth of the free colored population, while the second entails their exclusivity (both self-imposed and externally imposed). Lachance argues that not until the last decades of the antebellum era did New Orleans witness this second phase. Clearly the entrance of the refugees contributed to the first. Paul Lachance, "The Formation of a Three-Caste Society," *Social Science History* 18, no. 2 (Summer 1994): 222, 234–35.

58. Gwendolyn Midlo Hall, *Africans in Colonial Louisiana: The Development of Afro-Creole Culture in the Eighteenth Century* (Baton Rouge: Louisiana State University Press, 1992), 304; Kimberly Hanger, *Bounded Lives, Bounded Places: Free Black Society in Colonial New Orleans, 1769–1803* (Durham, NC: Duke University Press, 1997), 6, 26; and Thomas Ingersoll, *Mammon and Manon in Early New Orleans: The First Slave Society in the Deep South, 1718–1819* (Knoxville: University of Tennessee Press, 1999), 221–27, 248.

59. Hall, *Africans in Colonial Louisiana*, chapters 10 and 11.

60. Lachance, "The Politics of Fear: French Louisianans and the Slave Trade, 1786–1809," *Plantation Society in the Americas* 1, no. 2 (June 1979): 165–70.

61. Ibid., 175–77.

62. Quoted in ibid., 183.

63. Quoted in Caryn Cossé Bell, *Revolution, Romanticism, and the Afro-Creole Protest Tradition in Louisiana, 1718–1868* (Baton Rouge: Louisiana State University Press, 1997), 29.

64. Ibid., 30–37; Hanger, 109, 124, 152.

65. Bell, 65, 75–76.

66. Lachance, "Three-Caste Society," 228–29.

67. Quoted in Robert L. Paquette, "Saint-Domingue in the Making of Territorial Louisiana," in *A Turbulent Time: The French Revolution and the Greater Caribbean*, ed. David Barry Gaspar and David Patrick Geggus (Bloomington: Indiana University Press, 1997), 217; see also Hanger, *Bounded Lives*, 134.

68. Peter J. Kastor, *The Nation's Crucible: The Louisiana Purchase and the Creation of America* (New Haven: Yale University Press, 2004), 81–85; Paquette, "Saint-Domingue in the Making of Territorial Louisiana," 217; Joseph T. Hatfield, *William Claiborne: Jeffersonian Centurion in the American Southwest* (Lafayette: USL History Series, University of Southwestern Louisiana, 1976), 180.

69. Ira Berlin, *Many Thousands Gone: The First Two Centuries of Slavery in North America* (Cambridge: Harvard University Press, 1998), 350; Dessens, 94–95.

70. Clarence Edwin Carter, comp. and ed., *The Territorial Papers of the United States* (Washington, DC: U.S. Government Printing Office, 1940) 9:855. Hereafter cited as *Territorial Papers*.

71. *Claiborne Letter Books*, 4: 360–61. See also George Dargo, *Jefferson's Louisiana: Politics and the Clash of Legal Traditions* (Cambridge: Harvard University Press, 1975), 23–24. On the problem of cultivating among Louisiana locals "attachment" to the U.S. government, see Kastor.

72. *Poulson's American Daily Advertiser* (Philadelphia), January 18, 1810.

73. Merton Dillon, *Slavery Attacked: Southern Slaves and Their Allies, 1619–1865* (Baton Rouge: Louisiana State University Press, 1990), 121–22.

74. Drexler introduction to Sansay, *Secret History*, 31.

75. *Claiborne Letter Books*, 4:304, 317. On the Burr conspiracy and its effects in Louisiana, see George Dargo, "Burr's Conspiracy and the Orleans Territory," in *The Louisiana Purchase Bicentennial Series*, ed. Dolores Egger Labbe, vol. 3, *The Louisiana Purchase and Its Aftermath, 1800–1830* (Lafayette: University of Southwestern Louisiana, 1998), 224–41; Dargo, *Jefferson's Louisiana*, chapter 3; and Nancy Isenberg, *Fallen Founder: The Life of Aaron Burr* (New York: Viking Press, 2007).

76. Dargo, *Jefferson's Louisiana*, 54, 72.

77. *New-York Evening Post*, December 23, 1809. Reports on the actual amount embezzled by the port collector varied from $90,000 to $160,000.

78. *Massachusetts Spy* (Worcester), December 27, 1809.

79. Dargo, *Jefferson's Louisiana*, 106; Kastor, 57–61, 80.

80. For a biography of Claiborne, see Joseph Hatfield, *William Claiborne*.

81. Quoted in Rothman, *Slave Country*, 15; on French land claims, see ibid., 39–40.

82. Dargo, *Jefferson's Louisiana*, 28–33.

83. *Alexandria Gazette* (Virginia), September 12, 1809; on the system of patronage and loyalty that shaped political appointments in Louisiana, see Kastor, 95–108.

84. *Claiborne Letter Books*, 5:14–17; Dargo, *Jefferson's Louisiana*, 38–41; Dessens, 86–87, 131.

85. *Claiborne Letter Books*, 4:352.

86. Ibid., 4:365.

87. Ibid., 4:367.

88. Lachance, "The Politics of Fear," 192.

89. Petitions, ca. May 20 and July 8, 1809. *The Papers of James Madison*, 1:197, 283.

90. Quoted in Lachance, "The Politics of Fear," 188.

91. *Claiborne Letter Books*, 4:372.

92. Ibid., 4:380.

93. Ibid., 4:388–89.

94. Ibid., 4:389.

95. Ibid., 4:407. The number of free colored and black men is based on the mayor's reports to Claiborne dated July 18, 1809. See ibid., 4:409.

96. Ibid., 4:402.

97. Ibid., 4:403, 422–23.

98. Petition from the French refugees in New Orleans, ca. May 20, 1809. *The Papers of James Madison*, 1:197.

99. Rothman, *Slave Country*, 44–45.

100. Berlin, 343.

101. On the reasoning behind diffusion, see Jan Lewis, "The Problem of Slavery in Southern Political Discourse" in *Devising Liberty: Preserving and Creating Freedom in the New American Republic*, ed. David T. Konig (Stanford: Stanford University Press, 1995), 277; Rothman, *Slave Country*, 30.

102. *Claiborne Letter Books*, 4:406.

103. Chevalier Lejeune Malherbe and Others to James Madison, September 5, 1809, *The Papers of James Madison*, 1:352–53; *Claiborne Letter Books* 4:366, 417, and 5:30–31.

104. Quoted in Lachance, "The 1809 Immigration," 259.

105. Quoted in Ingersoll, *Mammon and Manon*, 257.

106. *Claiborne Letter Books*, 4:391.

107. Ibid., 4:391.

108. *Alexandria Gazette* (Virginia), October 9, 1809; reported in ibid., December 16, 1809.

109. Ibid., January 25, 1810.

110. Reported in the *New-York Evening Post*, October 12, 1809.

111. Reported in the *Alexandria Gazette* (Virginia), October 9, 1809.

112. *New-York Evening Post*, December 18, 1809. Also reported in *Poulson's American Daily Advertiser* (Philadelphia), December 16, 1809. Claiborne, too, worried about the smuggling of slaves under the ruse that they belonged to Saint-Dominguans on board. See *Claiborne Letter Books*, 5:1–2.

113. Reported in the *New-York Evening Post*, August 16, 1809.

114. *Alexandria Gazette* (Virginia), October 9, 1809.

115. Adam Rothman, "The Expansion of Slavery in the Deep South, 1790–1820" (Ph.D. diss., Columbia University, 2000), 210.

116. *New-York Evening Post*, August 16, 1809.

117. Reported in ibid.

118. *Louisiana Gazette* (New Orleans), January 12, 1810.

119. Thomas Hart Benton, *Abridgment of the Debates of Congress, from 1789 to 1856* (reprint; New York: AMS Press, 1970), 4:164. Hereafter cited as *Abridgment of Debates*.

120. *Abridgment of Debates*, 4:164. For a brief biography of John Ross, see *Biographical Dictionary of the American Congress, 1774–1927* (Washington, DC: U.S. Government Printing Office, 1928), 967. Representative John Ross is not to be confused with Senator James Ross, also from Pennsylvania, who served in Congress until 1803.

121. Donald L. Robinson, *Slavery in the Structure of American Politics, 1765–1820* (New York: Harcourt Brace Jovanovich, 1971), 324–36.

122. *Abridgment of Debates*, 3:496.

123. W. E. B. Du Bois, 96–97.

124. *Abridgment of Debates*, 3:498.

125. Ibid., 3:499.

126. Joanne Pope Melish, *Disowning Slavery: Gradual Emancipation and "Race" in New England, 1780–1860* (Ithaca: Cornell University Press, 1998).

127. *Abridgment of Debates*, 3:495.

128. Fehrenbacher, 152; W. E. B. Du Bois, 122.

129. Society Minutes, January 9, 1810, NYMS Papers.

130. *Poulson's American Daily Advertiser* (Philadelphia), January 24, 1810.

131. *Claiborne Letter Books*, 5:4; Bell, *Revolution*, 42.

132. *Poulson's American Daily Advertiser* (Philadelphia), September 27, 1809.

133. Quotation from Thomas Marshall Thompson, "National Newspaper and Legislative Reactions to Louisiana's Deslondes Slave Revolt of 1811," in Labbe, *The Louisiana Purchase Bicentennial Series*, 3:315; on the slave rebellion generally, see Bell, *Revolution*, 46; and Rothman, *Slave Country*, 106–17.

134. Lachance, "The 1809 Immigration," 261.

135. *Territorial Papers*, 9:850; *Claiborne Letter Books*, 5:3–5.

136. *Territorial Papers*, 9:882 n.71.

137. On the difficulties of enforcement in the early 1810s, see *Territorial Papers*, 9:888. Eventually, in 1818, the legislature altered the law so that the capturing captain received half the money from the sale, as a way to persuade ship captains to enforce the act. The same year, the federal government authorized the president to send armed patrols to catch slave ships. In 1820 violations of the slave trade act were deemed an act of piracy and hence punishable by death. Judith Kelleher Schafer, *Slavery, the Civil Law, and the Supreme Court of Louisiana* (Baton Rouge: Louisiana State University Press, 1994), 152.

138. Dessens, chapter 4.

139. Lachance, "Repercussions," 222–23; Kastor, 153–80.

140. Quoted in Dessens, 56.

CONCLUSION

1. All quotations from *Charleston Daily Courier*, February 11, 1804.

2. Examples of antebellum popular fiction referencing the Haitian Revolution are "Two Nights in St. Domingo," *Liberty Bell*, January 1, 1843; "The Flower Girl. A Tale of the Crescent City," *Ladies' National Magazine*, August 1844; "The Victim of Trifles," *Philadelphia Album and Ladies' Literary Portfolio*, April 2, 1831; "Nights at Sea," *Albion, A Journal of News, Politics and Literature*, October 6, 1838; "A Haytian Legend," *Yale Literary Magazine*, November 1839; "Constance de Martigny," *Godey's Magazine and Lady's Book*, January 1845; "A Most Remarkable Providence," *Christian Advocate and Journal*, June 22, 1827; and "Story of Philip Brusque," *Robert Merry's Museum*, January–June 1842.

3. On Saint-Dominguan influence in theater: *Spirit of the Times*, March 18, 1848; on markets: *North American Review*, January 1825; on sugar cultivation: *American Agriculturalist*, June 1944; on education: *The Knickerbocker; or New York Monthly Magazine*, September 1846; and on Girard, see *Spirit of the Times*, December 30, 1854.

4. On celebrations of refugee relief campaigns: *North American Review*, January 1825; and *The Knickerbocker; or New York Monthly Magazine*, September 1846. On Duncan McIntosh: *Christian Disciple and Theological Review*, January 1, 1821.

5. *Western Recorder*, January 16, 1827.

6. *The Knickerbocker; or New York Monthly Magazine*, September 1846.

7. A romanticized vision marked accounts of the forced migration of Acadians in the 1750s. John Mack Faragher, *A Great and Noble Scheme: The Tragic Story of the Expulsion of the French Acadians from Their American Homeland* (New York: W. W. Norton, 2005), 454–62.

8. Antebellum publications using derogatory terms for black and colored soldiers included: *The Knickerbocker; or New York Monthly Magazine*, September 1846; "Revolutions in Hayti," *Littell's Living Age*, August 17, 1844; and "Biographical Sketches," *United States Democratic Review*, August 1858. White refugee memoirs were often cited in these articles. See Jeremy D. Popkin, *Facing Racial Revolution: Eyewitness Accounts of the Haitian Revolution* (Chicago: University of Chicago Press, 2007), 31, 336–62.

9. Quotation is from "Biographical Sketches," *United States Democratic Review*, August

1858. On blaming Wilberforce, see "The Future of the South," *DeBow's Review of the Southern and Western States*, February 1851.

10. "Senator R. M. T. Hunter, of VA," *United States Magazine, and Democratic Review*, July 1851.

11. "History of Richmond," *Southern Literary Messenger*, January 1852.

12. Alfred Hunt, *Haiti's Influence on Antebellum America: Slumbering Volcano in the Caribbean* (Baton Rouge: Louisiana State University Press, 1988), 120; Chris Dixon, *African America and Haiti: Emigration and Black Nationalism in the Nineteenth Century* (Westport, CT: Greenwood Press, 2000), 30. For an important reinterpretation of the Vesey conspiracy, see Michael P. Johnson, "Denmark Vesey and His Co-conspirators," *William and Mary Quarterly* 58, no. 4 (October 2001): 915–76.

13. Alfred Hunt, 142.

14. "Southern Excitement," *Philanthropist*, June 10, 1836.

15. "Consequences of Immediate Emancipation," *Genius of Universal Emancipation*, October 1837. Also printed in *Religious Intelligencer*, November 30, 1833.

16. James Theodore Holly, *A Vindication of the Capacity of the Negro Race for Self-Government and Civilized Progress, as Demonstrated by Historical Events of the Haytian Revolution; and the Subsequent Acts of that People since their National Independence* (New Haven: William H. Stanley, printer, 1857), 33.

17. "Consequences of Immediate Emancipation," *Genius of Universal Emancipation*, October 1837. Also printed in *Religious Intelligencer*, November 30, 1833. For other positive revisions of the history of the Haitian Revolution, see "Alison's French Revolution," *Albion, A Journal of News, Politics, and Literature*, February 24, 1838; "St. Domingo," *National Era*, April 13, 1848; and "Reply to 'Ashmun' on Slavery," *Christian Register*, November 19, 1831.

18. "St. Domingo," *National Era*, April 13, 1848.

19. "More Slave Literature," *Liberator*, December 22, 1854; Alfred Hunt, 84–101; Matthew Clavin, "'Men of Color, To Arms!': Remembering Toussaint Louverture and the Haitian Revolution in the American Civil War" (Ph.D. diss., American University, 2005).

20. Gary Nash, *Forging Freedom: The Formation of Philadelphia's Black Community, 1720–1840* (Cambridge: Harvard University Press, 1988), 244; Dixon, 26, 39–40.

21. *Genius of Universal Emancipation*, August 1825. See also "Independence of Hayti," *Christian Watchman*, August 19, 1825.

22. *Genius of Universal Emancipation*, August 1825.

23. Dixon, 41–42.

24. Ibid., 96, 220–21.

The research for *Encountering Revolution* began with locating refugees, given the book's focus on interactions between Americans and Saint-Dominguans. The lack of consistent sources—immigration records, passenger lists, and so on—for this period (with the exception of the migration to New Orleans in 1809) made that task difficult. I tried to find as many exiles in East Coast cities as I could, and I turned to the sources of social history to do so. Wills, inventories, orphan court records, alien reports, city directories, church records (when open to the public), city and court records—all proved essential not only for identifying refugees but for examining their experiences in the United States.

Few caches of refugee papers exist in the United States. However, several important memoirs by white exiles give voice to their perspective: Mr. Gros, *An Historick Recital, of the Different Occurrences in the Camps of Grand-Reviere, Dondon, Sainte-Suzanne, and others, from the 26th of October, 1791, to the 24th of December, of the same year* (Baltimore: Samuel and John Adams, n.d.); Kenneth Roberts and Anna M. Roberts, trans. and eds., *Moreau de St. Méry's American Journey [1793–1798]* (New York: Doubleday, 1947); and Althéa de Puech Parham, ed. and trans., *My Odyssey: Experiences of a Young Refugee from Two Revolutions by a Creole of Saint Domingue* (Baton Rouge: Louisiana State University Press, 1959). In addition, Médéric-Louis-Elie Moreau de St. Méry's *Description topographique, physique, civile, politique et historique de la partie française de l'isle Saint-Domingue*, 3 vols. (1797; reprint, Paris: Société de l'histoire des colonies françaises, 1958) was printed during Moreau's stay in Philadelphia and reveals white colonists' views of the island.

Numerous letters from white refugees appear in the Stephen Girard Papers at the American Philosophical Society in Philadelphia, and several surface in the correspondence of major political figures (see citations below). The letters of the Rouvray family have been collected by M. E. McIntosh and B. C. Weber in *Une correspondence familiale au temps des troubles de Saint-Domingue: Lettres du Marquis et de la Marquise de Rouvray a leur fille, Saint-Domingue—États-Unis (1791–1796)* (Paris: Société de l'histoire des colonies françaises et Librairie Larose, 1959). The New York Public Library houses the papers of Pierre Toussaint, a black exile in New York City, but this material relates mostly to his antebellum years and so did not find its way into this project. Other significant collections for discussion about and by the exiles are the abolition society papers for New York City (New-York Historical Society) and Philadelphia (Historical Society of Pennsylvania); the Duncan McIntosh Papers, Joseph Despeaux Papers, and the Dubois-Martin Papers at the Maryland Historical Society in Baltimore; and the Francis James Dallett Papers at the Historical Society of

Pennsylvania in Philadelphia. Finally, the microfilm collections at the Church of Latter-Day Saints Family History Center at Lincoln Center in New York City facilitated research in genealogical records from cities all along the East Coast.

Newspapers provided crucial insight into the refugees and into American reactions to them. Most of the titles cited in the endnotes can be accessed through the digital (and, thankfully, searchable) version of Early American Newspapers (although when I started this project, microfilm editions were the order of the day). The print sources related to the Saint-Dominguans encompass also pamphlets, political tracts, broadsides, summaries of debates, and cartoons. I found such materials in the holdings of the John Carter Brown Library in Providence, Rhode Island; at the Library Company of Philadelphia; and in the digital resources of Early American Imprints Series 1 (1639–1800) and Series 2 (1801–1819). The exiles found their way into several popular novels and plays. Leonora Sansay's *Secret History; or the Horrors of St. Domingo* (1808), recently edited by Michael Drexler and reprinted by Broadview Press (2007), is the best-known fictionalized account from the period of the Haitian Revolution by an American and has extensive commentary on Saint-Dominguans. Refugees appear in Charles Brockden Brown's 1799 novel, *Arthur Mervyn*, as well and in the works of amateur playwright, John Murdock, especially his *Triumphs of Love* (1795).

Government documents were helpful for thinking about the American response at the state and federal levels (and they sometimes included appeals from refugees): Thomas Hart Benton, *Abridgment of the Debates of Congress, from 1789 to 1856* (reprint, New York: AMS Press, 1970); *The Debates and Proceedings in the Congress of the United States* (Washington, DC: Gales & Seaton, 1834–56); and the proceedings of various state legislatures (available on-line). The published personal papers of key government officials were crucial for exploring the exiles' influence on politics, slavery, and territorial expansion: *The Papers of Thomas Jefferson*, 35 vols. (Princeton: Princeton University Press, 1950–2009); *The Papers of Alexander Hamilton*, ed. Harold C. Syrett, 27 vols. (New York: Columbia University Press, 1961–87); *The Papers of James Madison*, Presidential Series, 5 vols. (Charlottesville: University Press of Virginia, 1984–2004); and *Official Letter Books of W. C. C. Claiborne, 1801–1816* (New York: AMS Press, 1972). Finally, some French consular correspondence from the 1790s has been compiled and reprinted in "Correspondence of the French Ministers to the United States, 1791–1797," Frederick J. Turner, ed., *Annual Report of the American Historical Association for the Year 1903* (Washington, DC: Government Printing Office, 1904), and the New-York Historical Society has the diary of Alexandre Hauterive, French consul in New York City in 1793 and 1794.

This research was supported by a rich secondary literature, and I have been fortunate to build on scholarship that investigates Saint-Dominguan exile communities in the United States and in other sites in the Atlantic world. Excellent studies of the Saint-Dominguan refugees include Winston C. Babb, "French Refugees from Saint-Domingue to the Southern United States, 1791–1810" (Ph.D. diss., University of Virginia, 1954); Susan Branson and Leslie Patrick, "Étrangers dans un Pays Étrange: Saint Domingan Refugees of Color in Philadelphia," in David P. Geggus, ed., *The Impact of the Haitian Revolution in the Atlantic World* (Columbia: University of South Carolina Press, 2001); Carl A. Brasseaux and Glenn R. Conrad, eds., *The Road to Louisiana: The Saint-Domingue Refugees, 1792–1809*

(Lafayette: University of Southwest Louisiana Press, 1992); Frances Sergeant Childs, *French Refugee Life in the United States, 1790–1800: An American Chapter of the French Revolution* (Baltimore: Johns Hopkins Press, 1940); Gabriel Debien, "Les colons de Saint-Domingue réfugiés à Cuba, 1793–1815," *Revista de Indias* 13, no. 4 (1953–54): 559–605, 11–36; Nathalie Dessens, *From Saint-Domingue to New Orleans: Migration and Influences* (Gainesville: University Press of Florida, 2007); Paul Lachance, "The Formation of a Three-Caste Society," *Social Science History* 18, no. 2 (Summer 1994): 211–42; idem, "The Politics of Fear: French Louisianans and the Slave Trade, 1786–1809," *Plantation Society in the Americas* 1, no. 22 (June 1979): 162–97; R. Darrell Meadows, "Engineering Exile: Social Networks and the French Atlantic Community, 1789–1809," *French Historical Studies* 23, no. 1 (Winter 2000): 67–102; idem, "The Planters of Saint-Domingue, 1750–1804" (Ph.D. diss., Carnegie Mellon University, 2004); José Morales, "The Hispaniola Diaspora, 1791–1850: Puerto Rico, Cuba, Louisiana, and other Host Societies" (Ph.D. diss., University of Connecticut, 1986); Gary Nash, "Reverberations of Haiti in the American North: Black Saint Dominguans in Philadelphia," *Explorations in Early American Culture: A Special Supplemental Issue of Pennsylvania History* 65 (1998): 44–73; Jennifer J. Pierce, "Discourses of the Dispossessed: Saint-Domingue Colonists on Race, Revolution and Empire, 1789–1825" (Ph.D. diss., Binghamton University, 2005); Joseph George Rosengarten, *French Colonists and Exiles in the United States* (Philadelphia: J. B. Lippincott Company, 1907); Bertrand Van Ruymbeke, "*Refugiés* or *Émigrés?* Early Modern French Migrations to British North America and the United States (1680–1820)," *Itinerario* 30, no. 2 (2006): 1–17; and Philip Wright and Gabriel Debien, "Les colons de Saint-Domingue passés à la Jamaïque (1792–1835)," *Bulletin de la Société d'histoire de la Guadeloupe* 26 (4e trimestre 1975): 3–216.

   While the literature on the refugees was indispensible for understanding my subjects, three broader historiographies have been important in shaping my interpretation of them and their impact on the United States: works on the Haitian Revolution, those about the Atlantic world, and studies of the early U.S. republic.

   Although the English-language literature on the Haitian Revolution dates back as early as C. L. R. James's trailblazing monograph from 1938, *Black Jacobins: Toussaint L'Ouverture and the San Domingo Revolution*, 2nd ed. (New York: Vintage Books, 1989), the recent outpouring of outstanding research has radically changed the way we think about this seminal event in world history. Essential monographs include Joan Dayan, *Haiti, History, and the Gods* (Berkeley: University of California Press, 1995); Laurent Dubois, *Avengers of the New World: The Story of the Haitian Revolution* (Cambridge: Harvard University Press, 2004); idem, *A Colony of Citizens: Revolution and Slave Emancipation in the French Caribbean, 1787–1804* (Chapel Hill: University of North Carolina Press, 2004); Laurent Dubois and John Garrigus, *Slave Revolution in the Caribbean, 1789–1804: A Brief History with Documents* (Boston: Bedford/St. Martin's, 2006); Carolyn Fick, *The Making of Haiti: The Saint Domingue Revolution from Below* (Knoxville: University of Tennessee Press, 1990); John D. Garrigus, *Before Haiti: Race and Citizenship in French Saint-Domingue* (New York: Palgrave Macmillan, 2006); David Barry Gaspar and David Patrick Geggus, eds., *A Turbulent Time: The French Revolution and the Greater Caribbean* (Bloomington: Indiana University Press, 1997); David Geggus, *Haitian Revolutionary Studies* (Bloomington: Indiana University Press, 2002); idem, *Slavery, War, and Revolution: The British Occupation of Saint-Domingue, 1793–*

1798 (New York: Oxford University Press, 1982); David Geggus and Norman Fiering, eds., *The World of the Haitian Revolution* (Bloomington: Indiana University Press, 2009); Jeremy D. Popkin, *Facing Racial Revolution: Eyewitness Accounts of the Haitian Insurrection* (Chicago: University of Chicago Press, 2007); Madison Smartt Bell, *Toussaint Louverture: A Biography* (New York: Pantheon Books, 2007); and Michel-Rolph Trouillot, *Silencing the Past: Power and the Production of History* (Boston: Beacon Press, 1995).

The first book-length treatment of the Haitian Revolution's effects on the United States was Alfred Hunt's 1988 *Haiti's Influence on Antebellum America: Slumbering Volcano in the Caribbean* (Baton Rouge: Louisiana State University Press). Lately, historians have begun to delve into unexplored facets of American reactions: Robin Blackburn, "Haiti, Slavery, and the Age of Democratic Revolution," *William and Mary Quarterly* 63, no. 4 (October 2006): 643–74; Gordon S. Brown, *Toussaint's Clause: The Founding Fathers and the Haitian Revolution* (Jackson: University Press of Mississippi, 2005); Matthew Clavin, " 'Men of Color, To Arms!': Remembering Toussaint Louverture and the Haitian Revolution in the American Civil War" (Ph.D. diss., American University, 2005); James Alexander Dun, "Dangerous Intelligence: Slavery, Race, and St. Domingue in the Early American Republic" (Ph.D. diss., Princeton University, 2004); idem, " 'What avenues of commerce, will you, Americans, not explore!': Commercial Philadelphia's Vantage onto the Early Haitian Revolution," *William and Mary Quarterly* 62, no. 3 (July 2005): 473–504; Donald Hickey, "America's Response to the Slave Revolt in Haiti, 1791–1806," *Journal of the Early Republic* 2, no. 4 (Winter 1982): 361–79; Daniel G. Lang, "Hamilton and Haiti," in *The Many Faces of Alexander Hamilton: The Life and Legacy of America's Most Elusive Founding Father*, ed. Douglas Ambrose and Robert W. T. Martin (New York: New York University Press, 2006); Rayford Logan, *The Diplomatic Relations of the United States with Haiti, 1778–1841* (Chapel Hill: University of North Carolina Press, 1941); Tim Matthewson, "Abraham Bishop, 'The Rights of Black Men,' and the American Reaction to the Haitian Revolution," *Journal of Negro History* 67, no. 2 (Summer 1982): 148–54; idem, "George Washington's Policy toward the Haitian Revolution," *Diplomatic History* 3, no. 3 (Summer 1979): 321–36; idem, "Jefferson and Haiti," *Journal of Southern History* 61, no. 2 (May 1995): 209–48; idem, *A Proslavery Foreign Policy: Haitian-American Relations During the Early Republic* (Westport, CT: Praeger, 2003); James Sidbury, "Saint-Domingue in Virginia: Ideology, Local Meanings, and Resistance to Slavery, 1790–1800," *Journal of Southern History* 63, no. 3 (August 1997): 531–52; George D. Terry, "A Study of the Impact of the French Revolution and the Insurrections in Saint-Domingue upon South Carolina: 1790–1805" (M.A. thesis, University of South Carolina, 1973); and Michael Zuckerman, *Almost Chosen People: Oblique Biographies in the American Grain* (Berkeley: University of California Press, 1993). These studies are complemented by considerations of the revolution's impact throughout the Americas: Sibylle Fischer, *Modernity Disavowed: Haiti and the Cultures of Slavery in the Age of Revolution* (Durham: Duke University Press, 2004); David Geggus, ed., *The Impact of the Haitian Revolution on the Atlantic World*; and Geggus and Fiering, *The World of the Haitian Revolution*.

Although these titles are impressive, we have just begun to appraise the implications of the Haitian Revolution, and the paradigm of the Atlantic world is central to this endeavor. Classic studies like R. R. Palmer's *The Age of Democratic Revolution* (Princeton: Princeton University Press, 1959–64); and Eric Hobsbawm, *The Age of Revolution, 1789–1848* (1962;

New York: Vintage Books Edition, 1996) have been influential for setting the interpretive stage for this age. More current assessments of the period, such as Jeremy Adelman, *Sovereignty and Revolution in the Iberian Atlantic* (Princeton: Princeton University Press, 2006); Robin Blackburn, *The Overthrow of Colonial Slavery, 1776–1848* (London: Verso, 1988); David Brion Davis, *Revolutions: Reflections on American Equality and Foreign Liberations* (Cambridge: Harvard University Press, 1990); and Peter Linebaugh and Marcus Rediker, *The Many-Headed Hydra: The Hidden History of the Revolutionary Atlantic* (Boston: Beacon Press, 2000), have deepened our conceptualization of this historical watershed. Works that focus on the colonial Atlantic world have also informed my approach: David Armitage and Michael J. Braddick, eds., *The British Atlantic World, 1500–1800* (New York: Palgrave Macmillan, 2002); April Lee Hatfield, *Atlantic Virginia: Intercolonial Relations in the Seventeenth Century* (Philadelphia: University of Pennsylvania Press, 2004); and Joseph Roach, *Cities of the Dead: Circum-Atlantic Performance* (New York: Columbia University Press, 1996), to name but a few.

All that said, I have found the scholarship on the black Atlantic to be the most compelling aid in contemplating the relationship between the United States and revolutionary Saint-Domingue. Specifically, this book draws from Paul Gilroy's singular analysis, *The Black Atlantic: Modernity and Double Consciousness* (Cambridge: Harvard University Press, 1993). Gilroy defies essentialist categories of race and evidence in order to ascertain "the pattern of movement, transformation, and relocation" that informed black intellectual currents—and modernity at large—in the nineteenth and twentieth centuries. Certainly, there are aspects of this process that are unique to populations of African descent and to the later period he considers, yet Gilroy's characterization of the Atlantic and his emphasis on "intermixture," "instability," and "mutability" are suggestive for the age of revolutions as well, when, some claim, "modernity" began (xi). David Brion Davis's *The Problem of Slavery in the Age of Revolution, 1770–1823*, 2nd ed. (New York: Oxford University Press, 1999); and Julius Scott's "The Common Wind: Currents of Afro-American Communication in the Era of the Haitian Revolution" (Ph.D. diss., Duke University, 1986) are two models for demonstrating the centrality of black Atlantic currents to this era.

It is worth mentioning a rival paradigm for characterizing this period. Some scholars have contended that the early republican United States is best described as "postcolonial." This term is provocative in that it highlights the continuities between the colonial and revolutionary epochs but so far, interpretations in this vein tend to insulate the thirteen North American colonies/states from transnational frameworks, potentially reinforcing the very exceptionalism that postcolonial studies purport to debunk. Interesting critiques of the postcolonial approach can be found in Joyce E. Chaplin, "Race," in Armitage and Braddick, eds., *The British Atlantic World*; Christopher L. Miller, *The French Atlantic Triangle: Literature and Culture of the Slave Trade* (Durham: Duke University Press, 2008); and Michael Zuckerman, "Exceptionalism after All; or, The Perils of Postcolonialism" in the roundtable on the application of postcolonial theory to early American history in the *William and Mary Quarterly*, 3rd series, 64, no. 2 (April 2007).

Any attempt to place the United States of this era into a broader context would have been futile without the bevy of superb works about various facets of the early republic. The endnotes to this book testify to my enormous debt to the scholarship on everything from high politics to period fashion, but that which treats a few subfields warrants more extended acknowledgment. It will come as no surprise that studies of slavery and abolition are central to my analysis: Ira Berlin, *Many Thousands Gone: The First Two Centuries of Slavery in North America* (Cambridge: Harvard University Press, 1998); Sylvia R. Frey, *Water from the Rock: Black Resistance in a Revolutionary Age* (Princeton: Princeton University Press, 1991); David N. Gellman, *Emancipating New York: The Politics of Slavery and Freedom, 1777–1827* (Baton Rouge: Louisiana State University Press, 2006); Joanne Pope Melish, *Disowning Slavery: Gradual Emancipation and "Race" in New England, 1780–1860* (Ithaca: Cornell University Press, 1998); Gary Nash, *Forging Freedom: The Formation of Philadelphia's Black Community, 1720–1840* (Cambridge: Harvard University Press, 1988); Adam Rothman, *Slave Country: American Expansion and the Origins of the Deep South* (Cambridge: Harvard University Press, 2005); and Shane White, *Somewhat More Independent: The End of Slavery in New York City, 1770–1810* (Athens: University of Georgia Press, 1991).

The literature on politics and nationalism is prolific. Some works important to my reading include Stanley Elkins and Eric McKitrick, *The Age of Federalism: The Early American Republic, 1788–1800* (New York: Oxford University Press, 1993); Don E. Fehrenbacher, *The Slaveholding Republic: An Account of the United States Government's Relations to Slavery*, completed and edited by Ward M. McAfee (New York: Oxford University Press, 2001); Simon P. Newman, *Parades and the Politics of the Street: Festive Culture in the Early American Republic* (Philadelphia: University of Pennsylvania Press, 1997); Peter S. Onuf, *Jefferson's Empire: The Language of American Nationhood* (Charlottesville: University Press of Virginia, 2000); James Roger Sharp, *American Politics in the Early Republic: The New Nation in Crisis* (New Haven: Yale University Press, 1993); and David Waldstreicher, *"In the Midst of Perpetual Fetes": The Making of American Nationalism, 1776–1820* (Chapel Hill: University of North Carolina Press, 1997).

Lastly, social, cultural, and literary analyses have given critical texture to this era. A few significant titles are Richard Bushman, *The Refinement of America: Persons, Houses, Cities* (New York: Alfred A. Knopf, 1992); Robert A. Ferguson, *Reading the Early Republic* (Cambridge: Harvard University Press, 2004); Sean Goudie, *Creole America: The West Indies and the Formation of Literature and Culture in the New Republic* (Philadelphia: University of Pennsylvania Press, 2006); Bernard L. Herman, *Town House: Architecture and Material Life in the Early American City, 1780–1830* (Chapel Hill: University of North Carolina Press, 2005); and Julia Stern, *The Plight of Feeling: Sympathy and Dissent in the Early American Novel* (Chicago: University of Chicago Press, 1997).

INDEX

exiles, 2, 38–42, 44–47, 49; clothing of, 40–41,
148; and French consuls, 62; housing of, 23–
26; immigration of, in waves (1793, 1798,
1804, 1809), 5, 87, 101, 142–43, 167, 168–69,
188; and naturalization, 113–15; newspapers
of, 31–32, 97–98, 189; and religion, 28–30;
property brought by, 26–28; social networks
among, 28–32; work done by, 32–34. *See also*
black and colored exiles; enslaved exiles;
white exiles

Fabre, Danse, 27
factionalism, 108–9, 123; danger of, as lesson
from Haitian Revolution, 89, 100, 109, 111,
123; deepening of, in U.S., 109–13. *See also*
party politics
Federalists, 64, 89, 102, 106, 109–10, 160,
164–65, 187; and naturalization debate, 114–
15; and trade with black-led Saint-Domingue,
160, 164–65. *See also* Adams, John; Hamilton, Alexander
Fond, John de la, 93–94
Fondevielle, M. (member of exile delegation to
France), 116
France, 17, 19, 48; and American Revolution,
73, 101; National Assembly of, 3–4, 70–71, 73,
74, 94, 105–6, 112, 145; National Convention
of, 115–16; prerevolutionary government of,
19, 73, 101; representatives of, in United
States, 91, 99–100, 101, 103, 106–8, 117, 123,
152; U.S. relations with, 73, 74, 101, 121, 160,
161, 186; views expressed in, on white Saint-
Dominguans, 54–55, 90–92, 99, 118–20; war
of, with Great Britain, 92, 101–2, 106, 120–
21. *See also* French Revolution
Franklin, Benjamin, 20, 48
"freedom principle," 17
free people of color: African Americans as, 15,
16–17, 48, 112; in Louisiana, 167, 181, 183–85,
191–92, 249n57; among Saint-Dominguan
exiles, 23, 30–31, 32, 44, 167, 175, 191–92. *See
also gens de couleur*
French consuls, 62
French language, 32, 35, 37–38
"French Negroes." *See* black and colored exiles
French Revolution, 4, 91, 101, 134–35, 203; U.S.
views of, 35, 37, 91; white exiles and, 89–95,
97–99, 105–6

Frères Réunis, 30
Fronty, Michael, 34

Gabriel's Rebellion, 144, 153, 207
Galbaud, Thomas-François, 56, 101, 102–4, 117,
123
Gallatin, Albert, 159
Gauvain, Peter, 73
Gazette française et americaine, 31, 82–83,
116–17
gender stereotypes, 53–54, 67–68
Genet, Edmond Charles, 99–100, 101, 103,
106–8, 117, 123
gens de couleur, 4, 15, 16, 20, 22, 42; in exile, 23,
30–31, 32, 44, 175; in Haitian Revolution, 81,
88, 100; as slaveowners, 142. *See also* black
and colored exiles
George III, 92
Georgia, 149, 174–75
Giles, William Branch, 75, 113–14, 115
Gilmer, Robert, 64
Girard, Jean, 39–40
Girard, Stephen, 38, 54, 87, 155, 206; as master,
39–40, 148, 155
Girondins, 91, 106, 107
Godefroy, Maximilian, 83
Grand, Lewis John Baptist, 27
grands blancs, 3–4, 91
Great Britain; anti–slave trade movement in,
131–32; policies of, on slavery, 17, 177; priva-
teers sponsored by, 102, 150–51, 155; and
Saint-Domingue in 1790s, 92, 119, 120, 122,
141; war of, with France, 92, 101–2, 106,
120–21
Grégoire, Henri, 79
Gros, Mr. (author of *Historick Recital*), 85,
156–57
Guadeloupe, 112–13

Haig, David, 147
Haiti, independent, 146; U.S. embargo against,
164–65, 172
Haitian Revolution, 1, 4; and abolition of slave
importation to United States, 133–34; and
British invasion, 92, 119, 120, 122, 141; and
enablement of Louisiana Purchase, 163–64,
168; and fear of factionalism, 89, 100, 109,
111, 123; French interpretations of, 90–92; as